*f*P

THE EMERGING MARKETS CENTURY

HOW A NEW BREED OF WORLD-CLASS COMPANIES
IS OVERTAKING THE WORLD

Antoine van Agtmael

FREE PRESS

New York London Toronto Sydney

Disclaimer: This book contains the opinions and ideas of its author. It is sold with the understanding that neither the author nor the publisher, through the publication of this book, is engaged in rendering investment, financial, accounting, legal, tax, insurance or other professional advice or services. If the reader requires such advice or services, a competent professional should be consulted. The strategies outlined in this book may not be suitable for every individual, and are not guaranteed or warranted to produce any particular results. No warrant is made with respect to the accuracy or completeness of the information contained herein. Both the author and publisher specifically disclaim any responsibility for any liability, loss or risk, personal or otherwise, which is incurred as a consequence, directly or indirectly, of the use and application of any of the contents of this book.

Readers should know that the author founded and currently serves as Chief Investment Officer of Emerging Markets Management, L.L.C. (EMM), an investment advisory firm focused exclusively on emerging markets. The author currently serves as director of several commingled funds managed by EMM, and is also a director of Strategic Investment Group (a group of related investment advisors), a member of the investment committees of the Brookings Institution and NPR Foundation and holds various directorships in not-for-profit organizations.

FREE PRESS
A Division of Simon & Schuster, Inc.
1230 Avenue of the Americas
New York, NY 10020

For information about special discounts for bulk purchases,
please contact Simon & Schuster Special Sales:
1-800-456-6798 or business@simonandschuster.com

DESIGNED BY ERICH HOBBING

Manufactured in the United States of America

5   7   9   10   8   6   4

Library of Congress Cataloging-in-Publication Data
Is Available

ISBN-13: 978-0-7432-9457-7
ISBN-10:   0-7432-9457-2

For Emily, Jenny, and Peter
My anchors in a nomadic life

Contents

Introduction: The Emergence of Emerging Markets   1

Part I

GLOBALIZATION HAS NO BORDERS

Chapter 1: Who's Next?   9
How emerging multinationals you've never heard of could eat
your lunch, take your job, or possibly be your next business
partner or employer

Chapter 2: Against the Odds   28
The strategies that propelled twenty-five emerging multinationals into world-class corporations

Part II

THE NEW BREED: TWENTY-FIVE WORLD-CLASS EMERGING MULTINATIONALS

**Chapter 3: From Under the Radar Screen: Building
Emerging Global Brands**   59
Samsung and Concha y Toro are setting new trends

**Chapter 4: Other Roads to Brand Leadership: Buy It or It
May Drop in Your Lap**   82
Lenovo buys IBM ThinkPad, Haier tries to buy Maytag, and
Corona Beer has its accidental iconic brand

**Chapter 5: China's Largest Exporters . . . Are Taiwanese:
Building a Global Presence Behind a Veil of Anonymity**   99
Hon Hai and Yue Yuen make your computers, cell phones,
and shoes

Chapter 6: From Imitators to Innovators   119
Taiwan's TSMC and High Tech Computer win by reinventing
industries and products

Chapter 7: Your Next Global Employer?   140
Hyundai and CEMEX want to be close to their customers
everywhere

Chapter 8: Turning the Outsourcing Model Upside Down   163
Brazilian plane maker Embraer stays in the driver's seat with
suppliers in the developed world

**Chapter 9: Commodity Producers that Redefined their
Industries**   183
Aracruz, CVRD, and POSCO defied conventional wis-
dom . . . and the odds

Chapter 10: Alternative Energy Producers   205
South Africa's Sasol makes oil out of coal and gas, Brazil's cars
use biofuels, and Argentina's Tenaris makes pipes seamless
enough to be used deep under the ocean or in Arctic climates

Chapter 11: The Revolution in Cheap Brainpower   227
India's Infosys and Ranbaxy transform the worlds of software
design and generics

Chapter 12: New Global Media Stars   248
Mexico's Televisa, India's Bollywood, and Korea's game makers appeal
to worldwide audiences

Part III

TURNING THREATS INTO OPPORTUNITIES

Chapter 13: A Creative Response   271
Don't be defensive or stick your head in the sand—develop new
policies and strategies

Part IV
AN INVESTOR'S RESOURCE

Chapter 14: Investing in the Emerging Markets Century:
Ten Rules   293
   A long-time investor looks at pride and prejudice in emerging
   market investing

Appendix: Financial Profiles of 25 World-Class Emerging
Multinationals   321

Notes   349

Bibliography   359

Acknowledgments   361

Index   363

The Emergence
of Emerging Markets

"There *are* no markets outside the United States!"

The year was 1974. I was a young banker, still wet behind the ears, working at Bankers Trust Company in New York. I had been asked to conduct a study on recycling petrodollars. Helping governments overseas to invest on a truly global basis seemed like a logical concept. But when I interviewed the bank's trust department (at the time among the largest in the United States), an intimidating executive tugged on his red suspenders and wrathfully snarled: "There *are* no markets outside the United States."

The man had at least two decades of experience in the banking industry on me. My own perspective was, for better or worse, different. I had grown up in Holland and had owned a few shares of Philips, Shell, and Unilever as a boy. Little did my interlocutor at Bankers Trust (nor I, for that matter) know that the great inviolable institution we worked for would one day be taken over by Deutsche Bank—a global rival from one of these "nonmarkets."

Experiences like this made me skeptical of conventional wisdom. They taught me to rigorously scrutinize faulty assumptions that even the experts—in some cases, *particularly* experts—all too frequently make as a matter of course. Ever since taking a course in development economics at the Netherlands School of Economics from Professor Jan Tinbergen (a brilliant econometrician who later became the first Nobel Laureate in economics) I had been fascinated with the fate and fortunes of what was then known disparagingly as "The Third World." Later, as a graduate student in Russian and East European studies at Yale in the late 1960s, I realized that central planning and communist ideology had little future, and longed to find out how foreign investment might help or hurt Third World development.

At Bankers Trust, I gained some exposure to a few of the more exotic forms of Third World economic development. I helped Iran Air lease airplanes and hire crews in Ethiopia, was involved in financing Ghana's cocoa exports, and grew wise to the ways—many of them laughably one-sided—that developed nations interacted with what were in many cases recent European colonies. Less than a year into my first job at Bankers Trust, I surprised no one more than myself by becoming suddenly, uncharacteristically, and inexplicably bored with analyzing American companies for the bank's credit department. For some reason, the dynamism of the world seemed to lie elsewhere. I managed to convince my open-minded superiors at the bank that it would be useful—not just to me personally, but also to the bank—for me to take a trip to Asia to study foreign investment in the region.

My trip turned out to be, as the popular parlance of the time had it, a mind-blowing experience. At the Seoul airport in 1971, the military policeman at immigration cocked his gun when he mistook the sunglasses in my pocket for a weapon. Seoul looked like a city in the Soviet Union, which I had just crossed on the Trans Siberian railroad: shabby, chilly, and poor. No skyscrapers yet loomed over the cramped center city and antiaircraft guns were starkly visible on just about every street corner. Even after a decade of 9 percent growth, Korea's per capita income stood at a dismal $225 (it is now over $10,000) although that was already three times higher than that of India. Still, the executives I met were already dreaming of export markets when they were not conducting their compulsory military training exercises.

That first trip to Asia took me to an exotic continent in which the war in Vietnam was still raging, to a Japan stuck in its first postwar slump, to a China still closed to outsiders like myself, and to an India nervously watching Bangladesh separate itself from Pakistan. Cars that looked like throwbacks to the 1950s were the only ones to be seen on the roads in New Delhi. Yet I could already feel the dynamism of many companies I visited, and their determination to make it big. I heard how companies from Hong Kong and Singapore were beginning to relocate their most labor-intensive operations to their lower-cost Asian neighbors. I intuitively grasped during that youthful Asian sojourn that multinationals would one day be attracted to subcontracting labor-intensive operations to countries with an abundant, cheap labor supply rather than merely assembling components in protected, local mass markets.

Upon my return to New York and Bankers Trust, I went to work for the International Department, an island of like-minded souls, but elsewhere there were few who shared our enthusiasm for the booming business prospects of Asia. This abiding sense of being outside the loop provided an important motivation for my acceptance, several years later, of an offer to move to Thailand to manage a local investment bank, majority-owned by Bankers Trust, which I chose over a rival offer to run the bank's branch in Paris. Bangkok or Paris? After my Asian trip, the choice seemed obvious to me, but one that many of my colleagues at the bank found hard to understand.

I spent the next four years in Bangkok happily learning the ins and outs of foreign markets as the managing director of the premier Thai investment bank. We were instrumental in bringing some of the first shares issues of local companies to the stock market, while riding like a bucking bronco one of the perennial boom-and-bust cycles of the Securities Exchange of Thailand. My turbulent tenure in Bangkok taught me that foreign investors would be better off hedging their bets by investing in a basket of markets in developing nations as opposed to a single one. Equally important, I observed the astonishing rapidity with which local firms absorbed international lessons, from raising chickens or producing textiles to assembling cars, and how they often managed to add their own local innovations to the mix.

In 1979, I left Bangkok for Washington, D.C., to join the International Finance Corporation, the private sector arm of the World Bank. Initially, I was taken aback to learn that the idea of portfolio investment in developing economies was regarded with suspicion, as fundamentally unsound. The knee-jerk reaction of the majority of development experts at the World Bank Group was surprisingly dismissive and resistant to the idea of investing in immature economies. How could these tiny and volatile casinos, my colleagues wondered out loud, possibly exert the slightest impact on real economic growth and development? How could these fledgling economies ever gain traction or attention or sizable investment flows from serious investors? This was my second lesson in how seriously flawed conventional wisdom can be.

Under the leadership of my courageous and decidedly unbureaucratic director and later friend, David Gill, another former investment banker, and with a handful of colleagues we gradually convinced the skeptics at IFC and the World Bank that increasing portfolio investment in developing countries might help entrepreneurs succeed and make companies less dependent on foreign aid and debt. My stay in Thailand had convinced me that a number of interesting new companies in the Third World were simply being ignored by major investors. But as David Gill used to say, correctly, "Finding one single successful example of people making money will be more convincing than a hundred academic papers." That is precisely what we proceeded to do.

Yet even sympathetic listeners tended to raise eyebrows when we brashly proclaimed that, in the near future, foreign portfolio investment would become more important than the World Bank as a source of funds for developing economies. At the time, IFC only invested *directly* in a strategy that requires an investor to take a major stake in companies and often a seat on the board of directors. To IFC's lasting credit, any number of major emerging market blue-chips would never have evolved to their current size without its seed money and perhaps more importantly, strategic and technical advice. Yet surprisingly little had been accomplished in the area of *portfolio* investment, which requires an investor to purchase shares on the open market after the company has been listed and gone public.

In a speech to the local Thai-American Chamber of Commerce before leaving Bangkok, I first proposed the idea of creating an investment fund that, as opposed to investing in a single country, would pursue a *diversified* strategy of investing in a group of countries to minimize the risk of one economy crashing and taking the entire fund down with it. We were acutely aware that the very idea of portfolio investment in still rudimentary capital markets would continue to invite skepticism without hard data to back it up. One of my first self-assigned tasks at the IFC was to commission a study of the stock performance of leading firms in a number of developing economies. Those returns, computed for the years 1975–1979 with the help of Professor Vihang Errunza of McGill University, turned out to be quite attractive. Now, well armed with good data, we were determined to present them to the investment community in as dramatic a fashion as possible.

HOW "THIRD WORLD" BECAME "EMERGING MARKETS"

In September 1981, I stood behind the lecturn at Salomon Brothers headquarters in New York City, preparing to pitch the idea of a "Third World Equity Fund" to a group of leading investment managers. Our central message to prospective investors was that our data demonstrated a real possibility of making real money in emerging markets, despite their admitted volatility. Developing countries, we argued, enjoyed higher economic growth rates and boasted a rich set of hitherto-ignored promising companies. We persuasively demonstrated that investing in a *basket* of companies and countries would provide the diversification required to mitigate the risk of investing in individual stocks and countries.

Twenty to thirty fund managers, including representatives from TIAA-CREF, Salomon Brothers, J.P. Morgan, and other major institutions, attended that conference. Judging by the faces in the crowd, I could sense that some were clearly intrigued, others were skeptical, and that just possibly we might win over one or two confirmed skeptics to our cause. At the conclusion of my presentation, Francis Finlay of J.P. Morgan remarked: "This is a very interesting idea you've got there, young man, but you will *never* sell it using the name 'Third World Equity Fund'!"

I immediately knew he had a point. We had the goods. We had the data. We had the countries. We had the companies. What we did not have, however, was an elevator pitch that liberated these developing economies from the stigma of being labeled as "Third World" basket cases, an image rife with negative associations of flimsy polyester, cheap toys, rampant corruption, Soviet-style tractors, and flooded rice paddies.

Over the weekend, I disappeared into one of the mental isolation spells my wife and children so heartily dislike, but which I often find oddly productive. Racking my brain, I at last came up with a term that sounded more positive and invigorating: *Emerging Markets.* "Third World" suggested stagnation; "Emerging Markets" suggested progress, uplift, and dynamism.

The following Monday, I sat down at my desk at IFC and dashed off a memo that made my message explicit. From now on, we would consistently refer to our Third World database as the Emerging Markets Data Base and the first index we created for emerging markets would be the IFC Emerging Markets Index. Thus, a phrase was coined. Born from conviction and based on firsthand observation in Asia, it was also a branding maneuver at a time when brands remained the exclusive province of consumer goods companies like Procter & Gamble. In the following years, we spent a lot of time negotiating with governments and convincing investment bankers as well as investors to create various country funds. And finally the diversified "Third World" equity fund became a reality as the Emerging Markets Growth Fund managed by Capital Investment, Inc., the first and soon largest fund of its type with a group of prestigious institutional investors from all over the world. Templeton, another candidate to manage the IFC-inspired fund, soon set up its own New York Stock Exchange listed fund.

Just weeks before the October 1987 stock market crash on Wall Street, with a group of colleagues from the World Bank, I founded a new firm,

Emerging Markets Management, focused exclusively on investing in emerging markets. Over the years since, we have actively participated in the often-dizzying ups and downs of those markets and companies together with such other pioneers as David Fisher and Walter Stern of Capital, Mark Mobius of Templeton, and Nick Bratt at Scudder.

In the initial years, we were often the first analysts to interview companies' managers. My former experience as an interrogator in the Dutch Army stood me in good stead when I attempted to sort the wheat from the chaff while deciphering and discounting often inscrutable management spin. We learned that companies in many emerging markets were often heavily protected by their local governments, not very competitive, and all too quick to take on crippling loads of debt. The traumatic crises of the 1990s in Mexico and Asia changed all of that. Leading companies were forced to become competitive not just in their domestic markets, but on the global stage. Some did precisely that; others perished. The survivors in this struggle for survival of the fittest became better, leaner, more finely focused, less dependent on debt. The groundwork was laid for the best of the lot to become fiercely competitive and, in a word, world class.

Twenty-five years ago, most sophisticated investors considered the notion of putting even a tiny portion of respectable retirement funds or endowments into shares of "Third World" countries as nothing short of preposterous. Today, a number of those countries have gone from Third World to Emerging, while a few are even recognized as major economic powers. Yet in the minds of even knowledgeable observers today, the firms that form the foundation of these economies are still widely regarded as third-rate, at best second-rate, and certainly by no means world class. The evidence suggests otherwise.

The companies portrayed in the following pages are in many cases models to be emulated, examples to learn from, and repositories of skills and knowledge that we in our comfortable cocoons may not even imagine exist. Being newcomers in the global competitive race, these firms have found niches others ignored and have conceived innovative strategies others disdained but that are, in fact, better suited to an interconnected world and volatile new markets. They all followed different roads to success, but most of us in the developed world know neither the companies nor the people who run them nor the strategies they employed to claw their way to the top of fiercely competitive industries.

I hope to change that with this book.

PART I

GLOBALIZATION
HAS NO BORDERS

"World history, with its great transformation, does not come upon us with the even speed of a railway train. No, it moves in spurts but then with irresistible force."[1]

—OTTO VON BISMARCK

CHAPTER 1

Who's Next?

How emerging multinationals you've never heard of could eat your lunch, take your job, or possibly be your next business partner or employer

For a few minutes, I held the future in my hand. Suddenly my Blackberry looked like a Model T Ford. I was trying out a prototype of a new third-generation cell phone. It certainly looked stylish, but more intriguing was the fact that this was a video phone that actually let me see the person on the other side of the line. And that was not all: on a bright screen that easily fit in my pocket, I could check local traffic, watch breaking TV news, and play interactive group computer games. Naturally, I could access the Internet, email, update my calendar, and listen to downloaded CDs. This was a *smart* phone indeed.

Was I visiting Verizon, Apple, or Nokia? No, it was January 2005 and I was standing in the research lab of High Tech Computer Corp. (HTC), a Taiwanese company that with its 1,100 research engineers had invented the iPAQ, sold it to Hewlett Packard, and gone on to make a successful series of state-of-the-art handhelds and smart phones for the likes of Verizon, Vodafone, Palm, and HP. All around me were young, smart, ambitious engineers from Taiwan and China, hard at work testing everything from sound in a sophisticated acoustics studio to new antennas, drop impact, and the scratch resistance of new synthetic materials. Designed in Taiwan, these high-tech video phones would shortly be mass produced, and one day soon sold around the world.

I was not just looking at the prototype of a new smart phone, but making a pilgrimage to the prototype of a new kind of company—savvy, global, high-tech (as its name suggests) and, most importantly, well ahead of its nearest competitors even in the United States and Europe. My experience at High Tech was not as unusual as you might expect. For thirty years I had been visiting little known companies all over Asia, Latin America, Eastern Europe, and Africa, convinced of the long-term potential of these unknown markets and companies even if few firms or economies were as yet globally competitive. Managing an investment portfolio that has since grown to over $16 billion has only confirmed my belief that just as conventional wisdom wrongly depreciated emerging *markets* twenty-five years ago as "Third World," today's all too common error is to underrate the leading *companies* from these markets. Largely unnoticed in the mature economies, the firms profiled in this book have succeeded against the odds and become battle-hardened survivors of tough crises and Darwinian competition. With the rising power of China, India, and other emerging markets, and the resultant shift of consumer demand from the West to these markets' exploding middle class, we have now formally entered the Emerging Markets Century.

THE EMERGING MARKETS CENTURY

Instead of being peripheral, as they have been since the first Industrial Revolution,[1] key economies of the former Third World will soon reemerge as the dominant economies of the future. In about twenty-five to thirty years, the combined gross national product (GNP) of emerging markets will overtake that of the currently mature economies (see table). Although comprising about 85 percent of the world's population, low per capita incomes in many emerging markets have kept their share of global GNP to about 20 percent. But this ratio is bound to change as the emerging economies continue to grow at a rate nearly twice as fast as their more mature cousins. This second industrial revolution will constitute nothing less than an economic landslide, causing a major shift in the center of gravity of the global economy—away from the developed to emerging economies.

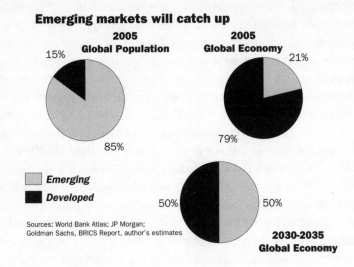

Emerging markets will catch up

2005 Global Population — Emerging 85%, Developed 15%

2005 Global Economy — Developed 79%, Emerging 21%

2030-2035 Global Economy — 50% / 50%

Emerging
Developed

Sources: World Bank Atlas; JP Morgan;
Goldman Sachs, BRICS Report, author's estimates

The Rise of BRICS and other Emerging Markets in the Global Economy (In Trillions)

	G7	All Developed	BRICs	Next 11	All Emerging
2005	27.3	32.4	4.2	2.9	8.9
2015	33.0	39.6	10.2	5.6	19.0
2030	43.0	51.6	28.2	12.5	46.8
2050	64.2	77.0	90.0	35.5	138.0

Source: Author's calculations based on Goldman Sachs projections for the four BRICs and eleven other major emerging markets and J.P. Morgan data for other countries. Goldman Sachs assumes that growth in emerging markets will slow and exchange rates in these markets will generally appreciate as their purchasing power increases, as has been the general experience in economic history.

According to Goldman Sachs projections, just four of the largest emerging markets (known as BRICs, for China, Brazil, India, and Russia) will overtake the seven largest industrialized countries, the G7 (United States, Japan, Germany, France, UK, Italy, and Canada) by 2040.[2,3] Including the next group of eleven major emerging markets,[4] the fifteen leading emerging markets will together be larger than the G7 soon after 2030. Their combined GNP is projected to reach $41 trillion, compared with the G7's $43 trillion after taking account of a probable slowing in China to less than half its current growth rate. Adding in the remaining developed and emerging nations, my own projections show that emerging markets as a group will overtake the developed world by around 2030–35. By the middle of this century, the emerging markets, taken in aggregate, will be nearly *twice* as large as the current developed economies.

A new breed of companies will play a critical role in producing this shift, a select number of which truly deserve to be regarded as world class. In the face of these firms' vigorous emergence onto the world stage, there will be a temptation to go into protective panic mode, as some American politicians began to do after Chinese companies made a few runs at long-established Western brands, and as European politicians did after Mittal Steel, the world's largest steel group with its Indian-born CEO, made a strong takeover bid for #2 steelmaker Arcelor, a major European conglomerate. But if we fall prey to a defensive response, we do ourselves a profound disservice by ignoring potentially attractive opportunities for business partnerships and investments. Anyone who wants to play in this global game needs to know the strengths and weaknesses of the players on the opposing team.

During that same multiweek tour through Asia, I visited a number of other corporations that would surprise those who still regard "Third World" companies as raw material producers or imitative makers of cheap electronics. I toured Bumrungrad hospital in Thailand where patient information is entirely paperless (in sharp contrast to even the most advanced hospitals elsewhere in the world) and to which hundreds of thousands of patients from all over the globe flock each year for treatments ranging from heart operations to cosmetic surgery, all obtainable at a fraction of the price in the United States. I spoke with petrochemical engineers no longer interested in producing cheap polyester but focused on developing sophisticated new synthetic materials. I listened to researchers speak excitedly about applying nanotechnology to flexible computer screens that could be folded and rolled up. And most importantly, I tested out a whole host of new products that based on the quality of their design, sophistication of function, and durability, were equal if not superior to competing products made in the United States, Japan, or Europe.

The broader phenomenon I had witnessed during my sojourn to the future could, of course, be loosely labeled with the tired term "globalization." But as Moises Naim, editor of *Foreign Policy* magazine, not long ago observed to me, "Globalization is not an abstract notion but driven by real actors who are pushing these changes." He has a point. It was plain as day that a number of the companies I visited on my last trip were no longer bit players, but leading actors, even budding international superstars, on this new global stage.

By now we have all heard *ad nauseam* about globalization, the startling rise of the Asian Tigers, China and India as economic powers, outsourcing and offshoring, both pro and con. Yet in the "West" (as the developed nations of the United States, Europe, Japan, Australia, and New Zealand continue to be conveniently, if not correctly, called) we go on clinging to the comforting notion that at least "our" top companies continue to lead the world—in global presence, in technology and design, and above all, in brand recognition and marketing prowess. But is this still true? Are the leading corporations headquartered in Korea, Taiwan, China, India, Brazil, Mexico, and Russia *really* so far behind their counterparts in the industrialized West? Can we consider our complacency—occasionally shattered by periods of anxiety verging on panic—justified at a time when:

- Korean Samsung's powerful global brand is now better recognized than Sony's, its R&D budget is larger than Intel's and its 2005 profits were higher than those of Dell, Nokia, Motorola, Philips, or Matsushita.
- The regional jets we fly are made by Embraer in Brazil.
- Mexico's CEMEX has become the largest cement company in the United States, the second largest in the UK, the third largest globally, and the leader in many other markets.
- Computers are now not just made but largely *designed* in Taiwan and China.
- We get most of our advice about how to fix those computers from India.
- Russia's Gazprom's gas reserves are larger than those of all the oil majors *combined* and its market capitalization rivals that of Microsoft. Europe would freeze in the winter without its gas supplies, as was pointedly demonstrated when it briefly turned off the tap. Meanwhile, Russian Lukoil's gas stations (bought from Getty Oil) can be found near the White House, the New York Stock Exchange, and all along the East Coast.
- Modelo, a Mexican company, sells more beer (Corona) to Americans than Heineken. And a Brazilian CEO became head of Inbev-Ambev, the world's largest beer company, in a merger in which "old" European beer companies were amazed at the efficiency of their Brazilian partners.

> *Often overlooked when people speak glibly of "globalization" is that a new kind of firm is fast arising and flexing its muscles in the nations of the former Third World.*

That is not all—not by a long shot. Today, Korean engineers are helping U.S. steel companies modernize their outdated plants. New proprietary drugs are being developed in Indian and Slovenian labs no longer content to compliantly turn out high volumes of low-cost generics for resale in the mature economies. New inventions in consumer electronics and wireless technology are moving from Asia to the United States and Europe, as opposed to the other way around.

The era of emerging markets companies being nothing more than unsophisticated makers of low-cost, low-tech products is rapidly coming to a close. Something different and dynamic is happening in these new economies, blessed with robust rates of growth our mature economies can only envy. What is often overlooked when people speak glibly of globalization is that a new kind of firm is fast arising and flexing its muscles in the nations of the former Third World. These companies frequently serve dual roles of competitor *and* business partner with established First World multinationals. It would be naïve for us to dismiss them for deriving their competitive advantage "unfairly" from "cheap labor." More often than not, factors other than price or cost have been the prime determinants in their arduous climb to world-class status. Chief among these "man-made" factors are: (1) an obsessive focus on quality and design, (2) brand building, (3) logistics, (4) being ahead of competitors in adapting to changing market trends, (5) acquisition savvy, (6) sustaining an edge on competitors in information technology, (7) clever niche strategies, and (8) unconventional thinking. These companies and their leaders represent the next big economic superstars of the Emerging Markets Century.

> *The era of companies from emerging markets which were nothing more than unsophisticated makers of low-cost, low-tech products is rapidly coming to a close.*

THE INVISIBLE CHAMPIONS

It is time to start getting used to the idea that the household names of today—whether we are speaking of IBM, Ford, and Wal-Mart in the United States; Philips, Shell, and Nestle in Europe; or Panasonic, Honda, and Sony in Japan—are in danger of becoming the has-beens of tomorrow.

After all, most of us were blissfully unaware that companies from emerging markets were already playing a major part in our lives. They make much of what we eat, drink, and wear, in addition to providing us with energy and raw materials. Fifty-eight of *Fortune* magazine's top 500 global corporations are headquartered in emerging markets. Many of these are not less but *more* profitable than their peers in the United States, Europe, or Japan. Emerging world-class multinationals have a number of things in common. They

> *The household names of today are in danger of becoming the has-beens of tomorrow.*

- Are widely recognized as leaders in their industry on a *global,* not just national or regional basis.
- Have a truly *global* presence in exports and, often, production.
- Have a top-three market share in enough countries to be a global player.
- Are globally competitive not just in price but in quality, technology, design, and management.
- Can be benchmarked against the biggest and best in the world.

Ten years ago, I would have been hard put to name even one such company, but *today* there are at least twenty-five emerging multinationals that are already world-class. And within a decade, I expect this number to grow to well over 100. In succeeding chapters, I will focus on themes—from building global brands to turning the outsourcing model upside down—which explain the secrets behind their success and are often *unique* to emerging markets. Each year, more and more of these world-class companies emerge into the mainstream. Among these new entrants are producers of some of the basic commodities on which all of us in the world economy depend, from oil and gas to iron ore, pulp, steel, and cement. But also among these new entrants are emerging-markets-based representatives in a broad range of technology-oriented, capital-intensive industries represented *in the Fortune 500 list.* Some industries boast more than one company that can be classified as "world-class" (Korean Samsung and LG in electronics, for example, or Indian Infosys and Tata Consulting in IT services). For the sake of clarity and cohesion I have chosen to include only the leader in each industry. The list also

> *Nearly one in ten of* Fortune *magazine's top 500 global corporations comes from emerging markets.*

excludes a number of smaller niches in which emerging market companies happen to excel, from pianos to textiles.

One reason that emerging multinationals have remained below the radar of so many executives, as well as the general public, is that companies such as Yue Yuen and Hon Hai remain deliberately hidden in the shadows cast by better-known brands such as Nike, Dell, or Nokia. Even though they are the actual producers of products for those companies, bigger brand names continue to control the distribution and marketing. When will they emerge from the shadows? These firms' prevailing invisibility—a conscious stealth strategy in some cases— does not mean that they are powerless, less profitable, or that they will be content to take the low-profile road forever. It won't be long before the biggest companies you have never heard of become household names.

> *Just as the rise of the United States after the Industrial Revolution turned American companies from imitators into innovators, emerging market multinationals will increasingly do the same.*

Companies like Samsung, LG, and Hyundai began by making products efficiently and cheaply but now have recognized brand names, a high quality image, world-class technology, and appealing designs. China's Haier and others are following in their footsteps. In fact, they are already better known than GE, Sony, or Toyota by hundreds of millions of consumers in China, India, and other emerging nations. Some are bound to find the ways and means to distribute their products globally without having to rely on the big brand names to handle the consumer end. As time goes on, more emerging-markets firms will take over long-established Western companies, including those they now supply. We are seeing this trend played out as global supply chains turn upside-down, with Western companies selling components and services to global giants from emerging markets. General Electric sells jet engines to Brazilian plane builder Embraer. Other smart firms will soon follow suit.

> *In the nineteenth century, aristocrats looked down on the new entrepreneurs and emerging middle class without understanding that a new era had begun. Analyzing the evolution of the twenty-five companies in this book is a first step toward making sure that we don't make that same mistake again.*

TIME TO FACE REALITY—
AND EXPLOIT ITS OPPORTUNITIES

Our ever-shrinking world is poised on the threshold of a new period of competitive threat, but also one of thrilling opportunity, when the global playing field is not just leveling (as Tom Friedman has persuasively argued in his book *The World Is Flat*) but tilting away from its former owners. Tracing the contours of this tilting field is the subject of *The Emerging Markets Century.* While globalization has achieved enormous prominence as a social and economic trend, our profiles of the twenty-five emerging multinationals can teach us valuable lessons about the real actors in this new world.

We can learn from these upstarts in emerging markets about:

- Competitiveness
- Process innovation
- Adaptation to new markets
- Future industry trends
- The types of jobs we should be training for
- The future of trade deficits
- Strengthening basic research and infrastructure
- New ways to deal with the aging of populations, and
- Shifts in political and economic power

World-class emerging multinationals are the foot soldiers in today's global competitive battle. Just as the rise of the United States after the Industrial Revolution turned American companies from imitators into innovators, emerging market multinationals will increasingly do the same. In the nineteenth century, during the first industrial revolution, aristocrats looked down on the new entrepreneurs and emerging middle class in America and Europe without comprehending that a new era had begun. As we now face a second industrial revolution, analyzing the evolution of the twenty-five companies discussed in this book can be a first step toward insuring that we don't make that same mistake again.

REVERSAL OF ROLES

Decades of good times created innumerable legacy problems for many long-established multinationals, but brutal crises in recent years squeezed out many emerging markets companies that had pinned their hopes on protection. The ensuing Darwinian struggle for survival left only battle hardened survivors still standing. As newcomers, emerging multinationals had to fight for shelf space and against preconceived notions of inferior product quality (not always without justification). In the end, the world-class companies described in this book carved out leading roles. These are not overnight wonders.

THE THREE WAVES

There have been, in my opinion, three distinct waves defining the commercial relationships between the former First and Third Worlds in the past century.

Wave 1: Foreign Direct Investment in Overseas Plants

During the postwar period, an American, Japanese, or Western European company would set up a manufacturing plant in an emerging market and import virtually everything except labor from the home country, including its own managers, machinery, capital, technology, and management techniques. They would operate copper mines or oil fields, assemble cars, run agri-businesses or make televisions or disk drives. Their purpose was to turn out inexpensive products for export using low-cost local labor and raw materials, while participating in the growing local market for their products. It was the logical business model for its time because home-grown companies in emerging markets typically had little or no track record, the technology on which they depended needed to be imported, there were few trained managers available, local capital markets were non-existent, and banks would only lend to them on a short-term basis. Some played up these overseas plants as crucial modernizers who brought much needed capital and technology to the Third World. Others decried them as neo-colonialist outposts who operated in splendid isolation and simply substituted commercial for political and social control. Ideologues on both sides of the debate misunderstood their *real* impact. Over time, these overseas plants familiarized a local labor force with global technology, trained local managers, set rigid standards for efficiency and service, and introduced management methods that spread quickly to their local suppliers and competitors. All of which, in turn, set the stage for . . .

Wave 2: Outsourcing and Offshoring

Over the past two decades, many traditional multinationals realized that it was no longer necessary to set up overseas subsidiaries: local corporations enjoy easy access to the capital markets, and could easily buy the latest technology themselves and learn how to operate sophisticated machinery in huge plants. Local schools and universities produce an ample supply of skilled workers and engineers. At a later stage, the Internet allowed instant communications and easy dialogue. Long-term business relationships developed the trust needed to rely on overseas suppliers rather than in-house operations. First a single component or cheap, low-tech part, then whole modules or products, then finally the design of entire sophisticated, high-tech products, were increasingly "offshored." True, the client in the United States, Europe, and Japan remained in the driver's seat and this symbiotic relationship seemed to remain between the mother ship and its dependent partners. Yet even as multinationals distributed and stamped their brand name on the products, they in turn became dependent on the process technology of the companies to which they "offshored." In the meantime, the outsourcing companies were able to earn excellent margins, often higher than those of their clients.

Wave 3: Peer-to-Peer Emerging World-Class Competitors

We are now entering the early years of Wave 3: *the emergence of world-class multinationals from emerging markets.* In some cases, a powerful emerging markets firm, a Samsung or High Tech in consumer electronics, a Modelo in beer, or an Embraer in aviation, has risen to a status that thrusts it into the same class as traditional multinationals. India's Infosys (IT) or Argentina's Tenaris (oil pipes) rank as global competitors. Brazil's Companhia Vale do Rio Doce (mining) and Mexico's CEMEX (building materials) have learned how to cleverly become global players without losing the particular advantages of their location in low-cost markets.

Emerging Multinationals Benefit from Role Reversal

- Just as good times create bad habits, serious crises leave only battle-hardened survivors.

- Decades of experience easily turn into the burden of "legacy" and without this burden, emerging market companies sometimes leapfrog.
- The "home market" advantage is shifting to faster-growing emerging markets with more middle-class consumers than in the West.
- Suddenly, China is more admired by many in Asia than the "West."
- A new world of consumers is making its presence felt.

FROM HEADWIND TO TAILWIND

We all sense—and those who travel frequently know from experience— that the pulsing center of the 24/7 global economy is shifting rapidly away from the cosmopolitan cities of London, Paris, and New York to the equally cosmopolitan cities of Shanghai, Mumbai, Seoul, and Mexico City. Today, while the so-called industrialized nations continue to produce 80 percent of the world's gross national product, they represent a mere 15 percent—a small and shrinking fraction—of the world's population. As a consequence of these unalterable demographic facts, the ongoing dominance of the former First World (for so long an immutable economic given) can last only so long as the rest of the world remains poor. Who truly believes that this deep disparity is likely to continue indefinitely, or that it would be desirable in the long run to maintain it?

While so many in the poor countries remain poor, today there are far more middle-class consumers in the world's emerging market nations than in the West. Their combined purchasing power, sophistication, and confidence are growing by the day. Middle-class educated consumers in Shanghai, Seoul, and Bangalore in Asia, Moscow and Prague in Eastern Europe, Sao Paulo, Buenos Aires, and Mexico City in South America—to name just a few emerging metropolises—are confidently buying more cell phones, refrigerators, televisions, or beer than their middle-class counterparts in the West. U.S. multinationals like General Electric, Procter & Gamble, DuPont, and General Motors soberly expect *more than half of their future growth* to come from emerging markets. For so many decades, these markets were peripheral to these companies, but they are counting on them over the next decade to keep their shareholders content. Jeff Immelt at GE, a bellwether U.S. conglomerate if ever there was one, has committed his firm to doubling its revenues derived from emerging markets from its current 15 percent ($25 billion) to 30 percent by 2010.[5]

This sometimes boisterous yet dynamic state of affairs stands in sharp contrast to the anemic growth forecasts by mainstream economists for many products in traditional markets. If current growth trends continue unchanged, China and India will be solidly diversified middle-class economies well before mid-century, much as Korea and Taiwan are today. Could travelers landing at New York's bedraggled JFK Airport in recent years, flying in from sleek modern airports in Shanghai, Seoul, or Singapore, be forgiven for wondering whether they have just landed in an underdeveloped country or a developed one?

IT IS THE NEW ECONOMIES, STUPID!

Only a decade ago, it was the fervent conviction of many a long-range visionary in the United States and Europe, from former AOL Time Warner chairman Steve Case to Vivendi Universal's grandiose Jean-Claude Messier, that the world-class companies of the future would exclusively arise from the bright and shining "new economy." Today, as the reality of the current global dynamic gradually sinks in, it is more likely that many if not most of the world-class firms of the future will come from the "new economies" of Asia, Latin America, and Eastern Europe—perhaps even the Middle East and Africa.

> *Many of the world-class firms of the future will come from the "new economies" rather than the "new economy."*

CHINA AND INDIA: NEW MEGA-MARKETS SPROUT NEW MULTINATIONALS

Before the middle of the twenty-first century, China's economy alone will be not only the largest in the world (as it was before the Industrial Revolution) but this time around it will not live in splendid isolation but will become the *anchor* economy of the world—the leading global importer, exporter, as well as trendsetter. China will not only dominate its region but also become an important investor overseas, rather than the largest destination for foreign investment as it is today. With the gap between rich and poor countries fast eroding (even if disparities within countries remain), the industrial nations led by the United States will no longer be the exclusive arbiters of taste, standards, and technology. Just as third-generation mobile telecommunications will flourish in Asia before the United States, new fashions in clothing and retailing will begin to move from East to West rather than the other way round. In China, for the young set, Korean rather than Western cosmetics, clothing styles, video games, and rock bands are now "cool." Hyundai cars, LG air conditioners, and Samsung refrigerators have become leading brands in China. While the best-selling Chinese cars today are still largely made by multinationals or are copycats, within a decade the Chinese will export well-engineered cars to Europe and the United States.

In India, at the Tata Institute of Fundamental Research in Mumbai, research on "string theory"—the universal theory that proponents suggest can be used to explain black holes and the origin of the universe—is among the most advanced in the world. India is also one of only six nations in the world capable of building and launching satellites. While ancient India was known for knowledge, innovation, and discoveries (including the mapping of planets and the solar system, as well as the invention of the zero), it took nearly ten more centuries for India to enjoy a second Golden Age, marked by internationally recognized software and pharmaceutical industries, which today no longer rely on the crude economics of sheer cost advantage but on intellectual capital to advance globally.

R&D activity in India is increasing rapidly, while improving laws on intellectual property rights offer protection for innovation to excel, particularly in the pharmaceutical industry. Private equity funding is now available in India, angel and seed funding are on the rise, and the government generously supports departments of science and technology as well as funding research at over forty high-tech institutes. In addition to pharmaceuticals and software—currently the leaders of economic growth—aerospace, defense (India's current president, Dr. A. P. J. Abdul Kalam, is best known as the father of India's missile program), and automobiles are increasingly driving new innovation and discovery.

A DRAGON UNLEASHED

In May 2005, after flying home to Washington, D.C., from Asia, I opened up *The Wall Street Journal* to read the announcement that IBM had agreed to sell its iconic PC Division and esteemed ThinkPad brand name to low-cost Chinese computer producer Lenovo. Curiously, the news elicited little more than a mild sense of unease in the business and policy communities, even though IBM was the company that had first mass-marketed a PC twenty-five years before, sparking a personal computer revolution that continues to this day. More attention was paid when—in rapid succession—the Chinese appliance maker Qingdao Haier Ltd., together with two American private equity funds (Blackstone Group and Bain Capital), sent the Maytag Corporation an indication of interest and the Chinese government oil company CNOOC made a bid for Unocal. Now Chinese companies were not only producing goods at low prices and even competing with American firms on their home turf, but they were trying to take over venerable American brand names and resources. Suddenly, what had been viewed as a convenience became seen as a threat. As *The Wall Street Journal* perceptively noted in July 2005:

> Whether successful or not, Haier's emergence represents an inevitable push by Chinese manufacturers to get hold of well-known Western brand names. Having clawed into the marketplace with ultra-low-cost manufacturing, these companies are acquiring both the sheen and the substance of global players, and they increasingly have financing to realize their global ambitions.

The chorus of questions inevitably raised by Haier's surprise bid for Maytag—*Who* was this Chinese appliance manufacturer? *What* did they want with Maytag? *Was* the storied Maytag repairman slated to lose his job to a counterpart from Shanghai?—remained remarkably restrained, in part because it was so easy to cast Haier in the role of savior of this faltering icon as opposed to an alien invader seeking to steal a crown jewel from the heartland of America. As Andrew Ross Sorkin pointed out in *The New York Times,* "Haier was less likely than its earlier suitors to lay off the Maytag repairman, not to mention thousands of his co-workers, so that it could flip the firm to yet another private equity firm."[6] Haier was also more likely to perpetuate "the Maytag brand, its culture and its legacy" than a domestic bidder. Only later, after venerable white goods brand Whirlpool entered the bidding war for Maytag, did Haier reluctantly fold its cards. This was not a sign that the Chinese hunt for brand names and resources was likely to slow down. The Chinese would learn from their mistakes, and polish their game for yet another run at key American companies and brands.

Yet the complacency with which Americans greeted the IBM and Maytag bids was abruptly shattered in late June 2005, when the 70 percent state-owned Chinese oil company CNOOC made a strong bid for the U.S.

oil firm Unocal—founded in 1890 as the Union Oil Company of California—in an attempt to top Chevron's rival $16.4 billion offer. At precisely this point, the supposedly level playing field suddenly seemed (to some) to be tilting too sharply toward Asia. Murmurings and rumblings about "national security" amplified into a howl of protest. Impolitic demands from the Chinese Ministry of Foreign Affairs for Congress to refrain from interfering in a "strictly commercial transaction" only served as a proverbial red flag waved before an onrushing bull.

Political grandstanding, irrational fears, and some undoubtedly valid concerns began to form an incendiary mix. Part of the outrage and protest was prompted by a sense of "how dare they?" based on antiquated twentieth century superpower notions as opposed to twenty-first century realities. When American oil companies were angling for control of Russia's Yukos as another "strictly commercial transaction," few concerns were raised on this side of the pond as to how a change in ownership of strategic Russian oil resources would play in Moscow. Lost in the rhetoric was also the fact that little of the oil from Unocal's wells ever reached American shores, or that the technology of deep water drilling was no longer an American preserve. Most of Unocal's reserves were, in fact, in Asia, and today the technology of drilling in 3,000 meters of deep water and a further 5–10 kilometers down into the rock is well mastered by Brazil's Petrobras. The drilling pipes used are as likely to come from the Japanese subsidiary of the Argentinean company Tenaris as from anywhere else. Even after the CNOOC bid was ultimately withdrawn as the political risk of a protracted national security review of the deal threatened to defer it indefinitely, it was no longer possible for Americans, along with others in the former First World, to ignore the issue. More recently, an international firm controlled by the government of Dubai gained control of the venerable British P & O, the largest operator of shipping ports in the world, sparking an artificially stoked outcry from politicians and the public. Many cooler heads viewed this as thinly veiled xenophobia masquerading as post 9/11 anxiety. The upshot was that Dubai Ports World agreed to sell off its American assets, rather than endure the suspicions of Americans regarding its ability to adequately secure vulnerable U.S. ports.

Despite occasional setbacks, takeover bids initiated by emerging multinationals, flush with money from higher commodity prices or eager to get access to technology, brands, or design, have been increasing steadily over the past years. French electronics giant Thomson was purchased by Chinese consumer electronics TCL. Taiwan's BenQ acquired Siemens Mobile.

Turkish appliance maker Beko recently acquired the German brand Grundig. During 2005 alone, emerging multinationals spent a record $42 billion in takeover deals in Europe (more than twice the previous year) and another $14 billion (in ninety-six separate deals) in the United States, well above the $10 billion previous peak in 2000.[7] It should be pointed out that this phenomenon is not confined to the United States or Europe. Canadian oil producers are being bought by the Chinese and Brazil's CVRD made a $17.6 billion takeover bid for Canadian nickel giant Inco, Ltd. Indonesian mining reserves have fallen into Chinese hands. China's Petrochina as well as India's Oil and Natural Gas Corporation (ONGC) are drilling in Sudan. Chinese firms are also buying mining and oil drilling rights all over Africa.

Interestingly, the largest buyers of U.S. assets have been Indian as opposed to Chinese companies, but the latter have finally arrived at a point when such transactions represent a logical strategic move and therefore a genuine competitive threat. Despite its huge local market, Chinese appliance maker Haier understands that it needs to be global and is following in the footsteps of Samsung by focusing on developing a global brand. Even as the latest rounds of bids failed, they were undoubtedly the leading edge of a trend. "The Chinese government has been preparing its top 100 to 150 companies to go overseas and expand," noted Jack J. T. Huang, chairman of the China practice at the large international law firm Jones Day. "The government wants to use [the recent bids] as a testing ground, to see how well the companies stand up to competition."[8]

The response on the part of the target societies to the sudden emergence of powerful and competitive firms in the emerging markets can be regarded as remarkably reminiscent of Elisabeth Kubler-Ross's famed delineation of the sequence of emotional stages people undergo when confronting the prospect of life-threatening changes: First denial, then fear, then anger, then acceptance.

As of 2006, America and Western Europe have not quite arrived at the stage of acceptance of the Emerging Markets Century and the global ambitions of emerging multinationals. We have at last grudgingly accepted that these firms do exist, and that some of them are growing very strong, along with their governments. Yet we still have trouble coming to terms with the twenty-first century reality that the former First World no longer rules the global roost unchallenged. When it comes to emerging multinationals, we still lack knowledge. And where knowledge is lacking, fear, anger, and anxiety will rule.

THE COMPETITIVE THREAT IS ONLY HALF THE STORY

Those who can clearly recall the Cold War may be forgiven for entertaining a sense of déjà vu regarding the emerging threat of emerging multinationals, because the frisson of tension aroused by takeovers from the world's former basket cases is distinctly reminiscent of earlier anxieties prompted by the launching of Sputnik. After that fateful night in October 1957, fears arose that the Russians were winning the Cold War, or at least the space race. Two decades later, the overwhelming success of Toyota and Sony prompted a similar alarmed battle cry that "The Japanese are winning." Now, in the early years of the twenty-first century, it is the Chinese and the Indians who are winning. Yet those who speak exclusively of losers and winners clearly regard a global economy as a zero-sum game. What if, instead, the rise of emerging markets and emerging multinationals were to become a win-win for both sides?

Just as Sputnik touched off the creative response of the space program and all the products and technologies it spawned; just as the Paul Revere cry of "The Japanese are winning!" led American companies to adopt TQM (total quality management), Six Sigma, and just-in-time inventory processes, so today's cry of alarm, "The Chinese, the Indians, the Taiwanese, and the Koreans are winning!" may well induce in the formerly complacent, suddenly anxious nations of the former First World a comparably creative response. There is ample scope for such a response, not based on naïve internationalism or misplaced fatalism but on the well-justified belief that the global economic scene is not a zero-sum game.

Emerging multinationals are no longer interested in being perceived as Korean, Mexican, Taiwanese, or Chinese companies. They aspire to be truly global, to operate globally, think globally, manage globally, and grow globally. This goal is rapidly becoming a reality for many, a reality to which both the emerging multinationals and the rest of us are only gradually beginning to adjust. Many emerging multinationals are already owned by shareholders from all over the world: Samsung is owned 52 percent by international shareholders, CEMEX 71 percent, Hon Hai 57 percent, Infosys 54 percent, and the emerging multinationals as a group about 50 percent. Moreover, emerging multination-

> *"The Russians are winning!" (1950s and 60s), "The Japanese are winning!" (1970s) and now, "The Chinese and Indians are winning!"*

als are becoming significant employers in the United States and Europe and attractive prospective employers for business school graduates, designers, and scientists. The Mexican cement producer CEMEX ploys over 30,000 in the United States and Europe, more than it employs in Mexico.

CEMEX's management meetings are conducted in English, while more than half of the firm's employees worldwide do not even speak Spanish. Hyundai just opened a plant in Alabama employing 2,000, while its regional suppliers employ an additional 5,500 workers. Haier makes most of its refrigerators for the U.S. market in a plant in North Carolina. Embraer obtains many of the components for the planes it builds from the United States, Japan, France, Spain, and Russia. When I recently asked to interview the CEO of the Indian pharmaceutical company Ranbaxy, I found myself greeted by CEO Brian Tempest, from the UK. Since 1995, Samsung's Innovative Design Lab (IDS) has served as an in-house school where promising designers can study under experts from one of the top U.S. design schools, the Art Center College of Design in Pasadena.

As a long-time investor in emerging markets, I have seen these companies survive the crises that hit them when, in short order, Mexico and Asia devalued, went into deep recessions, and seemed to get lost on their road to success. I have seen them turn problems into platforms for global success. I have watched the best of them grow in front of my own eyes from small, second-rate producers of cheap goods to well managed, globally competitive, large-scale, state-of-the-art corporations that are leaders in their industries and top-ranked in their market niches. Many of the next Microsofts, General Electrics, and McDonald's are more likely to appear in emerging markets than in the United States, Europe, or Japan.

The Emerging Markets Century tells the stories of how twenty-five companies made it to the top of the global heap, and how others in the same industries and countries fell by the wayside. It details what it takes to become a world-class company in an emerging market and what we—and other emerging market companies—can learn from that often harrowing experience. Formulating a *creative* as opposed to a *defensive* competitive response to this dramatic and often painful shift of power has become *the* central economic challenge of our time.

CHAPTER 2

Against the Odds

The strategies that propelled twenty-five emerging multinationals into world-class corporations

When the Russian composer Piotr Ilyich Tchaikovsky premiered his bold, highly colored Concerto for Violin and Orchestra in D Major (Opus 35) in Vienna in 1881, the most influential Viennese critic of the period wrote disparagingly that "For a while [it] moves soberly, musically, and not without spirit. But soon vulgarity gains the upper hand. . . . [The] finale transfers us to a brutal and wretched jollity of a Russian holiday. We see plainly the savage vulgar faces, we hear curses, we smell vodka. . . . Tchaikovsky's Violin Concerto . . . stinks to the ear."[1]

The most striking aspect of that review is not that a major musical critic could have missed the artistic boat by such a wide margin, but that the writing reeks more of cheap prejudice than Tchaikovsky's concerto did of cheap vodka. Yet this attitude of reflexive superiority on the part of an Austrian connoisseur to a presumably low-born composer from Russia is not so different from the unconscious biases still harbored by many citizens of the First World when thinking about the companies of today's developing nations.

The main reason that investing in emerging markets over the past quarter century has been so rewarding is that conventional wisdom based on outdated perceptions proved to be so wildly off the mark. The idea that dozens if not scores of potential global competitors might one day arise out of those markets, and be worthy of respect, emulation, possibly even fear, from established firms in the industrialized lands was widely dismissed as absurd. But in the words of George Soros, successful investing takes advantage of the "gap between perception and reality."[2] Often that gap may simply go by the name "prejudice."

Supposedly efficient markets continue to undervalue and assign an excessive risk premium to many of the companies portrayed in this book. The path to success of many emerging multinationals is full of examples of the irrational prejudice to which their founders and managers have been routinely subjected. To cite just a few:

1. In 1969, assessors for the World Bank advised the South Korean government that their proposed construction of an integrated steel plant in Korea was "a premature proposition lacking economic feasibility."[3] By 2005, the Pohang Iron and Steel Company (POSCO) built by the Korean government with the help of Japanese technical advisors was honored by the editors of *Fortune* as a "globally most admired company" and named "the most competitive [steel company] in the world" by leading steel industry analysts.

2. In 1988, a procurement manager at Royal Dutch Shell advised the senior technical manager of the Argentinean steel-pipe maker Tenaris to "return to this office when you can do better than copying your competitors." Today, Tenaris has become the top supplier to Shell in ten countries.

3. In 1992, when the Mexican cement company CEMEX announced its intention to acquire two large Spanish cement companies, its stock promptly plunged 30 percent. Why? International investors, preferred debt repayment and questioned the feasibility of a Mexican company taking over a Spanish one. As CEMEX CEO Lorenzo Zambrano dryly observed, "They said a Mexican company couldn't manage in Europe." Today, CEMEX is not only one of the largest producers of cement in Europe, but leads in the United States as well.

4. In 1984, when Morris Chang, founder of the Taiwan Semiconductor Manufacturing Company (TSMC), approached Intel founder Gordon Moore (legendary for "Moore's law") with his notion of constructing a capital intensive pure foundry that would manufacture silicon chips under contract in sharp contrast to the tradition of electronics firms manufacturing them in-house, Moore airily dismissed the proposition as "a bum idea." Today, that bum idea has grown into the largest dedicated semiconductor foundry in the world, the market leader in an industry that in 2005 racked up over $27 billion in revenues, according to the trade association FSA.

In future chapters we will encounter multiple examples of these failings on the part of Western analysts to properly account for these brash new entrants. To overcome the prejudice displayed by so many experts and market participants, only palpable pride could have motivated many of

> *To overcome the prejudice displayed by so many experts and market participants only palpable pride could have motivated so many of these companies to attempt their Herculean climbs to the top.*

these companies to attempt their Herculean climbs to the top. Whether it be the triumph of Samsung Electronics or Hyundai Motors in Korea, Tenaris in Argentina, TSMC, Hon Hai, or High Tech Computer in Taiwan, or Infosys in India, in virtually every corner of our world *pride* has spurred workers and managers on to prevail against often daunting adversity, including prejudice. Again and again during my visits to these companies, I have seen, heard, and felt the sheer psychological force of their deep pride in taking on the best in the world in their ceaseless determination to become tops in their field.

These firms might never have achieved world-class success in the absence of the adversity, obstacles, and prejudice that they encountered along the way. A comprehensive review of these companies' often stellar performance over the past two decades reveals one common theme: they are *survivors who have thrived through unconventional thinking.* What in hindsight is often termed "strategy" could more accurately be described as *creative adaptation,* a series of decisive, often daring and imaginative adjustments to adverse market conditions, strategic mistakes, or setbacks. Prominent among these have been a number of severe financial crises that have buffeted these firms and their managers like "gales of creative destruction," including currency devaluations and nearly total economic collapses. From the ashes of these crises have emerged formidable firms whose attitudes have been fundamentally shaped by the narrow survival of these Darwinian struggles.

TALK ABOUT A REVOLUTION

As I was preparing for my annual presentation to our clients a few years ago, I asked my special assistant Nowshad Rizwanullah, a young Yale graduate from Bangladesh who went on to work for the Indian emerging multinational Mahindra & Mahindra, to research data on the aging and rejuvenation of companies in emerging markets. For some time, I had suspected that companies had appeared and disappeared more rapidly in emerging markets than most people realized. That year, I wanted to shift the focus of my presentation from a narrow discussion of what had occurred over the past year to the broader picture of how companies from emerging markets had progressed and evolved (or, in some cases, fallen ignominiously by the wayside) since we launched our firm fifteen years before. Among our more startling findings:

- Just ten years ago, there were no companies in emerging markets that could be considered world class. Today, emerging markets companies are among the leaders in twenty-five global industries.
- In 1988, when we launched our first fund, there were just twenty companies in emerging markets with sales over $1 billion. Many were banks and commodities producers, an overwhelming majority of which were based in Taiwan. By 2005, there were at least thirty-eight companies with sales over $10 billion and 270 with sales over $1 billion, all survivors of a shakeout quite unlike any seen in the West for decades, if not centuries.
- In fifteen years, a startling 80 percent of the companies that had dominated the index for emerging markets had disappeared from the top 100 list.[4]

Interestingly, twelve (or about half) of my list of twenty-five world-class companies were among those twenty survivors. This was not just Darwinian survival in practice: it reflected the tremendous dynamism of these new markets with eighty new names.

What, to cite just one example, was Hua Nan Bank? Back in 1990, it was the third largest company in emerging markets, but practically nobody recalls it today. Then again, who would have believed back in 1990 that the Soviet energy company Gazprom would be capable of literally sending a chill down the spine of Western Europe by briefly turning off the gas taps to the Ukraine, or that by 2005 it would become the largest emerging market company in the world by market capitalization?

In the early 1990s, while attending a conference in Buenos Aires, I nervously ventured the dire prediction that the names of most of the blue chips on the Argentinean stock exchange would no longer exist (through failure, merger, or acquisition) within a decade. My audience of leading Argentinean executives was shocked. Ten years later, I was proven dismally correct. We now know that an overvalued exchange rate typically leads to perilous overborrowing in seemingly cheap foreign currencies, and that it is well nigh impossible in a world lacking protective barriers for any one company to be simultaneously competitive in oil and gas, construction, and numerous other activities.

Argentina was neither alone nor radically different from other emerging markets. By making annual visits to so many companies, I soon came to realize that the universe of emerging market firms was likely to constantly transform over time. Not only would crises and globalization inevitably take their toll, but government policies and other macroeconomic events would contribute to the awesome constructive and destructive power of these economies with new markets opening up, state-run companies being privatized, and new industries being born. The market capitalization table shows that *none* of the top ten companies in 1990 and 2005 remained the same. Fifteen years later, the top ten firms were all *at least* ten times larger than their predecessors. Of the twenty-five largest emerging market companies in 1990, only three firms made the Top Twenty-Five list again in 2005, all three from Korea (Samsung, then #20, Kepco, and POSCO). This was more than just change; this was a *revolution*.

Top Ten Companies in Market Capitalization

2005	Billion	1990	Billion
Gazprom, Russia	$170	Kepco, Korea	$14.0
Samsung Electronics, Korea	$107	Cathay Financial, Taiwan	$8.3
China Mobile, China	$93	Hua Nan Bank, Taiwan	$7.9
China Construction Bank, China	$78	First Financial Hld, Taiwan	$7.8
Petrobras, Brazil	$74	China Steel, Taiwan	$7.6
Lukoil, Russia	$51	ICBC, Taiwan	$7.1
Taiwan Semiconductor, Taiwan	$47	Changh Hwa Bank, Taiwan	$6.7
Surgutneftegaz, Russia	$46	Akbank, Turkey	$4.6
Vale do Rio Doce, Brazil	$46	Telmex, Mexico	$3.2
Oil and Natural Gas Corp, India	$37	POSCO, Korea	$3.0

Not only companies but whole countries and industries are new to the list of industry leaders. Banks, securities and cement companies in Korea and Taiwan, steel and glass companies in Mexico, car and gambling companies in Malaysia were among the leading players that lost their dominance over the past fifteen years, giving up their places in the sun to oil and gas, technology, mobile telecommunications, and resources. Today, firms in the BRICs (Brazil, Russia, India, and China) dominate the top ten instead of Taiwan, Malaysia, and Korea. While Korea and Taiwan remain important, technology companies have replaced many then-dominant financials and utilities on the 1990 list.

In retrospect, these results should not be so surprising. When our firm Emerging Markets Management started to invest in 1988, China, Russia, and Eastern Europe were still tucked away behind their impenetrable "iron curtain" while energy, telephone, and power companies—not to speak of roads and trains—remained in the seemingly permanent grasp of government hands virtually everywhere. Argentinean companies were being crushed by untenable rates of inflation. The South Korean market was dominated by a few local conglomerates (*chaebols*) which specialized in excluding foreign competitors and stymieing the emergence of smaller fry in the domestic sphere.

Most emerging markets companies were small, made second-rate products, were protected from competition, or—if they were bigger—were trying to do too many things at once. In Asia, more often than not, firms' balance sheets were wildly overburdened with debt. In Latin America, interest rates tended to be so daunting that even the finest firms were unable to attract financing at anything close to reasonable cost. As an active investor in emerging markets, I could not help but be attuned to the dramatic changes in our investment universe that occurred over the next decade and a half. To highlight just a few of the most transformative macroeconomic forces:

- The elimination of hyperinflation in Brazil and Argentina entailed *privatizing* many economic sectors, from telecommunications to electricity distribution; even water and roads that were traditionally held in state hands became publicly held companies, subject to the discipline of market forces.
- A rapid shift from centrally planned, Communist economies to *market orientation* in Russia, Eastern Europe, and China not only added major countries and many privatized companies to the list of emerging markets (and oligarchs to the list of the world's billionaires) but opened up many new arenas for local entrepreneurship and foreign investment.
- The Mexican, Asian, and Russian crises forced countries to get their *macroeconomic house in order.* Gone are the huge budget and current

account deficits, inflation and interest rates are way down, and emerging markets now own most of the world's foreign exchange reserves, led by China, Taiwan, and Korea. The whole macroeconomic picture is completely different and much more stable today.

- Over the past decade, key developing countries like China and India yearned to become members of the World Trade Organization (WTO). But in order to qualify for membership in that exclusive club, nations had to be willing to slash import tariffs and eliminate protective quotas. Soon, noxious licensing requirements and cumbersome local monopolies came under general attack, although of course many have survived the assault. Along with those other vestiges of a vanishing era, the cozy feeling that being part of the local industrial club would keep competitors out was consigned to the "trash heap of history."

- *Outsourcing* was an unknown concept in 1990 but has become an important driving force by exposing many companies to demanding customers and high standards. Before not very long, products manufactured for local consumption also dramatically improved.

Undergoing such sweeping change has been neither automatic nor easy. In many cases, the intellectual and policy lights went on only after countries and companies suffered through devastating crises which are nearly too numerous to enumerate. A complete collapse of the banking system in 1982 forced Chile to change course following the ill-advised introduction by that nation's military junta of a fixed-exchange rate. A precipitous drop in India's foreign exchange reserves to near-bankruptcy levels in 1991 led to long-overdue structural reforms. Argentina and Brazil could only battle hyperinflation and economic stagnation in the early 1990s by privatizing significant swathes of their economy. The 1994 Tequila Crisis in Mexico forced companies to either reform their old practices or wither away under the onslaught of heightened competition. The 1997 Asian financial crisis persuaded Korean, Thai, and Indonesian companies of the need to de-leverage their bloated balance sheets and deprived them of their belief that they could do everything well. In Russia, the 1998 collapse of the bond market made the newly minted oligarchs finally feel vulnerable, and grudgingly willing to adjust their farflung and often flabby operations to market realities.

IN A WORLD WITHOUT BORDERS,
ONLY GLOBAL COMPETITIVENESS IS GOOD ENOUGH

With all of these disparate developments in progress, only those companies that aspire to be competitive *globally* can hope to attain a sustainable competitive advantage. This has become not just a desirable option but a necessity. To be globally successful, companies need to be fiercely determined to be the best within their industry, not just as measured against local competitors but against the best the world has to offer. Those firms that turn out not to possess the right globe-straddling stuff will simply fail to survive. Personally, I find it ironic that the same global investors eager to apply this iron law of survival for companies in the major market economies often mentally excluded emerging markets companies from this seemingly immutable rule. Given the legacy of past protection, many investors—even some corporate managers—firmly believed that companies in emerging markets could slide by on their merits just as long as they remained competitive in their domestic markets. They had not learned the most critical lesson of globalization: stern market forces, by definition, enjoy and suffer no borders.

As my colleagues and I continued to crunch the data and ruminate on their implications, what I found most intriguing was that some emerging market winners had become as large and profitable as their counterparts in the United States, Europe, and Japan. On top of that once unimaginable feat, they had become as operationally efficient, conducted as much R&D, earned as many patents, and conceived of equally innovative designs as their First World counterparts. The best of the best worldwide were now in a class by themselves, not just in scale but in quality. Two simple tables illustrate this profound evolution from domestic to global competition. The table below depicts a straightforward comparison of the earnings among global companies. Clearly, the leading emerging market companies are no longer small, while their earnings approach—and at times even exceed—those of better-known names in developed markets. In addition, their revenues and profits have tended to grow at a rate significantly higher than their First World peers.

Earnings in Million US$

Companies		Developed Markets			Emerging Markets	
		1996	2005		1996	2005
Technology	Intel	5,157	8,664	Samsung Electronics	137	7,467
	Nokia	711	4,493	TSMC	707	2,909
	Dell	272	3,043	Hon Hai	67	1,268
	Sony	305	1,091			
	Texas Instruments	63	2,324			
	Micron	594	188			
Software	Microsoft	2,195	12,254	Tata Consulting Svc	N/A	518
	Computer Science	109	846	Infosys	10	511
	Accenture	N/A	940	Wipro	17	401
Cars	Toyota	1,893	10,930	Hyundai	66	2,429
	GM	4,963	-10,567	Tata Motor	199	297
	Volkswagen	438	1,320			
Telecom	ATT	5,908	4,786	China Mobile	543	6,545
	Verizon	3,402	7,397	America Movil	N/A	2,969
	Nippon Tel	2,256	6,630	SK Telecom	248	1,829
Oil and Gas	Shell	5,836	25,311	Petrochina	3,783	16,225
	BP	N/A	22,341	Gazprom	1,826	11,432
				Petrobras	665	9,753
				Lukoil	753	4,248
Steel	Arcelor	N/A	4,779	POSCO	738	3,922
	Nippon Steel	259	3,037	Shanghai Bao Steel	N/A	1,573
	US Steel	273	910			
	Nucor	248	1,310	Gerdau	62	1,142
Mining	BHP Billiton	N/A	6,398	CVRD	324	4,481
	Alcoa	515	1,233	Anglo-American	N/A	3,521
Cement	Lafarge	141	1,362	CEMEX	1,014	2,059
Beer	Anheuser Busch	1,190	1,839	SAB Miller	340	1,440
	Heineken	389	946	Modelo	210	669
	Inbev	N/A	1,123	Ambev	N/A	636

The table below concisely illustrates the forward and upward thrust toward the top ranking in global market share among a select group of emerging multinationals. Today, a significant number of emerging multinationals have attained the *#1 global market share* in their respective industries, which are no longer limited to a narrow slice of resource-based, low-tech activities. In fact, world-class emerging multinationals now maintain dominant market positions in some of the world's fastest growing markets. For example, Samsung (followed by Hynix, another Korean company) is the global market leader in flash memory cards used in popular iPods, cameras, and mobile phones. This market skyrocketed from $370 million in 2000 to $13 billion in 2006, according to estimates by the trade group World Semiconductor Trade Statistics.

Emerging Multinationals with #1 Global Market Share

Technology

Memory semiconductors	Samsung Electronics, Korea
Flat screens	Samsung Electronics, Korea
Logic semiconductors	TSMC, Taiwan
Electronic contract manufacturing	Hon Hai, Taiwan
Motherboards	Asustek, Taiwan
PC Notebooks	Quanta, Taiwan
Regional jet aircraft	Embraer, Brazil

Capital intensive

Oil pipes	Tenaris, Argentina
Shipbuilding	Hyundai Heavy, Korea

Consumer

Athletic and casual shoes	Yue Yuen, China / Taiwan

Materials and energy

Iron ore	CVRD, Brazil
Market pulp	Aracruz, Brazil
Gas	Gazprom, Russia
LNG gas shipping	MISC, Malaysia
Synthetic fuels	Sasol, South Africa

BIG IS NOT THE SAME AS WORLD CLASS

Each year *Fortune* draws up a list of the world's largest corporations ranked by revenues. Among the fifty-eight largest emerging market companies that made the Fortune Global 500 list in 2006,[5] each boasted in excess of $12 billion in sales. But I have included only six of these firms among the twenty-five world-class industry leaders in this book. Many emerging Fortune 500 companies are government-owned companies, often in the energy industry, that have attained global scale but are not yet world class in industry leadership, efficiency, market share, global orientation, or technology. The six on the Fortune 500 list that also made my list of twenty-five world-class contenders are: Samsung Electronics, Hyundai Motors, POSCO in Korea, Petrobas in Brazil, Hon Hai in Taiwan, and Reliance Industries in India.

The industry leaders in emerging markets are well represented among the largest *publicly traded* companies in emerging markets whose shares can be purchased by international investors. Of the twenty-five world-class emerging multinationals, eleven enjoyed sales of over $10 billion in 2005[6] and only one (Concha y Toro) had less than $1 billion in sales. Thirteen had at least $1 billion in net earnings.[7] Their market capitalization ranged from over $100 billion (Samsung Electronics) to $3 billion (Ranbaxy) and $1 billion (Concha y Toro).

The growth in emerging markets has been nothing short of astounding. In 1981, the total value of *all* stocks listed on emerging markets stock exchanges was $80 billion. That was less than the market capitalization of the largest emerging market firm,[8] Samsung Electronics, in 2005. Over the past quarter century the total market capitalization of emerging markets as a group has risen to over $5 trillion.[9] In 1981, portfolio investors had invested less than a few hundred million in emerging markets firms. Today, record annual portfolio investment flows of over $60 billion[10] constitute the leading edge of a trend.

As a value investor, I am intrigued by the prospect of analyzing why certain companies turn out to be attractive long-term *investments* while others, which at one time may have *seemed* promising, never really pan out. *Why* do some companies—even in the same country or the same industry—become successful while others fail? Understanding the traits that these successful companies have in common will aid us in determining which firms will be in the ascendant among the *next* generation of successful companies and investments.

METHODOLOGY FOR PICKING
WORLD-CLASS COMPANIES

Relying not only on my own research and many years of company visits but also on judgments by industry peers, other leading executives in emerging markets, and broker analysts, I began by analyzing which companies stood out in their various industries in terms of size, long-term growth, and industry reputation. I followed up on this raw data by interviewing many CEOs, CFOs, COOs, and other senior managers. Later, I further narrowed down the group in a more systematic and rigorous fashion by screening them for the five criteria specified below to pick the companies that were not merely big or well-known but had earned truly world-class credentials.

- a leader in its industry globally
- global presence in exports and, often, production
- top-three market share in enough countries to be a global player
- globally competitive not just in price but in quality, technology, and design
- benchmarks itself against the biggest and best in the world

A SUCCESSION OF STEPS TO WORLD-CLASS STATUS

In my discussions with the CEOs and in my related research, I found that not one single step but a succession of steps prompted emerging multinationals to make the lion's leap into the world-class category. The process of learning typically began with adopting unconventional thinking and moving beyond the comfort of infant industry protection to surviving brutal (even life-threatening) crises that led to greater focus and the need to deleverage the company's balance sheet. Bold management decisions frequently made the difference between wallowing in mediocrity and attaining the high honor of world class. An intuitive understanding of the need for quality, design, and technology helped companies like Samsung, Embraer, Hyundai, Infosys, and High Tech Computer: Instead of shying away from high-tech, high-stakes arenas they eagerly embrace them, despite the higher risks. Finally, either building or buying a brand has become the capstone for consumer-driven companies to establish themselves on the global scene.

THE POWER OF UNCONVENTIONAL THINKING

Emerging multinationals did not enter the world-class club by just follow-ing textbook practices and solutions. *Unconventional thinking* challenged (and even leapfrogged) well-established industry practices as a success driver for nearly every one of these companies. More than half of the twenty-five emerging multinationals created a quiet (or sometimes noisy) revolution in their own industries, by introducing innovations that were often widely ridiculed as simply not feasible at their inception. As new entrants, these firms frequently had little choice when attempting to gain market share from deeply entrenched incumbents but to attempt audacious solutions.

Surprisingly, a strong-willed government official was sometimes responsible for pushing through a new idea by selling it to entrepreneurs who in turn would sell it to backers and customers. In Taiwan, a far-seeing government minister (Mr. K. T. Li), determined to move the island beyond making televisions and other low-tech electronic products, persuaded Mor-ris Chang after a lifetime of experience in Silicon Valley to launch a semi-conductor plant lacking its own, in-house clients. What was once a gleam in the eye of that government minister became—under the guidance of entrepreneur Chang—TSMC, the largest independent pure foundry silicon-wafer fabricator in the world.

A young Norwegian who had fought in the forests during the Resis-tance in World War II and had been admitted to the Harvard Business School without ever going to college, landed in Brazil in the early 1950s. Erling Lorentzen became convinced that he could produce better and cheaper fibrous pulp from fast-growing eucalyptus trees than from the slower-growing Scandinavian pines of his home country. Just as the Korean government ignored the advice of the World Bank that construct-ing a steel mill lacking proximate reserves of iron ore, coal, or experience was insane, Lorentzen was not in the slightest bit discouraged when the World Bank's private sector arm IFC beseeched him to forget about mak-ing pulp from Brazilian eucalyptus, because the idea would never work.

HOW LIFE-THREATENING CRISES FORCED COMPANIES TO ADAPT AND REFORM

In some cases, it took a life-threatening crisis to shake up companies with sufficient force to oblige them to transform themselves—or die. The Mexican crisis sparked new ways of doing business all over Latin America. Faced with plummeting demand and a lack of credit, companies needed not only to cut staff and idle factories but to rethink their entire business model. As Paolo Rocca, the CEO of Tenaris in Argentina, succinctly put it: "Only companies that were able to adapt to the crisis survived." When Rocca's major client, Mexico's national oil company Pemex, suddenly stopped all purchases of drilling pipes, Tenaris's Mexican subsidiary TAMSA used superior information technology to help Pemex forget its inventory woes and began to deliver pipes only when needed—a capable and impressive twist on by-then-fashionable Japanese-style "just-in-time delivery." Similarly, the Asian financial crisis acted like a tsunami in swallowing up many uncompetitive companies but left standing those that had already begun to change. Samsung's CEO Jong Yong Yun candidly admitted to me that "the Asian crisis made it clear to everyone that we had no choice but to change."

FROM SURVIVAL TO GLOBAL LEADERSHIP

While surviving a crisis certainly concentrates the mind, a major setback does not automatically translate into a rousing success story. In Korea, the largest conglomerate, Daewoo, virtually vanished from the map while the smaller Samsung and Hyundai groups seized the opportunity to radically restructure and focus their ambitions and build major global brands. In Mexico, in the wake of the 1994 Tequila Crisis, large Monterrey-based companies such as the leading conglomerate Alfa, chemical producer Cydsa, and glass manufacturer Vitro never fully recovered or were unable to adjust to the resulting more open economy. In contrast, Mexican entrepreneur Carlos Slim Helu built a massive empire out of privatized companies (including Telmex), starting out before the crisis and only gaining strength from having survived the slowdown. In the process, he became the world's third richest man, according to *Forbes* magazine.

The difference between "world class" and "also ran" was frequently the product of management's willingness to take ambitious but disciplined gambles aimed at moving the firms into new business areas that demanded a combination of super-high quality and a willingness to jettison second-rate product lines. These entrepreneurs were not afraid of first-class technology and innovative design. Samsung in Korea set its sights on becoming the world's largest, most efficient and technologically advanced maker of memory chips in the world. It later entered the brand-new world of mobile phones with its own technology. Hyundai Motor's chairman Mong Koo Chung made the bold claim that "the only way to survive is to raise our quality to Toyota's level" when its American sales were still reeling from scraping rock bottom in the J.D. Power quality surveys. Yet another now independent part of the Hyundai Group evolved into the world's largest shipyard. All three companies were major but not dominant players in their domestic market before the Asian crisis. After the crisis, both emerged as world leaders in their respective categories, once their less adaptive domestic competitors bit the dust. As exporters, they were at first viewed as producers of cheap and respectable low-quality products. But in the wake of the crisis, they emerged as top-notch respected brands after overhauling their product lines and relentlessly focusing on quality.

THE TWENTY-FIVE WORLD-CLASS EMERGING MULTINATIONALS

More than half of the companies of world-class status operate in capital intensive or technology-oriented industries requiring high rates of spending on research and development to remain competitive. Most but not all of these high-tech and financially sophisticated firms are located in emerging Asia. My list includes **fourteen high-tech or capital-intensive companies** among the Top Twenty-five.

Samsung Electronics	Korea	The premier emerging market brand
Hyundai Motor	Korea	Competitive car brand
Hyundai Heavy	Korea	Largest shipbuilder in world
POSCO	Korea	Efficient, high quality steel manufacturer

TSMC	Taiwan	First independent semiconductor foundry
Hon Hai	Taiwan	#1 electronic contract manufacturer
High Tech Computer	Taiwan	Leading smart phone/PDA designer and maker
Lenovo	China	#3 global computer maker, bought IBM ThinkPad
Infosys	India	Successful IT services provider
Ranbaxy	India	A leading generics drug maker and researcher
Embraer	Brazil	Leading small jet maker
Tenaris	Argentina	World leader in pipes for oil industry
Sasol	South Africa	Leader in synthetic fuels
MISC	Malaysia	Leading LNG shipper

Five others are basic **commodity producers,** of which just two are truly resource-based: iron ore for CVRD and eucalyptus trees for Aracruz. The other three are increasingly sophisticated producers of cement, petrochemicals, and energy but their resources are abundant and each has had to develop its own special edge—both technological and logistical—in order to remain globally competitive.

CEMEX	Mexico	#3 global cement producer, #1 in the United States
CVRD	Brazil	#1 iron ore producer with global exports
Aracruz	Brazil	#1 market pulp producer, innovative and low-cost
Petrobras	Brazil	Oil and gas company strong in deep sea drilling
Reliance	India	Global-scale petrochemical producer

The remaining **six** emerging multinationals are **consumer firms and service companies**, producing a wide range of products from shoes to refrigerators, beer, and wine, and providing telephone service (both mobile and land-line) and media and entertainment.

Yue Yuen	China/Taiwan	Athletic and casual shoes for leading brands
Haier	China	Leading brand in China, #3 globally in refrigerators
Modelo	Mexico	Maker of Corona beer, a leading global brand

Concha y Toro   Chile   A leading wine brand
Televisa   Mexico   Hispanic soap operas attract a
                                        global audience
Telmex/America Movil   Mexico   Latin American telecom with
                                        global aspirations

Country of Origin of Emerging Multinationals					
Asia	14	Latin America	10	Africa	1
Korea	4	Brazil	4	South Africa	1
Taiwan	3	Mexico	4		
China	3	Chile	1		
India	3	Argentina	1		
Malaysia	1				

STILL A LONG WAY TO GO IN SOME INDUSTRIES

My list of world-class global competitors does not include members of such labor-intensive industries as textiles, toys, food, and retail. Finance and banking are also conspicuously absent. While there are indeed plenty of good-sized textile and food companies in emerging markets, most have yet to graduate into global superstars. The textile and toy industries remain so deeply fragmented that even fierce competition has not given any single company, or even handful of firms, a chance to rise above the fray. In food and retail, some companies (including the chicken and meat processor Sadia in Brazil and the retail chain Shinsegae in Korea) have been able to build local brands or even gain a significant level of exports, yet still lack the sophistication and global scope of Nestle, Unilever, Carrefour, or Wal-Mart.

In banking, the Hong Kong and Shanghai Bank (HSBC) originated in China but expanded much later on a worldwide basis away from its traditional Asian roots. HSBC, for example, acquired control of the Marine Midland Bank in the United States, and in the wake of the 1997 handover of Hong Kong to China, relocated its world headquarters to London. The Indian mortgage and real estate lender Housing Development Finance Corporation (HDFC), along with the HDFC Bank and ICICI Bank, all qualify as innovative financial institutions of sizable scope, which to their credit have shaken up the sleepy, clubby, state-dominated banking sector in India. Yet none has taken the necessary steps out of their local markets onto the global stage that would justify inclusion in a selective list of world-class players. Hyperinflation combined with the resulting strato spheric interest rates made Brazilian banks like Banco Itau highly efficient and respondent to external stimuli. Nevertheless, no bank originating in emerging markets has succeeded in establishing a global presence or leading its industry in innovation.

SURPRISES AND MYTHS

The resulting carefully culled list of twenty-five world-class emerging multinationals may shatter some comfortable myths and contain more than a few surprises. The following observations are apparent from the mass of data and thematic conversations with principals:

- Only a handful of emerging multinationals rely on natural resources or cheap labor as a major competitive edge.
- Many have held their own—or even leapfrogged previous industry leaders—in highly capital-intensive or high-tech industries.
- The competitive edge of these companies typically includes "man-made" factors (driven by management) rather than merely "natural" factors.
- World-class companies can be found not just in emerging Asia (14) but also in Latin America (10) and in South Africa (1). They are still missing in Russia and Eastern Europe.
- While some of the leading Russian and Chinese energy and telephone companies are global in size, they are not yet world class in either market share, efficiency, or technology.

It is widely but erroneously believed that emerging multinationals typically rely on cheap labor to form a critical facet of their competitive advantage. Even if that was true early in their history, that is rarely the case today. The same holds true of another emerging markets environmental factor: being sheltered by government policies of

Unconventional thinking, an ability to adapt to life-threatening crises, a global mind-set, and disciplined ambition are crucial ingredients for virtually all companies that succeed in attaining world-class status.

infant-industry protection. Although many (but not all) firms were at one time heavily government subsidized, promoted, or protected, few would have become successful on a global scale if they had failed to wean themselves of this clumsy shield or had not tested themselves in the demanding arena of export markets. None of the world-class companies on my list currently benefits from government protection in any significant way. Nor do natural resources score high on the list of key success factors for the top twenty-five.

Key Success Factors

An early commitment to export markets	21
A relentless focus on superior execution and quality	20
Emphasis on technology and design	15
Inventing a new industry model	13
Spotting a niche overlooked by established players	12
Using cheap brainpower as a competitive edge	12
Acquisition strategy	11
Fast-to-market	9
Branding	7
Organizational model/logistics	6
Natural resources	4
Cheap labor	4

Source: Interviews and research by author

This makes the primary success drivers different from general perception. "Manmade" factors turn out to be more important than natural resources or the advantage of low-cost labor in determining whether a firm wins or loses over the long haul. It turns out that unconventional thinking, an ability to adapt to life-threatening crises, a global mind-set, and disciplined ambition are crucial ingredients for virtually all companies that succeed in attaining world-class status.

A GLOBAL MIND-SET: BREAKING OUT OF THE INFANT INDUSTRY PROTECTION SHELL

An early and strong *export orientation* emerged as the major success factor for a whopping twenty-one out of the twenty-five world-class companies. Even firms like Sasol, Reliance, Petrobras, and Telmex, which for a long time catered to domestic customers, learned that lesson eventually. Such international contacts helped some companies to find companies in the United States and Europe that were ready to outsource some of their production.

Most companies found that exporting was not easy and, in fact, many overseas ventures did not work out in the first foray. Hyundai's first entry in the American car market, to cite just one prominent example, ended in disaster, with a long list of customer complaints about poor car quality followed by the ultimate humiliation of becoming the butt of Jay Leno's late night talk show. The major international oil companies were reluctant to buy Tenaris's drilling pipes at first, until Tenaris vastly enhanced its quality and service. Infosys spent nearly a decade wooing American customers before the first companies were willing to outsource some of their IT services. Before long, though, a trickle became a flood.

Getting a lucky break can be crucial. For Samsung Electronics, an antidumping suit against Japanese semiconductor producers gave it its first inroad into the U.S. market. For Infosys, the widespread fear of a millennium software bug brought it new business. For CEMEX, yet another antidumping suit drove it to go on an acquisition spree in Europe and Asia, ultimately leading it to buy the company that launched the dumping suit against it. Today, CEMEX and its U.S. subsidiaries are the largest producers of concrete products in the United States. In the end, however, taking clever advantage of opportunities spurned by others is often of greater importance than luck. A different way to say the same thing might be that great companies, like great people, have a way of creating their own luck.

OBSESSION WITH EXECUTION AND QUALITY

A far more critical ingredient for sustainable success than the vision and strategy so beloved by management and investment books is a relentless and even obsessive focus and drive to achieve superior execution and quality. This drive must come straight from the top, but only succeeds if it becomes deeply ingrained in the corporate culture. At all levels, managers and employees in successful companies not only shout service, execution, and quality (sometimes literally) as their mantra but, more importantly, take a palpable pride in making products that are regarded as world-class by substantial groups of objective observers.

Samsung chairman Kun Hee Lee went as far as to declare that "product defects are cancers that must be completely eradicated." This is the pride that counters the prejudice. Nearly every manufacturing company in our survey seemed to have a similar story about poor products literally getting smashed or burned on the assembly line, to serve as near-biblical reminders that there are dire consequences attached to shoddy or careless work.

An emphasis on technology and design tends to go hand-in-hand with execution and quality. Most emerging multinationals recognize that the era of "reverse engineering" and other forms of blatant imitation (if not piracy) are coming to an end. They are enormously eager to have their own R&D, develop their own engines, conceive their own designs, and—in short—transform themselves from imitators into innovators.

Of course, such a relentless focus on execution, quality, technology, and design is not unique to emerging markets. It is common to just about every successful company everywhere. What is surprising is how early and fast emerging multinationals have learned this crucial lesson and have learned to apply it in new ways. Sometimes we tend to forget that sloppy execution and second-rate quality were the general rule among many emerging markets companies as recently as ten to fifteen years ago. Just as "Made in Japan" was a term once widely associated with cheap shoddy goods. "Made in China" or "India" still carries a stigma today, but not for long. Korea shed that stigma with astonishing rapidity in just a few years.

LEAPFROG COMPETITORS BY INVENTING A UNIQUE NEW, LOGISTICS-BASED ORGANIZATIONAL MODEL

A critical discovery for smart entrepreneurs in emerging markets has been that producing low-cost products may be a good short-term shot in the arm, but does not provide a sustainable competitive advantage. As soon as a company succeeds at something, hundreds of new imitative competitors will jump into the fray, impose new efficiencies on a replicable product or process, and force profits to rapidly disappear. Something extra is needed to maintain attractive profit margins. This "extra something" typically has little to do with cost, scale, efficiency, or flexibility—although all are important. The crucial difference often has to do with *logistics,* as in helping a client solve a problem in managing the supply chain rather than with the production process itself. For example:

- Terry Gou, CEO of the consumer electronics firm Hon Hai in Taiwan, makes everything from Sony PlayStations to entire modules of components found inside Dell computers or Nokia handsets. When Dell introduced its direct distribution model, Gou immediately foresaw that a one-stop shopping model would soon be needed and that the future would be in joint design.
- CEMEX combined its early focus on information technology with the example of Domino Pizza's quick delivery policy to deliver ready mix to construction projects within half an hour.
- Argentina's Tenaris introduced "just in time" inventory management at the wellhead for global oil companies as far away as Nigeria well before its competitors because "we are completely in tune with an interconnected world," according to CEO Paolo Rocca. These types of innovations turned out to make the difference not only in establishing good client relations but in maintaining a sustainable advantage against global competitors.

Such "man-made" as opposed to natural competitive advantages have been critical to the success of world-class companies such as Embraer, Tenaris, and CEMEX, all of which have employed the power of advanced information technology to create a sophisticated—even unique—organizational model that has helped them leapfrog over their slower competitors in serving clients. These firms frequently found a way to dispense with a legacy of old habits, ossified ways of doing things, outmoded management concepts, and outdated plants to create new business practices that combine the immediacy of the Internet with the intimacy of family business.

STRATEGIES: FROM "TRIED AND TRUE" TO "EMERGING MARKETS TWIST"

Successful companies everywhere know the tried-and-true textbook policies and disciplines. These are Corporate Strategy 101:

- Focus on core activities, outsource noncore activities
- Become a market leader in major economies
- Keep costs low and product quality high

- Service customers well
- Invest in R&D
- Hire the best and brightest and keep them motivated
- Build a strong brand
- Motivate employees through options and other incentives

Like great companies everywhere, emerging multinationals first followed these textbook rules, but then learned to move conceptually beyond them. Not only are they better at operating in other emerging markets—with their poorly developed distribution channels, much needed courting of government officials, erratic regulation, and constant pirating—but as newcomers in global markets, they have learned that in a world replete with well-established brand names, they need to offer a special angle to differentiate themselves. To prevail against stiff and often intense competition, they learned to improve on the textbook "best practices" and develop new and/or unique business models and different strategies with a special "emerging markets twist."

Emerging Market Twist #1:
"Unbundle" an industry by taking advantage of "legacy thinking"
to create opportunities for newcomers.

Mines *must* be kept close to steel plants. Paper plants *must* be located near forests. IT services *must* be kept in-house to provide quick help. Fabrication of computer chips *must* be set up adjacent to the final product. All of these were immutable industry principles for decades before the world changed. Huge ships made it possible to ship commodities cheaply. Computers transformed inventory management. Virtually cost-free Internet communications rendered the question irrelevant of whether a programmer was sitting in the next cubicle or the next continent. Eager newcomers spotted these opportunities faster than well-established companies, whose legacy thinking had created old habits they found hard to shake.

In Korea, POSCO dared to build a huge steel mill without having any raw materials—iron ore or coke—nearby. Taiwan's TSMC built its semiconductor plant as an "independent fab" without ensuring a captive market of customers, bucking the trend of industry leaders like IBM and Intel. Aracruz in Brazil ignored the standard industry practice of its Scandinavian, Canadian, and American competitors, which supplied pulp to their own paper mills. Instead, it made a name for itself by servicing clients unable to produce enough pulp to supply their own mills or (in the case of tissue producers) required a different kind of pulp tailored to meet their special needs. Aracruz *vertically dis-integrated* by producing pulp on a massive scale for a global market and shipping pulp halfway around the world, even if that meant disregarding conventional wisdom, which stated that keeping costs low demanded shipping pulp only to customers within a region. All of these companies became successful by *unbundling* (or as some would say, "disaggregating") their industry.

Emerging Market Twist #2:
Vertically integrate the supply chain by building on related expertise.

Focusing on core activities (Corporate Strategy 101 lesson #1) works well when there is a network of reliable suppliers nearby able to pick up the other pieces. Lacking such a proximate network, the consumer electronics firm Hon Hai in Taiwan (which prospered by manufacturing components under contract) decided to *vertically integrate:* it first discovered that it could use its molding expertise for more than a few components, then that it had an edge in combining its mechanical and electrical engineering talents to produce even larger modules for computers and mobile handsets. Finally, having absorbed the lesson that its clients like Dell, HP, Sony, and Nokia increasingly preferred one-stop shopping, Hon Hai moved into producing entire component sets for better-known names, while hiding its own contributions from consumers' eyes under a modest veil stitched together from bigger brands.

Emerging Market Twist #3: *Be a chameleon*

The "gun that won the West," the Winchester rifle produced in New Haven and made popular by Teddy Roosevelt and John Wayne, is a classic example of a great innovation that became an outdated technology. Its factories at one time employed 19,000 but that fell to 200 before the company finally closed.[11] Similar lessons have not been lost on Samsung or, for that matter, virtually every technology company in Taiwan, Korea, and China. While the Asian financial crisis taught them the hard lesson that it is impossible to be good at everything, to simply narrowly focus on core activities does not make a winning strategy either.

Instead, many Asian companies follow a deliberate *chameleon* strategy, taking care to move incrementally up the value chain until they reach the stratosphere of high-end branded product. Take Samsung Electronics, for example, which relentlessly moved from toasters and televisions to semiconductors, handsets, and flat screens. While all companies adapt to survive (or die if they don't), East Asian companies have a history of being quicker on their feet than virtually any others around the world.

Emerging Market Twist #4:
Turn the outsourcing model upside down.

Instead of producing parts for other plane manufacturers in the United States and Europe, and becoming an outsourcing service and product provider for bigger clients, Embraer of Brazil insisted upon remaining in the driver's seat by designing two generations of sophisticated small jets from scratch. In effect, Embraer turned the outsourcing model upside down by becoming the *outsourcer* as opposed to the *outsourcee*. By enlisting sophisticated U.S., European, Russian, and Japanese companies as its subcontractors—or "production partners"—Embraer produces top-quality regional jets that have been market best sellers while competitors like Fairchild-Dornier and Fokker went bankrupt and Canada's Bombardier has had a tough time keeping up.

Emerging Market Twist #5:
Follow a South-South strategy.

Once upon a time, if you wanted to make it big in the world, you had to first make it big in the United States and Western Europe. But today, and increasingly in the future, if you want to make it big, you will need to make it big in China and, to a lesser degree, in India. China is well on the road to becoming the world's anchor economy in the twenty-first century, just as the United States was in the twentieth. Emerging multinationals grasp these trends far more acutely than many of their First World counterparts and competitors. They understand where their long-term future lies: often closer to home than ever before. As formerly peripheral economies become the world's rising economic powers, the primary markets will no longer be limited to just the affluent Western economies. Their own experience with volatile, poorly regulated markets lacking sophisticated distribution networks helps them to adapt quickly and has taught them how to seduce and cajole often resistant (and even corrupt) government officials.

Plane builder Embraer sells its regional jets in Saudi Arabia, India, and China knowing that it has an edge in these countries because none of them wants to be dependent exclusively on U.S. suppliers. Pharmaceutical company Ranbaxy developed a "BRICs" strategy to expand its generics sales in Brazil and Russia where it has a better chance to become a market leader even if its current sales in the United States are still much higher. Hyundai Motor recently upped the ante in the United States by constructing a billion-dollar factory in Alabama but has also built equally large new plants in China and India, where it reasonably aspires to vault into a top-three market position. While it does not have similar hopes for the United States and Europe, it does aim to build its global reputation in those markets. Samsung has turned itself into a premium brand in China, well ahead of local and even international brands. In developed markets, Samsung is content to be recognized among the leading brands; it does not need to become Number One.

Mexico's Televisa uses *the emerging markets wavelength as a competitive edge* in exporting its telenovelas to over one hundred countries. Televisa is so finely attuned to Hispanic culture and language that its soap operas (*telenovelas*) often attract higher audiences than major network stations in the United States. Its television series focused on upwardly mobile heroines also appeal to many impoverished households.

Emerging Markets Twist #6:
Solve the zip code problem by going global.

As Roger Agnelli, the CEO of CVRD in Brazil, put it to me: "Brazilian companies suffer from being in the wrong zip code. Even though we sell globally, we pay more for finance. It took us a long time to convince the rating agencies." The fact is that having the wrong zip code can prove a massive obstacle to achieving true world-class status, particularly for companies in countries like Mexico, Brazil, and Argentina that have suffered from debt problems in the past. Difficulties in obtaining project finance and lines of credit can be as great a handicap as overcoming amateurish management, chronic nepotism, or less-than-optimal corporate governance.

One way to solve the problem is not only to *operate* but also to *borrow* in the mature markets of the United States, Western Europe, and other economic centers. CEMEX in Mexico took over leading Spanish cement companies in part to raise funds and borrow as a "Spanish" company. Tenaris in Argentina has European members of its group that can borrow on European terms. Both succeeded in changing their zip code.

> *New world-class companies are becoming employers of significance in* industrial *nations, driven by their global marketing efforts, their eagerness to work closely with their most demanding clients, and their search for the most up-to-date technology and design*

Emerging Market Twist #7:
Use a veil of anonymity by aspiring to be the largest company no one has ever heard of.

Samsung, Hyundai, and Grupo Modelo's Corona are all examples of emerging markets global brands. Other emerging multinationals, not quite so patient, including Lenovo with IBM ThinkPad and Haier with Maytag, have endeavored to buy brands on the open market by taking slow-growing businesses off their First World owners' often eager hands. Other even more obscure companies have methodically built a global presence behind a veil of anonymity. Hon Hai of Taiwan produces for Dell, HP, Sony, Nokia, and others; Yue Yuen produces athletic shoes for Nike, Reebok, and Adidas and casual shoes for Timberland.

Emerging Market Twist #8:
Translate the classic Chinese Sun Tzu war strategy into focusing on a niche ignored by market leaders.

Size can make all the difference. The planes built by Boeing and Airbus are often too large for regional routes but many travelers don't like the slow speed and weather-related bumpiness of noisy turbo props. Market deregulation and competition from new carriers provided an opening for small, regional jets that Brazil's Embraer spotted before most others. China's Haier exploited another niche to get noticed in the American market. Its mini-fridges for college students became so popular that big box stores like Wal-Mart began to notice the newcomer in the appliance area and sourced other models from Haier's product line.

Emerging Market Twist #9:
Offer cheap brainpower instead of cheap brawn power
(making R&D and software development more affordable).

The new economy came in like a lion and went out like a lamb: the great fanfare and sky-high expectations finally fizzled (at least in the short term) when it largely failed to deliver on its outlandish promises. Technology moved so fast that much less fiber optic cable was needed than was installed around the world. But in the meantime, the Internet—invented to allow the Pentagon to communicate even after a nuclear strike and first used by nerdy academic types—took the world by storm. All of a sudden, free and instantaneous digital communication allowed people everywhere to be in touch at virtually no cost. Even if pornography and sports headed the list of "information" people searched for as they browsed the World Wide Web, in the end, the Internet rendered it irrelevant whether the person you worked with was sitting in an adjacent cubicle or thousands of miles away.

Armed with the Internet, a college graduate in India with software expertise or even English language skills could do as good a job—sometimes even better—as a similar professional in the United States or Europe, while being paid one-tenth or one-fifth as much as his or her First World counterpart. Not only goods could be traded but services became frictionless and mobile. IT services companies like Infosys, Tata Consultancy Services, and Wipro in India were quick to take advantage of this unprecedented opportunity. Ranbaxy Laboratories and others soon followed suit by offering drug research to global pharmaceutical companies while also working hard at developing their own proprietary drugs. In the end, the secrets of becoming world class boil down to bold ambition, discipline, adopting a global mind-set, and making adaptability a core capability.

Lessons

- *Find the most (rather than least) demanding taskmasters as clients.*
- *Compete globally, not just locally or regionally.*
- *Expect trouble—and react in a decisive way to bounce back.*
- *It is OK to not get it right the first time, as long as you get it right the second time.*
- *Vision is important but execution is paramount.*
- *Patience and persistence rather than flamboyance are key.*
- *Build a brand—or buy one.*

PART II

THE NEW BREED
Twenty-five World-Class Emerging Multinationals

CHAPTER 3

From Under the Radar Screen: Building Emerging Global Brands

Samsung and Concha y Toro are setting new trends

Strategies

- *Set an early goal to build a strong brand and be ready for a long campaign*
- *Follow a strategy of brand leadership in growing emerging markets and brand recognition in first-world markets*
- *Use the success of a breakthrough product to enhance overall brand recognition*

Travelers racing through the Dallas/Fort Worth Airport, American Airlines' sprawling home hub, could be forgiven for being slightly distracted by an eye-catching fifty-foot sculptural advertisement depicting a giant golden hand clutching a twenty-five-foot-tall Samsung mobile phone. The crisp screen of the phone, executed in Samsung's distinctive clamshell design, displayed crystal-clear video images that alternately told the time, temperature, and showcased a panoply of Samsung products ranging from televisions to telephones to music players to digital cameras. This Texas-sized clamshell-shaped cell phone, fully five stories tall, was voted by locals "one of the area's most memorable billboards," according to *BusinessWeek*. Its first sculpture went up at Paris's Charles de Gaulle airport in 2002 and Samsung has, or plans, identical installations at twenty-five high-traffic airports across the globe.

Samsung's unconventional marketing campaign has already accomplished four critical missions.

1. It boosted the firm's brand recognition worldwide.
2. It was a subtle reminder of Samsung's clever early use of the clamshell design at a point when imitators outnumber innovators.
3. It underscored Samsung's increasingly strong global reach.
4. It visually reinforced the fact that, just two days before its Texas-sized phone was installed at Fort Worth, an Interbrand–Business-Week survey of the top global brands ranked Samsung at #20, while archrival Sony had fallen to #28. For the first time Samsung had overtaken Sony in a key metric of twenty-first century competitive success: *brand value.* Interbrand's ranking unambiguously affirmed that Samsung was not only the premier emerging market brand but that it had carved out a top spot in the global brand universe. With a 186 percent surge over the past five years, Samsung has risen faster in brand value than any other brand in the world. As press reports trumpeting Samsung's triumph reflected, few key performance indicators are taken more seriously today by managers and investors than brand value, brand equity, and brand growth.

One indicator of Samsung's surpassing strength going into the Emerging Markets Century was that it had not only beaten Sony but also outranked such global icons as Pepsi, Nike, Budweiser, the Gap, Ikea, Harley-Davidson, and Starbucks in the quest for brand value worldwide. Only Finnish phone giant Nokia, another example of a company that reinvented itself from a second-rate electronics company, still outstrips Samsung in brand equity in consumer electronics. "Tough times for the mobile-phone giant [Nokia] as its market share slips and younger buyers turn to rivals such as Samsung," *BusinessWeek* acidly observed. "No longer known just for undercutting the prices of big Japanese brands, the Korean consumer-electronics dynamo is suddenly cool," So cool, in fact, that Samsung ranked even higher than too-cool-for-school Apple, home of the hugely popular iPod, and easily besting consumer electronics rivals Siemens, Philips, and Panasonic, as well as Sony. In yet another indication of the swiftness of this reversal of fortune, in 2005 Samsung earned seven times Sony's net profit of just over $1 billion on revenues of $56 billion, that were lower than Sony's $66 billion.

> *Interbrand's ranking unambivalently affirmed that Samsung was not only the premier emerging market brand but that it had carved out a top spot in the global brand world. Over the past five years, Samsung has risen faster in brand value than any other brand in the world.*

THE POWER OF A BRAND?

As Warren Buffett observed at the 1995 annual meeting of Berkshire-Hathaway shareholders, "Wonderful castles surrounded by deep dangerous moats where the leader inside is an honest and decent person . . . we like companies with dominant positions whose franchise is hard to duplicate." Buffet recognized that a franchise—a well-defined niche that sets a company apart from its competitors and helps it sustain pricing power and profit margins—changes the game of competition. A strong brand provides such a franchise. This is why virtually every management guru and business book singles out a company's brand as key to sustaining market leadership, particularly for consumer goods companies. Not all great brands are made by great companies, but few great companies or great long-term investments are made in the absence of great brands.

> *Not all brands are great companies or good investments but there are very few great companies or great long-term investments that are not major brands.*

The power of a strong brand is rarely underestimated by global competitors in this day and age, no matter what category or industry they play in. It is now widely accepted today that people buy brands, not products, whether it be a Nokia handset, a Sony or a Samsung television, a GE refrigerator, a Coca-Cola or Pepsi soft drink, or a Starbucks coffee (still trailing Nescafe worldwide, but climbing fast). Though few people outside Brazil yet buy a Brazilian Guarana soft drink, the younger set in Asia, Europe, and the United States prefer Samsung handsets over Motorola[1] or Nokia, and snap up cute and convenient Haier fridges from China for their college dorm rooms. Delta and US Air fly Embraer jets instead of Boeings on many regional routes. Chile's Concha y Toro label has become a familiar brand even among wine drinkers in the United States and Europe. Mexico's Grupo Modelo's Corona, in its distinctive long-necked clear glass bottle, is one of the strongest beer brands in the world, beating former category leader Heineken among imported American brands.

The term "brand" derives from the stamp incised into the surface of a product to certify its purity, authenticity, and origin. Brands have been around as long as there have been products, but brands in the modern sense of the term only began to play a significant commercial role with the advent of mass distribution in the latter part of the nineteenth century. As American industrialization fostered the creation of mass markets and mass merchandise, the trust consumers formerly placed in local producers was increasingly transferred to producers of nationwide brands. Globalization is repeating this process in the Emerging Market Century

Cincinnati-based Procter & Gamble, purveyors of Tide, Dove, and other soaps and detergents, was the first firm to take the notion of sustaining and growing brands seriously. In 1931, Neil McElroy, a P&G lieutenant who later became secretary of defense under President Eisenhower, wrote a memo to his superiors proposing that each "brand" in the P&G stable should have its own "brand man," who would take charge of all activities related to promoting that product as its own stand-alone business. In the midst of the Great Depression, the modern era of brand management had begun as it became widely recognized that people would pay a premium for a branded product. Brands are a proxy for the intensity of consumers' *emotional* connection to a firm and its products, which in turn helps to define its long-term strength and leadership. Since Interbrand founder John Murphy performed the first brand evaluation in 1989, managers worldwide have understood the necessity of managing the intangible asset of brand equity—including brands, copyrights, patents, customer loyalty, distribution, and staff knowledge—as scrupulously as more tangible assets such as factories, inventories, and cash. Executives' often intense fixation on maintaining a strong brand is rooted in a realization that a strong brand offers protection against creeping commoditization. In today's competitive commercial environment, carrying the perception of producing, or less enviably, *being* a commodity can mean the kiss of death for a product or firm.

Historically, the vast majority of leading emerging market companies never had to worry about building brands, because in their home markets their names were well known to consumers. Instead, they relied on a different and more classic "moat"—protection from foreign competition, which provided local dominance not through quality and excellence but by the erection of tariff walls. That cozy protectionist world, however, has been rapidly vanishing before our eyes. With their old moat eroding, a handful of emerging markets firms have begun—and in fact, been forced—to focus on digging a new moat that provides superior protection from competition in a rapidly globalizing world: *brand franchises.* Emerging markets companies are increasingly under pressure to break out of their cocoons and build global brands, or face the dire consequences of remaining local fixtures or low-cost commodity producers. *They have discovered that brands matter.*

As of 2005, a handful of emerging markets multinationals qualify as major brands, having begun to develop global brand identities outside their domestic markets: The list is not long but growing fast. Samsung's steady presence on Interbrand-BusinessWeek's prestigious Top 100 list of brands was joined by two other Korean companies, Hyundai (#84) and LG (#97) in 2005. On a different yet arguably as important list of the top 100 brands compiled by the World Brand Laboratory, Chinese consumer appliance giant Haier (which recently gained notoriety in its bid for Maytag) recently entered the global list at number #95. Acer computers, Hongkong and Shanghai Bank (with its Chinese roots), Corona beer, and Concha y Toro wine are a few other brands enjoying widespread global appeal. Others such as San Miguel beer and Bimbo bread built a regional reputation in preparation for going global, with as yet mixed results. Quite a few others (such as Thailand's C.P. Pokphand) tried to build a big brand but failed.

For smart pioneers like Samsung, executing a sophisticated branding strategy that includes everything from marketing, product quality, and technology to design and fashion has become something of an obsession. As others follow Samsung's lead and consumers in emerging markets begin to set the tone and the measure of what's "cool" and what's "in"—particularly with the younger generation—brands from these nations will inevitably become more powerful.

Historically, it has taken time and significant amounts of money to build a brand from scratch, although in recent decades some major brands (particularly but not all high-tech and media companies) have exploded onto the scene with astounding velocity. During the early stages of their export drive, many emerging markets companies chose to remain anonymous, and to adopt a stealth strategy to achieve if not renown, at least a firm foothold in major markets. Yet any number of signs abound that this state of affairs is unlikely to continue indefinitely. Interbrand publishes an annual reader's choice award that assesses the impact on global brand value of *regional* consumer preferences. Choices in Asia and Latin America were, not surprisingly, starkly different from some of the top North American (Apple, Google, and Starbucks) and European choices (Ikea and Nokia) that made it onto the Top-Ten global list. In the Asian-Pacific region, the top four favorites were, predictably, consumer electronics and automotive firms Sony, Samsung, LG, and Toyota. In Latin America, the five top brands hailed from different categories: CEMEX (cement), Corona (beer), Bacardi (liquors), Bimbo (bread), and Concha y Toro (wine).

As consumer markets in emerging Asia and other regions grow in importance, global brand awareness is bound to shift. In China, more beer, handsets, and kitchen appliances are already sold than in the United States. This means that consumers in those countries will increasingly determine which brands take the leading spots in various brand rankings worldwide.

Now let's consider two contrasting companies with global brands. Huge Samsung Electronics represents technology-heavy Asia. Small Chilean winemaker Concha y Toro, far removed from the major centers of wine consumption, was able to establish a global wine brand and become a successful example of a traditional industry moving south.

SAMSUNG ELECTRONICS
The Premier Emerging Market Brand

"Were you ever scared that the Samsung Group could have gone bankrupt during the currency crisis of 1997–98?" I asked Jong Yong Yun, CEO of Korea's Samsung Electronics. For no more than a split second, he shifted uncomfortably in the big armchair of his spacious, formal reception room on the executive management floor before replying with disarming candor.

"Yes, in July 1998, I realized for the first time that, if our huge losses continued, our capital would be completely eroded in three to four years' time. Deep down, even before the onset of the crisis, some of us were aware that we had to make big changes and we had even started to make them. But internally, there was a great deal of resistance to enacting fundamental reforms. The crisis made it clear to everyone that we had no choice but to change."

In his starched white shirt, conservative tie, and dark suit, Jong Yong Yun did not look perceptibly different from many other Korean executives I had met. He is every inch the "Samsung Man." But I had also heard him proudly referred to as a "chaos maker." In the Korean context, this is something between a badge of honor and an epithet. Known to be impatient with easy conventional solutions, during the Asian crisis he displayed the boldness and strength of character to successfully steer his firm through the most harrowing point in its evolution. Yet he would be the first to admit that without the bracing tonic and stern market discipline—the "shock treatment"—of that crisis, Samsung would never have developed into a powerful global brand.

Samsung first exported fish, vegetables, and fruit to Manchuria and Beijing.

The origins of today's twenty-first century global consumer electronics powerhouse date back to 1938, when Byung-Chul Lee established Samsung General Stores as an exporter of Korean fish, vegetables, and fruit to Manchuria and Beijing. Following the Japanese occupation, Korean War, and two decades of nearly 10 percent annual economic growth, Korea's per capita income catapulted from below $200 (lower than that of Peru) to over $10,000, among the highest in the developing world. Samsung Electronics was established in 1969 and merged with Samsung Semiconductors in 1988 to become a key part of Korea's most influential conglomerate.

Before the Asian crisis, Samsung's activities (like those of other major Korean groups) ranged all over the map, from consumer electronics, brokerage, and insurance to cars, shipbuilding, and petrochemicals. As long as the Korean domestic market was effectively closed to foreign competition, Korean conglomerates could easily afford to compete with one another in virtually every product category. The prevailing emphasis was on gaining market share—even market domination—as opposed to profitability, quality, or global competitiveness. Money was simply no object.

By 1997, the Samsung Group's balance sheet had begun to resemble an overloaded container ship, with its debt-equity ratio soaring to close to four times debt to equity. Ominously, even more debt remained lurking in a murky network of foreign subsidiaries. In retrospect, it was a lifesaver for Samsung that the financial crisis brutally eliminated those luxuries. Credit lines evaporated, revenues dropped precipitously as the Korean and regional economy went into a tailspin, and Samsung's ambitious yet ill-defined investment plans could no longer be financially sustained.

NEAR-COLLAPSE AND TOTAL TRANSFORMATION

In the midst of the crisis, Samsung Group came close to collapse. Burdened by huge debt, a sharp downturn in the semiconductor industry, and a series of failed ventures (most notably its disastrous foray into passenger cars), Samsung's harrowing passage through the valley of death was, in retrospect, precisely the "blunt blow to the upside of the head" (as Nike CEO Phil Knight has cheerfully dubbed his own firm's many crises) that Samsung Electronics needed to place it on the path to

During the 1997 Asian financial crisis, Samsung came close to collapse, but greater focus on high-end electronics, de-leveraging, ambitious investment in technology, and winning handset design turned it into a world-class brand.

brand stardom. Sometimes, only when a company is threatened with its very survival can it embark on the profound, often gut-wrenching and fundamental transformations required to boost it to the next level.

At the depths of the crisis, the unenviable task fell on Yun's shoulders, as Samsung's Mr. Inside and its top non-family executive, to lay off more than one quarter of Samsung Electronics' workforce, slash costs, de-leverage (reduce debt) dramatically, and ruthlessly drop a whole range of sideline businesses like pagers and electric coffeepots. With a determination that was very Korean, Samsung Electronics engineered an aggressive shift from low-end electronics and commodity memory chips (DRAMs) to mobile handsets, flat-panel display screens, digital media, and specialized chips such as flash memory used in digital cameras, iPods, and cell phones.

Yun flattened the organization, drove responsibility for key decisions further down the chain of command, and aggressively streamlined Samsung's sluggish bureaucracy, enabling it to move faster on new market opportunities. To import fresh ideas, he recruited top managers and engineers from the United States and put them through a four-week boot camp in which they were awakened before 6 a.m. every day to martial anthems extolling the virtues of being a "Samsung Man." Marathon mountain hikes were part of the drill.

Survival of the crisis inspired new hope and a more realistic sense of confidence. Even more critically, it intensified Samsung's brand building efforts. Gregory Lee, Samsung's global chief marketing officer, traces Samsung's extraordinary brand campaign to a 1997 decision, made on the eve of the Asian crisis, by Samsung's current chairman Kun-Hee Lee "to build a brand, not just a product." The marketing officer directly attributes Lee's bold initiative to the economic crisis, when the company was first forced to come to grips with the fact that "it was not as efficient as it needed to be. Not having a strong brand was crippling." Curiously, the efficiency and de-leveraging drive underscored the need for not just a strong brand, but a "premium" brand strategy, one CMO Lee bluntly describes as "ditching low-end products" even if they make a profit and are selling well. The aim is to climb up the value chain.

SAMSUNG'S PIONEERING HISTORY OF BRAND BUILDING

While the Asian crisis was the catalyst for Samsung's brand success, its global brand campaign efforts actually started much earlier. In my travels around the world, I often noticed that Samsung advertising billboards were always strategically placed in city centers from Cairo to Shanghai and that the first advertising passengers would see upon arrival at many national airports would be the iconic Samsung name and logo on the luggage carts. The most likely explanation for Samsung's success in the global brand sweepstakes is that the firm first hit its stride as a producer of consumer goods, as opposed to a pure technology company. Consumer products firms—of which the first was brand-happy Procter & Gamble—possess an intuitive grasp of the importance of marketing and consumer acceptance to the development of brand strength.

Jealous of the success of its Japanese neighbors, Samsung was the first Korean conglomerate to grasp the fundamental fact that low-cost products would not sustain their competitive edge indefinitely. Without a determined effort to upgrade its image, Samsung would achieve skimpy margins at best, and would likely fall victim to the same cost advantage that decades before had fueled its rise to power. Along with equally farsighted Korean carmaker Hyundai, Samsung took the lead in emerging markets brand building during the 1980s. By the 1990s, the Samsung name slowly began to catch the eye of consumers who had earlier passed it by as "yet another cheap brand from Korea."

"Change" has been a constant watchword of Chairman Lee, who likes to say that Samsung employees should "change everything except their wives and children." Born in 1942, the third son of Samsung's founder and a graduate of George Washington University with a passion for American movies (of which he possesses a vast library), Lee never expected to take the top job. But once he took over the reins from his late father in 1983, he demonstrated a compulsive drive for placing his own stamp on Samsung while putting the company on the international map. One of his earliest major initiatives was to establish a "Second Foundation" for Samsung Electronics designed to turn his firm into one of the world's top five electronics companies and leading brands. The process began with the 1988 merger with Samsung Semiconductor, which allowed the two firms to consolidate their technological resources and expertise. This initiative neatly fit in with the technology-oriented industrial policy of the Korean government, which provided Samsung with considerable support for the maneuver through easy money and generous grants for research and development.

Even before the Asian crisis delivered its stern market discipline, Chairman Lee had taken to guiding senior executives on visits to major U.S. retailers, in an effort to turn their embarrassment at finding Samsung products tucked away on the bottom shelves into a passionate drive to make those products better (and better known) than those of their Japanese competitors. Years of determined focus on quality, design, and technology brought Samsung's products to world-class levels. But it took time for Samsung televisions and video recorders to be viewed by global consumers as being even in the same league as Sony's.

To level the playing field with its Japanese competitors, the Samsung Group has spent in excess of $10 billion (more than any other company from emerging markets) on building a corporate brand, with major expenditures on creative advertising and high-profile sponsorships at the Sydney, Seoul, and Beijing Olympics. By consolidating its advertising from fifty-four different agencies into one it has created a unified message and shifted its retailing strategy from discount retailers like Wal-Mart up market to specialty retailers. Yet the firm's success in creating a global brand name has not been based on glitzy advertising and marketing campaigns alone. Ultimately, the real breakthrough came with the stunning success of Samsung's distinctively styled and featured mobile handsets, which overnight turned its brand image around. In just a few years, Samsung moved to the #3 position in the world in handsets, and shipped over 100 million units in 2005 (about 15 percent of

> *Samsung was able to capture not just market share but the high end of the market, making it the world's most profitable handset maker.*

the total sold in the world) while closing in on Nokia and Motorola. Samsung was able to capture not just market share but the high end of the market, making it the world's most profitable handset maker. Samsung's handsets remain highly prized not for their price or even state-of-the-art features but for their design, a critical element of brand evolution, and a clear product differentiator in an era of constant clutter and cheap commodity products.

High-end design shifted Samsung from a second-tier electronics company to a world-class brand name. Design and style clinched Samsung's success in the global market when the firm pursued a bold design strategy of taking on Nokia's "candy bar" phones head on with its far more appealing "clamshell" phones. Samsung executives also like to emphasize ruggedness. Despite the fact that Motorola was a shareholder of the leading mobile operator, Samsung gained its #1 position with a 65 percent market share in Israel after Changsoo Choi, marketing senior vice president, decided to smash and trample a handset before asking the president

of the local company to make a call to the cell phone, which (surprise, surprise!) went through.

While Samsung's success with its handsets single-handedly lifted its
image to "world-class," the company also scored major hits with other
high-end electronics. It currently boasts nineteen different items that enjoy
the world's #1 market share, including TFT-LCD televisions, VCRs, and
color monitors. Now that consumers have begun to accept Samsung's
brand as world-class rather than cheap, Samsung intends to leverage its
well-deserved recognition in handsets to become the market leader of the
digital age in multimedia. Having set its sights on being the Sony of the
twenty-first century, and largely achieved that goal, its next aspiration is to
become the BMW of the branding big leagues in consumer electronics,
with its premium brand strategy.

Luckily for Samsung, it aggressively moved into the high-end electronics fray at a time when the introduction of new digital technologies and
new products left consumers more open to considering new brands as new
markets opened up. As Eric Kim, executive vice president for marketing
says, "That transition, and our strategy to move up-market very aggressively are the main reasons why our brand improved rapidly."

SAMSUNG'S GLOBAL BRAND STRATEGY

Samsung plans to leverage its well-deserved recognition in handsets to become the market leader of the digital age in multi-media. It has set its sights on being the Sony of the twenty-first century.

"We looked to the future to build the
Samsung brand as iconic," commented
brand marketing chief Gregory Lee in a
recent interview with *BusinessWeek*.
When Samsung looked around the
world at models to emulate, it settled
upon the unlikely example of BMW,
which Lee describes as a brand "that everybody would love to have."
Using BMW as a model, Samsung ditched not only low-end products but a
number of low-end subbrands, including Plano, Tantus, Yepp, and Wise-
view. It resolved to leverage its single brand by creating a consistent brand
image focused on a small number of flagship products, of which the
mobile phone was #1, and digital televisions #2.

The firm deepened its investment on the design side, beefing up its
design staff from 100 to 450 worldwide with a stated goal of "bringing

coolness into the category" of mobile phones, permitting the firm to "price up due to the coolness factor. Coolness is very much part of the strategy," Kim emphasizes. Design guidelines produced a uniformity of colors across product lines, similar user interfaces on all cell phones, and consistency even along the sonic dimension.

A distinctive Samsung sound greets the user opening up the interface of both televisions and mobile phones. This in turn matches the sonic effect accompanying the logo in Samsung's latest global advertising campaign. Articulating Samsung's brand essence across multiple consumer touch points—sight, sound, look, and feel—is all part of projecting Samsung's "brand essence," which Lee insists stems from a realization that design is about more than merely the shape of an object, "it's the color, the feel, the sound," and every dimension that appeals to human sensation. Lee regards Samsung's brand as still very much a work in progress. His own market research reveals that most people still cannot express what the Samsung brand means to them personally, except that it is "cool" verging on "cold."

Still, the more significant reasons for Samsung's success in building a high-quality brand lie much deeper than just design. One asset Samsung has effectively leveraged (and one that may prompt other emerging market companies to do the same) has been its reputation in fast-growing markets like China, as one of the top brands—if not *the* top brand—for a broad range of products from refrigerators to handsets, as reflected in various regional brand surveys. More generally, Samsung has demonstrated that a successful brand can be created *only* if a company (1) makes enormously bold strategic moves that may look crazy at the time; (2) has an obsession for quality in execution; (3) is able to marry technology, global distribution, and design; and (4) spends heavily on R&D. That is a tall order. Even then, the risk remains that success could go to the company's head—as happened to Samsung and other Korean conglomerates until the Asian crisis saved them from their own hubris.

HEAVY SPENDING ON TECHNOLOGY AND R&D

Samsung Electronics spent over $5 billion (more than Intel) on R&D in 2005, or 9 percent of its revenues. It spent a total of $35 billion over the past decade and plans to spend a whopping $45 billion over the next five years alone. That compares with the $250 billion by *all* of the top 100 R&D spenders globally in 2004.[2] Spending by Samsung and LG together gave Korea the highest growth in spending during the 2002–2004 period at 38 percent, in comparison to the more modest spending increase of 7 percent by the leading American corporations during this same period.[3] R&D spending has been a critical component in Samsung's phenomenal success. It allows the company to constantly create cutting-edge, reliable technologies that are among the first to market. Examples from the past years are the largest (82-inch) flat screen, the highest density flash card (16 gigabytes), a seven mega pixel camera, and numerous new handsets with sophisticated cameras, mobile TV, and other features.

Samsung Electronics was awarded 1,641 new U.S. patents in 2005, climbing in four years from eleventh to fifth place among corporations globally, ahead of Intel, Micron, Hitachi, Toshiba, and Sony. Only IBM, with 2,941 patents, was significantly ahead of Samsung, while other household names in technology such as Canon, HP, and Matsushita were only just ahead.[4]

BOLD DECISION MAKING

Samsung's history is full of examples of technological decisions that were unusual and risky at the time but to which it owes much of its current brand leadership.

- In the 1980s, at a time when Japanese semiconductor makers dominated the business, Chairman Lee decided to make an aggressive foray into semiconductors. Interestingly, a U.S. anti-dumping suit against Japanese chipmakers provided Samsung with the space to launch mass production of 256K DRAM (dynamic random access memory) chips, the type of memory used in most personal computers. Success in that initiative permitted the firm to clear off thirteen years of debt and move on and up with a clean slate.
- When Samsung began to make a new generation of semiconductors (4Mb DRAM), its choice of the so-called "stacking" method allowed it to pull ahead of competitors and consolidate its domination of the industry for more than a decade.
- In 1999, in the midst of a deep recession in the semiconductor industry, Samsung built not one but two new chip fabrication facilities, not long after the Asian crisis when no one else dared to expand. That move later consolidated its market position with an increase of its global share from 18 to 25 percent.

- Samsung moved aggressively into the NAND flash memory business (used in popular consumer gadgets like digital cameras and MP3 players) when Toshiba alone commanded a 50 percent market share, turning down a partnership with the market leader in favor of independent development. Today, Samsung has taken over the leadership role in that market with a global share of 60 percent. Samsung executives like to point out that Samsung bettered Moore's law in NAND by doubling density in twelve rather than eighteen months for six consecutive years. Some of these major moves were widely criticized at the time, but turned out to be gambles that paid off big time.

Not all of Samsung's best-laid plans and bold strategic moves worked out as well as the move into semiconductors or mobile phone handsets. The failure of Samsung's automotive initiative is well known. At one of his regular retreats with Samsung's top executives, this one in San Diego in 1996 (not long before the Asian crisis), Chairman Lee announced that Samsung would invest the colossal sum of $75 billion (at a time when the company's sales were only $21 billion) in multimedia and TFT-LCD flat-panel displays (areas on which Samsung ultimately focused) but also in such far-flung fields as bioengineering. Following in the footsteps of Sony, he also aimed to partner with Dreamworks to develop content for multimedia. But the personal chemistry obviously left something to be desired, and Steven Spielberg later commented that during their meetings "there was too much talk of semiconductors."

OBSESSION WITH QUALITY IN EXECUTION

Chairman Lee has compared product defects to cancers that must be completely eradicated. To the consternation of some old-time employees, he ordered that a pile of defective products be crushed and burned as a clear warning that defects would not be tolerated. During a 1993 visit to Frankfurt, he surprised even his staff with a vehement outburst about how the dangerous force of old habits still diverts attention from quality, which should be the most important goal. The foundation of Samsung's strength as a brand has clearly been its relentless focus on product quality, technological sophistication, and a *zero tolerance for defects*.

WILL OTHERS OUT-SAMSUNG SAMSUNG?

Samsung's goal of being the world's leader in the digital multimedia world and overtaking Sony on virtually all fronts is well within its view. Yet the future will largely depend on the success of large flat-screen TVs as high definition television (HDTV) comes on stream in the United States and elsewhere. Soon, HDTVs are expected to cost less than twice as much as traditional TVs and will thus become more attractive to consumers.

In the meantime, competition is heating up in the smart phone arena. Samsung's long-time Korean competitor LG has adopted a similar branding strategy in an apparent effort to "out-Samsung" Samsung. LG recently moved into the #4 global market share in handsets while pulling ahead of Samsung in introducing third-generation phones in Europe. Taiwanese companies such as High Tech Computer are developing advanced wireless PDAs and smart phones that allow video conferencing and downloading of music. Just as Samsung successfully challenged Sony, Philips, Motorola, Ericsson, and Matsushita's Panasonic, it will soon be challenged itself by large makers of electronics in China who have scaled up, are improving in quality, and benefit from a huge and growing domestic market. Of course, it takes years to build a brand, but low-cost production by competitors puts pressure on margins in much the same way as Samsung Electronics once edged out others for market share.

No longer the brash upstart, Samsung has demonstrated a newfound maturity by forging a strategic alliance with none other than its fiercest rival, Sony. The two companies have jointly invested $2 billion in a state-of-the-art factory in South Korea to produce "seventh generation" liquid-crystal flat panel displays, a key product category that Sony under its technological chief Ken Kutaragi ignored for too long. The companies have also partnered in the development of Blu-Ray technology, as members of a consortium hoping to establish a standard for the next generation of video discs and players. "Sony is one of the very few electronics companies whose brands are recognized as iconic," commented Woo-Sik Chu, Samsung's head of investor relations, in a telephone interview with *The New York Times*. "We have a lot to learn from Sony. Yet by the same token, increasingly in the digital era, everything starts on an equal footing. They also want to see why our brand is rising." Indeed, in a world where competition is frequently the most notable feature, Samsung and Sony are leading the way into a new era defined by collaboration as much as competition.

An Investor's View

The Bull Case

- *Samsung is the premier emerging market brand with strong global recognition.*
- *Known especially for its handsets, Samsung Electronics is also the global leader in memory chips, flat screens, and a variety of consumer products.*
- *Samsung's high-end brand reputation in key emerging markets and willingness to produce locally should help it to maintain leading market shares.*
- *Samsung is consistently more profitable than most of its competitors in its key business areas of semiconductors, handsets, and flat screens.*
- *Despite huge investment in R&D and new high-tech facilities, Samsung Electronics maintains a clean balance sheet, strong operating margins, and high return on investment.*

The Bear Case

- *Although less dependent on semiconductors than before, Samsung Electronics' earnings remain cyclical.*
- *Corporate governance of Samsung has improved enormously in recent years but still provides occasional surprises.*
- *Samsung Electronics' challenge will be to maintain its lead against LG and Chinese competition while leveraging its handsets' reputation to other products.*

Lessons

- *It may require a life-threatening crisis before a company changes its corporate culture enough to make the tough decisions often required to build a major brand.*
- *Much-needed bold strategic moves may be easier in a company where the founding family is still in control.*
- *Building a global brand can be achieved only by an obsession with quality, design, and technology.*
- *It takes determination, patience, and time to build a global brand but the payoff in profitability is high.*
- *An overhasty brand strategy may kill a company.*

VIÑA CONCHA Y TORO
The Silver Bullet Brand

Everyone at Concha y Toro, Latin America's premier winery, was in a state of high excitement. The tables were set with colorful tablecloths and flowers, the best cooks were hired to prepare Chilean dishes, and, of course, the very best wines were served. It was 1988, and a select group of British master wine tasters were on hand to explore Chile's fertile Maipo Valley just south of Santiago. Bounded by the spectacular snow-capped Andes mountains to the east, the rugged Coastal Range to the west, and the fast-flowing Maipo River to the north, the valley boasts a warm, desert-like climate. With less than a foot of rainfall per year and sandy, fast-draining soils, it is considered ideal for the cultivation of wine grapes.

Yet exquisite anticipation turned to intense disappointment when the first sip by one of the masters led to the sticky comment that there was "something strange" about the wine. It didn't take long for the master tasters to determine the source of the "off" flavor. Most of the huge casks used by Concha y Toro to ferment and age even its best wines were made of Chilean oak ("rauli"), not the vintage French or American oak to which the master tasters' delicate palates had long grown accustomed. The tasters' advice was to replace all of those casks with stainless steel and oak imported from France, to give the wine a more internationally acceptable taste and bouquet. Concha y Toro Vice Chairman Rafael Guilisasti told me how the shock he had felt quickly turned into pride at the firm's turn-on-a-dime reaction. "At considerable cost, we took this lesson to heart and within a year we had replaced all the old casks."

On his first visit to New York in 1987 to Banfi Vintners, the firm's new distributor and the leading U.S. wine importer, a Banfi representative confronted Guilisasti (then the export manager) with an unanticipated question: Could they deliver the barely imaginable number of 300,000 cases to New York for the coming season?

Exchanging nervous glances with his chairman, Guilisasti breezily assured Banfi that this would be no problem at all. "Actually," he later confided to me, "we had no idea whether we could deliver because we were shipping barely 80,000. But that marked the beginning of serious promotion of our brand."

Not long after suffering those two significant shocks to its system, Concha y Toro partnered with Banfi to speed up the modernization of wine-making technologies at its plants. The dual shock vividly reflected the dual pressures faced by major vintners hoping, on the one hand, to promote themselves as producers of high-end vintages for wine connoisseurs while on the other producing enough volume to satisfy rapidly expanding export demand. In pursuit of export volume, the firm doubled the acreage of vineyards under cultivation at a cost of $150 million. At the same time, it took care to hire separate distinguished wine experts for each of its vineyards. These coordinated steps helped the company's exports to grow at 16 percent annually since the late 1990s.

The industry-wide shake-up of the once-sleepy wine industry began, not surprisingly, in the United States where wine growers (particularly in California) proved willing to experiment with new grapes and automation of harvesting, storing, and branding. For centuries, French and Italian vineyards had been fragmented into tiny family-owned holdings. Wineries lived off their reputations, which inhibited innovation, while distributing their fine wines through a small club of stuffy and not very dynamic distributors.

Concha y Toro's century-old phylloxera-free roots dated back to 1875, when Don Melchor Concha y Toro, a distinguished Chilean lawyer, entrepreneur, and politician, acquired a substantial estate in the Maipo Valley, within a day's drive by horse from his home in Santiago. At the time, a passion for wine-making (along with everything French) had seized the upper crust of Chile, and Don Melchor contracted with the eminent French enologist de Labouchere to plant vines purchased in Bordeaux. The winery proved more than a passing fancy. Demand for the Chilean wine skyrocketed after the dreaded phylloxera fungus put a number of French vineyards out of commission just as Concha y Toro was being planted. While the quantity of wine produced by Don Melchor was small, its quality was famously high. Before long word spread not just among the Chilean elite but also among the local bandits that his wine cellars were ripe for the raiding. To keep a close eye on the cellar, Don Melchor ordered a deep tunnel dug between the cellar and his country estate so that he could personally keep watch over his reserve bodega. Frustrated by ongoing inventory shrinkage (some pilfering was undoubtedly committed by his own workers), Don Melchor took to wandering his dark torch-lit tunnel dressed in a long black cape and brandishing a pitchfork, deliberately spreading the legend among the superstitious local populace that the Devil himself was protecting Concha y Toro's fine wines. A century later, in honor of this legend and Don Melchor's cunning, one of Concha y Toro's most distinctive wines would be dubbed "Casillero del Diablo."

Concha y Toro's first exported crates arrived on the Rotterdam docks in 1933, but exports remained a small fraction of the firm's revenues until after World War II. While European vineyards and distributors labored to get back on their feet, imported wines from Chile and other Latin American countries enjoyed a brief vogue in the United States. Once the European wineries got back on track, Chile's wine industry returned to its traditional inward focus. The firm and industry languished in local obscurity until the socialist regime of President Salvador Allende seized many vineyards from their landowners, sending the industry into a tailspin.

For a decade following Allende's death at the hands of a CIA-inspired coup, more than half of all Chilean vineyards simply ceased production. In the case of Concha y Toro, the family vineyard fell into the hands of a group of Chilean entrepreneurs. Whatever one may think of the politics of the now personally discredited General Augusto Pinochet, his free-market economic policies (profoundly influenced by Chicago economist Milton Friedman) had the paradoxical effect of loosening the stifling rigidity of the social structure in Chile far more than Allende's progressive policies ever did. Under Pinochet, a sizable number of the crusty old Chilean elite actually had to start thinking about making a living. Hernan Büchi, Chile's boyish-looking, motorbike-driving finance minister between 1985 and 1989, presided over the enactment of new laws that stimulated the creation of new industries. As the world opened up to Chilean entrepreneurs, competition became not merely fashionable but inevitable. Technical and managerial competence replaced old family ties or distinguished names as a prerequisite for success in the new, more market-oriented Chile. Lacking protection from imports, Chilean agriculture and industry *had* to compete internationally to survive.

COMPETING IN THE GLOBAL WINE MARKET

Chilean winemakers, including Concha y Toro, began to aggressively target export markets in the mid-1980s. In 1994, the firm took the landmark step of becoming the first vineyard in the world to obtain a listing on the New York Stock Exchange, a sign of distinction not just for an emerging

A twenty-year export boom has propelled Chile into the #5 position in the world, giving it a global export market share of 5 percent, roughly in the same league as Australia but ahead of the United States, Germany, and South Africa.

brand, but for an emerging industry undergoing rapid transformation and consolidation.

Today, Chilean wineries export 30 million cases, 60 percent of their production, valued at $835 million, a substantial change from the miserly $10 million in 1985. That export boom has propelled Chile into the #5 position in the world, giving it a global export market share of 5 percent, roughly in the same league as Australia but ahead of the United States, Germany, and South Africa. More important than quantity in this industry, quality has improved dramatically in recent years, as long-established vineyards in Chile—led by Concha y Toro—have been developing a quality image in collaboration with such leading names as Bordeaux's Mouton-Rothschild and California's Robert Mondavi. With annual revenues in excess of $300 million, Concha y Toro is not only Chile's largest exporter, controlling nearly a third of the nation's production, but among the top twenty largest winemakers in the world.

ACQUIRING CACHET FROM UP-MARKET QUALITY AND PREMIUM BRANDS

Concha y Toro very deliberately embarked on what is known in the industry as a "silver bullet" brand strategy, by which a major brand launches a subbrand, or set of subbrands aimed squarely at connoisseurs, in the hope of elevating the master brand by association with the subbrand. Like Gallo, the mass-producer of both mass-appeal and fine wines in California, Concha y Toro produces large volumes of wine at an attractive price combined with a few select cachet labels that an elite club of wine tasters can appreciate. This two-pronged premium/mass strategy keeps retail prices at the higher end of the $5–10 range while removing from the mainstream product at least some of the taint of a pure commodity. Not unlike other emerging markets producers looking to gain greater acceptance in international markets, Chilean winemakers have struggled to cast off their image as a producer of cheap and boring wines.

"From Rothschild we learned how to 'coddle' our wines—everything from grapes to irrigation—and constantly aim for the high end of the market so that we could move our portfolio up, but to keep growing, we need to have a strong presence in all price segments."—Rafael Guilisasti, Vice Chairman

As a sophisticated global exporter, Concha y Toro has been acutely sensitive to the varying tastes and needs of individual markets. While Chileans prefer their wines to be older and sweeter, the American public is more partial to clean, fruity, fresh offerings. The British, meanwhile, prefer their wines to display more complex flavors. Each market requires a different blend of stainless steel and wood and a different distribution strategy. In the UK, the major wine outlets are the ten leading supermarket chains, which require a trendy image to lend a particular wine significant shelf space and in-store promotion. To respond to this need, Concha y Toro established a boutique-like vineyard, Cono Sur winery, in the mid 1990s. Its young staff pressed to come up with a fresh image and trendy, innovative ideas suited to the British market. In little over a decade, Cono Sur grew into Chile's fourth largest exporter, contributing 13 percent to the firm's exports, mostly to the UK where it is now the company's leading brand.

Besides the more popular Sunrise and Frontera brands, Concha y Toro offers the Trio and Casillero del Diablo marques while the Almaviva, Don Melchor, and Amelia brands float in the lofty premium segment. Crucial to Concha y Toro's success has been its recognition in leading industry publications. It was named the most important vineyard in Chile and Argentina in a 1999 survey conducted by the prestigious *Wine Spectator* magazine and as the best-selling Chilean wine in leading American restaurants in a survey by *Wine & Spirits*. Don Melchor's 2001 vintage won 95 points out of 100 in *Wine Spectator,* making it one of only three Chilean wines ever to have achieved that distinction. In 2004, Concha y Toro received the highest scores among all Chilean wineries in the super premium and ultra premium wine categories. As Guilisasti proudly notes, "demand for our better wines is greater than our capacity to produce them." In the same year, Concha y Toro was named for the tenth time as one of the 100 wineries of the year by *Wine & Spirits* and by *Wine Enthusiast* magazine as "New World Winery of the Year." Meanwhile, the company was invited to join the Club de Marques, a winemakers' association for some of the industry's top brands, including Baron Philippe de Rothschild, Laurent Perrier, Barton & Guestier, and Robert Mondavi. Concha y Toro was the first and only Latin American winery to achieve this distinction.

Together with the French Baron Philippe de Rothschild Winery, Concha y Toro created the Almaviva winery in Chile, explicitly to produce the first Primer Orden class of wines in the New World, the South American equivalent of Bordeaux's Grand Cru Classé. "From Rothschild we learned how to coddle our wines—everything from grapes to irrigation—and constantly aim for the high end of the market so that we could move our portfolio up,"

Guilisasti confided to me a decade later. "To keep growing, we need to have a strong presence in all price segments."

Concha y Toro has assiduously nurtured positive publicity to promote its brand-building efforts on the product side. As one step to build its global brand, Concha y Toro organized an International Distributor Summit in 2000 (a first for the Chilean wine industry) to introduce the winery's top sixty exclusive global distributors to new developments and marketing tools. The company paid special attention to raising the profile of two of its high-end labels, the Casillero del Diablo and Don Melchor brands, and in 2002 held the regional Asian launch of its wine at the Great Wall of China. These promotional efforts have paid off handsomely. Today the company is the world's most widely recognized Chilean winery, and Casillero del Diablo its best-selling wine. A regional reader's survey for Interbrand recognized Concha y Toro as the fifth best-known Latin American brand and the only one in the rankings from Chile.

> *"Demand for our better wines is greater than our capacity to produce them.*
> *—Eduardo Guilisasti, CEO*

An Investor's View

- *Concha y Toro has carved out a strong niche in the import markets of the United States, Latin America, and various European countries as a leading example of the north-south move of the global wine industry with Australia, Chile, and South Africa becoming major players in a once-stuffy industry dominated by French, Italian, and Spanish winemakers.*

- *Success in today's wine industry requires more than a favorable climate, experienced vinologists, good grapes, and cheap labor; scale, sophisticated branding, good publicity, and global distribution are equally important.*

- *Australian Yellowtail's sudden rise to the top of the American import market was a tough lesson for Concha y Toro in how fast brand leadership evaporates without huge scale, cost competitiveness, and a "trendy" image. Recovery of the #1 spot will be hard, especially with the strong Chilean peso.*

Lessons

- *A strong brand and constant attention to distribution are as important as cost competitiveness, scale, and stable quality.*

- *Building a brand helps in dislodging traditional producers who have ignored the need for innovation.*
- *Branding has made the wine industry global with a move from north to south.*
- *A "silver bullet" strategy helps the image of mass market brands.*
- *The next big challenge in global wine branding is China with its growing consumption.*

CHAPTER 4

Other Roads to Brand Leadership: Buy It or It May Drop in Your Lap

Lenovo buys IBM ThinkPad, Haier tries to buy Maytag, and Corona Beer has it accidental iconic brand

Strategies
- *Buying a brand is a risky but faster alternative to the slow process of building a brand over many years*
- *In a crowded brand field, an emerging market newcomer may need to establish an iconic image*

Not all emerging multinationals have the luxury of time to build a brand as Korea's Samsung and Chile's Concha y Toro have done. Chinese firms, in particular, appear anxious to prove themselves in the global marketplace even as foreign brands have begun to poach customers in their home market.

Samsung's two-decade-long rise to power and buzz is an example of taking the classic long road to global brand leadership by building a brand painstakingly and expensively from scratch. In its campaign to become a global brand, Samsung adopted a strategy clearly modeled on Sony. It began by undercutting competitors on cost, and strategically deployed the profits gained from its growing revenue stream to fund R&D and improve quality, features, and design to the point that it could compete fairly at the more profitable high end rather than just at the low end. Like Sony, Samsung grasped early on the importance of cutting-edge design and the "coolness factor" in adding value. Like Sony, it achieved market leadership in consumer electronics by being an early mover in breakthrough products (like the clamshell-shaped mobile handset) that distinguished its offerings from competitors. And like Sony's legendary co-founders Akio Morita and Masaru Ibuka, Samsung's Lee family never wavered from their firm conviction that their company could compete with the market leaders on every front, including even the generation of the ephemeral quality of "buzz." Grasping that brand building is a curious and idiosyncratic discipline, more of an art than a science, Samsung deliberately moved to the next step, beyond the product, to the brand.

For emerging markets companies seeking world-class status, two other possible roads to brand leadership beckon: "the shortcut" and "the back road." If Samsung's path represents the classic long road, a number of emerging markets multinationals have chosen to adopt the more accelerated strategy of the shortcut, a concentrated leapfrog over existing competitors into the brand big leagues by simply buying a brand outright. In some cases, such a strategy is rooted in anxiety that these fast-growing firms are lamentably late in the game and do not have the luxury of time. In other cases, it is driven by a lack of confidence that they will be able to build a brand new global brand on their own without the cachet of a widely recognized label.

Flush with cash from their rousing success as low-cost competitors, these emerging multinationals would rather buy established brands on the open market than go to the trouble and expense of building their own. The strategy is to graft those brands' long-nourished equity onto their own late-entrant brands. One example of a firm deliberately taking the short cut is Lenovo, the # 1 PC manufacturer in China, and now (since its takeover of IBM's PC business) the # 3 PC maker in the world, after Dell and HP. It was perhaps spurred to do so because Dell had briefly begun to outsell Lenovo in China, in part as a result of Dell's superior direct-sales and mass-customization model but also by trading on the strength of the Dell brand. Another leading Chinese brand, kitchen appliance maker Haier, made an ultimately unavailing attempt to buy the American Maytag brand but triggered not just consternation but a battle with Whirlpool from which Haier (together with American firms Bain Capital and Blackstone) was forced to beat a hasty retreat.

The *"back road"* is a third road to brand stardom cleverly used by brands such as Modelo's Corona Beer. Such brands gain brand status almost through luck. More accurately, they are able to translate a cult-like popularity (such as Corona's "beach, surf, and sun" image) into an iconic brand through careful marketing.

LENOVO
The Chinese Company that Swallowed IBM PC

In 1984 (the year Apple famously spoofed IBM in a Super Bowl commercial that depicted workers for Big Blue as faceless, Orwellian drones), the Computing Institute of the Chinese Academy of Sciences provided one of its administrative managers, Liu Chuanzhi, with $25,000, a staff of ten, and a modest one-story bungalow in which to establish the New Technology Development Company (NTD). With this private venture, the Chinese Academy envisioned to commercialize the institute's research with the hope of ultimately generating profits that would fund its future research. Cleverly spotting a domestic void in desperate need of filling, the Computing Institute developed a combination hardware-and-software product known as the "Legend Chinese Insertion Card," which relied on a unique and highly intelligent "association" technology that minimized the time users spent inputting Chinese characters. It did not consume a significant amount of then-scarce hard drive space, and permitted an adaptation of a standard Western keyboard for Chinese use.

In 1989, NTD changed its name to Legend as a means of capitalizing on the brand buzz the Legend card was creating, and began bundling its Chinese-language cards with imported PCs. By 1993 it was prepared to plunge into the PC business on its own. It announced its intention to compete head-on with foreign brands by manufacturing and selling its own branded computers in China. Few industry observers took the firm seriously, particularly after the firm missed its annual goal of distributing 30,000 units of imported PCs by 10 percent. As Chairman Liu ruefully recalled, "We were really not sure whether we could survive in PC manufacturing or not. Given our background, making our own PC was the dream of the whole company. Because we were still making good money from the distribution business, we decided to hang on to manufacturing for one more year."[1]

Fortunately for the firm, that one year was enough. By 1994, Legend was trading on the Hong Kong Stock Exchange. Recognizing it would need to substantially beef up its PC operations if it could ever dream of competing with foreign imports, Lenovo granted Yang Yuanqing, the newly appointed general manager of its new PC unit, wide latitude. He quickly moved to control costs and dumped the firm's ill-functioning direct sales system in favor of a distributor-run operation, with distributor incentives tied to cash collection. As a result, Lenovo astonished foreign rivals by boosting 1994 sales by 152 percent. This straight-out-of-the gate performance propelled the firm's rapid rise to # 3 PC manufacturer in China, trailing only Compaq and AST.

But the machine that truly made Lenovo's name in the burgeoning Chinese PC industry was the user-friendly Tian Xi PC, a slimmed-down version that came bundled with one year of free Internet access, and featured single button access to the Web. This was an enormously popular feature in a country still heavily populated with first-time drivers on the information superhighway. The Tian Xi included Chinese voice-recognition software and a graphics pad that made it easier to input handwritten Chinese characters into the system. After selling 200,000 Tian Xi's in the first six months, Lenovo executive vice president, Li Qin, explained that the firm had understood that its sole competitive advantage lay in creating machines with functions tailored to the domestic market.[2]

By 1998, Legend had produced its one-millionth PC. In 2003, it changed its brand name to Lenovo, taking the "Le" from Legend and adding "novo," the Latin word for "new," to reflect the spirit of innovation at the core of the company. Lenovo's shocking (to Western observers) December 2004 decision to purchase IBM's fast-fading PC business for $1.25 billion in cash and stock reflected a frank recognition that, if it ever wanted to fulfill its global ambitions, it could never do so saddled with a brand known only in China. Of course, the fact that IBM was willing to ditch the business which had given rise to the now-quarter-century-old PC era in 1981 spoke to the fact that, from an American corporate perspective, manufacturing had become a low-margin commodity business. For newcomer Lenovo the ThinkPad brand represented a shortcut to brand building, and global presence while old-timer IBM had clearly concluded that PCs were soaking up too much of its resources for far too little return.

The financial results since the takeover unfortunately shed little light on the burning question of whether Lenovo has been able to retain IBM customers. With approximately $13 billion in annual revenues, growth and profits have been disappointing since its acquisition of IBM's PC business in May 2005. In a conference call with analysts, chairman Yang Yuanqing freely conceded that the company's "current cost structure and competitiveness have not been optimized and our product portfolio is not complete enough. We should have higher aspirations." Lenovo's year-on-year PC shipment growth in 2005 was the worst among the top five global PC vendors, according to market researcher IDC, with just 13 percent compared to global growth of 17 percent and Dell's 20 percent increase. Acer, the Chinese company's main rival in Asia, also managed a much brisker 53 percent growth during 2005. Executives at Lenovo vowed to increase operational efficiency, boost its product line, and focus more on profitability. "In this industry, it's required of us to be best-of-breed in terms of operational efficiency," said William Amelio, the newly appointed chief executive officer and president of Lenovo, who had previously headed Dell's Asia operations. As recently as July 2005,[3] *The Wall Street Journal* had heaped praise on Amelio's prowess in reconfiguring Dell's famed direct-sales business model to the vicissitudes of Chinese market conditions. In poaching Amelio from Dell, Lenovo adroitly turned the tables on its archrival.

The jury is still out on the Lenovo-IBM PC combination. Taking the shortcut to brand building has posed a real risk that instead of brightening Lenovo's brand by association with IBM's, Lenovo may overextend or simply sully decades of hard-built brand equity for IBM and Thinkpad. Investors' skepticism regarding the long-term prospects of synergies arising from the deal was reflected in Lenovo's shares dropping 13 percent in the wake of the May 2005 merger. That said, investors have a long history of getting strategic moves wrong.

QINGDAO HAIER
Best Known Brand in China Goes Global

In 1984 (the same expansive year in China that gave birth to Lenovo) Zhang Ruimin, a senior manager at Qingdao Refrigerators, a plant owned by the municipal government of the city of Qingdao, noticed a large crowd of people milling around outside his facility. Knowing full well that his plant was notorious for producing inferior-quality, even shoddy household goods, Zhang was somewhat shocked to discover that this frenzied and impatient crowd had formed in the hope of acquiring new refrigerators straight from the production line, as opposed to from stores.[4] Qingdao is a beautiful seaside city and well-known summer and health resort whose tree-shrouded hills and red-tiled roofs overlook the deep blue of the Yellow Sea.

Following Mao Zedong's disastrous Great Leap Forward and the brutal Cultural Revolution of the 1960s, Deng Xiaoping had put plenty of money in consumers' pockets for the first time since the Communist takeover of

China. The gradual relaxing of constraints on the economy in the wake of Mao's death left Chinese consumers and their economy hungry for any sort of appliance, even bad ones. What type of feeding frenzy, Zhang wondered, not at all idly, might be touched off by a Chinese company that succeeded in producing *decent* refrigerators and other household appliances for the long-suffering Chinese consumer?

For the next quarter century, as China turned into a vast construction site and became a major manufacturing hub for the rest of the world, more and more long-suffering Chinese families could finally afford new apartments, and new appliances with which to furnish them. Plagued by inefficiencies and uncontrolled costs, Mr. Zhang's factory was verging on bankruptcy despite surging demand. Yet Zhang, an energetic and dynamic man who felt stifled and restricted by command economy mechanisms, saw these shortages as a golden opportunity to both prove himself and to try out the business ideas he had been brooding about but could not put into practice in the stiff bureaucracy of the massive, Communist-style plant. "I wanted to take just one factory, and make it the best,"[5] he said later, taking tiny steps first, before attempting The Great Capitalist Leap Forward.

After convincing his Communist colleagues in the municipal government to appoint him Haier's president, Zhang took over the company and quickly set about transforming its struggling operations. Within its first year, Haier just about broke even. By the next, the firm turned a solid profit. Twenty years later, Haier is now the leading household goods brand franchise in China and ranks fourth in the world in that category, with a global market share of 3 percent.

The folk legends of Asian companies (including Samsung) are replete with possibly apocryphal tales of senior executives smashing inferior products in order to demonstrate a zealous commitment to quality. Nevertheless, Zhang insists that shortly after taking over the operation, he pulled 76 flawed refrigerators out of 400 directly off the manufacturing floor, attached to each one the name of the employee who had been responsible for making it, and asked those employees to smash them to pieces with sledgehammers, in front of the entire factory. He even insists that he struck the first blows against the flawed refrigerators himself. His goal, of course, was to impress his employees (who possessed only the foggiest notions of quality control) that shoddiness would no longer be tolerated. "The message got through that there's no A, B, C, and D quality," he notes. "There's only acceptable and unacceptable."[6]

EAGER TO CONQUER NOT JUST LOCAL BUT GLOBAL MARKETS

Zhang's commitment to quality went well beyond simple dramatic gestures. Despite government regulations that limited imported components for Chinese-made consumer goods, Zhang began importing components from Germany when the Chinese equivalents failed to satisfy him. If an employee located a defect in a product received from the previous manufacturing stage, he had not just the right but the duty to reject that piece.

> *Before long, Haier was producing some of China's top quality refrigerators, with the Chinese public taking note and flocking to buy them. In time, Haier expanded into other household appliances, and by 1997 it was China's #1 brand.*

Before long, Haier was producing some of China's top quality refrigerators, with the Chinese public taking note and flocking to buy them. In time, Haier expanded into other household appliances. By 1997 it was China's #1 brand in this area and the market leader in refrigerators, washing machines, microwave ovens, and freezers.

In June 2005, Haier teamed up with two prestigious U.S.-based private equity firms (Bain Capital and Blackstone Group) to make a surprise $1.3 billion bid for the Iowa-based Maytag Corporation. Until then only a few Americans had even heard of China's largest home-appliance producer. Even fewer were aware that Haier had already built a substantial plant in South Carolina to serve its burgeoning American market, and that its primary interest in Maytag was not for its *hard* assets (factories, offices, physical plant, and the like) but rather its *soft* assets: its expertise, intellectual capital, and tarnished yet well known American brand.

What Haier's bid for Maytag (ultimately withdrawn under pressure from a rival bid by Whirlpool) revealed about the famously secretive firm was that Haier, in the face of stiff competition from some of the world's most famous brands in its home market, was evidently impatient with building its own brand by the slow route, after the fashion of Japan's Sony or Korea's Samsung. As *The New York Times* bluntly put it, "Many [Chinese] companies appear to be acting partly out of desperation, as more foreign brands line the shelves of retailers in China."[7]

Haier's eventual withdrawal from the fierce fray over Maytag did not, most observers agreed, signal any long-term retreat on its part from embarking on a global brand strategy. In the same month that Haier made and retracted its offer for Maytag, *China Entrepreneur* magazine asked its readers in a widely reprinted cover story, "Should China Buy Wal-Mart?"

BUILDING A STRONG BRAND

As was the case with Samsung, Zhang realized early on that quality improvements alone would not propel his firm to world-class status. Fulfilling its global aspirations would require building a global brand, and for consumers to covet the cachet that went along with it. "Once I attended a banquet in Germany," Mr. Zhang later recalled. "I asked the wife of a manager there if she had ever heard of Haier refrigerators. She said she had heard about them. Then I asked if she would buy a Haier refrigerator. She answered no. She would choose Miele, a famous German brand of refrigerator. The reason is that Miele has become an art craft in the consumers' view. That is just what Haier aims to achieve."

Only by testing itself in the global marketplace—by building a brand— would Haier find out if it ranked as world class. "While our domestic market is essential for stability, it is not enough. We have to march into the global market, otherwise we will never become powerful. We need to do it in three steps—go out, go inside, and then go up in reputation."[8] According to Zhang, only by immersing itself in this baptism by fire, forced to compete with the best of the best, would Haier ever grow strong enough to survive as a global brand. He set out pursuing this goal with characteristic determination, launching his campaign by opening a Haier manufacturing plant in the United States in South Carolina in 1999, with an initial investment of $30 million. Well aware that moving production from China to the United States was bucking the tide of American firms moving operations to China to take advantage of cost savings, Zhang insisted that, no matter how much it cost, making appliances in America was the only way for his company to shed its cheap "made in China" image.

In America, Zhang and Haier defined a lucrative market niche that no other consumer appliance company had exploited up to that time: mini-fridges suitable for college dorm rooms and hotel mini-bars. After rapidly snapping up 30 percent of that fast-growing niche, Wal-Mart began selling Haier refrigerators and freezers more widely and in more sizes. Other leading retailers also carry their brand. We found them even in Pittsfield, Massachusetts, once the heart of GE land. Haier went on to build a solid reputation in small electric wine cellars, chest freezers, washing machines, dishwashers, and beer dispensers. Haier has also made a point of competing not simply on the basis of cost, or even quality, but also on pursuing genuine product innovations—the surest route to producing a brand. The firm combined innovative technology with meticulous consumer research, enabling it to define new niches and enter new markets in complete confidence that it would prevail.

FROM CONFUCIUS TO JACK WELCH

Zhang insists that his management models are Western business leaders such as GE's Jack Welch, Harvard Business School's Michael Porter, and MIT's Peter Senge and that he follows the principles of total quality management, time operation research, and Six Sigma. In fact, he has blended Western management thinking with his own passion for Chinese philosophy. He draws from such disparate sources as Laozi, Confucius, and Sun Tzu. Haier's factory walls are plastered with slogans such as "Never Say No to the Market," "Specialization, Zero Defect," and "Watch the Market Closely and Create Superior Quality." His philosophical writings exhorting his employees to better performance, which are regularly reproduced in his original calligraphy in company newsletters, employ this curious blend of ancient Confucian philosophy, old-fashioned Chinese communist techniques, modern management methods, and Japanese-style executive training. Haier combines an employee "point wage" evaluation system that directly links performance and quality improvements to wages and promotions with Communist-style indoctrination techniques complete with the mind-numbing use of slogans and discussion groups.

> *"First we observe and digest [a new method]. Then we imitate it. In the end, we understand it well enough to design a new product independently."*
> —*Haier CEO Zhang Ruimin*

Yet Haier management also makes it *mandatory* for employees to conceive of innovative ideas and insights. Such genuine product innovations as the mini-fridge and electric wine cellar, see-through vegetable crispers, and extra space in door shelves to fit gallon jugs have served to differentiate Haier products. Chairman Zhang insists, these innovations arose directly from management's insistence on spurring innovation at all costs.

Haier and Zhang have carefully emulated other emerging markets companies, from Sony to Samsung to Hyundai, by scrupulously absorbing the lessons acquired, and then benchmarking themselves against those models, as a way of ultimately outclassing their mentors. "First we observe and digest [a new method]," Zhang reveals. "Then we imitate it. In the end, we understand it well enough to design a new product independently."[9] And, it goes without saying, attempting to beat the unwitting model at its own game.

Not long after taking over Haier, Zhang established an alliance with Germany's Liebherr-Haushaltsgerate, which injected modern manufacturing technology into the plant and allowed the company to produce technologically advanced goods. Such was the extent of their relationship that the word "Haier" is a direct translation of the German word "Liebherr," meaning "Dear Sir." Still later, Haier collaborated with Mitsubishi, licensing refrigeration technology from the Japanese powerhouse. Through these alliances, Haier slowly picked up examples and lessons in producing quality goods, en route to producing its own.

THE FUTURE AND ITS CHALLENGES

Haier's ambitions to become a global Fortune 500 company within a few years may or may not be realized. Zhang's soaring ambitions—to build a strong finance capability modeled on GE Capital while building a global brand either by the short route or the shortcut—could also be Haier's downfall, as the firm's public relations seem inevitably to focus on Zhang's personal vision in a way curiously reminiscent of the now-discredited personality cult of Chairman Mao. "I don't want Haier to become like the Titanic,"[10] Zhang insists, paying at least token homage to the risks of overexpansion. Yet at the same time, he has found few fields and categories, from plasma TVs and air-conditioner compressors to entering the glutted Chinese market for mobile phone handsets, in which he feels Haier cannot compete. Much as was the case in Korea prior to the Asian crisis, a certain amount of hubris has crept into the expansion plans of many Chinese companies who—largely protected from the tough lessons of the Asian crisis—have never known a down cycle. There are still Chinese business leaders who seem captive to the naïve belief that, with their unique combination of competitive advantages, they can be all things to all people. While Korean conglomerates were forced to focus after the crisis, many Chinese firms (including Haier) appear to be committing some of the same mistakes as their Korean models, even as they emulate their quality and brand strategies.

Zhang, characteristically, uses a brand strategy to justify a brand strategy. He has claimed in interviews that handsets and washing machines may be different on the surface, but both are used by consumers who know the Haier brand. That said, Haier's foiled bid for Maytag certainly suggests that Zhang clearly grasps the limitations of his nascent brand. While likely pursuing other targets to acquire, Haier has thus far failed to develop a sophisticated brand strategy of the sort that defines Samsung. Nor has it yet pulled off the sort of juicy coup Lenovo did by picking up an iconic American brand at a fire sale price.

An Investor's View

The Bull Case

- *Haier has established a brand leadership position in China, is becoming better known in India, and is making an ambitious and impatient move to become a global brand.*
- *Following a successful "niche" strategy in the American market with mini-fridges and wine coolers, Haier is now broadening its distribution channels (including Wal-Mart and other major retailers).*

The Bear Case

- *Financial information on Haier remains inadequate to make sound financial judgments as an investor.*
- *A serious investment risk is Haier's lack of restraint in moving into many different products where it does not have a proven competitive edge.*

Lessons

- *Building a brand requires a long-term focus on quality, design, and distribution.*
- *For most emerging multinationals, tired brands will be easier to buy than vibrant ones.*
- *Expect stiff competition from competitors to any efforts to buy a brand.*
- *The difficulty of taking advantage of an existing brand without diluting its reputation is easily underestimated.*
- *Purchasers of a brand should have realistic expectations and not dilute their own brand-building efforts.*

GRUPO MODELO
How Corona Became an Iconic Brand

In the 1970s, a local distributor for the Mexico City–based Grupo Modelo, in the Pacific Coast Mexican city of Mazatlan, could not figure out why so many empty bottles of Corona beer were going missing from his returned boxes. Sales were rising robustly, yet a sizable number of Corona's distinctive long-necked, clear-glass, fully return-able bottles were not making their way back to the distributor.

> *Corona's beach and surf image together with its distinct, long-necked bottle made it into the #1 imported American beer brand.*

After making a few inquiries among his retail accounts, he quickly solved the mystery: Corona beer had become enormously popular among young American surfers visiting Mexican beaches, so much so that they had started taking home entire cases—and failing that, empty beer bottles—as souvenirs. Although it had not been an element in any deliberate strategy, Corona beer did stand out, less for its taste than for its distinctive long-necked, flint glass bottle, which was dramatically different from the more traditional, expensive amber glass bottles in which its rivals came packaged. The Corona beer bottle had become, quite inadvertently, an iconic brand image, as much a symbol of sunny Mexico (replete with associations with surf, beach, and a carefree holiday paradise) as Coco-Cola's curvaceous green glass bottle had become a symbol of America.

The birth of one of the world's great beer brands occurred more by luck than as the result of some carefully crafted brand strategy—the result of a "bottom up" cult status as opposed to "top down" marketing—Grupo Modelo's headquarters was sufficiently savvy to jump on this golden opportunity. As CEO Carlos Fernandez later told me, "During the late 1970s, we spent quite a bit of time and money developing a bottle for export that had amber glass, aluminum-and-gold foil on the neck, and an elegant paper label. To us, it spoke 'premium brand.' It was exactly the same beer that we sold in Mexico in the flint glass bottle, repackaged for the American market."

No one could have been more surprised than Fernandez and his colleagues in senior management when they learned that what the younger set in America yearned for was not a "premium" brand, but the same popular beer they had enjoyed on their Mexican vacations. Before not very long, bartenders in U.S. cities adjacent to Mexican vacation spots popular with the young—San Antonio, Texas, and San Diego, California, in particular—began serving Corona in volumes that piqued the interest of headquarters in Mexico City.

The timing of this lucky brand breakthrough was certainly fortuitous for Grupo Modelo. During the late 1970s, one of Mexico's routine devaluations of the peso had left the company without the dollars it needed to pay for loans and equipment. If Grupo Modelo could capitalize on Corona's popularity and cult status among the California surfer crowd, the company could obtain those dollars, and gain a foothold in the enormously lucrative North American beer market.

Among connoisseurs of the fine modern art of brand building, what had just happened to Grupo Modelo and Corona was the equivalent of manna from heaven: an "accidental brand" being the best kind of brand, since it wins, in effect, by popular demand. In another example, no one at Nike headquarters in Beaverton, Oregon, would ever have predicted that Nike sneakers would become popular in inner-city neighborhoods, even after the signing of an exclusive endorsement agreement with basketball legend Michael Jordan. The coronation of Corona as a great brand was not the result of a calculated strategy, but more closely resembled the success of the Swatch watch or the Volkswagen Beetle: a popular product, popularly priced, touches a cool nerve among the young trendsetters that even the savviest of marketers can spend billions pursuing to no avail. Corona had captured the heart and soul of the younger set in California and Texas without, as yet, spending a peso on advertising.

The decision to aggressively pursue an export drive in California and to market Corona as the Mexican beach beer par excellence was, however, a deliberate strategy. When one American bar owner, confusing Corona with a different Mexican beer he had been served in Mexico City, began serving Corona with a slice of lime on top—an expedient and stylish way to avert Montezuma's Revenge in Mexico—he unwittingly completed Corona's ascent to bona-fide cult status. Starting with a firm foothold in California, Modelo systematically expanded its distribution state by state, enhancing the popular image it began to enjoy with higher margins along the whole distribution chain.

Everything was going swimmingly for Grupo Modelo and Corona in the United States until 1986, a banner year in which—Fernandez informs me—Corona's U.S. sales reached a dizzying plateau of one million cases per month. It was no coincidence that just as Corona was hitting its stride in the States, mysterious rumors of uncertain origin began circulating in bars and cafes that the bright yellow Corona beer actually contained trace amounts of human urine. This diabolical rumor, far-fetched as it was, proved difficult for Modelo to quash without calling more attention to it. Yet the rumor proved repulsively effective, causing an immediate plunge in export sales, and a crisis mood at home in Mexico.

"It nearly killed off the brand," Fernandez recalls. This was particularly vexatious because the company had always been obsessively quality oriented and meticulous about the clarity and purity of its barley, its malt, and above all, its water. The rumor also proved tough to stamp out because it fed on irrational prejudices regarding the purity of all food in Mexico. When Modelo's crisis management team was able to trace the source of the rumor to a Nevada distributor of rival beer brands, Modelo's crisis management team sprang into action, inviting scores of journalists to visit the firm's clean, modern state-of-the-art breweries while also—as Fernandez delicately put it—"initiating a legal process" against those believed to be behind the rumors, which soon stopped them.

The positive publicity that supplanted the negative publicity eventually built even greater demand for the brand and ultimately aided Modelo's efforts to expand into export markets. By the late 1980s, volume began to trend sharply upward in the United States, once again achieving annual rates of growth in the 30–40 percent range. Yet according to Fernandez, "Corona could still have been a fashion brand, a flash-in-the pan." When the infamous "Tequila Crisis" in 1994 plunged Mexico into recession and domestic beer sales stagnated, Modelo had no choice but to pin its hopes for recovery on its neighbor's market.

A NEW CEO WITH AMBITIOUS PLANS

In 1997, the year Corona became America's leading beer import, dislodging Heineken from its long-held position, Carlos Fernandez became at age thirty-one the new chairman of Grupo Modelo, inheriting the post from his uncle. In 1925, Pablo Diez Fernandez had founded the firm in the bustling industrial town of Mexico City. Beer was not yet a popular drink in Mexico, in part because the local fermented cane concoction *pulque* was cheaper and stronger, and in part because ice and refrigeration were not widely available.

Ever since Pablo Diez Fernandez's day, the five families that own Modelo have maintained a tradition of allowing the younger generations to work in the company. Instead of stepping into plush jobs at headquarters, however, they are sent to work as interns in new plants or in the roughest sales districts. Those without stamina, people skills, or burning ambition soon fall by the wayside. Grupo Modelo's young CEO is a mechanical engineer who has known the aroma of malt from his high school vacation days, when he manually opened and closed steam valves, cleaned tanks, carried fifty-kilo sacks to the hoppers, and learned the tricks and nicknames of the workers. Later, he was put to work building new brewing plants and in 1989 he traveled with Modelo's engineers to Germany and Italy to see the newest automated plants. At one of them he vowed, "You know what? One day we're going to have a factory like this one." True to his word, he opened Modelo's newest, state-of-the-art brewery eight years later.

Since Carlos Fernandez took over as CEO of Grupo Modelo, sales have doubled, and exports have grown even faster, from 17–2s8 percent of sales. Imported brands, typically sold at higher prices and margins than American beers, make up 12 percent of the American beer market and Corona enjoyed 30 percent of this market in 2005, well ahead of Heineken's 19 percent. The third most popular imported beer, Canadian Labatte Blue's brands, is now owned by Modelo's rival brewer, Ambev from Brazil.

Corona has also become the leading imported brand in NAFTA partner Canada, and is currently expanding exports to 150 countries. Fernandez wants to be one of the world's top five brewers (from #7 currently), pushing ahead of such competitors as Carlsberg.

FROM LOCAL MARKET LEADER TO GLOBAL BRAND

Modelo's international success as a beer brand has been built on the systematic pursuit of the following four strategic steps:

1. Dominate the home market

Modelo's success abroad would not have been possible without its dominance of the Mexican market. Not only did its first enthusiastic followers "discover" Corona there, but it also allows the scale and cash flow to be competitive elsewhere. The company jealously guards its franchise through the use (common in several countries but outlawed in others) of exclusive arrangements with bars, and other retail outlets. Some view its ownership of a sporting arena, a soccer team (sponsoring another nine) and two baseball teams as an expensive tradition but others see it as key to brand promotion. Modelo, unlike other brewers, does not have breweries in other countries. It finds that "imported" beer possesses a snob appeal to trendy consumers that disappears as soon as it becomes known that the beer is locally bottled. Interestingly, the success of Corona abroad has allowed Modelo to reposition itself at home where it now has a more upscale image and pricing than it had before. While the Mexican beer market has grown sluggishly at 2 percent in recent years, Modelo's brands have gained market share with close to 3 percent annual growth.

2. Build a distinct, international (rather than Mexican) brand

While people order Tsingtao beer in Chinese restaurants and Singha with Thai food, Corona deliberately promotes an association with surfing and sunny beaches rather than with Mexico as a country. Its advertising slogan is "Change your whole latitude." Corona is less bitter than other beers, which only makes beer drinkers drink more. It advertises itself as a *"cerveza sin fronteras,"* or "beer without borders." But then, the best known refried beans are Taco Bell, made by Kraft, while the largest Hispanic food company in the American market, Goya, is Cuban-American.

3. Beat Heineken and go global

Modelo did not stop with the success of Corona Extra in the U.S. market. It later introduced Corona Light which is now the #8 import and Modelo's Especial that has climbed to the #4 import spot. As the leading import, Corona sells over $900 million worth in the U.S. market and has now turned its attention to the rest of the world where it currently sells over $160 million. In Australia, it is now the #1 import in a nation known for its beer consumption, though it has found the European and Chinese markets very competitive.

4. Join the top global brands

The global beer market is rapidly consolidating with many mergers in recent years. Brazil's Ambev has tied up with Belgium's Interbrew. South African Breweries (which bought Miller beer from the food arm of Phillip Morris) is another emerging market brewer with a large presence in other countries, from Africa to Russia and China.

Modelo's key challenges are to keep control of its home market in an age of more open markets and to make sure it remains large enough in the top league of producers to count as a survivor rather than being acquired. The merger of Brazil's Ambev with European Interbrew to form global leader Inbev poses a potential challenge to Modelo in Canada, Latin America, and even Mexico itself. Ambev is a highly efficient brewer with many more breweries in Latin America and has followed a very different brand strategy, focusing on local brands rather than one major global brand. The combined Inbev is strong in Eastern Europe, a market that is rapidly consolidating, and has a sizable presence in China. SAB-Miller has a strong head start all over Africa but also in Eastern Europe and China. Heineken sells more beer in Nigeria than in Holland or the United States. In contrast, Modelo has focused on the developed world in its global marketing efforts and has not yet made significant inroads in the most populous emerging markets.

An Investor's View

- *Modelo's future success rests on keeping dominance in Mexico while preserving its distinct brand image in global markets.*
- *The jury remains out on whether the top global brewers will win market share with "local" brands or global brand strategies.*
- *The consolidation of the beer industry will continue and brewers have little choice but to compete for dominance.*
- *The Inbev-Ambev combination (with its Brazilian CEO) as well as the South African Breweries merger (SAB-Miller) have overtaken Modelo in size.*

Lessons

- *An iconic brand needs some special story that fixes its identity in people's imagination.*
- *Dominance even in a hopelessly competitive market can be achieved through a careful brand strategy.*
- *Well-established market leaders can be dethroned.*
- *Success with branding in one market can be used to achieve success in others.*

CHAPTER 5

China's Largest Exporters . . . Are Taiwanese: Building a Global Presence Behind a Veil of Anonymity

Hon Hai and Yue Yuen make your computers, cell phones, and shoes

Strategies

- *Don't stick to your knitting but vertically integrate to allow "one-stop shopping."*
- *Like a chameleon, build on existing expertise and constantly move up the value ladder.*
- *Don't build a brand too early but achieve a global market presence by hiding behind the veil of global brands, leaving the distribution to others while focusing on cost-efficient manufacturing.*

After Chiang Kai-shek fled the Chinese Mainland to Taiwan in 1949, in rapid retreat from the overwhelming advances of Mao's armies, only the intervention of the U.S. Seventh Fleet prevented an invasion of the newly declared island bastion of capitalism in the South China Sea. The Chinese army began shelling Quemoy and Matsu, two small islands in the Taiwan Straits, first heavily, then intermittently, then on odd numbered days, finally with propaganda shells. The Taiwanese reciprocated in kind.

Nearly six decades later, the rhetoric between the two formal adversaries remains heated. China continues to regard Taiwan as a renegade province that must sooner or later be brought to heel while President Chen Shui-bian of Taiwan has made no bones about his long-term ambition of one day declaring Taiwanese independence. Yet for all the saber rattling and political posturing between the two former foes, Taiwan is now the largest investor in China and Taiwanese companies also count among the largest exporters in China.

Total Taiwanese investment on the mainland has swelled to the tune of $80 billion over the past 15 years,[1] well ahead of other nations with substantial stakes in China such as Japan and South Korea.[2] Today, while heated phrases occasionally fly over the Straits, hundreds of thousands of Taiwanese quietly manage factories, run restaurants, and own apartments in Shanghai (even if they still have to fly there through Hong Kong). Whole industrial estates in Southern China are filled with Taiwanese factories. Virtually every Taiwanese electronics company now maintains manufacturing operations in China. And after much hemming and hawing, even Taiwanese semiconductor giant TSMC recently received government permission to build an advanced semiconductor plant on the Mainland. Yet Taiwan remains a much-misunderstood driver of China's economic miracle. According to *BusinessWeek,*[3] "No one knows for sure how much of China's exports in information and communications hardware are made in Taiwanese-owned factories, but the estimates run from 40 to 80 percent. As many as 1 million Taiwanese live and work on the mainland." In the same issue Russell Craig of tech consultants Vericors Inc. observed that "all the manufacturing capacity in China is overlaid with the management and marketing expertise of the Taiwanese, along with all their contacts in the world."

The best examples of the reality on the ground are two companies most consumers have never heard of, even if they use their products every day.

1. Hon Hai produces more parts and components for more computers, mobile phones, and game consoles than any other firm in the world. Headquartered in Taiwan, today Hon Hai remains a Taiwanese company in name only, as over 100,000 of its worldwide work force of 160,000 are employed in China and only 5,000 remain in Taiwan.

2. Yue Yuen is another giant company you've never heard of, even though it produces over 186 million pairs of shoes a year, more than any other firm in the world. Like Hon Hai, Yue Yuen employs several armies of workers in a network of plants all across Asia. Yue Yuen's four factories in Guangdong province in Southern China alone employ more than 160,000 people.

CHINA: MANUFACTURING HUB
OF THE EMERGING MARKETS CENTURY

It has become a cliché to say that China is now the manufacturing center of the world, just as Great Britain was in the nineteenth century and the United States in the twentieth. But being a cliché does not make the phenomenon less remarkable. For decades, China was one of the most closed economies in the world. Yet to put China's belated entry onto the world economic stage in historical perspective, Deng's reforms of the 1970s opened up the Chinese economy to the influences of "foreign devils" *far earlier* in its drive toward industrialization than Japan and Korea did before it.

Mass education, a seemingly infinite and low-cost labor pool, the potential of a market with 1.3 billion people, a stable currency, and enormous investment in infrastructure have made China so attractive to foreign investors that foreign direct investment (FDI) of $60 billion in 2004 exceeded that of the previous largest recipient, the United States. In fact, direct foreign investment in China has *grown* continuously from $40 billion in 2000 while global **FDI** *dropped* from $1.4 trillion to $560 billion during the 2000–2003 period.[4] In total, China has attracted over $550 billion in FDI with foreign investors employing over 22 million Chinese workers, exporting over half of China's total, and paying 20 percent of all taxes.[5] When China joined the WTO in 2001, even more investment opportunities for multinationals were created, not exclusively oriented around low-cost manufacturing. In recent years, multinational interest has spread beyond manufacturing. Between June 2003 and June 2004, no less than 200 R&D centers were set up by multinationals in China.[6]

With an export sector growing at 30 percent or more per year for several years in a row, China has become the world's fifth largest exporter. In fifteen years, China has moved from a barely noticeable blip in the landscape of world trade to becoming a larger exporter to the United States and Europe than Japan. Half of China's 200 largest exporters in 2004 were foreign-backed companies; together, these 99 companies contributed $72 billion or 15 percent to all China's exports.

BUILDING A GLOBAL PRESENCE HIDDEN BEHIND
WELL-KNOWN BRANDS

While Dell, Apple, IBM, and Nokia may get all the credit for leading the world into the digital age, contract manufacturers like Hon Hai or designers of smart phones like High Tech Computer are playing a growing role not just in the manufacturing but also the development and design of these complex instruments of consumer desire. Although just a few household names are known worldwide for superior design, quality, reliability, and technical innovation, the average consumer is hardly aware that the quality and ingeniousness of the products themselves may have much more to do with the contract manufacturers' fulfillment of their obligations than with the technical sages at the head offices in Austin, Santa Clara, Armonk, or Helsinki.

More often than not, the Apple iPods and Motorola cell phones we all use every day are produced by little-known third party manufacturers in remote corners of China, Korea, and Thailand. And while this brute fact is now commonly known, the *identity* of the firms behind these labels and logos remains deliberately obscure to the consumer. Exhibit A of the outsourcing movement is the consumer electronics giant Hon Hai, which is only barely better known by the name of its Hong Kong subsidiary, Foxconn. Hon Hai currently serves as the overseas manufacturer of—among other consumer goodies—Sony's PlayStation 2, Apple's Mac mini, Power Mac G5, AirPort Express wireless base station, and parts of the Apple iPod as well as parts of Nokia and other phones. Hon Hai is not alone. Taiwan's Quanta Computer, for example, manufacturers Apple's current line of iMac G4 computers, is the No. 1 global maker of notebook PCs, and like Hon Hai, is a key supplier to Dell and Hewlett-Packard. Yet another Taiwanese contract manufacturer, Asustek Computer, produces the iPod shuffle and the G5 iBook for Apple.

Not every Taiwanese consumer electronics manufacturer has elected to go the anonymous Brand X route. BenQ, a spin-off of Acer, recently purchased Siemens Mobile and has invested significant sums into building a global brand, with as yet uncertain results. Acer itself has also enjoyed a modest success in its quieter quest for greater name recognition.

CHEAP LABOR FOR HOW LONG? AND WHAT THEN?

While the labor pool in China will always be vast, there are already shortages of trained labor in specialized industries such as electronics. Wages have also been steadily climbing at double-digit rates in recent years. Longer term, China's one-child policy and the resulting graying population (unusual in developing countries) will contribute to a gradual erosion of China's huge labor-cost advantage, probably far more dramatically than the proposed adjustments to its currency pushed by U.S. policy makers.

Smart emerging multinationals like Hon Hai and Yue Yuen know that their low-cost labor advantage will provide them with an edge in global markets for only so long. Hundreds of ambitious local entrepreneurs are likely to outdo them on the cost front if they do not identify means apart from low wages and other financial efficiencies to stay ahead.

Staying Successful in the Outsourcing Game
- *Economies of scale in production and sourcing*
- *Product design and R&D*
- *A broad assortment of products, constantly moving up the value ladder*
- *Vertical integration rather than "sticking to knitting"*
- *Speed-to-market*
- *Flexibility in adapting to the whims, fashions, and technology breakthroughs of their industries*

HON HAI PRECISION INDUSTRY CO. LTD., TAIWAN
The Largest Consumer Electronics Firm You've Never Heard Of

Hon Hai's conspicuously low-key headquarters in Tucheng, a gritty suburb of Taipei, looks and feels different from the sleek modern head offices of the more famous electronics companies located at the other end of the famed Sun Yat-Sen Freeway in Taiwan's high-tech Hsinchu Science Park. After passing through a cramped entrance hall and reception area in which engineers were animatedly discussing blueprints, I was escorted through a series of dimly lit corridors

Hon Hai became the world's #1 electronics contract manufacturers in 2004, surpassing Flextronics.

with bare floors to a small, sparsely furnished meeting room. This was, I was told, the anteroom of the executive offices of Hon Hai founder and chairman Terry Gou, now Taiwan's richest man with a net worth of $3.2 billion.[7]

The drabness of that executive office fit Terry Gou's preference for a Spartan, no-frills look. The "mega-sites" of Hon Hai in China looked much more impressive. I briefly wondered whether this strict imposition of a low-rent executive style risked coming off more like a pose than a policy given the size and strength of his company. I understand that Tucheng means "dirt city" in Chinese, yet I couldn't help thinking that the firm could easily afford to upgrade its furniture and install a few yards of new wall-to-wall carpeting without being accused of decadence.[8] After all, Hon Hai had recently surpassed the Singapore-based Flextronics and Silicon Valley–founded (Singapore-based) Solectron to become the largest electronics contract manufacturer in the world, with $17 billion in 2004 sales. It had more patents to its name than any other Taiwanese company apart from TSMC.

Yet again, these shabby offices and gritty surroundings seemed like an accurate reflection of Gou's successful stealth strategy, which over the past three decades has propelled "the biggest company you have never heard of" into not just one of the largest but one of the most profitable electronics manufacturers in the world. Like the wealthy man who affects shabby dress because he can afford to, Terry Gou (who personally owns a quarter of Hon Hai along with a medieval castle in the Czech Republic) has capably shrouded himself and his company in a veil of anonymity that permits him to produce a vast variety of components and products for competing companies like Dell, Apple, IBM, Nokia, and Sony without ever appearing to threaten their hegemony as world-class brands. Just as TSMC discreetly insists that it will never "compete with its customers"—and goes to enormous lengths to barricade the chip designs and other intellectual property of one customer from another—Hon Hai's competitive edge lies in the fact that it can serve many masters, like a Swiss bank, while promising utmost discretion and security when producing goods for competing firms.

A more accurate impression of the firm's vast scale and scope may be gained not from the vantage point of the unprepossessing head office in Tucheng, but rather from touring one or more of Hon Hai's "mega sites" in Mainland China. Some 100,000 Hon Hai workers are employed producing "the three C's" (computers, communications, consumer) including PCs, handsets, game consoles, and other consumer gadgets at these sprawling industrial parks, which like similar facilities elsewhere in China resemble small cities. Hon Hai's huge city-within-a-city in Shenzhen, bordering Hong Kong, is close to major ports and employs more than 30,000. It is just one example of Hon Hai's ability to maintain a strategic competitive advantage as a creator of economies of scale in China that simply swamp comparable attempts by rivals. These are not factories in the Western sense of the term, but industrial cities executed more on the Soviet model, with their own dormitories, medical clinics, shops, cafeterias, and a medley of other support services. During the SARS epidemic, these factory-communities were kept virtually insulated from the outside world until it was clear that the situation beyond their gates was under control by the government. Speed and efficiency rather than fun and creativity would appear to be these proletariat paradises' true stock in trade. According to *BusinessWeek,* assembly line wages at these Taiwanese-owned plants in China currently average about $120 a month, a living wage in China yet low by Western standards.

Words like "tough, battlefield, and cost conscious" lie at the heart of Hon Hai's Spartan corporate culture, evidently a natural outgrowth of the founder's no-nonsense personal style. Gou himself has favorably compared his plants to army camps, and is proud of being known as a demanding, hands-on manager who runs his business with military discipline and equally rigid expectations. As he has said on more than one occasion, "You need real discipline. A leader shouldn't sleep more than his people; you should be the first one in, last one out." Unlike most of the other leading executives of Taiwan's hi-tech industry, Gou was trained as a merchant marine rather than as a PhD at a top American university. He is equally proud of never having received a dollar in government support or tax breaks, unlike many of his Taiwanese contemporaries.

Queried in an interview by a local Taiwanese publication[9] as to the seeds of Hon Hai's success, Gou chose to single out the firm's "plain and assiduous buffalo culture," which he favorably contrasts with the "high-tech" culture of leading firms, both in Taiwan and abroad. "Hon Hai has always been working hard like a buffalo in the field of precision components." He pointedly contrasted Hon Hai's buffalo culture with "students [in America] just stepping out of campus (who) hold shares and get high salaries too easily." As he proudly expounded to a meeting of Hon Hai shareholders later that year, "Only a long journey can test the riding strength of a steed."

AN EARLY MOVE INTO CHINA RIDING
THE PC OUTSOURCING WAVE

Hon Hai is a classic example of a high-tech company founded in a garage by a workaholic entrepreneur with ten subordinates, which has retained its "garage culture" and the brash attitude of a start-up to triumph over adversaries long after becoming an incumbent and fixture in its own industry. In 1974, Terry Gou and colleagues began turning out plastic switches and other parts for cheap black-and-white Taiwanese TVs. By 1981, the company had gained the attention of the blossoming computer industry by producing an efficient and reliable socket for snap-on memory expansion in home computers. As the PC boom took off in the 1980s, Hon Hai's sales soared along with it. Before long, the company was branching out into manufacturing entire modules and circuit boards for nearly every name-brand PC producer on the planet.

Listed on the Taiwan Stock Exchange in 1991, Hon Hai's key strategic move occurred in 1993 when it became one of the first Taiwanese electronics companies to shift production to China on a massive scale. Unlike others, Hon Hai built its own vast plants instead of buying outdated items second-hand from customers, leading to even greater efficiencies and economies of scale over the long haul. As it proceeded to the pinnacle of PC success, founder Terry Gou continued to lead the way for his troops, working fifteen-hour days, six days a week, and spending more than half of his time overseas, either at Hon Hai's multiple production sites or meeting with clients. In contrast to many CEOs, he is notoriously press-shy and rarely meets with reporters or broker analysts, in keeping with the firm's discreet "no-brand" image.

Hon Hai is the undisputed king of outsourcing but, like its founder, remains full of restless energy and always eager to get on to the next stage. By the turn of the century, the firm's vast plants in China accounted for 80 percent of its total capacity, a far higher ratio than its main competitors Singaporean Flextronics with 40 percent and U.S. founded (now Singapore based) Solectron with 27 percent mainland Chinese production. Access to a vast pool of cheap labor has obviously been fundamental to Hon Hai's success, but it would be naïve to assume that its *continuous sales growth of over 35 percent for each quarter between 1998 and 2004* (except for the SARS outbreak in the second quarter of 2003) can be attributed solely to its strategy of shifting the bulk of production to China.

Even during downturns in the industry, when all of its competitors were losing money, Hon Hai has maintained its earnings growth and is by far the world's most profitable contract manufacturer. While the other top four electronics contract manufacturers all lost money in 2004, Hon Hai virtually doubled its share of the *global* contract manufacturing market to 15 percent[10] by gaining market share from other leading players like Flextronics and Solectron, with shares of 21 percent in PCs and 13 percent in handsets, despite being a latecomer in the telecom area. In 2001, Hon Hai surpassed TSMC in sales to become Taiwan's largest manufacturing company. In 2002, it became the largest exporter *from* China, shipping $4.4 billion in goods from the mainland to locations all over the world.[11]

IT TAKES MORE THAN JUST CHEAP LABOR

I remember when my colleague Rita Lun, who follows Taiwanese companies for us, returned from a conference in New York where she met with Terry Gou. He had shown her a copy of *BusinessWeek* magazine with a cover story on Dell's new direct distribution model. "This is the wave of the future," he had exclaimed, not hiding his excitement. He clearly wanted Hon Hai take part of this important revolution and he was true to his word. The fact is that Gou's Hon Hai has managed to say on top by developing the "one-stop shopping" concept into a revolutionary, new organizational model for contract manufacturing. This model is entirely in tune with his clients' needs for just-in-time delivery, a lean supply chain, and Dell's direct distribution model. All of that on top of moving faster on its feet than competitors and constantly cutting costs to remain the lowest-cost producer while continuing to move up the value chain.

> *Hon Hai has managed to stay on top not just by being faster, remaining the low-cost producer, and moving up the value chain, but also by developing into "one-stop shopping," a revolutionary organizational model that is completely in tune with Dell's direct distribution model.*

One-stop shopping means moving from individual components such as connectors to making the outside shells or "enclosures," to whole modules of numerous different products. Hon Hai was the first electronic component manufacturer (EMS or Electronic Manufacturing Services) to move toward vertical integration.

Once Gou understood how the Dell direct distribution model would radically revamp the global supply chain throughout the computer industry, Hon Hai's ability to integrate mechanical and electrical engineering, combined with its legendary molding expertise, permitted this radical move. Gou knew that in the new world inaugurated by Dell, minimizing lead and design times would be critical to maintaining success. Only through vertical integration would he be able to satisfy the needs of his big brand customers.

Earlier, the speed with which Hon Hai designed complicated socket molds made it the first company to be certified by Intel for the wireless Pentium socket, leading it to capture 70 percent of Intel's mold business. This led to further contracts for Apple's curvaceous computers. Hon Hai calls its vertical integration model CMMS (components, modules, moves, and services), a system that permits it to nimbly skip on to new higher-margin products as older models downgrade into low-margin commodities.

THE SECRETS TO HON HAI'S SECRET SUCCESS

With thousands of smaller firms throughout China and Asia seeking to imitate his lightning fast and flexible execution, Terry Gou knows that his greatest task is to keep Hon Hai a tough act to follow. Over the years, I have met many of his senior executives but an interview with Gou himself has eluded me; his strategy of anonymity allows few opportunities to meet even for longtime shareholders. In discussions with our own and other analysts, seeking to pierce this impenetrable corporate veil, I have come to the conclusion that the key secrets behind Gou's efficiency, speed-to-market, and cost-competitive production are (1) scale, (2) seeking the most demanding customers who are leaders in their industry, (3) highly focused, high-yield "joint" design, and (4) constantly moving up the value ladder.

1. The sheer *scale* of Hon Hai's operations and its ability to quickly scale up operations are hard to beat. At the insistence of companies like HP, Dell, Intel, and Nokia, Gou has also gone global with plants in Europe (Hungary, the Czech Republic, Scotland) and Latin America (Mexico and Brazil), and soon India.[12]

2. Gou is a champion of seeking the most demanding customers in the belief that they force a company to stay ahead. Hon Hai consciously targets the top two–four customers in each of the industries it serves: Dell,

HP, Intel, and Apple in computing, Nokia and Motorola in handsets, Cisco and Sun Microsystems in networking, Sony and Nintendo in gaming play stations. As soon as he got wind of the stylish new iPod, Gou is said to have flown to his client Apple's head office because he recognized that consumers are as sensitive to high style as to technology. Armed with Hon Hai's mold expertise, he only aimed to work with the best.

3. Rather than trying to conduct R&D on his own, Gou has thrown in his lot with cutting edge *joint* design. He is determined to follow a different path from many other electronics companies. He knows that "pure manufacturing and OEM won't survive," and he prefers "to do joint design, because I know from day one who pays for it and who will be the client." Hon Hai's R&D centers in the United States, Japan, and Europe are deeply involved in early stage R&D and new product development while researchers in Taiwan and China focus on the hot wireless area and process engineering impediments. With 3,000 engineers including over 100 PhDs,[13] Hon Hai has received 13,000 patents and applied for 20,000, mostly related to bread-and-butter connectors but also to such new areas as optical and heat sink technologies. As opposed to quietly "sticking to his knitting," the chameleon-like Gou keeps relentlessly moving into new areas, building on his existing expertise. His next ambition is to become a major player in electronic auto parts although he cautiously admits that "car makers and their first tier suppliers still do their own thing. Outsourcing of electronics isn't growing fast yet and will take another five years" to get off the ground.[14] Gou is constantly on the lookout for new opportunities and a major competitive edge for his firm, which even as it has gained in scale has managed so far to remain nimble enough to identify and stay ahead of new industry trends. "We don't buy orders or relationships but our internal data base tells us quickly when others can't do something. We see that as a potential growth niche and will move quickly to develop that area, buy a team or even a whole company as long as the niche is big enough." While he maintains that "we focus on organic growth," he recently bought Ambit, a Taiwanese company known for its networking and wireless expertise, as well as Eimo in Finland for its cutting-edge nanotechnology techniques employed in ultra-precision molding.[15]

> With 3,000 engineers including over 100 PhDs, Hon Hai has received 13,000 patents.

STAYING COST-COMPETITIVE

Scale, modern machinery, and experienced engineers are all part of Gou's fanatical cost control system—his proudly proclaimed "buffalo culture." Hon Hai has gained a reputation not only for quoting production costs 10–30 percent below rivals but also for having the industry's shortest time-to-market, an essential advantage for an electronics contract manufacturer. For example, Hon Hai was able to ramp up Acer's 2003 line of computers faster than Acer itself by taking just two months to move from order to volume production for its PCs.

FUTURE CHALLENGES

Hon Hai is well-positioned for growth and has kept up its explosive pace but has lagged behind the model of "world class" in the corporate governance and transparency sweepstakes. In Hon Hai's corporate culture, clients come first, and outside shareholders are expected to trust the management rather than understand the business and its financials. Gou has stated publicly that he views investment bankers as people who could not succeed in manufacturing but just "fly around first class and stay in luxury hotels." Hon Hai's plants and business units are run by professional managers and engineers, but the company remains heavily dependent on its hands-on chairman. Eventually, Hon Hai's suppliers may catch up and its Chinese competitors will squeeze its margins more than they are able to do now. And Gou has pointedly neglected to tackle the one major job he may find hardest of all: training a successor to himself.

Since its inception three decades ago turning out switches and other small plastic parts for TVs, Hon Hai has always been able to adapt quickly and move assiduously up the value chain. Hon Hai's strategy and drive has paid off in spades. It is now the world's largest electronics contract manufacturer by sales, and has maintained profitability in periods when the industry as a whole and its main competitors were all in a downturn.

Lessons

- *Cheap labor is a crucial but only temporary advantage.*
- *Pure manufacturing is migrating to joint design and even original design.*
- *Leadership at the top is key to success in execution and cost control.*

An Investor's View

The Bull Case	The Bear Case
• An ambitious early move into China	• Others are trying hard to imitate Hon Hai
• Huge plants with modern machinery	• Lack of financial transparency
• Aggressive and dynamic management	• Corporate culture after succession?
• Unique expertise in molding	• R&D spending lower than others
• Offers one-stop shop/vertical integration	• Difficult to integrate major acquisitions
• Strong relationships with industry leaders	• No brand name
• Superior execution	• Little independent design
• Rapidly growing	• Organic growth will eventually slow
• More profitable than peers	• Always margin pressures

YUE YUEN
The Largest Shoe Company You've Never Heard Of

As a business school student at Stanford in the 1960s, Phil Knight, the future CEO of Nike, wrote a paper on the advantages of outsourcing. He postulated that low-cost, high-tech athletic shoes produced in an efficient Asian economy like Japan might one day make real inroads on German industry leader Adidas. Within a few decades, outsourcing of shoes rapidly migrated from Japan to Korean and Taiwan, on to Thailand, and today to China, Vietnam, and Indonesia. Thousands of shoe manufacturers sprang up in these areas but the largest of them all, a Taiwanese company with most of its production facilities in China and others in Vietnam and else-where in Asia, is the obscure Yue Yuen.

The first time I visited one of Yue Yuen's facilities in China's Guang-dong province (where you will find more high-rises and big factories sprouting up seemingly at random than cows prowling its grassy fields), I was impressed by the massive scale of the venture spread out before me on the former site of a lychee plantation. This vast industrial complex employs in excess of 50,000 young, mainly female workers at a cluster of twenty modern factories. Here, workers spend endless hours (although not nearly as many as was common practice a decade ago) sitting silently at sewing and cutting machines, gluing and stitching together different types of shoes. What is most striking is that a manufacturer like Yue Yuen is not married to any single client or brand. Instead, each brand—Nike, Reebok, Adidas, and New Balance running shoes or Timberland boat shoes—has its own separate building, in a perhaps naive attempt to keep designs and other high-tech innovations from spilling over from plant to plant.

Of the roughly one quarter million workers employed by Yue Yuen worldwide, about 160,000 work at three sites a few dozen kilometers apart in South China. The one I have toured, Huang Jiang, is by Yue Yuen standards a medium-sized plant. Yet it boasts its own reservoir, power plant, telephone exchange, distilled water plant, fire station, dormitories, post office, and shops. And, as I was proudly informed by a spokesperson from management, the world's largest tannery, all owned and operated by the same Taiwanese parent company. Above my head, countless dry, tanned hides swirled on meat hooks, ready to be turned into running shoes, boat shoes, even leather furniture. I was told that over eight thousand hides are imported there every day from Brazil and the United States, then aniline dyed and finished within a record six minutes, a process that not long ago took hours of soaking in stinking vats.

In the showroom, an impressive variety of the firm's eclectic footwear collection was on display, beneath posters in English and Chinese that lay out precisely the rules governing labor, safety, and the environment. This is the legacy of an uproar that caught Nike, Reebok, Adidas, and other committed outsourcers in its grip, but which has also made Yue Yuen, once part of Nike and others' brand problems, currently part of the solution.

During lunch break, I saw groups of young women strolling the grounds, girlishly gossiping while making a few quick purchases in the factory stores. Many hail from poor, rural areas in the northwest of China, live here in dormitories for several years and earn a few dollars per day, low by Western standards but a generous improvement on what they could make at home.

A NEW SET OF STANDARDS

On May 12, 1998, Nike CEO Phil Knight stood shamefacedly at a podium at the National Press Club in Washington. With great fanfare he announced the formation of a six-pronged plan to improve labor conditions in the approximately six hundred contract facilities around the world that manufactured Nike footwear, mainly in Asia. Three decades earlier, Knight, a former University of Oregon track team member, and his track coach, the legendary Bill Bowerman, had founded a firm dedicated to turning out the world's finest shoes for competitive athletes. Focused initially on track teams, Nike eventually branched out to other sports.

Independent as Nike was, by 1980—having captured an astonishing 50 percent share of the running shoe market in the United States from Adidas—the firm was as wedded as ever to its original outsourcing model, in order to gain maximum cost advantage over its domestic and European rivals. Phil Knight was proud of the innovation he had helped spark, which in his view kept his own employees' attentions focused on the design, promotion, and distribution of footwear, while production was handled by contract manufacturers, first in Japan, then elsewhere in Asia. It took until the late 1980s for an enterprising journalist from *The Oregon Weekly,* published in his own hometown of Eugene, to start casting aspersions that the true source of Phil Knight's growing wealth and prestige—cheap Asian labor—was doing bad things to its iconic brand.

By that point, Nike's prominence as a consumer icon meant that investigations by a variety of activist groups of its labor practices in exotic locations like China and Indonesia were likely to gain maximum exposure in the media. Labor activists in Asia, particularly skilled at fanning the flames, found their stories picked up first by the media in the UK—including Thames TV and *The Economist*—and eventually by progressive U.S.–based outlets. By 1997, Nike felt under sufficient consumer pressure to hire former UN Ambassador Andrew Young to tour Nike's Asian factories and issue a report that it hoped would clear it of allegations of participation in labor abuse. Knight, for his part, was not shy about publicizing his own aggrieved view that Nike was unfairly taking a hit for the multiple ills of outsourcing and globalization.

The contrasting rallying cry of activist non-governmental organizations (NGOs) and the media was that Nike and other multinationals seeking to outsource production to low-cost labor countries should regard themselves as responsible for every link in their global supply chains. Even if the workers who made the shoes or other consumer goods were not directly employed by the firms in question, concerned consumers were increasingly demanding that the firms doing the outsourcing exert some influence and control over the labor policies of the contract manufacturers it hired to handle production.

By the late 1990s, the issue was posing a sufficient peril to the integrity of the brand and its popularity among fickle young consumers that Phil Knight and Nike ceded critical ground to their critics and began taking steps to rectify the situation. Yes, they agreed, Nike *was* responsible for the health and livelihood of its workers in Thailand, Vietnam, China, and Indonesia. Over the last several years, Nike has conducted more than a thousand interested observers from the media, organized labor, NGOs, and investment groups on tours of its Asian factories, including those owned and operated by footwear colossus Yue Yuen, whose vast factories in China, Indonesia, and Vietnam produced one out of six pairs of branded athletic shoes sold worldwide in 2005.

Under mounting pressure from Reebok, Nike, Timberland, and other American firms, Yue Yuen terminated a number of practices conducive to the production of bad brand karma overseas. It abolished a controversial system of fining workers for misbehavior and stopped paying mainly by a piece rate. The concerns expressed by the global firms "have helped us pay more attention to human rights issues," Edward Ku, executive director of Yue Yuen, told a reporter from the *San Francisco Chronicle* in 2000.[16] Similar pressure brought to bear by activists induced the company to switch from toxic formaldehyde-based to less toxic, water-based glues on all its production lines. The *Chronicle* reporters observed slogans plastered on walls everywhere in the plant exhorting workers to, among other things, "Work diligently because life is hard and short (The spirit of Yue Yuen)."

In a recently published book[17] on corporate social responsibility, Pou Chen Group Chairman Tsai Chi-jui noted that when the big American footwear brands first began pressuring him and other suppliers to improve their labor practices, the moral suasion caused those suppliers to impose superior standards on *their* suppliers. "This has set a good example for the industry," Tsai Chi-jui maintained. "In fact, some of the brands with which we work have adopted our CSR (corporate social responsibility) policies as their standard and have introduced our CSR practice to their subcontractors."

Under withering criticism from NGOs on labor and environmental conditions, the major brands have been concentrating their production among a more select group of suppliers that are willing to comply with strict rules of conduct and can be audited effectively. As a result, Yue Yuen has been growing at twice the industry rate. The environmental and social audit process undergone by many contract manufacturers in Asia is well described in *The Financial Times:*[18]

> Big US and European companies, particularly in the footwear and apparel industries, send staff and third-party auditors to determine whether their Chinese suppliers are complying with the multinationals' codes of conduct and national labor laws—which for China stipulate a 40-hour working week with a maximum of 36 hours of overtime a month. Auditors talk to factory managers and examine records to check for working hours longer than the legal limit and sweatshop conditions. They tour the factory, looking for everything from under-age workers to exit doors and fire extinguishers to the number of workers sharing factory dormitory rooms.

Such audits can pose a chilling prospect for many Chinese factories, because failing an audit can mean a potentially crippling loss of business. In 2000, Reebok shifted a major contract away from Yue Yuen to another firm until it could demonstrate that it had completely cleaned up its act. Compliance can require a costly overhaul. When audits began, "we'd go to the factory, we'd see they did not meet lots of standards,[19] says Steve Li, executive director of Hong Kong–listed Yue Yuen Industrial. Mr. Li adds that improving social compliance is a continuing effort at his factories. "This is a pretty long journey. It's not ended. There is still a lot of room to improve."

Yue Yuen/Pou Chen founder Tsai Chi-jui was raised in Taiwan in an artistic household where both parents were weavers of traditional Chinese fabrics. He majored in art at Taichung Normal University before teaching elementary school for several years in central Taiwan. On the side, he began working as a part-time designer for local footwear makers, and in 1969 he and his three brothers founded Pou Chen in Taiwan. In the 1970s, the firm made its first substantial inroad into global outsourced footwear manufacturing by landing a major contract with New Balance. This coup was more dramatically followed in 1980 with an even larger contract with German athletic shoe firm and longtime industry leader Adidas. Over time, these contracts opened the door to close relationships with more than forty major international brands as Pou Chen began sprouting sprawling production facilities all over Asia.

In 1988, Tsai founded Yue Yuen and registered the firm in Hong Kong to better manage his fast-growing firm's production lines. He appointed his brother Tsai Chi-neng chairman, and embarked on a massive migration comparable to Hon Hai's into mainland China. By 2002, of Yue Yuen's 279 production lines, 156 were located in China, 72 in Vietnam, and 51 in Indonesia, while the firm maintained only a residual five lines in Taiwan, mainly for final assembly processing for the local market.

Very discreetly, Yue Yuen exploded into the world's largest maker of athletic and casual shoes for all the major brands with a 17 percent share of the global market, well ahead of all competitors. In 2005, it produced 186 million pairs with total revenues of $3.2 billion. Yue Yuen accounts for 20 percent of Nike's orders, over 25 percent of Adidas's, and over 20 percent of Reebok's after a remarkable eleven consecutive years of growth in revenues and earnings.

THE YUE YUEN DIFFERENCE

Yue Yuen's early move into low-cost production centers such as China explains only a part of its raging success. There are thousands of small shoe factories in China and other countries that are no more than sweatshops, eking out a marginal existence but never making it into the big league. What makes Yue Yuen different are its prior experience making shoes in Taiwan, huge economies of scale from its massive plants, quality control through vertical integration, huge versatility in product assortment, flexibility in adapting with lightning speed to the rapid fashion changes in the shoe industry, and a savvy willingness to play by the rules.

What makes Yue Yuen different is its prior experience, huge economies of scale, quality control through vertical integration, huge versatility in product assortment, flexibility in adapting with lightning speed to the rapid fashion changes in the shoe industry, and a savvy willingness to "play by the rules."

Maintaining and protecting brand secrets is one of Yue Yuen's greatest challenges, as well as a critical success factor. Preventing any leakage of intellectual property from brand to brand is part of the job of Jackson Lee, who runs Yue Yuen's R&D center and makes a point of never letting Adidas and Nike development teams come into contact. I learned during my visits that even casual photography near production lines is strictly *verboten*. Industrial espionage is not unknown in Taiwan or elsewhere in Asia, and is a problem that affects shoe manufacturing as well as high-end semiconductor chip design.

Production efficiencies and low cost are certainly not the only keys to Yue Yuen's explosive growth. Developing long-term partnerships with key customers and suppliers has been an even greater success factor. In a recent attempt to foster even closer and more creative collaboration with clients, Pou Chen has joined Nike in founding a research and development center at its new global headquarters complex in Taichung City, located near prestigious Tunghai University. This joint venture signals Yue Yuen's aspiration to partner with clients not merely in cutting costs, but in the more value-added aspects of the footwear business: research and design.

From its vast and efficient in-house tannery to its stakes in more than sixty different suppliers, Yue Yuen (and parent company Pou Chen) assures clients that it can provide the quality and economies of scale that it promises. Its scale allows it to scout the world for raw materials, buy them in bulk, and negotiate low prices. In an industry where raw materials comprise 50 percent of the total production cost, such savings comprise a critical competitive advantage.

Yue Yuen sources many materials from nearby suppliers to minimize transportation costs. From athletic shoes, it has branched out into casual shoes and ladies' shoes but has pulled back from diversification into leather car seats and furniture. Its wealth of relationships with virtually all the major brands allows Yue Yuen to spot fashion trends quickly while its long experience in the shoe industry has taught the company that the manufacturer who gets its shoes to the sales racks fastest wins. In its R&D labs, young designers are trying out new features that its clients can promote in their advertising.

Athletic shoes remain Yue Yuen's major product with 65 percent of sales but casual shoes and shoe soles are increasing in importance with 17 and 15 percent. The American market has always been Yue Yuen's largest, at 42 percent, but Europe and Asia are growing markets. Yue Yuen now has six hundred shoe stores in China.

In February 2005, Yue Yuen announced that it was ahead of schedule to achieve its goal of opening up to one thousand sporting goods retail outlets in China by 2008 when the Olympic Games are held in Beijing. The two Tsai brothers who run the company make sure they leverage their decades of experience in the shoe industry. They are not afraid to constantly try new initiatives. Besides its ambitious retail plans, Yue Yuen also hopes to go into sportswear. When asked about this new venture, David Tsai says simply and modestly, "It complements our footwear business."

An Investor's View
The Bull Case
- *The competitiveness of Chinese labor costs faces few challenges for the medium-term future.*
- *Yue Yuen has well-established relationships with all the major brands in athletic and casual shoes.*
- *Very few of the world's numerous shoe manufacturers can compete with Yue Yuen in scale and ability to source materials.*

The Bear Case
- *High turnover and rising wage rates caused by China's rapid development as a manufacturing center are costly for Yue Yuen.*
- *The athletic and casual shoe markets in the United States and Europe are mature, forcing Yue Yuen to go into new areas where it has less dominance.*

Lessons
- *Global brands will increasingly hold their suppliers responsible for operating under a rigid code of conduct, posing both challenges and opportunities.*
- *Even in industries dependent on cheap labor, only a few rise to world class status by differentiating themselves through scale, quality, adaptability to fashion and design.*

CHAPTER 6

From Imitators to Innovators

Taiwan's TSMC and High Tech Computer win by reinventing industries and products

Strategies

- *Surprise industry insiders by dis-aggregating activities, relieving small design houses from the need to spend billions*
- *Move up the value ladder from simple manufacturing to sophisticated design*
- *Cooperate with customers by sharing technology libraries*

After losing the Chinese Civil War (1945–1949), the displaced Nationalists dreamt they could harness the traditional Chinese entrepreneurial juices to create a competing market-based model on the nearby island of Taiwan that would form a favorable contrast to the ascetic Communist society and planned economy being erected by Mao and his disciples on the mainland.

Not that Chiang Kai-shek's Republic of China wasn't rigid and oppressive in its own way, but the plucky little island nation, bolstered by massive infusions of U.S. foreign aid, succeeded in realizing its lofty ambition of becoming a shrine to the capitalist spirit in Asia. At the bustling heart of this audacious little enterprise stood Taiwan's consumer electronics industry. But after more than two decades of robust growth, K.T. Li (minister in charge of technology for the fledgling Republic of China) considered it neither as sophisticated nor cutting edge as it could be and in dire need of an appropriate stir of the pot from above.

Not every great business idea springs fully formed from the hyperactive minds of rugged, lone-ranger entrepreneurs, even if they are the ones so vital to making it work. Quite a few audacious, blue-sky ideas for major companies, particularly in the emerging markets, originated as

little-celebrated "ah-ha" moments experienced by government bureaucrats inhabiting drab offices off long dusty corridors into which no natural
light will ever shine. One such visionary bureaucrat was K.T. Li, a former
finance minister and graduate in physics from Britain's Cambridge University, who took it upon himself and his government in the mid-1980s to
boost Taiwan's complacent consumer electronics industry to the next
level.

Taiwan's tech companies had been muddling along turning out cheap
transistor radios and air conditioners with barely a thought given to driving
innovation. They had become quite adept at churning out tons of inexpensive consumer goods, from knock-off, no-name digital watches to pocket
calculators and TVs. Yet there was no Taiwanese Sony, no Taiwanese Samsung, Motorola, or TI.

Imitation—not only the sincerest form of flattery, but a key shortcut to
economic success—was the name of the game in Taiwan. As was true for
the United States in the nineteenth century, Japan in the early twentieth
century, and the Asian Tigers and China today, successful imitation had
too often been conducted by means of flagrant violation of intellectual
property (IP) rights. Just as today's emerging multinationals' copycat pasts
may still trip them up in the minds of consumers, complacent European
industrialists at first looked down on their American followers. More
recently, Americans and Europeans woefully underestimated the ability of
Japanese automobile and steel producers to not merely compete but overtake them in quality, design, and technological innovation.

As K.T. Li was aware, virtually all companies and countries pass
through a phase of mimicry during the early stages of industrial development. But there is always a catch. Like infant industry protection, imitation
provides critical cover during the incubation phase. Yet over the long haul,
imitation can be corrosive to progress if companies grow dependent on
easy pickings. Firms in emerging markets with world-class aspirations
need to make a break with their imitative pasts to have any hope of establishing themselves as leaders in the future. At a recent conference in India,
I heard Ratan Tata, the visionary chairman of the Tata Group in India,
challenge other corporate leaders when he observed, "No company
becomes world class until it stops reengineering and starts innovating on
its own." He has insured that Tata Motors remains firmly in the forefront of
innovation in India with its new compact family car, the Indica.

Ever since the era of Thomas Edison, continuing up through the present
ascendancy of Steve Jobs, Bill Gates, and other tech tycoons, innovation in

the fast-paced consumer electronics industry has not been a luxury but a prerequisite for survival. Every year a steady stream of new products is brought to market in a pattern of continuous displacement that calls to mind the Austrian-American economist Joseph Schumpeter's dread "gales of creative destruction." Within a blink of an eye, cathode-ray tubes gave way to multimedia flat screens, mainframe computers were supplanted by stand-alone PCs, then by desktops and notebooks networked through servers, then finally by a dizzying array of wireless devices that keep us connected to the Internet and each other just about anywhere in the world.

Desk telephones and land lines have been largely displaced by the most popular consumer gadget of recent history, the mobile phone. Yet even mobile phone manufacturers are contending with the onslaught of cell phones that have miraculously morphed into multifunctional "smart phones" combining video capability, Internet access, a keyboard for portable email, an electronic calendar, gaming, an MP3 player, and a digital camera.

Most of the manufacturing of the world's consumer electronics is conducted in Asia, especially China, to which such intellectual and capital-intensive activities as design and development (still perceived as a bastion of value-added activity for the industrialized world) have been migrating, not just for cost savings but to gain strategic proximity to one of the world's most dynamic economies. Original equipment manufacturers (OEMs) located in emerging markets (once best known for churning out products cheaply and quickly, based on designs provided by customers) now pursue a strategy of clambering friskily up the value chain to the more hallowed status of original design manufacturers (ODMs).

The most widely accepted measure of technological innovation has traditionally been a firm's or a nation's intellectual wealth, as reflected in its storehouse of new patents. At the outset of the twenty-first century, the wellsprings of intellectual property rights remain dominated by the former First World[1] but new additions are added every day from former colonial backwaters. With 1,641 patents, Samsung Electronics ranks #5 globally in 2005, ahead of Micron, Intel, Hitachi and Toshiba but still behind IBM and HP.[2] Measured as a percentage of sales, research and development (R&D) activity in many world-class companies approaches that of their competitors in the developed world.[3]

From Korea, Singapore, and Taiwan to China and India, the drive to become innovators not imitators is particularly strong in emerging Asia. China has set itself the goal of boasting two of the ten leading universities in the world by the end of this decade. Comparisons of engineering graduates and test scores in science and mathematics underscore the progress Asian emerging markets have made in building the foundations of innovation and intellectual originality for the future.[4]

According to the *Global Information Technology Report* (published by the World Economic Forum), Singapore has pushed the United States (now #5) out of its customary leadership spot as a result of the quality of its science and math education, telecommunications costs, and Internet access.[5] Hong Kong now ranks ahead of Japan, the UK, and Germany, Taiwan ahead of the Netherlands and France, and Israel, Korea, and Estonia ahead of Belgium and Spain.

Besides spending massive amounts on R&D, leading companies from emerging markets benefit from getting better results for the same amount of money spent, as their researchers still cost only 10–20 percent of their American, European, or Japanese counterparts. A stunning 70 percent of the design of new models of wireless PDAs, 65 percent of notebooks, and 30 percent of digital cameras is conducted by Taiwanese and other Asian companies.[6]

TAIWAN SEMICONDUCTOR MANUFACTURING COMPANY (TSMC)
Reinventing the Way the World Makes Semiconductors

It may have been homesickness, it may have been patriotism, it may have been restlessness, it may have been long-suppressed entrepreneurial zeal, it may have been a classic midlife crisis, but when Taiwan's minister of technology K.T. Li came calling on Dr. Morris Chang, a U.S.-based pioneer of the semiconductor industry, Dr. Chang felt that the job being dangled by Li was an honor he couldn't refuse. The year was 1985, and the Shanghai-born Dr. Chang had just turned fifty-four. After nearly a quarter century with Texas Instruments, he had recently transfered to TI's archrival General Instruments. Despite the fact—as he confided to me over a leisurely breakfast of bacon and eggs at the Sherwood hotel in downtown Taipei—that he had held top positions in one of the most dynamic growth industries of the twentieth century, as an American-educated Chinese he still felt a glass ceiling.

I had grown bored with corporate life in the U.S. I had been the man responsible for the semiconductors business at Texas Instruments but not CEO. I formulated the semiconductor strategy, but it had to be examined, critiqued, and modified by my boss and by his boss. I never felt I had enough freedom of action. We were making a lot of money with semiconductors at that time but the company was using our business as a source of funding for other activities like consumer calculators, educational toys, and digital watches. I felt frustrated that I could not keep the cash we were making to reinvest in semiconductors.

For Chang, the prospect of heading up Taiwan's Industrial Technology Research Institute (ITRI) being established by Minister Li seemed like the perfect antidote to midlife malaise. The new institute was being launched in the hope of luring native Chinese back from U.S. academia or Silicon Valley to further the technological development of a homegrown consumer electronics industry. In an attempt to replicate the incubator status of Silicon Valley, Minister Li was in the advanced stages of establishing the now-renowned Hsinchu Science Park in a suburb of Taipei.

FROM DEVELOPMENT ENGINEER IN SILICON VALLEY TO ENTREPRENEUR IN TAIWAN

Chang had survived a childhood spent evading the brutalities of the Japanese overlords who invaded China in the late 1930s and were not driven out until 1945 following their defeat at the hands of the Allies. Their withdrawal left a void that Chiang Kai-shek and Mao Zedong violently vied to fill for four brutal years. With the fall of China to Mao's forces in 1949, Chang and his parents fled to the United States just as Chiang Kai-shek and his followers were defensively digging themselves in on Taiwan. After arriving in Massachusetts at eighteen, Chang spent a year gaining his social and intellectual bearings at Harvard before transferring to MIT in his sophomore year. In 1952, he graduated from MIT with a BS degree, earning his MS in mechanical engineering the following year.

Before returning to MIT for his PhD, Chang took a job as a junior development engineer with now-defunct Sylvania Electronics, seven years after Dr. William Shockley and colleagues at Bell Laboratories announced their invention of the transistor on December 23, 1947. The first commercial use of the transistor was to miniaturize electronic circuits in products for the hearing impaired. While Motorola's 1953 patent application for radio transistors was gathering dust unexploited, it took the visionary genius of Sony founder Akio Morita in the then emerging market of Japan to commercialize Bell Labs' invention and popularize the pocket-sized transistor radio.

In 1958 (the same year Texas Instruments' legendary senior engineer Jack Kilby filed his first patent for a "solid circuit" semiconductor) Chang accepted a job as a development engineer with TI. Founded in 1930 as a provider of seismic exploration equipment to the petroleum industry, TI gained a foothold in the infant electronics industry after acquiring the Massachusetts-based Geophysical Service Incorporated (GSI), which manufactured precision electronics components and measuring devices for the U.S. military during the Second World War.

During the 1960s, TI developed the first IC (integrated circuit) based computer, pioneered transistor-transistor logic (TTL) chips, commercialized the first hand-hand calculator, produced the first single-chip microcomputer, and was first to market with a single-chip microprocessor developed in conjunction with Intel. At Motorola, IBM, and other major chip developers and manufacturers, ever-faster computers and chips were laying the solid-state foundations of the Information Age.

Morris Chang was present at the creation, yet after three decades in the United States, he still felt a deep emotional bond with his Chinese homeland. While the prospect of returning to Communist China was clearly out of the question, assisting Nationalist Taiwan in making the next great leap forward in technology possessed a tangible patriotic and adventurous rather than just financial appeal.

Chang's nostalgia and fondness for Chinese culture and customs only deepened every time he traveled "home" to Taiwan for an interminable sequence of job interviews. "Here was a group of government people who seemed so eager to build up their country's economy," he recalled affectionately. In one fell swoop, he was not only reentering the Chinese culture of his youth, but recapturing the sense of excitement, ambition, and adventure that had filled the corridors of brash start-ups like TI when both they and Dr. Chang were in their roaring twenties.

One of the most alluring aspects of his new position as president of the Industrial Technology Research Institute (ITRI)—"one of the key instruments of Taiwanese industrial policy at the time," he assured me—was that his staff of over four thousand employees, more than half of whom were crack engineers and scientists, would be answerable solely to him. "While the nature of the job was similar to what I was doing in the U.S.," he noted, the critical difference was that in Taiwan it would be possible to do "similar things with a very large budget" without having to have his numbers relentlessly reviewed by senior management. Now, *he* would be senior management.

Only after he returned to Taiwan did his powerful patron see fit to inform him that he had lured Chang to Taiwan on false pretenses. Minister Li had all along been secretly hoping to persuade Dr. Chang to use ITRI as a base to launch something less governmental and more entrepreneurial. He wanted the estimable Dr. Chang to jump-start the equivalent of a TI or Motorola in Taiwan.

Unbeknownst to Chang, a team of topflight engineers and technicians had been working day and night on a semiconductor pilot line for several years prior to his arrival. At first Chang resisted the idea because "they lacked the first requirement of a successful business: a concrete product concept!" Yet he knew that if he and his Taiwanese colleagues were ever to succeed against keen competition from European, Japanese, and American semiconductor companies, the key ingredient of success would have to be a radically different approach to the problem.

As Chang explained his dilemma, "I didn't want to disappoint this minister because he had been very active in recruiting me. Even if he recruited me on the pretense that I was going to be president of ITRI, he had in mind all along that he wanted me to transform a pilot project into a real business through a spin-off. The more I hesitated, the more enthusiastic he became. After all, he had started it all and felt he needed to find a place for his people to go to after they were trained. Basically, he let *me* realize the dream *he* had. I always admired him greatly for that."

In a particularly emerging-markets twist, Minister K.T. Li had not the faintest idea of how Dr. Morris Chang would actually go about jump-starting a private enterprise. Dr. Chang, for his part, would never have *dreamed* of taking on such an overambitious and frankly ludicrous project in the absence of substantial public-sector support. If it failed, the venture might well have made Chang and Taiwan a laughingstock throughout Asia.

A REVOLUTIONARY NEW CONCEPT

No one on Taiwan could have been more aware than Dr. Chang that K.T. Li's concept was (not to put too fine a point on it) close to stark raving mad. Difficult as it may be to recall today, in the mid-1980s nearly all integrated circuit (IC) or "chip" manufacturers were full-fledged "integrated device manufacturers" (IDMs) like Intel, Compaq, DEC, IBM, Texas Instruments, Motorola, and Siemens. As a matter of course, these and other firms custom designed, fabricated, and marketed semiconductors from scratch. But Dr. Chang knew, based on a quarter century of experience at IT, that of the five phases of manufacturing to which every integrated circuit is subjected (specification and design, silicon fabrication, testing, assembly, and packaging) by far the most difficult and complex is the fabrication and etching of the silicon wafers themselves.

Silicon wafers are fabricated in superclean facilities (called "fabs") in a pristine process that combines thin, polished, round six-to twelve-inch plates of silicon (formulated from sand vacuumed off Australian beaches) with tiny electrodes into integrated circuits. Once the silicon surface has been coated with a thin layer of aluminum or copper (which connects it to the circuits in the underlying layer), the wafer is broken down into individual chips that are tested in place, plugged into the customer's product, and tested again. Needless to say, the capital investment required for a "fab" is higher per square inch than any other industry. At roughly a billion bucks a pop, fabricating a "fab" is anything but a cheap labor operation.

But what if, Dr. Morris Chang wondered, a pure foundry contract manufacturer could develop the skill and capability to relieve independent chip designers of the trouble and turmoil of fabricating the silicon wafers and chips by themselves? What if, lacking a fabrication plant of his own, an independent designer could fail or succeed in the market not based on his or her ability to properly process the chips, but rather on the value and creativity embedded in their individual design and internal logic?

As Dr. Chang informed me over breakfast in Taipei, the idea for an independent foundry had originated with an American professor at Caltech, Carver Mead, who wrote a book describing the potential for more generic chips that he called ASICs (application specific ICs) at a time when all integrated circuits were custom designed. The revolution in the semiconductor industry that Dr. Chang envisioned was already occurring in a small way, yet it was limping along in low gear until Chang came along to jump-start it backed by the clout and resources of the Taiwanese government.

Chip designs are so proprietary that good designers justly live in fear that their irreplaceable intellectual property may be purloined by some unscrupulous fabricator. But TSMC solemnly assures customers and prospective customers on its website, "Our charter prevents us from designing or making our own brand-name IC products. TSMC therefore is a partner, not a competitor, to our customers."

> *TSMC was the first company to spot the innovative opportunity of being a dedicated IC foundry while leaving the designing and branding of chips to others.*

Morris Chang also knew from experience how easily the semiconductor business could be starved of much-needed capital when the end products of its parent suddenly went out of fashion. He decided that in the evershifting world of new product development, an independent fab would possess the flexibility to shift its output from a languishing to a flourishing sector, minimizing impact on capacity utilization. He also entertained the wild notion that an entire new industry of fabless designers might one day emerge from the successful execution of his plan. On this last point, he was right. Today, nearly a thousand fabless chip designers have sprouted up in the world, constituting the bulk of TSMC's four hundred clients and 60 percent of its revenues, proving crucial to its existence.

"I think it was serendipitous to set up a foundry in the late '80s," Chang reflected over breakfast. "I don't think it would have happened or succeeded had I not been here, because the first years we survived with orders from the big brands. We would not have received them if I hadn't been at TSMC because they trusted me from my days at TI. Our main clients during the first years were big companies that didn't need us but used us as a secondary source because we were cheaper when they ran out of capacity themselves. But beginning in 1991–92, the fabless companies began to come to us in droves. Suddenly, our technology was truly competitive."

SUCCESS FOLLOWED RIDICULE AND A TOUCHY START

Even if the existence of this market niche seems obvious in retrospect, most of the founding fathers of the industry assumed that Dr. Chang had gone off the deep end. "When I went around looking for capital, even Gordon Moore [founder of Intel, and famous for "Moore's law" predicting doubling in chip power every eigteen months] told me he didn't think this pure foundry concept would work. He called it a 'bum idea'!"

Bum idea or not, the concept "was born out of desperation that we didn't have an actual *product* idea to sell," Chang breezily assured me. Taiwan possessed substantial numbers of skilled and eager workers and engineers, but "had no clients lined up and was still two generations behind California."

The herd mentality's unshakeable belief that the independent foundry was a nonstarter made it practically impossible to raise money, build a plant, or find clients. Both 1985 and 1986 were bad years for the semiconductor industry, and most companies were in no shape to invest in a big new plant. In despair, Chang began contacting companies with whom he had strong prior relationships. He canvassed Intel, TI, Motorola, Siemens, Thomson, and a few Japanese chip makers, but all professed to be so short of cash they lacked the capability to invest on the scale Chang was seeking. He had been hoping for a commitment of $220 million over a three- or four-year period, of which the Taiwanese government was willing to put up roughly half (49 percent), yet he was still on the hook to raise the rest from private investors.

In the end, the Dutch consumer electronics giant Philips (which already maintained a large and growing operation in Taiwan with nearly 15,000 employees) ended up Chang's only primary investor. And this was mainly because, as Chang advised me, "it wanted to stay on the Taiwanese government's good side." It possessed "a global strategy," but was weak in transforming innovation into viable businesses. Alone among the chip firms, Philips was willing to be persuaded by Chang and strong-armed by Taiwan into regarding Chang's "bum idea" as a growth opportunity.

Yet even the Philips deal nearly broke down when the Dutch proved inflexible negotiators—a national characteristic with which I am familiar. "They kept demanding all kinds of concessions, including an option to convert their initial 27 percent share into a 51 percent controlling interest at the end of three years if TSMC was successful." In the end, Chang kept the dialogue with Philips open and was able to modify the more onerous conditions.

The remaining investment funds were gleaned from a group of local investors whom the government heavily leaned on to lend a helping hand. After nine months of tense negotiations, TSMC broke ground on its first plant in June 1986.

It took TSMC more than a decade to ascend to a level where the company could be considered capable of offering truly "leading edge products." While just a few years ago Chang regarded TSMC as "still fifty to a hundred steps behind IBM and Intel," today he sees the firm as "at least on a par with Intel and IBM. In a few areas, such as immersion technology, we are actually *ahead* of the competition."

Key Success Factors of TSMC

- *Developing a new industry model—relieving design houses from the burden of semiconductor fabrication*
- *Economies of scale*
- *Continuous focus on technological innovation*
- *Lowest break-even point in industry thanks to high operational efficiency*
- *Obsession with superior quality*
- *Strong balance sheet*
- *Focus on customer service—helping clients to innovate*

HIGH OPERATING EFFICIENCY TRANSLATES INTO A LOW BREAK-EVEN POINT

Morris Chang was determined from the outset to keep fixed costs low and production cycles short. TSMC controls costs while accelerating the production process by permitting multiple customers to use the same "mask" (used to protect areas that are not being treated) for their wafers. By achieving this and other operating efficiencies, TSMC's *break-even level is as low as 40 percent* of capacity utilization, in comparison to 65–70 percent for its three top competitors UMC of Taiwan, Chartered of Singapore, and SMIC of mainland China.

STAYING AHEAD OF TECHNOLOGY

Resting on one's laurels is always a surefire recipe for disaster. But for companies like TSMC, whose existence depends upon repeatedly challenging the prevailing wisdom and existing order in their industry, it can be the kiss of death. Industry upstarts and new entrants *need to constantly innovate* or fall victim to a new breed of upstarts. In mid-2005, TSMC announced its intention to be the first foundry to produce the "X Architecture" chip in cooperation with Silicon Valley–based Cadence Design Systems and fabless 3D graphics design house ATI Technologies. This revolutionary graphics processor for computers uses diagonal interconnects to enhance performance, reduce costs, and require less battery power. According to R&D vice president Dr. Ping Yang, "we are now developing sixty-five-nanometer design rules" that vividly display TSMC's enduring strength in this promising area of nanotechnology.[7]

A BROAD ARRAY OF SERVICES WITH CUTTING-EDGE TECHNOLOGY FOR USE BY ITS CLIENTS

TSMC grasped early on that it was not enough for it to be at the technological cutting edge but that it needed to ensure the same for its clients. TSMC scrupulously maintains this edge by developing and even acquiring technology files and libraries for use not only by its own engineers but also by its customers. These files facilitate clients' design services while the libraries permit customers to quickly design sophisticated semiconductors based on the industry's newest process technologies. Through constantly expanding agreements with other library providers and intellectual property services, TSMC provides access to a worldwide network of expertise and designs. Chang has even tried occasionally to further bind his customers by investing in them. "We will consider making an investment if we can see we can enhance the company's business, but if it's just a passive investment, we will not make it."

CHALLENGES OF THE FUTURE

Apart from the sheer cyclicality of the semiconductor industry, TSMC's greatest challenge will be the ramp-up of increasingly sophisticated independent foundries in China, accompanying a likely migration of much of the electronics industry. TSMC is still ahead of its Chinese competition Chang admits openly, "If I were to start TSMC today, I would probably do it in China. Not because of cheap labor but for the greater talent pool." The Taiwanese government finally granted TSMC permission to invest $900 million for its own plant in China. Of course, TSMC and other Taiwanese companies hope to control design and innovation while giving over much of their manufacturing to China. "I don't think Taiwan is in the driver's seat anymore," says James C. Mulvenon, co-author of a 2004 Rand Corporation study on Taiwan's and China's chip industries, which concludes that European and Japanese chip makers

> *Our key innovation was in not competing with our customers.*
> —Morris Chang

will provide China with technology the Taiwanese refuse to share. In reality, the Taiwanese, at least for now, remain key players in the development of China's semiconductor industry.

By refusing to slavishly follow the example of others TSMC created two entirely new models for the semiconductor industry—that of the "fabless" chip fabricator and the independent design house. It is not often that a single company is able to establish two entirely new industries. In the process, Morris Chang and TSMC created not only new models for its own industry but a role model for innovation and change in emerging markets as a whole.

Partnering with the world's leading chip companies, TSMC is able to create a product quicker, cheaper, and better than its competitors in a way that keeps it profitable even during times of duress. To Morris Chang, who spent two decades in the United States helplessly watching Asia attempting to chase "the end of the train," it is something of an accomplishment to have created a company embodying Asia's and the emerging markets' broader transition from imitator to innovator.

An Investor's View

The Bull Case
- *Fabless model has proven to be viable*
- *Technological leadership*
- *Continued strong demand growth*
- *Strong but volatile growth trend of earnings*
- *Strong human capital; invests in its future*

The Bear Case
- *Chinese competition is heating up*
- *Hard to maintain as electronics industry moves to China and money is no object*
- *Highly cyclical industry*
- *TSMC's quality is well recognized in its market valuation*
- *Is drive of new generation as strong?*

Lessons
- *Revolutionary ideas derided by experts (especially if they have an axe to grind) may shake up an industry and create a whole new path to success.*
- *It is not enough to innovate at the outset; the need is constant.*

- *Initial government support is often crucial to get a new industry off the ground but becomes stifling when continued too long.*
- *Strong founders with broad experience are needed in most new businesses.*
- *Highly capital-intensive industries can succeed in emerging markets if companies have a strong capital base, generate significant cash flow, and operate in a low-interest-rate environment.*

HIGH TECH COMPUTER CORP. (HTC)
On the Cutting Edge of Wireless Communications

On Friday May 10, 2005, at the Mandalay Bay Resort and Casino in Las Vegas, Microsoft chairman Bill Gates unveiled the hotly awaited Windows Mobile 5.0 during his keynote address at Microsoft's Mobile & Embedded DevCon 2005. "We're here to talk about a big advance in the mobile platform and our embedded operating system that, combined with new tools, will let you build applications that weren't possible before," Gates told his rapt audience. "The whole mobile space is incredibly hot. We're moving well beyond just doing voice calls and SMS [systems management server] messages to a whole range of applications that will take media, location, and productivity information and present it in new and rich ways."

Holding aloft two microcomputers, one made by Samsung and a second from Taiwan's lesser-known High Tech Computer Corporation, he announced that the brand-new High Tech Universal PDA (personal digital assistant) phone he was clutching in his right palm was "the first Windows Mobile 5.0-based." Within seconds, he received an email attachment combining a mobile version of Word, a mobile version of Powerpoint, and a mobile version of the Excel spreadsheet. More impressively, High Tech's Universal carried a mobile version of Windows Media Player 10 that synchronized with Bill Gates's desktop PC, permitting him to transfer music, pictures, videos, and podcasts from his PC to his PDA.

Taiwan's High Tech Computer Corp. (HTC), developer of the Universal, is an original design manufacturer (ODM) that designs and manufactures devices not only for HP, iMate, Audiovox, and other Windows Mobile equipment vendors but for most major telecom operators in the United States and Europe. It also produces Palm's wildly popular and versatile new Treos that use both Palm and Windows operating systems. The HTC Universal is a 3G (third generation) device equipped with a full keyboard and an unusually bright and crisp 180-degree pivoting screen that slides smoothly from landscape to portrait mode at the flip of a wrist. It permits users to create and edit files using Microsoft Office applications as well as wirelessly send and receive photo and video files at rapid connection speeds. Dual speaker stereophonic sound lets owners watch and listen to high-resolution videos sitting in airports or during other down times. The device's clever hinge design allows the screen to be protected by folding it flat over the keyboard, and enables owners to answer a phone call without opening the cover by pressing a talk button.

COMPLETELY PORTABLE—THE WAVE OF THE FUTURE

Although still comparatively small in size with sales of $2.3 billion and net earnings of $366 million in 2005. HTC is today one of the world's best positioned companies to take advantage of the growing trend toward "convergence" in handheld wireless devices that bundle a mobile phone, Internet access, email, camera, MP3 player, TV, and tiny entertainment center into one portable package.

Within the near future, most if not all of the traditional functions of the old personal computer will be replaced by this new kind of PC. Cheap, global, always handy, always on, these handheld "personal communicators" will soon overtake cell phones in popularity. We will use such devices to make video phone calls, look up "light" information on the Internet, play games, listen to music, watch TV video clips and even daily segments of soap operas, make reservations, remind us of appointments and birthdays, and pay our parking meters and tickets. Software designers will be quick to allow users to engage in the already fashionable "content snacking"—watching selected snippets of programs while surfing and riffing among multiple media platforms at will. Sports events ranging from World Cup soccer matches to the Olympics will be conveniently condensed into brief segments, as will lowbrow pornography and highbrow news, the most popular items on the Internet. Soon, we will no longer be tethered to our desktop computers or telephones, be obliged to port unwieldy cameras to social functions, or keep stacks of CDs for our CD player. Like Bill Gates in Vegas but without the crowd, we will use our handheld devices to stay connected wherever we are in the world.

When I asked HTC's soft-spoken CEO Peter Chou what motivated him and his ambitious young engineers to create the next generation of handheld PCs, he made no secret of his firm's burning desire to innovate. "What drives me," he said simply, "is pride in being at the cutting edge of design in wireless technology."

"Show me what you are developing in your labs," I couldn't resist asking, curious to see some of the new products this innovative company's 1,100 research engineers were working on. At first reluctant, he soon gave in and conducted me through HTC's labs, to an acoustics studio where you could literally hear a pin drop (developed with help from German and British acoustic engineers) and then to a room where new antennas were being tested followed by yet another room full of engineers intensely fiddling with elaborate RF (radio frequency) testing equipment.

"We need to solve our own problems rather than having to run to Qualcomm or Texas Instruments," Chou said brightly. "We can even work with different operating systems now." It is true that HTC has shown itself to be as adept with Windows as with Palm and has succeeded in integrating Blackberry's "push" email technology. Cleverly, HTC has invested in the same equipment used by certification boards to replicate their tests in-house, allowing the company to send off a product for certification with "over 90 percent" confidence of receiving approval.[9]

In another building as crisp, clean, and brightly lit as one of his firm's screens, young designers and other creative types were working on models for the upcoming years. A beaming Chou showed me "our BMW," proudly pointing to a souped-up version of the recently unveiled Universal that integrates Bluetooth, WiFi, and third-generation phone reception "together with the usual goodies. With this one here, you get not only an MP3 player but also a GPS, with Internet access and video capability. We like to maintain a broad product portfolio," he noted mildly. "Last year we brought out twenty new products and only one flopped."

CLASSIC SUN TZU LEADS TO MODERN INNOVATION

In 1997, a team of engineers from Digital Equipment Corporation's (DEC) operations in Taiwan decided that, after spending fifteen years working at DEC, they understood the intricacies of taking a product idea and turning it into a reality. DEC fostered an environment of innovation and discipline that HTC's founders carried into their new venture. During their DEC days, a product had to be built from the ground up, all the way from the chips on the inside to the design of the outside. This proved a valuable lesson when the founders designed their first PDA.

Founder Chou and his team were brilliant research engineers who believed that Taiwan's traditional high-tech expertise, making notebooks and computer peripherals, would shortly be obsolete and that the industry would soon see margins threatened by creeping commoditization. As an antidote to such a fate, these ambitious entrepreneurs focused instead on what they fervently believed would be the technology of the future. After being turned down by Palm, they consoled themselves by quoting to each other from the Chinese classic, Sun Tzu's *The Art of Warfare,* which teaches its students that an overwhelming enemy can only be conquered by smart tactics.

Fortunately for them, Cher Wang, chairwoman of the company and daughter of Taiwan's richest man (petrochemicals billionaire Wang Yung-ching, founder of the Formosa Plastics Group), was also chairwoman of VIA Technologies, a listed IC design house. Having worked with some of HTC's management during their DEC days, she exhibited faith in this small group of talented Taiwanese engineers by funding their start-up, faith which has since paid off to the tune of many billions in revenues.

When I visited the company the first time, one of its engineers told me how he and his colleagues had scratched their heads trying to figure out how HTC could possibly break into the popular PDA (personal digital assistant) market. They knew all of the "big guys" had been outmaneuvered. Hypercompetitive Microsoft was smarting because its Windows CE operating system had failed to catch on with early adopters, who preferred Palm by a margin of at least two to one. Intel's microprocessor chips were not used in the Palm Pilot, while Sony also felt left out of a market it considered its own following the success of its Walkman and PlayStation game box.

HTC decided to please all the marginalized players by assembling a device that would look stylish and combined an Intel chip, Windows CE, and a Sony TFT-LCD screen. After they showed their completed prototype to Compaq (now HP) in 1999, it awarded HTC a contract as sole designer and producer and began to sell the device under its own name. The Compaq iPaq was HTC's first smash hit and briefly the world's best-selling PDA.

The iPaq was the first PDA to be validated by Microsoft's NSTL test lab, and won numerous "best product" awards in various major technology shows.[10] By 2003, the company was shipping nearly 1.5 million WinCE-based pocket PCs and two years later it was producing half of the Windows CE-based PDAs in the world.

ON THE CUTTING EDGE OF THE FUTURE'S GADGET

With an eye on the European market, HTC made sure it produced the world's first smart phone based on Microsoft's Windows operating system. Peter Chou is quick to point out that High Tech is close not only to Microsoft, Intel, Qualcomm, Hewlett-Packard, Palm, and Dell in the United States but to Toshiba and Sharp in Japan. Aware that telecom operators prefer customers to be loyal to them rather than a handset brand, HTC developed "private label" smart phones emblazoned with the carrier's brands, as opposed to its own, or those of potential rivals Nokia, Motorola, or Samsung. The firm has maintained close relations with virtually all major telecom operators in Europe, including Orange, Vodafone, Telefonica, and T-Mobile, as well as the majors in the United States from Verizon to Cingular to Sprint. As an insurance policy, it has taken the first steps to developing its own brand HTC, which it rolled out in mid-2006. Yet at present, while few have heard of HTC, its primary customers comprise all the brightest telecom brand names of the world.

Key Success Factors
- *Early focus on a rapidly growing niche of the mobile phone industry that will take off with the spread of third generation telecommunications*
- *Strong design talent*
- *Constant push for innovation and new models*
- *Excellent relationships with technology providers and telecommunications companies*

INNOVATION, INNOVATION, INNOVATION

A lack of strong R&D effort and spending has been the traditional Achilles heel of many Taiwanese companies. With a staff of over 1,100 R&D-oriented engineers (200 of them

> *HTC has an impressive list of "first."*

ex-DEC staffers), High Tech Computer provides a clear-cut exception to this rule. HTC's engineering development team dedicated entirely to the PDA market is the largest R&D team of its kind in Taiwan, large even by Korean standards. By providing employees with competitive compensation packages including stock in the company, and an open, relaxed but disciplined work environment, HTC has been able not only to attract top engineers, but to keep their extensive experience in-house, despite lucrative offers from abroad.

> *HTC is able to attract Taiwan's brightest and most dedicated engineers.*

HTC's List of "Firsts"

- World's first Windows CE, 64k, ultra-thin, palm-sized PCs with color screens
- First PDA using Intel's StrongARM processor
- First LTPS (low temperature poly-silicon) LCD panels
- First lithium polymer batteries
- First Chinese and GSM/GPRS wireless Pocket PCs
- First Windows-based smart phone, the SPV phone
- XDA was the first product to combine a PDA with a GPRS handset into one compact unit, providing Internet access in color, web-based email, and mobile phone capabilities.
- Among first manufacturers to add Blackberry capability to other applications

FOCUS ON DESIGN AND QUALITY

Like Samsung in Korea, HTC controls a large and growing design studio where artists and other creative minds experiment with various new models and materials in tandem with the innovation emanating from the engineering labs. Size, form, style, spacing of keyboards, swiveling of screens, placement of antenna are all tested in hundreds of new prototypes, and the best ones are selected for commercial launch.

> *"We tell our clients that, if a product doesn't meet our absolute quality standards, we will not ship it."*
> *—Peter Chou, CEO*

"We tell all of our clients that if a product doesn't meet our absolute quality standards, we will not ship it," Chou flatly assures me. Since the day of HTC's founding, the company's management has been determined that no product leave the line unless it is of unimpeachable quality.

STAYING CLOSE TO CUSTOMERS

Through constant dialogue with its clients that operate wireless networks, HTC is able to maintain a sense of what consumers look for in new products today and what improvements they would like to see in the future. This can range from such seemingly mundane issues as ease of text message typing to such critical issues as quality of reception (and the effectiveness of the unit's built-in antenna).

THE FUTURE OF THE HANDHELD/SMART PHONE

Once smart phones catch on beyond the business elite and status-conscious youth, pricing pressures are likely to become intense. Inevitably, wireless PDAs will become commoditized and mass producers will move into the space currently occupied by high-end first-movers. The current skepticism regarding the speed with which 3G communications will be adopted worldwide provides HTC with a bit of breathing space to establish itself as a leading producer in this area. Qualcomm's new 3G chip will make video conferencing from handsets far superior to what we have today. With its strong product portfolio, HTC has a head start, yet it knows that Samsung and others with big brand names and huge design staffs are breathing down its neck.

HTC is as much as twelve months ahead of others in its product development but many other Taiwanese companies like BenQ (which recently acquired Siemens Mobile), notebook makers Asustek and Compal, and GPS maker Mitac are all scrambling to get a slice of this profitable pie. Even if they can't compete on technology, they will undoubtedly compete on price.

High Tech Computer Corp. began its life as an improbable proposition: to build a tiny handheld device when the rest of Taiwan's tech industry was exclusively focused on becoming the notebook makers to the world. Through a staunch insistence on designing a top quality product, HTC carved itself a niche in the world of personal communicating, and arguably began a trend fueling the rapid growth in handheld converged devices.

That a small group of engineers from the tiny island of Taiwan could grow into one of the world's leading technology innovators has defied conventional wisdom and dire predictions.

An Investor's View
The Bull Case
- *HTC dominates the high-end market for Microsoft-based PDAs and smart phones.*
- *HTC is maintaining its technological lead despite efforts of others to catch up.*
- *Growth in revenues and profits are strong.*
- *Comparable in revenues to RIM's Blackberry.*
- *Higher operating margin than Nokia or Samsung.*

The Bear Case
- *HTC is only a small player in a highly competitive and R&D intensive industry.*
- *As smart phones become more ubiquitous, most consumers are paying less attention to features and technology but more to design and fashions.*
- *The spread of third generation telecommunications has been frustratingly slow and it is taking users time to embrace new features.*
- *HTC has only recently introduced its own brand names (HTC in Europe and Dopod in Asia).*

Lessons
- *Newcomers should seek an attractive, growing niche ignored by industry leaders.*
- *Even small companies with experienced researchers can come up with new products that defeat existing technologies.*
- *"Riding the wave" of new killer applications may be a quick road to success.*

CHAPTER 7

Your Next Global Employer?

Hyundai and CEMEX want to be close to their customers everywhere

Strategies

- *Build plants in strategic locations around the world to be close to customers while gaining flexibility to export everywhere*
- *Have the confidence to acquire or build production facilities in developed countries just as traditional multinationals have moved production to low-cost countries*
- *Ensure that design stays local even as production moves global*
- *Change the zip code to improve finance and image*

On May 19, 2005, a chartered Boeing 747 touched down at the Montgomery, Alabama, airport carrying a few hundred Hyundai executives from South Korea accompanied by the hugely popular (in Korea) three-girl techno-pop band Eleccookie. The top brass from Hyundai HQ in Seoul had jetted in for the day to preside over the opening ceremonies of a sprawling new $1.1 billion car factory on the outskirts of the former capital of the Confederacy.

It had taken three years to transform over 1,700 acres of pastureland into one of the most highly automated automobile manufacturing plants in the world. Covering over 2 million square feet of spanking-new factory floor, Hyundai's first manufacturing facility in the United States is a steel-and-concrete harbinger of tough times to come for the automobile industry going into the Emerging Markets Century. High legacy costs for pensions and health care, combined with work flow inefficiencies in the older plants of long-established companies, have prompted estimates that even modernized but still older plants in Detroit would require 25 percent more workers to produce the same volume of cars as an automated plant like that in Montgomery, Alabama.

During the opening ceremonies, images of shimmering steel sheets emerging fully formed but untouched by human hands from the stamping shop were projected onto gigantic screens as an audience of over 4,000 dignitaries and guests looked on. The sheets were pummeled into recognizable profiles by two 5,400-ton presses before being shot along sleek electro-monorails to the welding shop, where 250 robotic arms nimbly welded them onto unpainted exteriors. Inside the paint shop, every steel exterior was dipped and rotated 360 degrees ten times through a cathode bath to provide corrosion resistance. The bodies were then primed, painted with a topcoat, and provided with a clear coat by a process the company touts as "100 percent automated."

"Automation," a Hyundai press release helpfully explains, "prevents possible damage to the steel and also helps ensure quality and consistency." Of course, this high degree of automation also saves the firm and its shareholders untold millions in salaries and benefits straight off the bottom line. Automation keeps the 2,000-plus "team members" permanently on their toes, aware that at the stroke of a pen, their jobs could be replaced by robots who don't demand pensions, or outsourced to cheaper human workers overseas.

Nowhere are the twin challenges and opportunities created by automation and globalization more palpable than here at Hyundai's new plant in Alabama, where wages and benefits are roughly half those of comparable jobs in Detroit. When I visited Hyundai's even larger factory in the southeastern seaport of Ulsan in Korea (the largest integrated car plant in the world, measured by production volume), I learned that the 30,000-odd blue-collar unionized employees there consume more than eight tons of rice every day on Hyundai's tab, while the company bears the full cost of schooling for all employees' children, including fees at university. Even so, legacy costs are largely responsible for making the total labor costs in Detroit about twice those in Ulsan as Hyundai's Korean work force is younger. Even though the 1997 Asian crisis cut wage costs in dollar terms, total labor costs per car are roughly in line in Korea and Alabama. So why has Hyundai spent a billion and change to build a new plant in the new South?

- It is deadly serious about becoming a major presence in the American car market, following closely in the footsteps of Toyota and Honda and stepping into the ever-shrinking market share of the "Big Three."

- It hopes to put to rest doubters who claim it can't be as successful with U.S. made cars as with imported cars produced with low-cost Korean labor.
- It wants to demonstrate that it is a truly global producer with facilities that are anyone's envy.
- It wants to shorten the logistical supply chain stretching between it and millions of potential customers in the world's largest, toughest, most lucrative car market.

WHAT HAPPENED TO THE "GIANT SUCKING SOUND"?

The high point of the celebrations was a brief address by former president George H. W. Bush, who delivered his remarks following the sashaying cuties of Eleccookie performing a rousing chorus of Stephen Foster's "Oh Susannah." "You know, back when I was president, I worked with like-minded public citizens to help open the global market because of days like today. Simply put, I was convinced that there would *not* be a giant sucking sound of jobs leaving the country. Quite to the contrary, I believed that more companies like Hyundai would come here and enjoy access to the most advanced economy and the best workforce anywhere in the world."

So what ever happened to the "giant sucking sound"[1] famously forecast by industrialist and presidential candidate H. Ross Perot in 1992, when the Clinton administration was preparing the North America Fair Trade Agreement (NAFTA) for passage by Congress? This drain-like cyclone was supposed to accompany a massive migration of high-paying factory jobs from union strongholds in Michigan and Indiana to bustling *maquiladora* factories on the far side of the U.S. border with Mexico. While cross-border job migration has indeed taken place, the tangible effects of NAFTA in particular, and free trade agreements in general, on employment in the United States are more ambiguous than advocates on both sides have argued. Twelve years after the passage of NAFTA in 1994, the closest thing to a consensus on its long-term effects has been that neither its detractors (who predicted a massive flow of U.S. jobs across the border to Mexico) nor its boosters (who predicted resurgent economies on both sides of the border) have seen their dark or rosy scenarios prove true.

While the effects of any free trade agreement on employment are hard to quantify, few commentators a decade ago would have predicted that foreign companies, particularly firms based in emerging markets, would become growing employers of Americans in the first decade of the twenty-first century.[2] Despite the well-publicized rise in outsourcing and off-shoring of jobs from America and other mature markets like Western Europe to emerging economies, the car industry is just one example of how free trade and globalization have led foreign firms to *create* new manufacturing jobs in mature economies. Above and beyond the 2,000-odd jobs at the Hyundai facility in Montgomery, seventy-five related suppliers have constructed facilities elsewhere in North America at a total cost of over $500 million, creating an estimated 5,500 jobs associated with servicing Hyundai's Alabama operations alone. Thousands more are employed by Hyundai car dealers and the company's U.S. design facilities in California and Michigan.

While Hyundai press literature predictably features pictures of smiling "Team Members" merrily manning the assembly lines at Montgomery, impromptu comments made by workers and managers to the press are harder to dismiss as pure propaganda. Take Hyundai production director John Kalson, who walked away from a similar job with Ford in Detroit for the greener pastures of Hyundai's Montgomery facility. "Is Ford building a new plant? No. Is GM? No. Is Daimler? No." Kalson posed these obviously rhetorical questions to a bevy of reporters being conducted on a tour of the facility. None of his listeners had a response, because the questions spoke for themselves.

> *Contrary to popular perception, emerging multinationals did not ship existing jobs overseas after they took over companies in the West but in fact added to the local jobs as a result of new expansions.*

What H. Ross Perot and other industry pessimists failed to forecast more than a decade ago was the rise of modern Michigans in once remote locales like Alabama and Slovakia. At first glance, Alabama and the less developed part of former Czechoslovakia would seem to have little in common. But explosive growth in both these regions in recent years can be directly traced to calculated decisions made by automobile producers and suppliers to shift the footprint of production to low-wage environments in close proximity to mature markets with large pools of high-paying consumers. What smart firms are doing is going with the flow, taking advantage of the pronounced cost-disparities within different regions inside those markets: Alabama as opposed to Detroit; Slovakia as opposed to Stuttgart.

JOB CREATION WILL BECOME
A TWO-WAY STREET

Hyundai is just one example of a new phenomenon likely to spread faster than we can imagine today: globalization will become a two-way street of job creation and destruction. As a pragmatic investor, long-time observer of globalization, and committed realist, I foresee no likely alternative to this ceaseless flux of regional job loss and gain. A complex welter of factors including cost, logistics, red tape (and its elimination in fresh market economies), and the comparative flexibility of work rules and work ethics will force traditional and emerging multinationals to shift production nimbly among facilities strategically scattered all over the world.

HYUNDAI MOTOR
Persistence Pays Off

HYUNDAI'S GLOBAL GAMBLE

With the benefit of hindsight, Hyundai's decision to spend $1 billion-plus on its Alabama facility seems like a classic no-brainer. Yet back in the spring of 2001, two years before the first spade had broken ground outside Montgomery, Hyundai managers in Seoul had flatly informed me that they still had plenty of unresolved questions about the obvious risks involved in taking this massive gamble on a foreign continent where they had dismally failed to make it in the past. More than five years ago, the American dollar was still strong and the Korean won was weak. Memories of the Asian crisis remained fresh in many minds, car markets in Asia were just starting to take off, and the loyalty of American customers to Hyundai was close to zero due to persistent quality problems. Yet Hyundai CEO Mong Koo Chung and his top management team were ahead of their middle managers in believing that it was critical to the firm's future to establish a major presence in the United States, where the customers are discerning and the profit margins seductive.

AN INAUSPICIOUS BEGINNING

Hyundai Construction was founded following World War II by the idio-syncratic Ju-Yung Chung, a man of modest means and little formal education whose brother spoke English passably enough to enable him to make contact with American military authorities eager to grant civilian construction contracts. The fledgling company's road to riches began with paving roads and constructing buildings located on or near U.S. military bases in South Korea. Hyundai gained early expertise by learning to meet the famously tight specs to which U.S. military contractors are bound, competing for contracts let by the tough-to-please U.S. Army Corps of Engineers. The onset of the Korean War in 1950 provided the fast-growing firm with more plentiful cost-plus contracts in furtherance of the U.S. military mission on the embattled Korean peninsula. In the 1960s, servicing construction contracts with the U.S. military—to which the South Korean government maintained notoriously tight links—provided the firm with 70 percent of its profits and a quarter of its revenues.

In accordance with Korean commercial custom, Hyundai blossomed into one of the most powerful *chaebols* in the country, branching out into cement, steel, and (two decades after the firm's founding) auto manufacturing in 1967. The family ties between the group's affiliates remained sufficiently strong that the first president of Hyundai Motor was a former president of Hyundai Cement. In 1973, Hyundai Heavy Industries (HHI) built its first ship. Less than a decade later, HHI had become the world's largest shipbuilder, with cumulative deliveries exceeding 10 million tons.

Hyundai Motor began modestly by producing a Korean Cortina in a joint venture with Ford, a partnership that enabled it to transfer technology from an automotive leader while gaining additional prowess from licensing and technical assistance agreements from Japanese manufacturers, including Mitsubishi. Inspired by its Japanese partners, Hyundai Motor instituted quality control circles, a practice later transferred to Hyundai's ship-building arm, laying the foundation for its later success.

A DISASTROUS FOREIGN FORAY

After spending more than a decade humbly manufacturing other firms' designs, Hyundai's big breakthrough came in 1975 with the success of the subcompact Pony. Korea's first independently designed and manufactured car was a huge hit in the still heavily protected domestic market, propelling newcomer Hyundai into the top ranks of Korean carmakers. In February 1986, Hyundai introduced its subcompact Excel to U.S. car buyers, hoping to capture a niche at the low end of the American market the Japanese were abandoning. First-time car buyers unable to afford average sedans snapped up 100,000 Excels in seven months, and 169,000 in the first year. Buoyed by its sudden success, Hyundai management in Korea laid ambitious plans to construct its first overseas factory in Bromont, Quebec.

But by the time the Quebec factory was up and running in 1989, irate American consumers had caught on to the fact that the low Hyundai price tag did not come with Japanese quality. Already weak customer loyalty in the U.S. plummeted. Hyundai's brand image hit a low point when *Tonight Show* host Jay Leno compared Hyundais with Yugos, the Communist-era rattletraps imported from Yugoslavia. "With gas prices so high," he quipped, "most people want a car that you spend most of your life pushing anyway." As Hyundai sank to the bottom of J.D. Power & Associates' quality rankings, Jay Leno bitingly observed that Hyundais had "no room, you have to push it to get going, and it only goes downhill."

FROM THE BOTTOM TO THE TOP

So how did Hyundai, within just a few years, drive itself from being the fodder of late-night comedy to seeing its brand recognized in 2005 by *BusinessWeek*-Interbrand on the list of the top 100 in the world? Hyundai boasted the distinct advantage of having ample room for improvement. Starting out at a dismal 272 problems per 100 cars in the late 1980s, it rose to the top nonpremium brand position in the 2006 rankings of the J.D. Power's Initial Quality Survey with 102 problems, for the first time ranking ahead of traditional leader Toyota (106). It ranked only behind premium brands Porche and Lexus but ahead of such venerable names as Jaguar (109), Honda (110), General Motors (119), Volvo (133), and Mercedes (139) as well as the industry average of 124. The widely respected J.D. Power Survey measures the number of complaints reported by consumers within the first ninety days of ownership.[3]

This remarkable victory was the culmination of years of intensive quality-building efforts driven by stubborn persistence, national pride, and breathtaking ambition. Korean engineers I queried regarding progress in quality shrugged when I mentioned monetary compensation or stock options, but expressed their pride at not "feeling behind as a nation and company." Those same engineers recalled a young colleague whose marriage coincided with the discovery of a barely audible wind noise in a new model. He rarely went home for the next six months to visit his young bride until he had fixed the problem. His compensation? Two days of vacation.

THE WISDOM OF CHAIRMAN CHUNG

In March 1999, the mild-mannered Mong Koo Chung, then sixty-three, gained control of the firm from his founding father. Expectations were that the founder's eldest son would prove to be an ineffective and transitional figure, possibly paving the way for an eventual passage of control to a management not dominated by family members. Having spent the greater part of his career in the unglamorous after-sales service division (the automotive equivalent of Siberia), the notion of Mong Koo Chung turning into a hard-driving turnaround champ seemed far-fetched.

Yet Hyundai employees who had often gone out on strike against previous managements were stunned to see Chung not long after assuming the CEO's mantle stopping the assembly line in Ulsan to express irritation at the Sonata he was inspecting. According to the plant manager, Chung shouted: "You've got to go back to basics! The only way we can survive is to raise the quality to Toyota's level."[4] No mean task, as Toyota was the undisputed global quality leader. In fact, James E. Press, a U.S. based director of Toyota Motor Corporation, readily conceded: "Hyundai has done a remarkable job of accelerating the learning curve and development cycle of their products. They've closed the gap faster than anyone ever thought they would."[5]

Today, Hyundai plays in the same league as car industry leaders and has bested such better known names as Volkswagen, Volvo, Chevrolet, and Suzuki. When I spoke to Hyundai's quality control engineers at Ulsan, they pointed out that this obsessive focus on quality *saves* rather than loses money, because problems are tackled before a single vehicle leaves the production lines, rather than after consumers dis-

> *"The ten-year, 100,000-mile warranty allowed us to get on people's shopping list—we're moving from a brand of last resort to a brand of choice."*
>
> *—CEO of Hyundai USA*

cover them, prompting recalls and costly repairs often covered by warranties.

Aware that it needed to make a bold move to convince buyers that its quality problems were behind it, Hyundai began offering an unprecedented ten-year, 100,000-mile drive-train warranty in the United States, an aggressive demonstration of confidence that persuaded American consumers to give the company a second look. "The warranty allowed us to get on people's shopping list," noted Hyundai Motor America's former president Finbarr O'Neill. "We moved from a brand of last resort to a brand of choice."[6] The actual cost of this initiative turned out to be lower than the reserves set up, while positive press and word of mouth more than made up for any additional funds laid out.

The Asian financial crisis of 1997–98 nearly destroyed the Hyundai Group. Car sales plummeted by half and its healthy profits turned into stomach-churning losses. Yet the crisis turned out to be a blessing in disguise for the Group because (1) the automobile company emerged strong and independent from what was left of the Group and was no longer forced to serve as the piggy bank for underperforming affiliates; (2) the huge devaluation of the won made Korean cars affordable again in foreign markets; (3) Korea's severe recession gave Hyundai an opportunity to snap up its major competitor, Kia Motors, for a song while simultaneously taking its archrival, the Samsung Group, out of the car market; (4) the collapse of the domestic market compelled it to redouble its export efforts; and (5) the company was forced to become leaner and meaner to compete globally.

Breathtaking Ambition

Koreans, like the Chinese, like to summarize their corporate philosophy in simple-sounding slogans with breathtaking scope. Hyundai Motor's four objectives sound trite but show how high it is aiming:

- Best customer service
- Best technology
- Best quality product
- Best value for people

Or to put it simply: the best in everything. Hyundai means it, even if it has not always delivered on its promises in the past.

Key Success Factors
- Relentless focus on quality after initial false start
- Developing in-house technology rather than remaining dependent on licensing
- Active brand-building efforts

- *Recognition that local design and styling are crucial to success*
- *Daring move to produce in all key markets*

GLOBAL MIND-SET, LOCAL DESIGN CAPABILITY

Companies like Honda and Hyundai may be trendsetters in shifting car production to the "new Detroit" in the South. But something else is happening on the design front, which now ranks with quality near the top of the list of consumer priorities. No less of an authority than Bob Lutz, vice chairman of General Motors, has stated that the modern car industry has entered the business of "entertainment."[7] Design and styling are becoming as important as technology—and not in the car industry alone. Emerging multinationals are rapidly absorbing the lesson that being attuned to the more ephemeral matters of taste and "buzz" moves merchandise. Only those with their creative and cultural antennae out who remain immersed in local culture are able to succeed in conceiving designs and styles that not only appeal to consumers but cater to their hidden and still unexpressed desires.

Take the $30 million, 90,000 square foot Hyundai-Kia Design & Technical Center in Irvine, Orange County, California. "A California-based design staff has a better understanding of automotive trends and how to make them appealing to U.S. consumers on a big scale," insists Peter Butterfield, president of Kia Motors America, a Hyundai affiliate. Hyundai also maintains an America Technical Center in Ann Arbor, Michigan, charged with overseeing engineering activities in the United States.

Following the firm's naive first attempts to conquer the American car market, Chairman Chung realized that catering to Americans' ever-changing consumer tastes provided yet another key to cracking the toughest market on earth. Flooding the U.S. market with stripped-down "econocars" that moved nobody's hearts or minds was a strategy that had singularly failed. Chung oversaw a radical reengineering of the firm's flagship Sonata into a hard-nosed "Camry-killer."[8]

At a concept clinic conducted in 2000 in San Diego, more than two hundred American consumers were asked to rate the Sonata against its rivals on every conceivable attribute from esthetics to power and pricing. When consumers professed a hankering for the luxurious Audi A6, Hyundai made it a key benchmark for the Sonata. Inside Hyundai, the 2006 Sonata became known as "an affordable A6."

For the first time in its history, Korean executives were asked to take a back seat to their U.S. counterparts when it came to finalizing the design for the firm's first SUV. When Hyundai's Santa Fe SUV became an instant best-seller not just in the U.S. but around the world, that new design approach was vindicated. Unlike the fuel-conscious Koreans, the American team recognized that American consumers (at least before gasoline prices shot up) desired greater horsepower, so they gave the Santa Fe SUV a 2.7 liter, V-6 engine, compared to the 2 liter, 4-cylinder engine offered by the SUVs of Toyota and Honda. The team added muscular curves to the hood and door panels, a move vigorously attacked by company conservatives in Korea who thought the car looked "crumpled." This design point was so well received by U.S. customers it was later imitated by competitors.

Hyundai's young chief designer at the Hyunda-Kia Design and Technical Center in Irvine, Joel Piaskowski is the son of a veteran designer at Chrysler who himself worked for GM in the United States, Germany, and Japan. Piaskowski told me that the new Santa Fe is a California-inspired vehicle from hubcap to hood. "I don't think there's been a day where I haven't driven around Southern California and seen an exotic, custom, classic, hot rod, tuner or any other oddity of transportation on the local streets." The Sonata turned out in Alabama, while a global best-seller, is being heavily redesigned for the North American market. Part of the challenge faced by nearly all automotive designers these days is to reconcile the inevitable tensions that arise from balancing local tastes and requirements with the need to project and maintain global brands.

When I spoke with Hyundai's design engineers in Seoul, they proudly pointed to their own separate building, with state-of-the-art virtual reality capabilities shared by design centers around the world. Oh Sung Hwan, deputy general manager of production at Hyundai's Ulsan plant, put it most clearly, "We now try and make cars from a customer's point of view, not from an engineer's."

GLOBAL MANUFACTURING STRATEGY
WITH PLATFORMS IN ALL MAJOR MARKETS

With Hyundai sales of $57 billion in 2005 and a total global capacity of three million cars per year, the nearly fifty-year-old Hyundai Motor ranks (together with Kia) as the sixth largest car company in the world and aims to rank among the top five by 2010, a goal that will require more than doubling global production. Less than a year before it opened the new American plant, Hyundai completed construction of a 200,000 car plant in Beijing and a 250,000 car plant in India. Kia's car sales in Europe have been growing faster than any other car company because the Kia in Europe enjoys a fine reputation for fuel efficiency, reasonable quality, and is on average smaller than the Hyundai lineup. In June 2005, Kia signed an agreement in Slovakia to build a Euro 700 million plant.

> *With new plants in the United States, China, and India, Hyundai Motor plans to more than double its car production in a determined strategy to rank among the five largest car companies by 2010.*

GLOBAL CAR DEMAND IS SHIFTING HYUNDAI'S WAY

Underpinning Hyundai's long-range global ambitions is a major shift in global car demand. Over the past few years, the car market in the United States, Europe, and Japan has actually shrunk. *All* of the global growth of 3 million units has come from emerging Asia, especially China and India. Even with their low per capita income, these two already make up about 10 percent of the 57 million unit global car market. By 2015, more than 28 million cars will be sold in emerging markets, nearly 40 percent of the global total and more than double their current share.

In many newer car markets, the Hyundai brand is already admired, and the persistent quality problems that dogged it in America never became hot-button issues in those regions. In India, Hyundai is the second largest car maker after Maruti, a joint venture with Japan's Suzuki. With an 18 percent market share, Hyundai has even pulled ahead of Tata Motor's popular indigenous Indica.

Not surprisingly, Hyundai has saved its most ambitious plans for the largest emerging car market, in China. "In the increasingly global environment, it is critical to achieve an economy of scale, and China will help us achieve that," observes marketing chief Harry Choi.[9] Hyundai expects China to become its largest market outside Korea with 1.2 million cars at the end of this decade, more than the 1.1 million it hopes to sell in the United States and ahead of Europe. Hyundai's Elantra is already the mainstay of Beijing's taxi fleet and China's second-best-selling sedan after the Xiali, domestically produced by the Chinese partner of Toyota.

FUTURE CHALLENGES

In June 2006, the Korean prosecutor announced the indictment of Chairman Chung Mong Koo. He was charged with diverting $136 million from Hyundai companies to create a political slush fund, apparently a common practice among the *chaebols* before the Asian financial crisis, threatening what had recently become the sixth largest auto firm in the world with paralysis at the top, Chung Mong Koo's legal troubles were compounded by a parallel investigation into the activities of his son and heir apparent Chung Eui Son, president of Kia Motors. Chairman Chung "is the Moses who brought us where we are today," a Hyundai spokesman told *The New York Times.* The specter of the firm's powerful chairman son having to make decisions while languishing in jail cast doubt on the firm's ability to move as aggressively into new markets as it had been prior to the scandal.[10, 11]

Hyundai will need to prove it can keep utilization high and costs low in its new plants in the United States, China, and India. Unlike their predecessors, these are world-class plants in terms of size, technology, local content, and quality, rivaling those of the world's leading car companies. The jury is still out on whether this strategy of producing locally in major markets rather than exporting from Korea will pay off in the long run.

As Hyundai marketing manager Seo told me: "We used to be obsessed with the competitors who were ahead of us. Now we believe it is much more important to keep an eye on the new automakers in China and India. Having a top-notch brand is no longer a luxury but a necessity." Hyundai knows better than most that China will become a big car exporter in the future with costs that are hard to match. It plans to keep its edge through a strong presence in the Chinese market, sophisticated design, superior quality, and constant technology innovations. Over the next few years, Hyundai will introduce three new models in Korea, five in China, and six in the United States. Its success with these new models will be critical for its future, now that its brand is more widely accepted.

As the center of gravity of the global car industry shifts from the United States and Europe to Asia and other emerging markets, Hyundai has proved that with the right attitude and determination, quality, design, and R&D, even a developing country like Korea can produce a world-class product while becoming a world-class company. Its competitors in Detroit, Stuttgart, and Tokyo are keeping a close and nervous eye on this Korean giant's every step.

An Investor's View
The Bull Case

- *Hyundai Motor does not face the legacy problems of traditional carmakers in the United States and Europe.*
- *By positioning itself as a global car manufacturer, Hyundai has the flexibility of moving production around as and when needed while being prepared for the emerging car markets of the future in China and India.*
- *Obsession with quality enabled Hyundai to bridge the gap with leading Japanese car producers faster than most expected and regain the confidence of demanding car buyers. It has met its objective of matching Toyota's quality, based on the most recent J. D. Power survey.*
- *There is no match among emerging market carmakers for Hyundai. Most never rose above local protection or, at best, reverse engineering. The only exception is Tata Motors with its indigenously designed small car Indica but it remains way behind Hyundai.*
- *Hyundai has world-class scale, labor costs, efficiency, and quality; it is catching up in design and technology.*

The Bear Case

- *Production efficiency of new plants still needs to be proven.*
- *Selected Chinese carmakers will become a threat within a decade.*
- *Hyundai is late in introducing the hybrid technology pioneered by Toyota.*

Lessons

- *It is possible to succeed after failing on the first try.*
- *World-class status requires relentless pursuit of quality.*
- *Quality image and brand awareness may be quite different in emerging markets from traditional markets, giving emerging multinationals an edge.*
- *Flexibility of production platforms will be a key competitive factor in the future.*

CEMEX

"In Mexico we have world-class artists, architects, and photographers. Why shouldn't we have world-class businesses as well?" [12]
—Lorenzo Zambrano, Chairman and CEO of CEMEX

During a 1992 dinner at the Museum of Modern Art in New York, Cementos Mexicanos CEO Lorenzo Zambrano (a grandson and namesake of the company's founder) casually remarked to Citicorp's then-president John Reed, "Wouldn't it be great to strike back in Spain and take control of its cement sector five hundred years after the Spaniards conquered Mexico?" Beneath the self-consciously casual comment, listeners knew that Zambrano was not making idle chit-chat. A hard driving bachelor, Zambrano's track record to date made the notion of a Mexican cement company dominating its former colonial master's cement industry anything but far-fetched. Yet outsiders still wondered how a company from emerging Mexico could even *think* of dominating its industry in an advanced nation like Spain.

"It was the five-hundredth anniversary of the conquest of the Americas by Spain," the courtly, soft-spoken CEO of CEMEX recently recalled with a chuckle in his art-filled offices in midtown New York. "Five centuries before, Columbus and Cortes had conquered our country. We were looking to balance our Mexican-dominated portfolio." When two big Spanish cement companies came up for sale sooner than expected, Zambrano and CEMEX decided to pounce. Following an aggressive series of acquisitions the firm was the dominant cement maker in Mexico. But Zambrano did not relish the thought of having all his eggs in one basket, and vowed never to permit more than one third of his business to be located in any one country.

> *"Either we become large and international or we end up being purchased by a bigger player."*
> —Lorenzo Zambrano,
> CEO of CEMEX

Since major international cement players had been eyeing Mexico as an attractive place to do business, Zambrano's European expansion was also defensive. "Either we become large and international," he told his staff, "or we end up being purchased by a bigger player." [13] Not long after his casual conversation with John Reed, CEMEX acquired the two largest Spanish cement producers, with Reed's

Citibank providing the bulk of the financing. CEMEX stock promptly plummeted 30 percent as market analysts were working for debt repayments instead of further aquisitions and found the idea that CEMEX could be successful in taking on an industry dominated by a select group of European players too hard to swallow. "For Spaniards, the idea of a Mexican company coming to Spain and changing top management was unthinkable," Zambrano told me. "They said a Mexican company could never manage in Europe."

Wielding the axe like a surgeon, Zambrano and CEMEX set about proving the critics wrong. Both companies were, he told me, "in total shambles, with too many board members and top-tier executives." Zambrano put in his own "high potential people," a term he defines as "young and inexperienced people willing to work insane hours to achieve our financial goals. Still, the financial community remained skeptical, since most investors bought into the conventional wisdom that we had overpaid."

After cutting costs by one-third, streamlining management, reducing peak hour energy use, introducing alternative fuels, automating all plants, and dramatically cutting inventory levels, CEMEX's European expansion strategy raised the profile of the company and put it on investors' radar as a fast-growing firm. By 1997, CEMEX would be named "the most admired company in Spain" by the magazine *Actualidad Economica*. By 2000, the company had more than quadrupled its Spanish operating margins to nearly 33 percent, compared to the previous 7 percent. As Zambrano proudly reflected, "This was a make or break deal for the company. And I admit, in retrospect, we did it without having acquired a fair understanding of the operational risk. But we were willing to work very hard to put those two companies back on top of their markets."

Yet even those impressed by CEMEX's agile one-two Spanish punch would be surprised to note that by 2003, *Wired* magazine would rank the firm in fifth place on its top-forty list of "masters of innovation, technology, and strategic vision." Described as a "case study in transforming a hopelessly low tech enterprise into a model of info-age efficiency," CEMEX found itself listed just behind such high-tech brands as Google, Nokia, Yahoo, and IBM, and ahead of such companies as eBay, Amazon.com, Microsoft, and Cisco in a survey of companies the magazine declared were "reshaping the global economy."[14]

HOW AN ANTI-DUMPING SUIT TRANSFORMED CEMEX INTO A GLOBAL PRODUCER

CEMEX's Cortez-like "reconquest" of North America began with a serious setback. In 1989, eight local cement companies in the American Southwest joined two unions to form the Ad-Hoc Committee of AZ-NM-TX-FL [Arizona, New Mexico, Texas, Florida] Producers of Gray Portland Cement, a pressure group spearheaded by Southdown, the largest cement producer in the United States. Among the Ad-Hoc Committee's lengthy litany of complaints was that soaring imports of Mexican cement to the southwestern region—characterized as "unfair foreign competition"—had forced seven cement plants in the southern region to shut their doors. Petitioners alleged that dumping by low-cost Mexican producers had depressed the price of cement in the United States by more than 50 percent. "Our investigation to date convinces us that the Mexicans' success in U.S. markets is due to dumping and not to any other factor. We should not have to cede U.S. markets and U.S. jobs to unfairly priced imports from Mexico. If we lose out to *fair* competition from Mexico, so be it!" declared Southdown CEO Clarence Comer. The success of his suit was—some cynical observers surmised—not entirely unconnected to the firm's contribution to George H. W. Bush's 1988 presidential campaign.[15]

In November 1989, the International Trade Commission (ITC), an arm of the U.S. Department of Commerce, found in favor of the petitioners' charges, leaving Zambrano steaming, then scheming. "It was the only time in my job I ever felt furious enough to cry," Zambrano confessed to me years later. Yet CEMEX's nuanced reaction to the threat of federal litigation reflected its growing sophistication as a global competitor. It immediately hired a raft of top-notch legal and media advisors in the United States to explain its position in greater depth than bold headlines and cheap rhetoric. *The Wall Street Journal* and other media outlets weighed in in on CEMEX's side.

While legally contending that the ITC had virtually ignored CEMEX's greater costs in importing cement into the United States, CEMEX viewed the anti-dumping charges as simply an expedient way to stifle expansion there. Having consolidated as much as possible in Mexico, Zambrano considered expansion into the nearest viable market—the U.S.—as critical to the firm's survival. But after the International Trade Commission imposed anti-dumping duties of 58 percent[16] on all Mexican cement imports, the

Mexican government appealed to a GATT arbitration panel, which ruled in its favor, finding that the tariffs imposed violated global international trade accords. An odd loophole in the GATT agreement permitted the United States to unilaterally reject the aribitrator's ruling and maintain the 58 percent "countervailing duties."

One obvious way to circumvent the anti-dumping ruling would be for CEMEX to continue to import cement into the United States from third parties based in nations other than Mexico—even if those third parties were owned by CEMEX. As a major *trader* as well as *producer* of cement, Zambrano simply ramped up imports into the United States from operations in other countries. He routed many tons of cheap Chinese cement through CEMEX's own network of terminals on the U.S. West Coast.

Encountering this regulatory roadblock in the United States caused the firm to reconceive its international expansion strategy, and ultimately fashion itself into a stronger global competitor. As Hector Medina, executive vice president of planning and finance, put it: "The anti-dumping ruling made us realize that the U.S. was not the whole world." He flatly described the anti-dumping suit as "a blessing in disguise," because it forced CEMEX to "play with the adults."

SHOOTING YOURSELF IN THE FOOT

Let's take a moment to analyze the Pyrrhic victory achieved by the anti-dumping suit. Two decades ago, the United States imported one out of *ten* tons of cement. Today, imports account for one out of *four* tons of cement. As for CEMEX, it (along with a few other Mexican cement producers) exported five million tons of cement to the United States from Mexico ten years ago. Today, the U.S. continues to import the *same* five million tons of cement from CEMEX, nearly one quarter of its total cement imports, but less than two million tons originate in Mexico.

In an interview with *Cement Americas* in July 2002, Gilberto Perez, CEMEX's president of U.S. operations, defiantly maintained, "we haven't lost market share because of the dumping suit." Instead, CEMEX simply acquired companies in Venezuela, the Caribbean, and elsewhere that now do the majority of exporting to the United States. Today, in part as a result of the unintended consequences of the anti-dumping suit, CEMEX has transformed itself into *the largest cement producer in the United States*. As for Southdown, the Texas-based company that initiated the anti-dumping suit, it was eventually taken over by a foreign firm: CEMEX! "That was a bonus I really savored," Zambrano proudly told me many years later. In short, the anti-dumping suit transformed CEMEX into the global company it is today with only 21 percent of its sales from Mexico, 27 percent from the United States, 28 percent from Europe, and 24 percent from the rest of the world.

The U.S. consumer now pays higher prices for imported cement. And since nearly half of all cement consumed in the United States is purchased for infrastructure and other public works, the U.S. government and taxpayers have ended up footing the bill for this ill-fated attempt to save domestic cement producers from extinction.

THE GLOBAL PRODUCER

Since the suit, CEMEX has blossomed into a truly global company. Lorenzo Zambrano, a Stanford Business School graduate, insists that his experience studying abroad in California radically altered his outlook at an impressionable age. "I learned there are other ways of thinking—and also what the competition would look like later. I became convinced that it is important for future managers to spend some time outside their own country," a practice he has institutionalized at CEMEX.

Today, the president of CEMEX's Mexican operations is Spanish, the V.P. for human resources is a former engineer in charge of ready mix from Venezuela, and the head of European operations was previously in charge of South East Asian operations. When CEMEX took over Texas-based Southdown and began streamlining its operations, it appointed a Mexican plant manager in Louisville and a plant manager in Charlevoix, Michigan, from the Philippines.

A CEMEX PLAYBOOK FOR ACQUISITIONS
AND POST-ACQUISITIONS

In its bid to achieve a global presence, CEMEX has refined the art of the acquisition into a science. The first lesson learned the hard way was that it is easy to overpay when the business cycle for the local cement industry is strong. Not long after its high-profile Spanish acquisition, Spain went through its deepest recession in decades. CEMEX also learned from its 1992 Spanish takeover that it needed to institutionalize the acquisition process as well as to refine a post-acquisition integration strategy.

Once a country is identified for investment, CEMEX scours the market for specific companies that match its

> *"Strategy is execution. The way to a good opportunity is to study, study, study. We have found that the best companies have doers, not talkers."*
>
> —*Lorenzo Zambrano,
> CEO of CEMEX*

requirements: a controlling stake to give it enough flexibility in reforming operations and sufficient scope to increase efficiency or optimize capacity utilization. Besides a rigorous minimum criteria of 10 percent return on capital employed, time required to turn around the company is another critical factor when CEMEX analyzes a new acquisition candidate. After a suitable target is identified, a team of ten is sent on-site to perform one to two weeks of due diligence based on standardized methodologies (revised and updated every six months). Every aspect of the business is scrutinized from the age, education, and average years of service of employees to union affiliations, government involvement, and training programs. The CEMEX team also meets with government officials and competitors to learn if there are any bugs swept under the rug. As a competitor remarked to me admiringly, "Unlike Europeans, they don't suffer from analysis paralysis. Instead of endless committees, they

> *The key to CEMEX's success has been its well-honed ability to spot attractive acquisitions, to turn them around and quickly integrate them.*

have family control and strong executive management."

Once a new business is bought, CEMEX dispatches a post-merger integration team (PMI) responsible for thoroughly analyzing and suggesting areas in which the operation can be improved, based on past experience and practice. Before being dispatched from headquarters, the PMI team attends cultural awareness and teambuilding workshops to prepare to focus on operating improvements, the sharing of best practices, and the harmonization of cultural beliefs.[17] Regional managers visit the site every month while the country president personally reports back to Zambrano on a regular schedule.

"YOU CAN'T MANAGE WHAT YOU CAN'T MEASURE"

In 1988, then-IT manager Gelacio Iniguez persuaded Zambrano that CEMEX should become the first Mexican company to own its own satellite telecommunications network. At the time, it was an unusual move in an engineering-oriented industry. Today, CEMEXNet links all of the firm's global operations, providing executives from Monterrey to Manila with detailed on-time access to financial data. Sales figures are broken down to include the delivery routes of each factory's trucks in all countries. Operational data from individual plants and kilns are available, including data such as the granularity and chemical composition of each batch of cement produced. "I'm always surprised that our competitors have next to no computers," Gilberto Perez says. "It means that their headquarters has only last month's operating figures. I can look at last night's at the touch of a button."[18]

CEMEX is viewed as an industry leader in the use of IT to improve operational efficiency.

This attention to detail has helped CEMEX to keep its energy cost per ton stable even though oil prices have skyrocketed in recent years through energy savings and the use of alternative energies such as waste and tires.

CEMEX grasps that logistics are as important in cement as production. In Mexico, a network of 2,100 distributors and special customers (called Construrama) is connected wirelessly to provide ready mix within half an hour after an order is received, following the Domino Pizza model, which the firm hopes to replicate in other countries. The firm helps builders adjust to changing schedules and strives to provide the construction equivalent of one-stop shopping. While CEMEX reduces truck waiting times, customers gain confidence that the ready mix (and other building materials) will indeed be in the right place at the right time.

REAPING THE FRUITS OF EXPANSION

In an industry that produces two billion tons of cement every year, CEMEX ranks as the world's third largest cement maker with a capacity of 97 million tons and sixty-one of its own cement plants in eighteen countries. It is #1 globally in ready-mix and #2 in aggregates, making it the world's second largest producer of building materials after France's

Lafarge and ahead of Switzerland's Holcim. More impressively, CEMEX has consistently managed to be more profitable than its industry peers and is considered the benchmark in efficiency with a free cash flow growth rate of 21 percent over the last decade.

After seeking growth in emerging markets, CEMEX's strategy shifted significantly with its 2000 acquisition of Southdown in the United States and its March 2005 $5.8 billion takeover of #3 European cement and aggregate producer RMC, one of the oldest building material producers in Great Britain where it ranks #2 in the market. The boldness of the RME acquisition prompted *The Economist* to wryly observe, "Queen Victoria, whose subjects built or financed much of Latin America's infant infrastructure, would not have been amused." The RMC acquisition will nearly double its revenues to over $15 billion, its cement capacity to 97 million tons, in addition to 125 million tons in aggregates and 76 million in ready mix. The rationale behind the acquisition has been to optimize logistics, to strengthen its position in Europe and the United States, and to reinforce a broader move to develop a consumer brand by moving deeper into higher-margin ready mix and aggregates. Selling cement in CEMEX bags as opposed to in anonymous bulk provides the firm with an opportunity to compete on service and speed of delivery rather than just price. CEMEX's brand is already among the best known in Latin America and the company is determined to make it better known around the world. As I was driving to the airport in California with CFO Rodrigo Trevino, he pointed out the distinctive CEMEX logo on a company truck to bolster his contention that in the wake of the RMC acquisition CEMEX is no longer a commodity producer. That may still be a dream, yet this highly efficient producer is working hard to turn building materials from a commodity into a brand.

An Investor's view
The Bull Case
- *CEMEX is world class in turning around acquisitions, management, and IT use.*
- *CEMEX manages to be more profitable and efficient than its global competitors.*
- *CEMEX is a leader in a consolidating industry.*
- *The company has top-notch management and pays great attention to hiring highly qualified people.*
- *CEMEX has proven ability to give parochial local companies a global outlook.*

- *Each acquisition has brought significant savings from synergies or productivity improvements.*

The Bear Case
- *CEMEX has had a tough time establishing a major foothold in Asia.*
- *Some investors would like to see higher dividends or more debt repayments rather than continuous acquisitions.*
- *Shift from more rapidly growing emerging markets to slower growing markets in U.S. and Europe still needs to prove its sustainability.*

Lessons
- *Cement is no longer a local industry but one that is increasingly dominated by a handful of global players.*
- *Logistics are as important as efficient production.*
- *In a consolidating industry, those who do not acquire will be acquired themselves.*
- *Greater vertical integration helps not only the customer but the company's bottom line.*
- *"Branding" will be important for the future even for commodities like cement.*
- *Going global without being state-of-the-art in IT is a recipe for disaster.*

CHAPTER 8

Turning the Outsourcing Model Upside Down

Brazilian plane maker Embraer stays in the driver's seat with suppliers in the developed world

Strategies

- *As a newcomer, exploit opportunities created by legacy costs and regulatory changes (low-cost carriers taking on "legacy" airlines; modification of pilots' "Scope clause").*
- *Dare to take advantage of a fresh, outsider perspective on industry changes in developed markets (airlines moving away from the "hub" model).*
- *Follow Sun Tzu's mandate of finding a "weak spot" among opponents (Boeing and Airbus ignoring the regional jet market in their focus on building bigger planes).*
- *Put yourself at the center of the "outsourcing" model instead of being a supplier to a developed-world designer and integrator of planes.*
- *Take advantage of "cheap engineering brainpower."*
- *Play the "South-South" card with commercial as well as military aircraft sales.*

A heavy downpour and an unseasonably chill wind blowing off the Serra do Mar mountains failed to dampen the spirited fiesta being thrown in an airplane hangar at Sao Jose dos Campos, Brazil, in September 2005. Brazilian plane maker Embraer was celebrating the delivery of the first of a firm order of 100 E-190 twinjets into the eager hands of U.S. budget airline JetBlue. The mood in the huge space was casually upbeat as members of the team that had designed and constructed the 100-seat aircraft watched themselves perform in an amateur music video. Rollicking sounds filled the hangar where Embraer's spanking-new "E" family of jets was rolling off expanded assembly lines at a merry clip of a dozen per month.

At the conclusion of the musical ditty, the video screen slid away and a dark curtain opened to showcase JetBlue's sleek new plane, resplendent in the airline's distinctive blue livery. Immediately following the video, Jet-Blue officials confirmed their intention to absorb identical versions of the E-190 into their fast-growing fleet at a rate of eighteen per year between 2006 and 2011. The total cost would be $3 billion, with an additional $3 billion more if JetBlue was to option to buy an additional 100.

"Today is a day JetBlue customers and crew members have been looking forward to for years," exulted JetBlue CEO David Neeleman, proclaiming the E-190 "the plane of our future". . ."As I look at this beautiful new aircraft I see many new opportunities to bring the JetBlue experience to communities all over North America," he said. The 190 offered a "perfect" complement to JetBlue's existing fleet of eighty-one European Airbus 320s, COO Dave Barger added. "The 190 represents what I call our 'Pathfinder' with regards to opening up new routes."[1]

A few weeks after accepting its first E-190 from Embraer, JetBlue announced the inauguration of daily flights between New York's JFK and Boston's Logan Airport, and from Boston to Austin, Texas, the Bahamas, and West Palm Beach, Florida, all routes served by its newly acquired E-190's. *The New York Times* quoted Standard & Poor's airline analyst Betsy Snyder as expressing surprise that Embraer's new "big little" jets were so "plush" on the inside. "They can add whole cities they couldn't fill an [Airbus] 320 with," she observed. "[The Embraer 190] opens up a whole lot of new destinations for them."[2]

"We thought it was worth the risk given the hundreds of new routes we are going to be able to serve," Neeleman insisted. "In fact, when we looked at [the Embraer 190] it was like, not only is this *not* a risk, it's probably a risk if we *don't* buy it."[3] Embraer, for its part, had bet the ranch—an estimated $1 billion—developing the E family, convinced it spied a gap in the industry's line-up wide enough to fly an entire family of jets through. As of early 2006, the plane maker had racked up $10 billion in firm orders including 459 firm orders and 442 options for its E series, confirming realistic expectations of long-term demand over the next two decades approaching the 6,000 unit mark.

JetBlue CEO Neeleman's personal affinity for his new Embraer fleet was no doubt deepened by the fact that he had been born in Sao Paulo, son of a wire service correspondent, and speaks fluent Portuguese, a linguistic facility he demonstrated to the delight of the local journalists attending the press conference at Embraer headquarters. After growing up in Salt Lake City and dropping out of college—dogged by persistent ADD (attention deficit disorder)—Neeleman returned to Brazil as a Mormon missionary, converting more than two hundred Brazilians to the faith before earning his entrepreneur's wings flying Utah's large Mormon families on budget tours to Hawaii. After selling his share of the tour business to Southwest Airlines in 1993 for a cool $20 million, the ever-restless Neeleman worked briefly for Southwest's impulsive CEO Herb Kelleher before being shown the door. He sat on the sidelines for five years, saddled with a non-compete cause, before launching JetBlue, a deliberate rival to his former employer.

In going with Embraer, Neeleman was willing to abandon a pivotal part of JetBlue's legendary low cost structure, its single-plane strategy, a move that has saved it countless millions in training and maintenance costs and offered untold simplicities and efficiencies over the past five years. Yet the iconoclastic Neeleman proved willing to compromise his monogamous marriage to the 156-seat Airbus 320 out of a firm conviction that victory in the skies will come to those carriers able to fly more routes between smaller cities directly. *Business Week* quoted People Express founder Donald Burr: "The market is moving in [Embraer's] direction. The hubs are full, and a lot of people in leadership roles think that more personalized aircraft operating *directly* (italics added) between non-hub airports are the way to get people traveling faster again."[4]

LEGACY PROBLEMS CREATE OPPORTUNITIES
FOR NEWCOMERS

Mauricio Botelho, Embraer's CEO, a former mechanical engineer and veteran turnaround specialist, neatly summarized the challenge facing most major airlines today: "Airlines are operating with the wrong aircraft, and they're taking a loss." Assisting the struggling airlines of the world to "right-size" their aging fleets has been Botelho's overriding objective for the past decade. Relentlessly espousing this "small is beautiful" mantra has turned the Brazilian plane manufacturer from a nearly bankrupt basket case in the early 1990s into the world's fourth largest aircraft manufacturer. Only Boeing, Airbus, and Montreal-based Bombardier (known for building Amtrak's problem-plagued Acela luxury train) outsell Embraer in this cutthroat competition for survival.

Rather than compete to build the big planes that fly between the big hubs, Embraer and rival Bombardier have aggressively pursued the regional jet market. Manufacturing smaller jets that fly along the "spokes" radiating from such major hubs as Chicago, New York, Denver, London, Paris, Hong Kong, and Singapore has been a niche the two biggest players have to date been reluctant to exploit. The significance of the delivery of the first E-190 to JetBlue is that the E family stands a real chance of reshaping the commercial air industry worldwide. With budget carriers like JetBlue able to fly fewer passengers on shorter routes more economically, the inevitable result will be to put already reeling legacy carriers even further on the defensive.

Yet another case in point: in early October 2005, two weeks after the JetBlue delivery party, US Airways pilots reached a tentative accord with legacy carrier U.S. Air to operate the Embraer 190 with a new pay rate. Pilots' unions worldwide had stiffly resisted airlines' desire to shift to smaller aircraft, as compensation drastically declines with smaller plane size. But US Airways broke in its new E-170s with a flight from Pittsburgh to Albany the previous April and was now being grudgingly permitted by its pilots to modify the "scope" clause prohibiting the operation of aircraft the size of the 190 without their express permission. "All we had to do was to point to JetBlue," an airline spokesman was quoted as saying, to make the unions see reason. U.S. Air now has 57 E-190s on order.

> "This plane is our passport to the First World."
> —Geraldo Alckmin, Governor of the State of Sao Paulo

A VERSATILE PLANE FOR REGIONAL MARKETS

The accomplishment Embraer has been able to pull off with its best-selling E family is to provide aircraft in the 70–110 seat segment with nearly all the comforts and amenities of larger costlier planes. As guests and the press took a tour of JetBlue's 190, visitors gave the spacious interior an enthusiastic thumbs-up as they passed down a wide central aisle, on either side of which the airline's one hundred signature leather seats were laid out in a two-by-two configuration, with no dreaded middle seat to avoid like the plague. Clever fuselage design provides Embraer's new jets with the head and shoulder room typically reserved for the big boys, while soft shapes lacking visible edges and indirect lighting enhance an enveloping sense of space and comfort. When I recently flew the new E series plane on a U.S. Air flight from Washington, D.C., to Boston, both pilots and flight attendants raved about the roomy new plane.

PLAYING THE "SOUTH-SOUTH" CARD

While playing its best hand—size and cost—to the hilt, Embraer has been feverishly exploiting its natural advantage as an emerging markets player by selling loads of cost-cutting craft to *other* major emerging markets players. In December 2005, Saudi Arabian Airlines took delivery of the first of fifteen Embraer seventy-seat 170 aircraft, in a deal said to be worth $400 million. Panama's Copa Airlines (previously an exclusive Boeing customer) announced it was restocking its similarly aging fleet with new Embraers to increase flight frequency and serve more routes. Poland's flag carrier LOT announced Embraer 170 flights out of Warsaw to destinations throughout Europe. Also in 2005, the Indian Ministry of Defense announced its acquisition of a new fleet of Embraer Legacy business jets, luxuriously outfitted and equipped with the latest in high-tech avionics, to ferry government ministers and other VIPs around the subcontinent and the world.

Perhaps the most extreme example of this canny birds-of-a-feather strategy is the establishment of Harbin Embraer Aircraft Industry Company, a joint venture between Embraer, Harbin Aviation Industry Group Ltd., and Hafei Aviation Industry. Asked whether he was not worried about the Chinese copying the plane's advanced technological features, CEO Botelho shrugged his shoulders and replied "Otherwise, they could always buy one and simply re-engineer it." Based in Harbin (capital of Heilongjiang province), Harbin-Embraer specializes in manufacturing and selling the company's older thirty-to-fifty-seat ERJ 145 regional jets to Chinese airlines. The company's first sales have gone to China Southern Airlines, the largest airline in China, which ordered a total of six ERJ 145s in February 2004, and Sichuan Airlines, partially controlled by China Southern, which has been happily operating a half dozen ERJ 145s in China for the past year.

TAPPING THE GAP

Embraer's strategy to sell so many planes to so many airlines in so many countries in so short a time is so stunningly simple it borders on the deceptive. The firm freely discloses its game plan on its website, where Embraer has codified "The Rule of 70–110," with the magical numbers pointing to the number of seats on the plane as the sweet spot of the future. An earlier version of the same rule was succinctly expressed by the Chinese philosopher and strategist Sun Tzu: "Strike Where Your Opponent Is Weakest." Embraer puts it more literally.

Mainline aircraft with too many seats are flying smaller demand routes. Regional markets are expanding, pressing regional jets to carry more passengers more frequently. Passenger demand is trending toward the 70-to-110 seat segment, a range for which an efficient aircraft family didn't exist. The industry is facing an equipment gap. We present evidence of the gap, offer a strategy for profiting from the 70-to-110 segment and . . . help you to "tap the gap."

HIGH TECH HUB OF THE SOUTHERN HEMISPHERE

On a recent tour of Embraer's showcase factory, an easy forty-five-minute drive outside Brazil's industrial hub of Sao Paulo, I was ushered through a warren of well-lighted rooms filled with bright young engineers and designers working away at rows of computers in a cluster of squeaky-clean modern buildings. Embraer's campus-like headquarters was originally established by the Brazilian Defense Ministry in 1969 as a home-grown source of modern planes for its small yet ambitious air force. Today, Embraer's campus is home to over 12,000 employees, although as recently as a decade ago, the payroll had to be halved due to drastically declining orders, a sagging local, regional, and global economy, and rapidly skyrocketing costs.

The high point of my visit came when I was escorted into a dimly lit room tucked away in a remote corner of the building. My Embraer hosts enthusiastically asked me to don a pair of 3D spectacles of the multicolored, plastic-lens type that would have seemed more at home at an amusement park than in the offices of one of the world's largest jet manufacturers. My hosts were boyishly proud of the spectacle they were about to demonstrate. Not wanting to ruin their fun, and with my own curiosity piqued, I donned the 3D glasses, parked myself in the first of several rows of soft movie theater seats, sat back, and enjoyed the show.

Out of thin air, a scaled-down three-dimensional jet airplane appeared in front of me like some sort of conjurer's trick, hovering in space like a modern mirage. It was as though I had been instantaneously transported into a jet hangar without leaving the comfort of my chair. The detailed aircraft could be rotated left and right, flipped up or down, and zoomed in and out, allowing me to view it from every possible angle. I could open the door, enter the plane, tour a fully outfitted interior, sit in the pilot's seat, or inspect the inside of an engine. At a few touches of a button, the entire exterior of the jet was stripped off, exposing a complex network of wires, tubes, piping, and switches. Individual components, highlighted in different colors, were easily distinguished from one another inside the maze of circuitry and equipment. Connections could be inspected, measurements verified, designs approved. Every single wire, bolt, and nut that would appear in the real version was precisely recreated in full 3D before my very eyes.

Most impressive of all, teams of aviation engineers from across the world could examine this same life-sized 3D model from their respective locations using their own virtual reality equipment, collaborating on projects in real time, and defying physical limitations. Clients could view precise replicas of their finished purchases long before a single piece of metal was ever welded together. Every aspect of the manufacturing process could be simulated from start to finish in stunning detail, right down to setting up the manufacturing hangar, determining the layout of the aircraft, choosing seat cover fabrics, and designing an exterior paint scheme.

In the past, real models needed to be painstakingly built out of such cumbersome materials as wood, metal, and plastic. Now Embraer can save time and money by handling such tasks in the virtual world, relying on technology once reserved for Hollywood movies. As one of my hosts quietly informed me when I pulled off my 3D specs, "We were the first major airplane company to use the virtual reality tool with customers. We were quicker to acknowledge the benefits. We certainly have been quicker than the competition to take from the market what the market has to offer. Every day, we endlessly scour the market to see what is out there and what we can use to keep ahead of every possible shift in the industry."

INDUSTRIAL CHOREOGRAPHY

As a reality-based encore to this impressive virtual reality show, we were escorted into the production zone, home to a series of hangars filled wall to wall with assembly lines of planes at various stages of completion. My immediate impression was one of a quiet and confident industriousness more akin to laboratories than factories. I was struck by the delicate precision with which this complex assembly work was being conducted by highly trained, obviously well-motivated employees. As I looked on from the sidelines, I spied one worker, struggling with a pesky part, stop briefly as a managerial type stepped over to help him. He calmly showed him exactly what needed to be done, and quietly stepped away. The assembly line rolled on again.

The entire episode could not have taken more than a few seconds. But to someone like me who has visited hundreds of factories as part of my job, it possessed all the panache of a well-rehearsed dance step, a simple and elegant *pas-de-deux* that revealed the quality of Embraer's industrial operations, where engineers make up 25 percent of the work force. Here was cooperation and teamwork, not dull rote labor that causes workers to lose interest and quality to suffer. A similar sense of pride and confidence is exuded by Embraer's engineers, managers, and executives. As one of the topflight high-tech companies of the world, and a champion of the dynamic Brazilian economy, Embraer has long drawn the best, the brightest, the most talented graduates from the nation's top technical schools, including one conveniently located right in its own backyard the Instituto Technologico de Aeronautica (ITA).

Sao Jose dos Campos is a lively, livable, well-managed city that reflects the positive presence not just of Embraer but dozens of laboratories, universities, technical institutes, and a variety of firms, many founded by former Embraer employees to support Brazil's burgeoning aerospace industry. You would think Michael Porter, the Harvard Business School proponent of "clusters" of educational institutions and related industries, had designed the city himself. The Brazilian National Institute for Space Research (INPE), which coordinates intensive research in Earth observation, space sciences, and space technologies, has its campus nearby. Conveniently located between the two most active production and consumption regions in the country, Sao Paulo and Rio, the town and environs are bisected by the Presidente Dutra Highway. Embraer's headquarters' city has been rightly referred to as the epicenter of Brazil's "Silicon Valley." While it does lie in a valley, a more accurate analogy would probably be to the former farmland of New Jersey, between New York and Philadelphia, which also rapidly industrialized in the postwar period.

WAS A BRAZILIAN THE FIRST TO TAKE TO THE AIR?

Brazilians love to tell outsiders that the true father of aviation is Alberto Santos-Dumont, a wealthy and eccentric bon vivant, son of a Brazilian coffee baron, who gained fame throughout Europe in October 1901 for rounding the Eiffel Tower in a motorized airship (or dirigible), in a flight witnessed by twelve kings and queens, Jules Verne, and Gustave Eiffel. In contrast to the secretive Wright Brothers, who had no official observer on hand to confirm their first foray off Kitty Hawk, North Carolina, in 1903, the slight and frail Santos-Dumont, weighing in at just 100 pounds and impeccably turned out as always, took off in his 14-Bis and flew for 60 meters on the outskirts of Paris on November 2, 1906, in full view of a crowd of spectators. The strong winds that blew off Kitty Hawk further disqualified the U.S. inventors' dubious claim, in the Brazilian view, of having flown their plane "unassisted." To this day, Brazilians regard their rightful claim to this landmark of progress as stolen from them by greedy Yankees, who have glorified the Wrights'"chicken flight" while consigning Santos-Dumont's heroic feat to historic oblivion.

One of the new heroes of tumultuous Brazil between the world wars was another aviation pioneer, Casimiro Montenegro, the co-pilot on the inaugural flight of the Brazilian air mail system. Like Charles Lindbergh in the United States, Montenegro captured his people's imagination and pioneered the nascent aviation industry in Brazil on both the military and civilian sides of the fence. As a colonel in the Brazilian Air Force—established in 1941 under American influence, in an attempt to neutralize pro-German sentiment among the deeply conservative Brazilian officer class—Montenegro flew sorties over Italy in Brazilian bombers. He returned home convinced aerospace was the wave of the future, and that Brazil—with its vast scale, wide open spaces, and chronically underdeveloped road and rail infrastructure—was an ideal candidate for primacy in the air.

AN EARLY CENTER FOR AERONAUTICAL RESEARCH

Championing the creation of a training institute in Brazil for home-growing its own aeronautical engineers, Montenegro prevailed upon Richard Smith, then chief of aviation engineering at MIT, to plan an elite institution closely modeled on MIT in the fertile farmland of the Vale do Paraiba, where Montenegro once narrowly survived a crash landing in a rice paddy. The Aeronautical Technical Centre (CTA) became the new home of a contingent of German aeronautical engineers, including the famed Heinrich Focke, inventor of the FA-61, the first truly maneuverable helicopter, and founder of the Focke-Wulf Aircraft firm that supplied high-performance planes for the Luftwaffe. Although Focke's attempts to perfect a plane-helicopter hybrid in Brazil foundered, the powerful legacy of German craftsmanship and precision helped CTA get off the ground.

"It all began with CTA and ITA," engineering and development chief Satoshi Yokota told me, referring to the establishment of Embraer in 1969 by the Brazilian government. ITA continues to educate elite Brazilian engineers next door to Embraer and demonstrates how top-notch education is as crucial to the development of high-tech industry as it is in India, Taiwan, Korea, and China. During our recent visit, a shared sense of technical esprit de corps was transmitted between fellow ITA graduates Yokota and Clecius Peixoto, our company's analyst for Brazil, as they swapped stories involving the web of connections, economic and intellectual, linking the two institutions.

NATIONAL CHAMPIONS

A surplus of idled airplanes left over from World War II combined with an economic growth rate averaging over 8 percent annually (comparable to China's today) spurred transportation development in Brazil, linking the crowded coasts to the sprawling interior. During the 1960s and 1970s, Brazil was a powerhouse of optimistic, modernist—some would say surrealist—ideas, as the government created an entire new capital city, Brasilia, located in the central plains of the country far from the coastlines of Rio.

The fashionable economic development theories of the times, taught as gospel by nearly every major university on the planet, dictated that every developing nation should promote "national champions" to catch up with the First World. The enormous costs involved in jumpstarting "national champions" did not make commercial sense in the absence of heavy protection, but ideology triumphed over pragmatism. The Brazilian government established Embraer in the same expansive spirit it spawned the state-owned oil giant, Petrobras, along with native carmaker FNM, later acquired (or rather, bailed out) by Volkswagen, a local computer industry and nuclear research. In the heady spirit of the times, it seemed only rational for a rapidly developing would-be Latin American superpower to acquire the "technical autonomy" required to become expert in aircraft design and production.

STATE ENTERPRISE AND A COSSETED MILITARY DARLING

Empresa Brasileira de Aeronautica S.A., better known as Embraer—and 51 percent controlled by the Brazilian Ministry of Defense—began modestly in January 1970 with less than $2 million in seed money. Its first product was a cute little crop duster called the Ipanema, designed in cooperation with U.S. civilian manufacturer Piper. This was a classic case of infant-industry protection combined with technology transfer, as Piper competitors Beechcraft and Cessna (both of whom had enjoyed substantial market penetration in Brazil prior to the Ipanema) howled pitifully in protest. In keeping with its assigned role as an adjunct to the Brazilian military, Embraer's next product was a jet trainer, the Xavante, engineered in collaboration with the Italian firm Aermacchi.

The military arm of the business was lovingly nurtured by former Brazilian Air Force captain Ozires Silva, forty-one when he was appointed the firm's first CEO. Born into a poor country family, as a boy Silva performed odd jobs at an air club in his home town. At the age of fourteen he flew his first plane, without a license, and after graduating from the Air Force Academy three years after the end of World War II, Ozires Silva rose rapidly in rank, evolving over time from a top-notch pilot into a top-notch manager.

Although his strength was motivating an organization into making a product that was first and foremost superbly engineered and only secondarily commercially profitable, Silva was wise in the ways of exporting hard-to-sell products to global markets where the label "Made in Brazil" was anything but a door-opener. "When we designed our first plane," he later recalled, "a small simple [Ipanema], I thought that we should obviously try to sell it to other Third World countries. But I learnt that the First World likes simple planes, whereas the Third World only imports sophisticated models."[5] No doubt for the reasons described, the Ipanema sold better internationally than at home.

The 1970s witnessed an "economic miracle" in Brazil, during which, Captain Silva later recalled, the country "imagined it could produce everything." For a while, Brazil and Embraer succeeded beyond their founders' wildest dreams in growing explosively behind solid protective barriers. After three years in operation, Embraer hit a worldwide home run with the nineteen-seat Bandeirante, a nonpressurized turboprop primitive by present standards but well-equipped for its time. The origins of the plane dated back to 1965, when Silva—still employed by the Ministry of Aeronautics but already involved in the creation of Embraer—had asked visiting French aviation engineer Max Holste to design a light two-engine turboprop for the Brazilian military. The first prototype of the Bandeirante was designed using Holste's plans by engineers from the CTA in response to Silva's request.

By 1982, after nearly ten years of production, twenty-two commuter airlines in the United States were flying 130 Bandits on domestic routes, enabling it to capture an impressive 46 percent of the commuter turboprop market. Threatened by Embraer's inroads into its business, U.S. market leader Fairchild went so far as to file an anti-dumping complaint with the U.S. International Trade Commission (ITC) asserting that the whopping Brazilian subsidies justified the imposition of an equally whopping 40 percent countervailing duty on all imported turboprop aircraft.

Fairchild's claim of excessive subsidization was ultimately rejected by the ITC. While not wholly without merit, the suit conveniently neglected to mention that nearly every *other* country was deeply engaged in subsidies and export finance for aviation, from the United States and Europe to Japan and Canada. Without government-sponsored research and huge military contracts, most major plane companies would have long since gone under. Embraer was far from alone in enjoying an impressive array of handouts and subsidies from its patrons in Brasilia.

Yet within the bright clouds scudding along the horizon there lurked a dark lining. There has rarely been a government subsidy extended to any company that did not come without strong strings attached. Like a host of other state-sponsored enterprises over the years, Embraer suffered from dependency on a particular set of military customers. Like indulgent parents, the Brazilian Air Force rarely felt any urgency about reining in the firm's natural tendency to elevate technical and performance considerations—always of keenest interest to military buyers and politicians—over strictly commercial concerns.

CRISIS YEARS AND NEAR-COLLAPSE

As the high-flying 1970s melted into the downward spiraling '80s, the cracks in the Brazilian economy began to show. Embraer's destructive dependency on the lucrative relationship to the Brazilian military only added to its litany of woes. In 1985, Embraer's shaky situation took a pronounced turn for the worse when, after two decades of military dictatorship, a freely elected democratic government occupied Brasilia. As military contracts declined, a series of civilian administrations in Brasilia produced little of note aside from red tape and skyrocketing inflation. By 1990, Brazilian inflation had hit an all-time Weimar-like high of 6,800 percent on an annualized basis, amid a global downturn in military commerce following the winding down of the Cold War.[6]

As export subsidies evaporated and the nation's capacity to invest in new technologies hit bottom, Embraer's annual sales dropped from $700 million in 1985 to $200 million in 1995. Annual losses mounted despite the reluctant imposition of stringent cost-cutting measures, including a 50 percent work force reduction from 12,000 to 6,000 (implemented over the vociferous opposition of Congress).

The firm's shaky state was weakened further when, at the behest of the civilian government, it embarked on a disastrous joint venture with an Argentinean counterpart to develop a pressurized turboprop airplane. The primary raison d'être for this plane was to celebrate the recent rapprochement between two traditional adversaries. The CBA-123 (the initials stood for Consortium Brazil-Argentina) was a classic example of a high-tech, high-prestige, high-cost project beloved by the firm's engineers, but in no way demanded by prospective customers. It was the height of irony that, after mourning the loss of its sugar daddies in the Brazilian military, Embraer's greatest loss-producing project of all would be championed by the civilian administration of President Jose Sarney.

Captain Ozires Silva's departure in 1986 to run Brazilian oil giant Petrobras did little to improve Embraer's volatile fortunes as the costly pressurized turboprop project continued to consume foreign exchange at a terrifying rate. Embraer squandered millions building up a costly

CAD/CAM capability at a point when few other airline manufacturers boasted such a high-tech luxury. After an expenditure of tens of millions in development costs, not a single thirty-passenger twin-engine pressurized turboprop CBA-123 was sold. As orders for new planes plummeted, Embraer management stooped to churning out mountain bikes in an effort to keep its assembly lines rolling.[7]

By 1990, as inflation soared to an all-time high, Embraer's payroll hit an unsustainable peak of 12,700. The following year, Embaer suffered its cruelest blow yet when it lost out on a $7 billion contract to supply a Joint Primary Aircraft System (JPATS) jet trainer for the U.S. Air Force and Navy. Embraer had spent countless hours and millions ginning up a Super Tucano turboprop to fulfill the specs, only to be beaten by a European consortium. In the wake of this debacle, Captain Silva was rushed back from Petrobras in a last-ditch attempt to save his old sinking ship.

Silva had gone there hoping to turn the sprawling oil giant into a lean, mean, modern, efficient, market-oriented firm. Yet he had failed to take into account the awesome inertial power of the bloated bureaucracy in Brasilia to block even modest reforms at every turn. By the time he returned to Embraer, he had become a convert to the cause of privatization, a still controversial notion when talking about state-sponsored companies and major employers.

After Embraer ranked high on the list of impending privatizations in 1992, Silva firmly guided the faltering firm through two wrenching years of protests by labor, Congress, and the bureaucracy before the firm was finally sold in December 1994. It went for $265 million to the Brazilian financial services conglomerate Companhia Bozano Simonsen, two large public sector pension funds, and the U.S. private equity firm Wasserstein Perella. After Wasserstein Perella failed to come up with its share of the funds, Bozano Simonsen swallowed hard and took on the rest.

A STUNNING TURNAROUND

A tightly held financial services enterprise with interests in minerals, real estate, and agriculture as well as aviation, Bozano Simonsen had its work cut out for it turning Embraer around. Nine months after taking on Embraer, Bozano Simonsen and its partners hired Mauricio Botelho, a trained engineer, to engineer its recovery. In its final year as a state-sponsored enterprise, Embraer had racked up a stunning loss of $310 million on revenues of $250 million. As Botelho came aboard, the company's total backlog for new orders barely exceeded $200 million, or substantially less than its previous year's losses.

If Ozires Silva (who had gone on to head Brazil's national airline Varig) was the perfect founding leader of Embraer, Mauricio Botelho was equally a man of his times. A mechanical engineer by training, he graduated from the University of Brazil in 1965, and at age twenty-six signed on to build a saw mill on Marajo Island in northern Brazil. "There was nothing around," Botelho later recalled. "We had to attend to the employees, their families, and the surrounding communities. So we built a school. Children rowed their canoes on the river long distances to come to class. Seeing that was deeply touching. I learned that, if you give people an opportunity, they take it and blossom."[8]

After working as a manager and director responsible for business development and project implementation in power generation and transmission, steelmaking, mining, and petrochemicals for engineering giant Empresa Brasileira de Engenharia, Botelho's first leadership role was as president and CEO of Odebrecht Automacao e Telecomunicacoes Ltda., a company specializing in process control and telecommunications systems implementation.

Two months after taking over at Sao Jose dos Campos, Botelho persuaded the board that the first order of business must be to boost productivity. Despite the fact that the work force had already been slashed in half to just over 6,000 jobs, Botelho met with the firm's anxious union representatives to explain the need for additional work force reductions and a 50 percent drop in overtime hours. Once the firm returned to profitability, Botelho promised, he would return the force to full strength. At the union's request, Botelho agreed to take a 10 percent pay cut like every other employee, and with that symbolic commitment, the union conceded to Botelho's plan. "That event was a turning point," recalls Botelho. "Management proved it was seriously committed to obtaining results. The workers, in turn, embraced the cause of the company's recovery."[9]

SECRETS OF SUCCESS

So how did this remarkable firm steer itself from virtual bankruptcy in 1994 to being the fourth largest airplane maker in the world? Imagine surviving hyperinflation, an 80 percent drop in sales in a single year, a sudden loss of military orders after the end of the Cold War, government pressures to get involved in dead-end projects and overly ambitious technologies, bankruptcies of major customers, and the reversal of growing plane sales after 9/11. Not to speak of turning a state-owned pet project of the Brazilian military into an efficient, private sector maker of popular jets with suppliers and customers around the world. How did the only major player in the category located in an emerging market succeed in a highly competitive, capital-intensive, technologically advanced industry? How and where did it find its competitive edge?

BETTING BIG ON SMALL JETS

Privatization, new management, layoffs, debt reduction, substantial investments in IT systems, a flatter hierarchy, total quality management, a recovering global economy, improved market intelligence, and the introduction of system performance feedbacks all played a role in Embraer's impressive revival over its first decade in the private realm. But even the most avid advocates of relentless cost cutting and squeezing operating efficiencies out of existing programs understand that the permanent recipe for long-term sustainable strength is launching breakthrough products and finding new market niches.

Embraer's turnaround can be attributed to a single bold gamble that in 1995 looked like a long shot. Engineering the transition from producing twin-engine turboprops to regional jets was a laughably audacious goal at the time. At the point of privatization in 1995, Embraer's only adventure in the rarefied universe of pressurized planes had been the disastrous thirty-passenger CBA-123. Fortunately for Botelho and Embraer, in 1989 the firm had commenced planning for a regional jet in response to market pressures. The turboprops that had made so much of Embraer's volatile fortunes to date were aging fast, and their slowness and loudness was beginning to vex passengers accustomed to the quiet and comfort of larger jets. The hub-and-spoke system pioneered by Robert Crandall at American Airlines was undergoing revision as the spokes grew longer and flight frequencies tighter. One answer to the regional airlines' mounting headaches was a smaller jet, a market niche Embraer's longstanding rival, the Montreal-based Bombardier, was also moving aggressively to tap.

In 1989, Bombardier bet half its $250 million market cap on a fifty-seat regional jet that could outperform turboprops on the regional routes favored by commuter airlines. With its Canadair jet CRJ-200, which first took to the skies in 1992 and quickly racked up $4 billion in back orders, Bombardier was the first to market in that niche. But underdog Embraer, preoccupied with its loss-making turboprop, its labor woes, and the perils of privatization, suffered from the disadvantage—which it turned into an advantage—of having let its competing plane languish on the drawing boards.

As Embraer was being brought to the auction block, the bare-bones plan that ultimately turned into the best-selling seventy-seat ERJ-145 had been briefly revived by management as a form of "dressing the bride" to achieve the highest market price. While Botelho may not deserve sole credit for reviving the regional jet at Embraer, his leadership skills were sorely tested in bringing Embraer back from the brink to a level where it could capably produce such a sophisticated plane.

When designing the ERJ-145, Embraer's engineers were forced to start fresh because their experience was limited to producing a thirty-seater turboprop. Unlike Bombardier, Embraer had no older jet to reconfigure, which allowed engineers to accommodate customers' suggestions such as two-and-one seating to offer more cabin width per passenger. In yet another ironic twist, the beefed-up CAD/CAM capacity and other bells-and-whistles innovations that had added so much to the failed turboprop's development costs came in mighty handy when designing and constructing the ERJ-145.

Meanwhile, Bombardier simply took its existing business jet and stretched it out into a commercial fifty-seat jet, which meant that the new jet carried more than a ton and a half of extra weight, offered outdated systems, and had unnecessary operating features. The more modern and comfortable regional jet that Embraer brought to market three years after Bombardier's entry was two tons lighter, three million dollars cheaper, and 15 percent less expensive to operate than Bombardier's competing $21 million model. The ERJ-145, presented for the first time at the Farnborough Air Show in the UK in 1996, quickly secured a major contract with Continental Airlines' commuter subsidiary Continental Express. Over the succeeding three years, Embraer sold an additional 300 planes, as many as Bombardier had sold in seven. By 1997, the ERJ-145 accounted for 60 percent of Embraer's revived revenues. By 1998, following three years of privatization and eleven consecutive years in the red, Embraer was back in the black.

Restored profits permitted a gradual build-up of the work force to

11,000 plus, just under its peak level a decade before. In 2005, Embraer enjoyed sales of $3.8 billion and net profits of $291 million. Botelho championed a critical shift of focus at Embraer from a strictly technical orientation to a market-driven customer focus. Organizationally, he moved the firm closer to customers by creating five profit centers, three based on region and geography for commercial jets, one for light aircraft, and one for government sales. He placed an "entrepreneur" in charge of each division, with responsibility for developing and improving customer relations, and he permitted these divisional managers to operate their own P&Ls, shifting the decision making closer to the customer.

NICHE MARKETING

Identifying and then exploiting a yawning market gap ignored by the big plane manufacturers was clearly the key to Embraer's turnaround. Just as Henry Ford liked to sell his Model T in any color as long as it was black, industry leaders Boeing and Airbus had long been content to sell any plane as long as it was big. Airbus has even staked future market dominance on its mammoth, 600-seat double-decker A380. Other emerging market companies can learn from Embraer that it pays to follow the age-old rule of warfare: *Don't attack head-on but choose a weak spot where the attention of the opponent is not focused.* Embraer succeeded where scores of other well-known plane builders miserably failed, including Holland's Fokker, Japan's Mitsubishi, German-American Fairchild-Donnier, and Great Britain's BAE Systems.

TURNING OUTSOURCING UPSIDE DOWN

Like destroyers swarming protectively around an aircraft carrier, companies in emerging markets once made components for the "mother ship" in the United States, Europe, or Japan. Brazilian plane builder Embraer is the first example of a new type of company that, located in an *emerging* market, lies at the center of a large web of suppliers in *developed* nations. *It has turned outsourcing upside down.*

Ironically, its earlier obsession with technology as opposed to commercial viability provided the seeds for this later success. Embraer is able to design new planes from scratch at lower cost than its competitors, using

Brazilian engineers who are just as well trained but less costly than their counterparts in developed nations. Embraer builds global planes, yet remains in the driver's seat of integrating, designing, and assembling innovative regional jet planes in its huge hangars in Sao Paulo State while outsourcing many components.

The company encourages its "risk-sharing partners" to jointly develop components with its designers. The seventy-seat Embraer E-170, which made its first flight in February 2002, and the Embraer E-190, which made its maiden flight in March 2004, are powered by two newly designed GE engines and equipped with Honeywell avionics, wing stubs and pylons from Kawasaki in Japan, titanium plates from VSMPO in Russia, door and fuselage parts from France, Spain, and Belgium, and electronics from a variety of American companies.

Reverse-outsourcing enables Embraer to obtain the highest quality and cheapest components from all over the world, giving it a distinct advantage over its more vertically and horizontally integrated competitors like Bombardier. As Satoshi Yokota told me over lunch in Embraer's cafeteria, "We have a more flexible model. All our subassembly is done outside. Bombardier does it in-house. When we want to speed up, we flow more activities out while Bombardier's subassembly holds up final assembly and becomes the driver of the cycle. With our supply chain and assembly process it is very simple to build up the production rate. We need to make only minor investments to speed things up." Such flexibility helps immeasurably during inevitable market downturns such as the aftermath of 9/11. The outsourcing model also gives Embraer strategic alliances with component providers that keep it at the forefront of technology, speed up the development phase, and keep costs to a minimum. Co-production and licensing agreements also help Embraer sell planes and keep some competitors at bay. CEO Botelho likes to say that "when you've got only 100 customers, you have to focus entirely on what they want."[10] This is quite different from what his predecessor said: "We are engineering minded . . . not fanatical about the business side."

FUTURE CHALLENGES

Like those of nearly every other company in its industry, Embraer's revenues and earnings have always been volatile. That is unlikely to change in the future. The success of its new family of planes, despite an encouraging start, is not yet wholly assured. Plane builders tend to have just a few fickle clients and Embraer is no exception. A sudden downturn in a notoriously unstable industry could easily put the massive orders for its planes in jeopardy or cause an indefinite postponement in key orders, particularly since so many airlines in the United States and Europe have been teetering on the verge of financial insolvency. Rumors abound that Boeing and Airbus may turn their attention to the 100-seat market, although it could help that a French aerospace consortium holds a 20 percent stake in Embraer and may view it as "its" small plane manufacturer.

The primary question facing Embraer today is simple: Where does it go from here? The backlog of orders for the E family and estimates that the market may consume an additional 6,000 regional jets in the next two decades are all dependent on the aging of the E's turboprop predecessors coupled by a dramatic expansion in "spoke" flights from existing hubs.

Since in the airline business size clearly matters, Embraer's sweet spot—which currently occupies the midsection—can only expand in either direction so far. Recently, the firm has begun publicizing its interest in exploiting yet a new niche: the market for "light" and "ultra-light" jets quite a bit smaller than even the smallest in its current Legacy line of business jets, currently configured to seat eighteen passengers.

Over the next decade, nearly 10,000 business jets costing $144 billion are expected to be sold.[11] At between $2 and 7 million, Embraer reckons the global market for light and ultra-light aircraft at up to 3,000 planes over the next decade. With upfront development costs estimated at under $250 million, light may mean for Embraer in the next decade what midsized means in this one: an opportunity to achieve a strategic competitive advantage. It hopes that VLJs will constitute one-quarter of all units sold and contribute 4 percent to revenues. Embraer is also planning to leverage its partnership with its European shareholders EADS and Dassault in building an F-X supersonic fighter for the Brazilian air force. If that project bears fruit, Botelho has said that it will grant Embraer access to critical technology that could lead to the development of a Brazilian supersonic business jet, a super-fast ultra-light. Other long-range speculative scenarios include one in which Embraer would use its immense cost and training advantages to begin building big jets in Brazil for its largest competitors, including Airbus and Boeing.

CHAPTER 9

Commodity Producers
that Redefined Their Industries

Aracruz, CVRD, and POSCO defied conventional
wisdom . . . and the odds

Strategies

- *Defy conventional wisdom through sheer determination and leapfrog established producers by creating a new industry model.*
- *Take advantage of the ever-growing hunger for natural resources in the "new" industrial economies by establishing close south-south relations.*
- *Use modern science to improve yields and tailor products to customer needs.*
- *Make use of bulk vessels to ship raw materials to a seaside location and export finished products around the world.*

In 1817 the English economist David Ricardo wrote presciently of the "comparative advantage" enjoyed by wine producers in Portugal and textile manufacturers in England. Differences in the cost of production made wine cheap in Portugal and expensive in Great Britain and cloth cheap in Great Britain and expensive in Portugal. As Ricardo explained, shifts in a region's, nation's, or industry's relative prosperity tend to be closely related to changes in comparative costs of production and distribution of raw and finished materials.

As recently as the turn of the twentieth century, the backbreaking labor of 40 percent of the American population was required to maintain the agricultural sector at a level sufficient to feed the country. Today, 4 percent of the U.S. population can grow more than enough wheat, soybeans, and beef to go around, with plenty left over for exports. We tend to forget how much national economies have adjusted to these shifts while benefiting from these economies of scale, and to what degree consumers in the developed nations have profited from the low prices associated with them.

REVERSE SHIFT

As the rapidly industrializing nations of the future First World colonized Africa, Asia, and the Americas, those colonies provided the embryonic industries of Europe and North America with a seemingly endless supply of low-cost raw materials, along with the low-cost and sometimes even free labor required to grow and extract them. The first phase of globalization was defined by a brutally simple equation: the undeveloped regions of the world possessed the lion's share of natural resources and compliantly yielded up their wealth of resources to First World multinationals with the know-how, capital, experience, and global contacts to commercialize and refine those raw materials into finished goods.

China is now the world's largest—and fastest growing— steel producer with over 1,000 plants producing one quarter of all global steel but, like Japan and Korea, it needs to import many of its raw materials and energy.

Today not only has the know-how to grow, extract, and process both raw materials and finished products spread to emerging multinationals, but global demand has shifted with it to a new group of industrial powers. This fresh crop of emerging multinationals has achieved stunning rates of growth and profitability by intelligently exploiting its natural advantages: proximity to resources, a more efficient cost structure, an ability to leapfrog over old competitors with more modern technology, and no shortage of strategic wit and wisdom.

Over the centuries, the most salient characteristic of commodity products has been that they are fungible: tradable on open markets without regard to brand recognition or awareness. Even if basic commodities vary in quality, grade, and ease of extraction or production, one piece of pulp, iron ore, or steel is never dramatically different from another piece of pulp, iron, or steel. But today, far-seeing firms like Korea's POSCO (steel), Brazil's CVRD (iron), and Aracuz (pulp) have learned that being a low-cost or efficient commodity producer is no longer sufficient to beat out global competitors. To succeed today, commodity producers are required to advance the technology of production, use science for yield improvement, pioneer inventive logistical and information systems, and tailor and upgrade basic commodities to better meet customer needs.

ARACRUZ CELULOSE
Pulp Nonfiction

Before turning twenty-one, Erling Lorentzen (the scion of an old Norwegian shipping family) led eight hundred anti-Nazi guerillas to sabotage a plant suspected of producing heavy water for a possible Nazi atomic bomb. He later described this daring raid with characteristic modesty as a welcome break from spending long hours transmitting secret radio messages to the British. After spending his formative years fighting covertly for freedom, Lorentzen applied to Harvard Business School lacking the benefit of a college degree. Despite that deficit, Harvard accepted him. After tucking a crimson MBA under his belt and spending a few more years gaining experience in the family shipping business, the restless Lorentzen settled in Brazil, where his family maintained business ties.

Despite the vagaries of Brazil's politics and notoriously volatile economy, Lorentzen retained an incorrigible optimism regarding the possibilities of exploiting that nation's boundless natural resources to accelerate its development. After successfully operating a gas distribution business purchased from Exxon for twenty years, he had honed his entrepreneurial skills, knew the country, and was yearning to enter a new phase. When two Brazilian friends in the forestry business approached him for advice in implementing a scheme to export wood chips to Japan in boats that also carried iron ore, he succeeded in persuading them to "industrialize" the wood products in Brazil, and to export the finished commodity product (pulp) at a cost less than foreign competitors.

A neophyte in the wood products industry, Lorentzen knew that over the centuries increasing literacy had created an ever-rising demand for wood pulp, the essential raw ingredient used to produce paper for newsprint, books, coated magazine stock, tissue and Kraft, paper towel and plates. Traditionally, the pine forests of the United States, Canada, and Northern Europe have provided the bulk of the softwood used to produce pulp. But in the colder climates of the north, suitable trees can take up to four

decades to grow to maturity, while in tropical countries like Brazil and
Indonesia, eucalyptus hardwood trees grow twice as fast as their northern
equivalents, and can be harvested in five to seven years.

PUTTING BAZILIAN EUCALYPTUS ON THE GLOBAL MAP

Lorentzen established a company deep in the Brazilian rain forest to make
pulp from eucalyptus, taking full advantage of Brazil's tropical climate,
eucalyptus's fast growing cycle, the Brazilian government's generous
reforestation tax breaks, and a low-cost local work force. Lorentzen perse-
vered in the face of any number of experts who dismissed his scheme as
stark raving mad. The World Bank's private sector arm IFC went so far as
to dispatch a stern letter attempting to dissuade him from his folly. Fortunately for his future shareholders and the IFC (which years later extended
to him a substantial production credit) he blithely ignored their expert
advice.

An early convert to the doctrine of "sustainability," Lorentzen grasped
that eucalyptus was an infinitely renewable resource. He insisted on
imposing the strictest environmental standards on his operations, relying
on advances pioneered in his native Norway and other Scandinavian countries in addition to newly refined American statutes. A convert as well to
the manifold benefits of science and technology, he harbored a blind faith
that R&D and good forest management could increase yields and quality
well beyond current levels. This visionary also grasped the critical fact that
new opportunities existed for making eucalyptus pulp into tissue and sani-
tary napkins, while major producers like Kimberly Clark lacked the forests
and pulp to meet their own needs.

Lorentzen raised enough capital during a period of sky-high interest
rates in Brazil to build a plant nearly triple the size of standard mills of the
period. He planted his first trees in 1967, commenced construction of his
first mill in 1975, and launched production three years later with an annual
capacity of 450,000 tons. Today, nearly a quarter century after the first
pulp rolled off his presses, Aracruz remains the world's largest independent pulp producer, blessed with lower costs than anyone. Exporting virtually all of its production to five continents, it holds long-term contracts for
80 percent of its $1.4 billion sales in 2005 (on which it earned $477 million in net income) in a highly cyclical industry.

MARKET CYCLES ARE BRUTAL TASKMASTERS

The long road to success was ridden with potholes. As Aracruz CEO Carlos Aguiar told me in his office in Rio, "The original promoters of the project quickly learned that you cannot ship iron ore on the same ship as pulp. Oxidation negates the bleaching and causes black spots on the pulp. Road shows in the United States and Asia failed to convince skeptical customers until they saw much later that the eucalyptus fiber made paper machines run faster and gave better printing quality."

The pulp market is so fragmented and cyclical that even a leading producer enjoys minimal pricing power. When pulp prices are high, imitators flood the market, ruining prices and hastening the next downturn. "During 1993, prices were way down, our debt was huge, and the Brazilian economy was in terrible shape. We had no choice but to cut half of our six thousand jobs. I live close to the mill and play soccer with my workers every week. I had to cry every night when I couldn't do anything for my friends who had no more jobs and would not get them back. My family began receiving death threats. It was the most awful year of my life but I knew that this was the only way to survive. Today we produce more pulp with just two thousand people."

"We always aim to be the lowest cost producer in the world—always, always, always," Aguiar insisted, as if repeating a mantra. "I tell my people that costs are like fingernails. You cut them and they grow again, so you must cut them all the time." He contends that Aracruz's competitive edge has little to do with cheap labor. "We employ a lot of mechanization and our labor costs are not as low as people believe. We pay 125 percent in social benefits in Brazil in comparison to about 40 percent in the United States. But when I went to Finland for the first time, I was shocked to find they could run a mill with four hundred people when we had 1,200. I told our managers we had to do the same but nobody believed me." Determined to quell the doubters, Aguiar dispatched a group of engineers to Finland to search for innovative solutions that would make it possible for Aracruz to achieve Finnish productivity levels.

> "Our wood costs of $70/ton are only one-third those faced by our competitors in Northern Europe and North America. Of course, nature helps a lot but we always put enormous emphasis on forestry management to improve our yield."
>
> —Carlos Aguiar,
> CEO, Aracruz

DOUBLING YIELDS WITH SOPHISTICATED
FORESTRY MANAGEMENT

As critical to honing its edge as Aracruz's natural "eucalyptus advantage" has been, its enduring success has more to do with continual improvements in yield from state-of-the-art forestry management, innovative tailoring of its products to customer needs, and an obsessive drive for efficiency. "Of course, nature helps," Aguiar admits, "but Mr. Lorentzen always put enormous emphasis on forestry management to improve our yield. We still do a lot of R&D. Through genetic research, we are now growing 45 cubic meters per hectare each year, virtually double the 25 cubic meters when we planted our first plantations in 1970."

GENETIC SELECTION MAKES ARACRUZ WOOD
CHEAPER *AND* MORE DESIRABLE

In the 1970s, Aracruz followed standard industry practice by establishing commercial plantations from seeds imported from Indonesia and Australia. But by the 1980s, Aracruz had departed from industry practice by pioneering the science of clonal propagation to determine the species most adaptive to Brazilian environmental conditions, including disease tolerance and resistance.

Aracruz was the first forestry company to employ clonal propagation techniques on a commercial scale outside the laboratory. The goal is to create plantations that grow trees with the most genetically desirable traits, while maintaining a sufficient degree of diversity to avoid genetic vulnerability to disease. Modern management techniques permit Aracruz to breed trees that require less water to grow to maturity, at greater speed, and with greater density than their naturally cultivated counterparts. The primary objective is to increase productivity, or pulp yield, defined as cubic meters of pulp grown per hectare of plantation. A secondary goal of the breeding program is to reduce water use and industrial waste by minimizing the lignin content of the wood.

In the early 1990s, the company established a Microbacias ("microbasins" or "watersheds") project to study the ecological impact of the eucalyptus tree on water levels, soil, local vegetation and fauna. The point of this visually impressive practice is to gain a thorough understanding of the complex interactions between the eucalyptus and the environment. Aracruz forestry managers keep track of the amount of rainfall retained in the root of the tree and how much water is absorbed by the soil. Among other secrets of the rain forest, Aracruz has unlocked the fact that a hectare of land planted as a eucalyptus plantation consumes the same amount of water as the native forest surrounding it, yet the eucalyptus are more efficient at converting water and other nutrients into biomass than native forest. The firm has explored ways of naturally fertilizing forests by returning the residuals left over from harvesting back to the soil, including leaves, branches, and bark. As a result of these efficiencies, Aracruz's more than three-decades-old tropical hardwood plantations are vastly more productive than its competitors' in both the northern and southern hemispheres.

FUTURE CHALLENGES

The greatest challenge facing Aracruz is the ongoing consolidation of the paper industry. "Annual production of all market pulp is forty million tons," Aguiar explains. "Total Brazilian production is still pretty small, with eight million tons of which we make three [soon slated to rise to four] million. Paper machines are so huge now that just a few can supply an entire local market so there are fewer and fewer paper companies. I always say to my staff that if we don't make $1 billion in sales, we are nothing."

With the top four tissue manufacturers controlling 50 percent of the world market, pulp producers are more fragmented than their customers. When the demand–supply balance is unfavorable, pulp becomes a buyer's market. To counter this loss of leverage, Aracruz has consistently focused on building long-term relationships with major tissue and paper producers around the globe. About half of its pulp is used for tissues, 30 percent for printing paper, and 20 percent for photographic paper.

The firm has aggressively marketed its products to pulp-poor countries in Asia such as China, Korea, and Japan. Today, Asia is a growing part of Aracruz's sales with a 33 percent share, nearly double that of a few years ago, although Europe still tops it with 40 percent. Given China's huge impact in the pulp market, its needs and purchasing policies will be a major factor determining pulp prices, but pulp demand in other emerging markets like Korea, Taiwan, and India is also rapidly expanding.

Aracruz needs to grow if it hopes to improve its pricing power over the long haul. It must expand organic capacity, acquire or merge with other companies. VCP, one of the major industrial groups in Brazil, has purchased a stake in the firm, as well as other pulp operations but other shareholders (including founder Lorentzen) have thus far resisted selling out. Its joint venture with Finland's Stora Enso opens up other opportunities, but only the future will clarify whether Aracruz or others will be among the last survivors of this cutthroat consolidation.

An Investor's View
The Bull Case
- *Aracruz is the world's largest, most profitable, and lowest cost producer of short fiber market pulp.*
- *Eucalyptus pulp is low cost and particularly attractive for tissue.*
- *With China as the major demand factor in the future, there will be further expansion, takeovers, and mergers in the pulp industry.*

The Bear Case
- *The pulp industry remains highly cyclical.*
- *A sudden downturn in Chinese demand could have a devastating impact.*
- *The paper and tissue clients of the pulp industry are highly concentrated, putting them in a strong position except when the cycle is at a peak.*
- *Future success depends on whether Aracruz will end up on top in a consolidating industry that is currently fragmented.*

Lessons
- *Bulk carriers have changed the economics of many industries by allowing shipment of raw materials such as pulp and iron halfway around the world.*
- *Even industries in emerging markets can dramatically increase productivity through research on genetic selection.*
- *In a cyclical industry, the investor's typical valuation measures are of little use but competitive position and industry trends are key.*

COMPANHIA VALE DO RIO DOCE (CVRD)
The Leading Iron Ore Producer is Going Global

Flying into the company town of Carajas, one sees the open-pit mine below stretching to the horizon, a bloody scar slashed into the dark red clay beneath an otherwise pristine green rainforest canopy. The Carajas region, encompassing large swathes of the Brazilian states of Para and Maranhao, straddles the vast Amazon basin. Here lies the heart of CVRD's Northern System, where the largest single iron deposit in the world lies inches beneath lush publicly owned lands. The noise is deafening as enormous wheel loaders, hydraulic shovels, excavators, trucks, scrapers, tractors, and bulldozers move earth and rock. Mines may all look the same to the naked eye, but their scale and the grade of the ore being excavated make the difference between profit and loss.

There is so much iron ore in Carajas that even at today's pumped-up production levels, there is enough to last two hundred years. Consuming only proven audited reserves should take at least twenty. The 66 percent iron ore content of the Carajas mine, higher than the industry average, permits Carajas iron to escape the standard *beneficiation* (purification and refinement) process, reducing production costs even further.

Nearly as impressive, CVRD (Cia Vale do Rio Doce, or "Valley of the Sweet River") earned international environmental recognition in 2004 for the "sustainability" of this open-pit mine, the traditional target of environmental groups' most venomous ire. It is the first operator of an open-pit mine to receive ISO 14001 Environmental Management Certification, an honor CVRD contends is not only a showcase for its "green efforts," but an economic necessity. "At CVRD we are doing what we are doing not only because we love the monkeys, birds, and butterflies, but in order to keep the company competitive," Mauricio Reis, CVRD environment systems manager, assured a recent group of visitors to Carajas. "Our ecosystems are under the spotlight . . . Our clients, particularly from Europe, demand that our production uses clean methods."[1]

The company found that instituting environmentally sound practices makes good management sense by revealing operational defects and making auxiliary systems—including energy and waste disposal—more efficient. The World Business Council for Sustainable Development (established following the 1992 Earth Summit in Rio) has applauded CVRD's efforts to control the damage its operations cause in environmentally sensitive areas like Carajas. "We need raw materials and this is where you find them," the Council's vice president of operations, Eric Derobert, observed after a visit to Carajas. "It's very impressive to see these guys lost in the middle of nowhere taking such a progressive approach."[2]

CVRD's hard-earned environmental credentials are indeed a valid proxy for efficient management. But such plaudits reflect the sophistication of this global giant, which today ranks as not only the largest and lowest-cost but also the *best* all-around producer of iron ore in the world. The company's mines are merely nodes in a complex system of transportation and communications networks that are the envy of mining companies worldwide. At Carajas, a train carries up to 240 gondola cars round-trip every forty-three hours, ferrying up to 130,000 tons of ore every day to the company's marine port at Ponta de Madeira. A 100-kilometers-long natural channel provides access for ships of up to 420,000 dead-weight tons. A loading system fashioned from bucket-wheel reclaimers, conveyor belts, and single-boom ship-loaders operates at two modern company piers—all part of the firm's extensive network of integrated excavation, transport, and shipping facilities.

CVRD's Southern System, located in the state of Minas Gerais, consists of nine additional mining complexes, all with ready access by road or by rail to the Tubarao marine terminal, boasting storage facilities capable of holding up to five million tons of iron ore and pellets. The Southern System's iron, like Carajas's, is mined by the not very scenic open-pit method. Yet it too is extracted with considerable respect for its natural surroundings, yielding a wide range of varieties and concentrations that are amenable to being blended to client specifications.

CVRD is the world's #1 iron ore producer, the #2 producer of manganese and iron alloys, and currently the fourth largest player in the global metals and mining industry.

Thanks to sharp price increases in past years, CVRD has become the largest mining company in the Americas (bigger even than Alcoa, Phelps Dodge, Newmont, and other North American mining companies). It is Brazil's largest exporter and one of a very few Brazilian companies whose debt earns an investment grade rating. With iron ore reserves unmatched by size and quality in the world, CVRD's annual production of 200 million tons of ore accounts for a whopping 30 percent of global exports, more than double that of its nearest competitors, Australia's Rio Tinto and BHP Billiton. Vale is currently the fourth largest player in the global mining and metal industry with revenues of $14 billion, net profits of $4.3 billion, and a market cap of $46 billion in 2005. In August 2006, it made an all-cash $17.6 billion bid for Canadian Nickel giant Inco Ltd, trumping two other bids from U.S. copper producer Phelps Dodge and Canadian zinc producer Tech Cominco Inc. Although its other mining operations are still smaller than the more diversified Anglo American, BHP, and Rio Tinto, CVRD is more profitable with cash flow growing at over 30 percent annually over the past four years and an operating margin of 43 percent.

ANCIENT HISTORY

Despite later lectures by the United States on the virtues of enterprise, American pressure on Brazil following the U.S. entry into the Second World War prompted Brazil's military's government to form CVRD as a government enterprise. Bases in Northern Brazil were urgently required as refueling stops for aircraft flying to support the offensive in North Africa, and the American war effort suffered an insatiable appetite for iron and steel. The U.S. government had reason to harbor fears that some of the generals leading Brazil's military government were too pro-Nazi to be strictly trustworthy. It extended a supportive hand to Brazil's nascent steel industry as a not-very-subtle form of bribe to keep Brazil from favoring the Axis powers.

After the war, American interest in Brazil's mining resources subsided, making room for engineer Eliezer Batista (who later went on to become the minister of mines in Brazil, was fired after the military coup in 1964 and returned to CVRD in the '80s to create Carajas) to step in and pick up the slack. As Francisco Gros, a former central bank governor, later explained to me one night over dinner in Rio, "Batista saw how Japan was rebuilding its steel industry and needed to import most of its iron ore. He knew Australian suppliers were next door but believed that Brazil could become competitive if it built large ships and specialized ports. He used to say that CVRD was more a logistics company than a mine. The force and charm of his personality were such that he not only built close relationships with the Japanese but talked the Brazilian government into helping CVRD to build railways and ports to export to Japan even though it did not seem very practical."

> *CVRD's export success came from the gleam in a dreamer's eye: Eliezer Batista, who was in shipping rather than mining.*

In the 1970s, CVRD expanded its operations in Carajas, building a special railroad to transfer the ore to its new port and outfitting the port with new docks designed to service the company's growing needs. By 1974, CVRD had become one of the world's largest iron ore exporters, controlling 16 percent of transoceanic iron ore shipments. As cash flow grew, CVRD embarked on a helter-skelter diversification program into everything from other mines to completely unrelated activities, many of which siphoned off cash flow, creating a legacy of chaos and confusion that took strategists decades to reverse.

Today, CVRD continues to be as much a logistics company as a mine. Its 5,600 miles of rail and eight marine terminals account for over two-thirds of the total freight transported by Brazilian railroads. Subsidiary Docenave offers coastal and long-haul transport to customers nationwide. The firm's logistics network is more than a cash cow; it serves as a means to control and maximize the efficiency of every step between resource extraction and the end user.

PRIVATIZATION AND NEW MANAGEMENT TURN CVRD INTO A WORLD-CLASS COMPANY

The most surprising fact about CVRD is that for decades it merely muddled along as a rich but mediocre government enterprise until privatization prompted it to hit the jackpot. The firm was the hottest ticket in Brazilian President Cardoso's mid-1990s privatization program, but turned into one of the most controversial privatizations, as populists and activists lodged lawsuits and mounted fierce protests against the government's decision to "sell off its crown jewels." After laboriously clearing those hurdles, CVRD was sold in 1997 to a consortium led by Brazilian steel maker CSN for $3.3 billion. A key negotiator of this complex transaction was the investment banker Roger Agnelli of Brazil's leading private bank Bradesco, who succeeded in shrewdly outmaneuvering CSN and others for control of the board, which ultimately appointed him CEO.

Agnelli may be blessed with movie star looks, but during our interview he gave every sign of being a strong strategic thinker as well. His overwhelming goal was to privatize CVRD not just in name but in reality. Not beholden to the stifling traditions of the past, Agnelli modestly referred to himself as a "lucky guy" whose outsider perspective helped him find fresh solutions to vintage problems.

"Investment bankers," he observed with all due self-respect, "have a few crucial advantages over engineers trained as mining executives in this day and age: a sense of speed and urgency, a global perspective, a strategic bent, and a focus on the financial side of the business. The mining business was very traditional and closed to new ideas. Globalization pushes companies to be

> *Not bound to tradition, a new management team led by Roger Agnelli wanted to privatize CVRD not just in name but in reality, and turn the iron ore giant into a modern, diversified, world-class mining empire. And that was even before China's demand exploded.*

more efficient. The answer I used to get before I took over was 'we are studying this issue.' As an investment banker, I was used to asking for results, as opposed to more studies. It was not enough for me to hear that nobody could beat us in iron ore, I wanted to see more organic growth."

Agnelli was very young when he became managing director in Bradesco. Banking, like mining, was a conservative industry in Brazil. Because he was so young, people did not mind if he asked a lot of questions. "I learned it could be useful to ask a lot of 'silly' questions." Among the silly questions he asked after taking over CVRD was why two separate conveyor belts were required for the Northern and Southern Systems. Noting that one consumed far more steel than the other, Agnelli "first got the standard run-around with answers like the climate, ocean wind, or humidity. But after I probed a little deeper, the engineers finally admitted that this was just the way it had always been done." Operational consolidation of CVRD's Southern and Northern systems reportedly saved $2 million in operating costs in the first year alone.

NOT JUST FERROUS METALS
BUT COPPER, BAUXITE, AND NICKEL

Agnelli was not opposed to diversification, merely diversification without rhyme or reason. He jettisoned unrelated side businesses like pulp and paper and refocused the firm's activities into a coherent portfolio of metal and metal-related products, including bauxite, copper, nickel, potassium, and kaolin. The firm has since become the world's second largest producer of manganese (used in steelmaking and batteries) and iron alloys (with 11 percent of global seaborne trade). With the June 2004 opening of the Sossego Copper Mine next door to its existing mining operations in the

Brazilian state of Parána, CVRD is the fifth largest copper producer in the world.

Sossego is CVRD's first greenfield mining project in twenty years. José Auto Lancaster Oliveira, Executive Director, Non Ferrous Minerals and Energy, recalled how he had formerly worked for Phelps Dodge but that the U.S. copper giant had decided against investing in Brazil when copper prices were lower. Smiling at Phelps Dodge's unduly conservative concerns regarding Latin American copper, he volunteered that, "in Chile, we built the living quarters of the employees close to the airport so they could leave quickly if needed. When Phelps Dodge assessed the project, its engineers projected ten years for completion. CVRD finished in seven."

Agnelli is determined to turn Sossego into a model modern mine where employees are not cocooned in a special company enclave but immersed in the local community. "My engineers told me to forget this idea, that this was the equivalent of the Wild West. There was even a red light district with girls of ten years old, some suffering from leprosy. I went there and got the mayor to move this area. We brought in water and sewage treatment, a school, a police station, and technical training. Soon the town nearly tripled in size to over 15,000 people. As modern miners," Agnelli notes, "we can't just be technicians. We need to listen to the community and be less arrogant."

CVRD aims to become a major player in bauxite (a primary ingredient in producing aluminum) after its acquisitions of large mines in Brazil and neighboring Paraguay. Within a decade, its 20 million tons of production will put it in the same league as aluminum giant Alcoa. CVRD is also launching a $1 billion-plus nickel project and is quietly eyeing Cuba's nickel deposits, which amount to 30 percent of the world's total. If its proposed acquisition of Inco goes through, it would add the world's second largest nickel producer under its corporate umbrella.

CVRD views coal as ubiquitous but in November 2004, won an international bidding war to explore coal deposits in the Moatize region of northern Mozambique, home to the largest unexplored coal deposit in the world with an estimated 2.4 billion tons. "Coal is a strategic asset to a steel supplier," Agnelli contends. The Mozambique project is supported by the International Finance Corporation (IFC) and the Brazilian national development bank BNDES. CVRD plans to invest $1 billion for concession payments, mine development, and construction of a maritime terminal for ship loading, and will also link an existing local railroad to ports on the coast of Mozambique.

BECOMING A GLOBAL MINER

Only 10 percent of CVRD's current mining takes place outside of Brazil (where it is active in eighteen states) but Agnelli hopes to lift that to 30 percent within the coming decade. The Inco deal alone would enable Agnelli to surpass this goal. Currently it has a presence all over the Americas; France and Norway in Europe; Bahrain as well as Africa's Mozambique, Gabon, and Angola; and China and Mongolia in Asia. CVRD's worldwide scope is also reflected in the fact that it maintains sales offices in all major markets, from Brussels and New York to Shanghai and Tokyo. Agnelli sees a great future for CVRD in Africa, and believes Brazil has a natural affinity for the continent. He candidly hopes to preempt a Chinese takeover of the continent's resources. "The Chinese are invading the world, especially in high sovereign risk places." While cautiously optimistic about opportunities in China and Russia, he is flexible in wielding a strategy based more on practical opportunity than a theoretical grand scheme.

AN INNOVATIVE COMMODITY PRODUCER

Agnelli proudly showed me how, in the collegial style I remembered from visiting Bradesco, the bank he left to come to CVRD, all top executives sit together in one room without partitions or private offices. As he did so, he laughingly recounted how "a few years ago I met the CEO of one of the top mining companies in the world when we were only #9 or #10. He said that he loved CVRD and wanted to combine forces. I replied that 'my father already taught me as a child that you should not call a wolf to defend yourself against dogs. You are too big for us now and we are too small. Let's have the same conversation in four years. Maybe we can then talk as equals. Or perhaps we will *buy* your company.' I met the same executive again recently. 'We are not really interested any more in buying your company,' I said, 'but we are bigger now than yours.'"

An Investor's View
The Bull Case
- *An efficient, low-cost, global-scale mine is transforming itself into a leading diversified mining corporation with a global footprint.*
- *CVRD is a classic case of how privatization and new management*

*can, within a few years, turn a large but stodgy and overdiversified
company into a world-class corporation.*

The Bear Case
- *China's sudden, insatiable appetite for iron ore has created such a
  ballooning in CVRD's cash flow that it could create "bad habits."*
- *CVRD will need to prove that it can be as efficient in copper, bauxite,
  nickel, and coal as it is in its ferrous operations.*

Lessons
- *An unexpected windfall in demand may change the entire character of
  the company but also become a temptation to squander cash flow.*
- *Privatization often provides a unique opportunity to install new management, change corporate culture, create a sense of urgency, and
  adopt a new, more focused strategy.*

POHANG IRON AND STEEL COMPANY (Posco)
Against All Odds

The March 1969 report from the World Bank was unambiguous. The construction of "an integrated steel plant in Korea [was] a premature proposition lacking economic feasibility." If any reader of the report were inclined
to question its conclusions, its author spelled out the rationale behind his
thumbs-down verdict.

1. Korea lacked *iron ore,* an essential component in steelmaking, while
   the primary sources of a steady supply of iron were distant and
   costly to reach.
2. Korea lacked *coal,* the raw material for coke, a key component in
   steelmaking.
3. Korea lacked the *skills* and *complex engineering know-how* required
   for integrated steelmaking.
4. Korea lacked the ready *capital* required for integrated steelmaking.
5. Korea lacked a *large domestic market for steel,* while the most efficient steel producers in the world were located practically next door
   in Japan.

In any country other than South Korea circa 1969, under the repressive and autocratic regime of military strongman Chung-hee Park, such an unalloyed negative verdict from the all-powerful World Bank (a proxy for American sentiment and support) would have scuttled the project without further ado. But the Korean government was determined to succeed in even its wildest ambitions. It had placed top priority on developing self-sufficiency in steel manufacturing, an anchor industry it viewed as critical to the development of a full-fledged industrial economy.

Despite every rational argument against it, fierce determination and national pride took precedence over plain common sense. Even as the World Bank was issuing its downbeat assessment, road crews were clearing a site in the former fishing village of Pohang to make way for the nation's first modern steel plant. It would be the first since the Japanese— in their wartime role of overlords of Korea—constructed two plants in its former colony to supply strategically critical steel to their armies fighting in Manchuria and China.

Ever since the cessation of the Korean War in 1953, the South Korean government had energetically lobbied its allies abroad for support in constructing a local steel industry from scratch. It had every reason to suspect that at least some of the skepticism voiced in the World Bank report could be ascribed to pressure from America's Big Steel companies, which already faced stiff new competition from Japan. It is an irony of history that when the Americans failed to step up to the plate, Korea's ancient adversary, Japan, moved aggressively to take up the slack. The Japanese not only identified a promising commercial opportunity in South Korea, but found a tangible way of making amends for "thirty-six years of hardship under Japanese rule," as the Japanese government contritely conceded.

A legacy of suffering under Japanese colonial rule had finally paid dividends in the form of crucial cooperation between the two now friendly nations. Korea had remained a desperately poor country with a per capita income as low as Peru but had its eye firmly fixed on following Japan's footsteps. No wonder the original Korean procurement team dispatched to Japan enjoyed a scanty per diem of $10 per day. By day, they proudly purchased the then unheard-of sum of $175 million worth of the highest grade steel-

> *After the American refusal, the Japanese, led by Nippon Steel, saw an opportunity and became Posco's major technical partner, training ground, and day-to-day adviser.*

making equipment. By night, they remained confined to their shabby hotel, dining on bowls of store-bought instant noodles and hand-washing their underwear in the hotel room sinks.

President Chung-hee Park was obliged to personally intervene when his stiffnecked bureaucracy kept raising objections to the costly equipment purchases being agreed to in Japan. He signaled his imperial displeasure by signing a hastily drawn up note, famously called "Memorandum with the President's Handwritten Signature," to clear all future logjams with a presidential stroke of the pen. To ensure that the massive project would remain on track from then on, President Park appointed a top general, Tae-joon Park (no relation to the president but a key supporter in the coup that brought him to power) as the firm's no-nonsense, hard-driving chairman.

Like strongmen the world over, Chairman Park was not shy about setting an example of ruthless efficiency. When he discovered that the hole for an anchor bolt in some freshly poured concrete was set at the wrong angle, he blithely blew up the entire section in front of the assembled contractors. Not surprisingly, the first phase of construction was completed a month ahead of schedule. More surprisingly, the Koreans constructed the plant at an unheard-of low cost, primarily by subcontracting the work to low-wage local contractors.

In April 1970, ground was broken for Posco's first plant, boasting an annual capacity of 8.5 million tons. By July 1973, the concern was open for business. A second plant followed in 1986 with an 11.4 million ton production capacity. By the late 1980s, Posco was exporting nearly three million tons of steel annually, a figure that by the mid-1990s had doubled to 30 percent of total production, or six million tons. Today, the company is among the world's most efficient, largest and technologically advanced steel producers. In 2005, Posco was honored by the editors of *Fortune* as a "globally most admired company," called "the most competitive [steel company] in the world" by leading steel industry analysts, and named one of "the Masters of the Web" by *Business Week*.

HOW INFANT INDUSTRY PROTECTION HELPED AND HURT

That Posco was established and nurtured in its early years by a fiercely determined, autocratic government makes it a sterling example of the once fashionable policy in the developing world of *"infant industry protection."* There is no doubt Posco benefited enormously from being a pet project of a military strongman and his confidantes at the highest levels of the Korean government. Government support was critical to the firm's survival in its early years, as the generals kept the company from falling into the grasping hands of the powerful local *chaebols* (business groups) while reining in the country's legendarily militant trade unions.

Protection under President Park went so far as the drafting of a special Iron and Steel Industry Promotion Law, passed in 1970, which provided the company with access to long-term low-interest loans to purchase equipment and build a port, water supply facilities, an electricity generation station, roads, and a railroad line. This rich package of products and services, rendered at 20–50 percent discounts, is estimated to have added up to $42 million to its bottom line in 1970.[3]

Less acknowledged by those who have called for anti-dumping charges against Posco is that this wealth of subsidies and protections came at a cost. For most of its history, Posco was required to sell steel to domestic consumers at a "special" price set below the prevailing world prices it would have commanded if the same steel had been exported. Posco was subjected to constant government meddling, which became increasingly stifling as the firm grew. For years, the Korean government not only appointed top management but determined every last detail, from how much steel the company could sell abroad to what prices it could command in the domestic market to how much it could invest to what companies it was asked to bail out and which other "infant" industries it was required to help. On balance, government support was probably more of a burden than a help. Yet the Korean government took until 2001 to relinquish control.

Key success factors
- *Early export drive despite infant industry protection.*
- *From top to bottom, Posco's staff was driven by national pride in its determined effort to turn an unconventional idea into reality.*
- *Posco took lessons from the Japanese and then outdid them in efficiency.*
- *From the beginning, Posco invested in people, not just machinery.*
- *The company possesses a strong drive to "better the best" globally in technology.*
- *With a global mind-set from the outset, Posco recognized China's growing dominance in steel and has not only moved "up market" but is becoming a global producer with plants in China, India, and the United States.*

AN OBSESSION WITH TRAINING

Posco's management grasped early on that building a large steel plant on its own would not be enough to earn world-class status in a highly competitive industry. Acquiring world-class skills would require training and technological know-how from others. Before operations had even commenced, 597 of its staff had received training in Japan or Australia. Their Japanese coaches were surprised to see Posco's overseas trainees passionately taking notes and memorizing information in a fashion reminiscent of the Japanese themselves in the old days. So committed were they to their training that before they actually began work in the plant they rehearsed their jobs by shouting orders to each another in an open soccer field. Trained staff was required to remain with Posco for two years and to develop materials to train the next groups in-house. Technicians who reached a "sacred stage" of knowledge were highly praised and rewarded with special treatment. Posco also placed highly qualified college-educated engineers as foremen in the mill, a strategy that quickly paid off in improved productivity.

> *Posco stands out in its drive to become world-class for its huge commitment to training and technological innovation, making it a leader in productivity, efficiency, and costs.*

FROM TRAINEE TO TEACHER

Posco learned from the Japanese that top-tier productivity can only be achieved through continual fine tuning rather than relying only on high-technology machinery and IT. Minimizing downtime and rejecting batches of steel that fail to meet stringent quality requirements, preventive maintenance, and low employee hours per ton (now down virtually to Japanese levels from three times the number in 1975) are just as important. In a bid to shed its dependence on foreign technology, the Korean authorities worked tirelessly to link Posco, the Pohang Institute of Industrial Science and Technology (Potech), and the Research Institute of Science and Technology (RIST). Eventually, through much trial and error, POSCO developed several types of homegrown equipment and technology.

In the late 1980s, the firm's engineers developed an expert system to forecast wind pressure changes inside a furnace as well as systems for diagnosing furnace abnormalities and controlling furnace heat. In the 1990s, Posco engineers exported methods and proprietary technology to the United States, Europe, South Africa, and India. In 2006 Posco is opening a revolutionary new plant employing a breakthrough technology called Finex. Developed in-house, this new method of steelmaking dispenses with the traditional and time-consuming step of melting of coal and ore into chunks with hot air (so-called coking and sintering) thereby saving energy and cutting emissions by 90 percent.

Posco is strong not just in the steelmaking process but like any self-respecting world-class company, is a frontrunner in information technology. Starting in 1999, it networked not only its own eighty-one plants but also its suppliers and 19,000 customers. Everyone in the firm freely maintains access to the same on-line information, avoiding duplication, errors, and confusion and allowing suppliers to assess future needs and clients to obtain up-to-the-minute delivery times. In its first year of operation, 1,600 customers placed orders amounting to 5 percent of sales through the Internet.

GOING INTERNATIONAL

In yet another sign of changing times, Posco entered into a joint venture in 1986 with U.S. Steel to modernize—at an initial cost of $450 million—a vintage California steel plant with roots dating back to the 1910s. Today, a plant famed for providing the raw material to construct the San Francisco–Oakland Bay Bridge qualifies as one of the world's most technologically advanced mills of its kind, employing 1,000 Americans, shipping tons of cold-rolled, galvanized, and tin-mill products from hot-rolled steel daily to more than 150 customers primarily in the thirteen western states. Not unlike Hyundai's new plant in Alabama, USS-POSCO Industries provides Posco with a virtual insurance policy against trade sanctions and punitive tariffs against "foreigners" accused of dumping cheap steel on American soil. As part-owner of a U.S. steel mill that provides a livelihood for hundreds of Americans, Posco won an exemption from the 30 percent tariffs on steel imports into the United States days after their imposition by the Bush administration. While Posco has improved productivity at U.S. Steel and exported proprietary key technologies to companies such as Saldanha in South Africa, VSL in India, and Hoogovens in the Netherlands, it tends to be surprisingly modest about its achievements. One of its advertising slogans tells the low-key story: "We move the world in silence."

An Investor's View
The Bull Case

- *Posco is one of the world's largest, most efficient, and lowest cost producers of steel with special strengths in high-quality galvanized and stainless steel plates*
- *Posco dominates the Korean market with a 55 percent market share.*
- *Less than twenty-five years old, Posco does not face a legacy of high pension liabilities.*
- *New Finex technology will improve Posco's technological lead.*
- *Joint ventures in China and a huge new plant in India provide flexibility in a global market.*
- *Long-term contracts increasingly assure access to raw materials.*

The Bear Case

- *China's steel industry is coming up fast and will soon be the biggest and most modern globally.*
- *Posco's car and shipbuilding clients go increasingly global.*
- *Even younger plants in China are becoming increasingly world-class.*
- *Falling behind on size in rapid concentration, led by Mittal Steel, Posco may be forced to seek an alliance with one or more other leading steelmakers*
- *Posco was slow to move into low-cost countries with large markets.*
- *The fight for resources will become tougher.*

Lessons

- *Posco has demonstrated that it is possible to build a world-class, efficient, low-cost steel plant without the usual iron ore and coal resources based on sheer determination, strong government support, and a captive market of carmakers and shipbuilders.*
- *Building a greenfield plant without prior experience requires a huge commitment to training and the willingness of a world-class company to serve as a mentor.*
- *Constant efforts to achieve top-notch technology and extensive use of IT are useful only if careful attention is paid to "the small things" of operating a plant if the goal is to achieve world-class efficiency and the lowest cost structure.*

CHAPTER 10

Alternative Energy Producers

South Africa's Sasol makes oil out of coal and gas, Brazil's cars use biofuels, and Argentina's Tenaris makes pipes seamless enough to be used deep under the ocean or in Arctic climates

Strategies

- *With growing energy use, actively pursue research and experimentation with alternative energy sources.*
- *Instead of dismissing "emerging market" alternative energies, take them seriously.*

The state-controlled Russian energy giant Gazprom has quietly become not just the largest emerging market company, but also, far and away, the largest provider of natural gas to Western Europe. More noisily, on Sunday morning, January 1, 2006, in the midst of one of the coldest winters recorded in Europe, Gazprom abruptly cut off all natural gas supplies to neighboring Ukraine. Gazprom's explanation for this action was the Ukrainian government's decision to balk at paying Russia US $230 for 1,000 cubic meters of gas, a nearly fivefold increase over the long-subsidized price of just under $50. Though the Russians maintained with a grim poker face that this was a "fair market price" and a "purely commercial dispute," both the Ukrainians and the rest of the world saw a political element in Russia's high-stakes energy brinkmanship.

What sent a shiver down the stiffer spine of Western European nations was not only that Russian President Vladimir Putin and his allies within Gazprom seemed to use this as an opportunity to crack down on the Ukrainians for electing the Western-leaning Viktor Yushchenko as president over a strongly Kremlin-backed candidate. More ominously, their own natural gas supplies were threatened by the action, as most of the gas shipped through Ukrainian pipelines was destined for transshipment to clients elsewhere in Western Europe. Gazprom CEO Alexei Miller appeared on *Russia Today* (the first English-language satellite TV channel in the country) to insist that gas being shipped through pipelines across Ukraine to Europe would not be disrupted by his firm's move. But Europeans took small solace from those assurances after Ukraine threatened to siphon off enough supplies to meet its own needs, leaving only the leftovers to be sent across its territory to the West.

As oil and gas prices on world markets lurched sharply upward in response to the prospect of European capitals going dark due to power outages, the increasingly bitter dispute was ultimately resolved in a fluster of face-saving maneuvers. But this narrow escape from energy anarchy only underscored the frightening fact that the European Union was as beholden to its largest gas supplier, Russia, as the United States was dependent on imported Middle Eastern oil to meet its energy needs.

Barely had the gas started flowing through Ukrainian pipelines again when, on January 31, President George W. Bush stated during his annual State of the Union address that "America is addicted to oil, which is often imported from unstable parts of the world." Before waiting for the shock to wear off—a shock deepened by the fact that both presidents Bush had been oilmen long before running for office—President Bush confidently asserted that "the best way to break this addiction is through technology." Getting down to brass tacks, the president pushed, in his list of promising technologies, for "funding additional research in cutting-edge methods of producing ethanol, not just from corn, but from wood chips and stalks, or switch grass. Our goal is to make this new kind of ethanol practical and competitive within six years."

While some skeptics questioned the practical value of Bush's vow to reduce oil imports from the Middle East by 75 percent by 2025, environmentalist and energy experts alike applauded the president for putting the issue of energy dependence back on the front burner. Perhaps arcane references to using "wood chips and stalks, or switch grass"—a fast-growing plant that grows wild in the Great Plains—as fuel caused some observers to scratch their heads, but investors, policy makers, and politicians sensed a new openness at the White House to the promotion of alternative and renewable non-fossil fuel sources to meet the nation's energy needs.

A growing global consensus had taken hold that the economics of energy had fundamentally changed, not necessarily for the better and that global warming required drastic action to reduce the level of carbon dioxide emissions if not to stave off a major crisis then at least as a prudent insurance policy. Just about everyone of any political persuasion could agree that radical solutions were required to achieve "energy independence" for the U.S. and Europe in the foreseeable future. Yet the $64 trillion question remained: could a combination of energy conservation, cleaner coal, cheaper ethanol, wind power, solar energy, better batteries, hydrogen fuel cells to run pollution-free vehicles, and a renewed reliance on safer, cheaper nuclear power solve not just the United States's but the world's energy problems? What about the fact that with more cars and trucks crowding new roads in China and India, Brazil and Russia (to cite just the "BRICs") burning more gasoline and diesel oil, more factories and homes consuming electricity worldwide, and with more low-cost airlines transporting first-time fliers who could never afford to fly before, the use of energy *for transportation alone* was expected to grow nearly *three times as fast* in emerging Asia alone as in the rest of the world during the next twenty years? It was becoming increasingly clear that alternative energies and the need to avoid ecological gridlock would become central issues in the Emerging Markets Century.[1]

> *With more cars and trucks crowding new roads in China and India, Brazil and Russia (to cite just the "BRICs") burning more gasoline and diesel oil, more factories and homes consuming electricity worldwide, and with more low-cost airlines transporting first-time fliers who could never afford to fly before, the use of energy for transportation alone was expected to grow nearly three times as fast in emerging Asia alone as in the rest of the world during the next twenty years.*

With tribal strife in oil-rich Nigeria, unrest in Iraq, nuclear sword-rattling in Iran, populist rhetoric in Venezuela, a new government in Bolivia, and hurricanes Wilma and Katrina, even a market that produced and consumed 85 million barrels of oil a day appeared to have no slack left in the system. While it clearly didn't take much to upset the system, it would take an awful lot in the way of new investment, determination, and ingenuity to right it.

Amid the grab bag of energy alternatives being promoted as potentially viable, the president's pledge to make "cellulosic ethanol" (an alcoholic fuel derived from agricultural waste such as woodchips, switch grass, and rejected stalks from grain crops) a competitive and practical automotive fuel within six years caused the greatest reaction. Where on earth did the president get the idea that using ethanol was remotely practicable? It turns out he had recently paid a friendly visit to Brazil.

"When President Bush made a recent stop-over in Brasilia," *The Wall Street Journal* reported,[2] "Brazilian leader Luiz Inacio Lula da Silva hosted a barbecue and described to Mr. Bush how the country had reduced its oil import bill." Indeed, while the United States and Europe have heavily subsidized biofuels made from sugar beets, corn, and sunflower seeds, Brazil has developed low-cost solutions that are shockingly practical and economic. Brazil's car fleet currently consists of a majority of "flex-fuel" cars equipped to run on sugar-cane ethanol with lower emissions and at a lower cost than gasoline, all without the need for government subsidies that kick started the process but stopped many years ago. India and China have recently sent delegations of high officials to witness Brazil's innovative program firsthand. India, currently the world's third-largest sugar producer behind Brazil, mandated in 2003 that nine of its states add a 5 percent ethanol mixture to gas.[3] Indian companies like Praj and Uttam are hard at work developing more efficient processes to consume a variety of biofuels.[4] Suzlon, another Indian company, is among the world's leading makers of modern windmills and Chinese companies like Suntech are becoming major players in solar energy. Could it be that the solutions caused by the spiraling needs for energy will increasingly come from emerging markets themselves?

THE POWER OF BIOFUELS

In November 1976, three ethanol-powered cars (a Beetle, a Dodge, and a Brazilian car called a Gurgel) developed in the Brazilian Air Force laboratory of ethanol researcher Urbano Ernesto Stumpf sped off on an epic five-thousand-mile journey from the air force's research lab in the southeastern state of São Paulo to the northern city of Manaus in the Amazon Basin.[5] The background of that trip—billed by the Brazilian government as a "National Integration Rally"—was that the OPEC oil shocks of 1973 (prompted by an Arab-Israeli war that caused oil prices to practically quadruple overnight) had hit Brazil like a punch in the gut. The chronically cash-strapped country imported 80 percent of its energy supplies, causing it to consume 40 percent of its foreign-exchange income to pay for oil under the new OPEC regime.

Clearly something had to give, and Brazil's head of the junta at the time, General Ernesto Geisel, decided it was not going to be the Brazilian economy. At the stroke of a pen, he decreed that the country's gasoline supply be mixed with 10 percent ethanol, and that this modest level would rise to 25 percent over the ensuing five years, giving Brazil a thirty-year head start. Brazil's beleaguered sugar industry, already suffering from depressed sugar prices, became the grateful recipient of cheap loans to underwrite the construction of ethanol plants and generous price support for the ensuing product.[6] Infrastructure? Not a problem. The government issued a fiat to state-controlled Petrobras to construct the pipelines and other equipment required to distribute ethanol on a national basis. Presto! Foreign oil problem *nearly* solved.

Locally developed innovative technology played an equally important role in easing the Brazilian transition. The chief engineer at the Brazilian unit of Italian car parts company Magneti Marelli, Fernando Damasceno, invented a cheaper "flex-fuel" device by programming a standard car computer to constantly calculate the ethanol versus gasoline mixture in the tank and adjust the engine accordingly. In 2002, his team sold Damasceno's "black box" to Volkswagen, which used it in its flex-fuel Gol. Today, the Brazilian black box is routinely installed in just about every car made in Brazil.

Thirty years later, some 29,000 fuel stations—it no longer makes sense to refer to them as "gas stations"—in Brazil provide a steady flow of ethanol to fuel a home-grown fleet of "flex-fuel" cars equipped to run on ethanol, gasoline, or any mixture of the two. For a country whose vastness rivals that of the United States, Russia, and Canada, and where driving long distances (often at high speeds) has long been a national habit, the fact that ethanol provides an accelerant effect not unlike rocket fuel has made the spirit (comparable to the national drink, caipirinha) popular with Brazilian speed demons. At current prices, locally produced ethanol typically runs about 10 percent below that of gasoline. Even 300 small planes fly on ethanol. Before our very eyes, we have a nation that has achieved something approaching energy independence in our time.

Emulating the Brazilian experience particularly in North America or Europe, however, is not quite as simple as sending a team of experts in to copy its most appealing features. The triple key to Brazil's ethanol advantage is that the country, besides an abundance of sun, boasts cheap land, cheap water, and cheap labor. This combination makes growing the base feedstock (sugar) and distilling it into fuel a competitive alternative to pumping oil. Add in the fact that according to a recent Citigroup analyst's report, "Brazilian [sugar] plants are often very efficient not just [in] using the fuel generated by the ethanol production to run the plant but even sometimes [in] being able to sell the excess energy back to the grid. [This] suggests that the Brazilian competitive advantage may stick for at least a little while."[7]

Sugar-based ethanol is exported from Brazil to the United States but, contrary to WTO rules, is subject to a 100 percent duty of about 54 cents a gallon to protect American corn farmers from undue foreign competition. "It makes no sense to tax ethanol coming in from friendly countries like Brazil when we do not tax oil imported from countries like Saudi Arabia," insists Gal Luft, executive director of the Institute for the Analysis of Global Security, a Washington think tank that specializes in energy-security issues.[8] Rather than being encouraged to promote independence from foreign oil (of which 70 percent is consumed in transportation), the United States has historically caved to the politically connected farmers who produce 4 billion gallons of ethanol annually from corn feed stocks.

Despite the duty, Brazilian ethanol is currently being produced at the oil-equivalent price of $25 a barrel.[9] It can be sold in New York for $1.10 per gallon, a bargain at current gasoline prices.[10] Unless oil prices plummet, trade in biofuels is likely to skyrocket from its puny base of 1.8 million tons in 2004. Brazil and India have led the way in biofuel costs, which have been steadily falling and are currently between $0.15 and $0.20 per liter as compared to $0.60 per liter in Europe, where ethanol is processed from sugar beets.[11] Scientists believe that new enzyme technologies could make "cellulosic" ethanol made from grain and cellulose (wood chips, switch grass, etc.)[12] competitive with the current Brazilian costs for sugar-cane-based ethanol by the end of this decade.

SASOL
Converting Dirty Coal and Flared Gas into Oil

On March 23rd, 2004, during a signing ceremony at the Ritz Carlton in Doha, Qatar, Abdullah Bin Hamad Al-Attiyah, the energy minister of Qatar, welcomed South African energy company Sasol and its partner, U.S.-based Chevron, in its new joint venture. To a polite smattering of applause, he encouraged the foreign firms to "work hard to realize the ambition of the State of Qatar to become the GTL (gas-to-liquid) capital of the world."

ADDING TO THE NATURAL GAS SUPPLY

According to *World Oil* magazine,[13] huge volumes of flared and other types of "stranded" (otherwise wasted or unused) gas amounting to just under 10 percent of the world's total gas reserves could be brought to market without undue strain to the system. Instead of simply flaring this now-wasted gas, which is also an ecological hazard, South Africa's Sasol has discovered how to turn it into oil, a modern form of alchemy quite different from that of the medieval chemists who hoped to turn coal into gold.

Using gas in this innovative way would add substantial supply to the two more commonly used ways of transporting gas—by pipeline and in liquefied form (LNG). Another emerging multinational, Russia's Gazprom (not yet a world-class company but certainly global in size), is easily the world's largest and (as the Ukrainian experience suggests) most powerful gas producer. It now supplies through huge pipelines over one quarter of Western Europe's gas (as much as 40 percent of Germany's and over one third of Italy's) in addition to providing heating and electricity to most of Eastern Europe. The vast majority of this fuel is currently transported westward through a complex system of pipelines crossing the Ukraine, and it is building facilities to export gas to the United States and China.

Besides Gazprom, other emerging multinationals are also leading players in the increasingly important global gas market. Nearly one quarter of the world's gas exports are shipped in liquid form from countries such as Algeria, Qatar, Nigeria, and Trinidad with new facilities planned in Angola and Venezuela. Among the 25 world-class emerging multinationals (see Financial Profiles at end of this book) are the world's largest shipyard (and leading builder of sophisticated LNG carriers), Korean Hyundai Heavy Industries, and the world's largest shipper of liquefied natural gas, Malaysian International Shipping Company (MISC). MISC plans to go beyond the profitable but dull long-term contracts to ship LNG all over the world and is aiming to use more of the gas found offshore by converting old supertankers into floating gas liquefaction plants.

LIQUEFYING COAL

In contrast to oil, which is becoming scarcer, more expensive, and harder to drill for in risky and remote places, coal is one of the most *underutilized* sources of energy. The world's over 1 trillion tons of coal reserves worldwide would be adequate to provide for the world's fast-growing energy needs for at least another century. Coal is conveniently located in many large and growing consumers of energy such as China, India, and the United States. More importantly, coal's dirty image is no longer always up to date because companies like Sasol are refining modern coal-to-liquid processes that are able to scrub out CO^2 and other offensive pollutants which can be "sequestered," used in commercial by-products or stored underground rather than being released into the atmosphere. Efficient, low-energy sequestering of carbon-dioxide will be the key to a wider use of coal.

Of the new technologies that promise to alleviate the global energy shortage, one of the most intriguing is Sasol's two-step "coal-to-gas" (CTG) and "gas-to-liquid" (GTL) process, which converts coal into gas and later gas into clean, liquid hydrocarbon products.

The coal-rich United States is finally jumping onto this hard-to-beat bandwagon. In September 2005, Pennsylvania governor Edward Rendell announced a venture with Waste Management and Processors Inc. to license Sasol's Fischer-Tropsch (FT) process to build a huge plant to convert so-called "waste coal" (leftovers from the mining process) into low-sulfur diesel fuel at a site outside of Mahanoy City, just northwest of Philadelphia. The state of Pennsylvania has committed to purchasing a significant percentage of the plant's output and, together with the U.S. Department of Energy, has offered over $140 million in tax incentives. Governor Brian Schweitzer of Montana has also proposed developing a plant that would use the FT process to turn his state's coal reserves into fuel in order to help alleviate the United States' dependence on foreign oil. Two other coal-producing states are exploring similar plans with Sasol.

A 1923 DISCOVERY ONCE FUELED GERMAN TANKS

In 1923,[14] Franz Fischer and Hans Tropsch of the Kaiser Wilhelm Institute in Berlin perfected a chemical reaction that converted carbon monoxide and hydrogen into liquid hydrocarbons using catalysts, such as iron and cobalt. The Fischer-Tropsch process, as their discovery became known, proved capable of converting even the cheapest, lowest grade coal into high-grade synthetic oil, a technique that proved a significant boon to oil-poor but coal-rich Germany during the waging of World War II.

Just four years after the Fischer-Tropsch process was first published, a South African government white paper strongly recommended its use in that coal-rich country. In the early 1930s, Anglovaal and the British Burmah Company established a joint venture to mine oil shales. In the late 1930s, Anglovaal acquired the rights to the German process, and appointed Etienne Rousseau research engineer to apply the process to converting South African coal into oil. In 1938 Franz Fischer visited South Africa to lend assistance to the venture, but the outbreak of World War II put a damper on commercial ties between Germany and South Africa, and the South African coal conversion experiment went into hibernation for the duration.

During the war, Germany and Japan employed the Fischer-Tropsch process to produce alternative synthetic fuels as a means of evading the strategic consequences of Allied blockades of their access to natural oil. In 1944, Germany's yearly synthetic oil production reached more than 90 million tons and used it as fuel in its battle tanks. After the war, captured German scientists continued to perfect the science of synthetic fuels in the United States as part of the controversial Operation Paperclip.

FROM IDEA TO LARGE-SCALE OPERATIONS

In September 1950, the South African government established the South African Coal, Oil and Gas Corporation Ltd. (SASOL) and appointed Etienne Rousseau managing director, a position he held for the next eighteen years. Not far from Anglovaal's original coal mines, Sasol established a coal-to-oil conversion plant and an adjoining company town, appropriately named Sasolburg. "I must tell you honestly that there were times in Sasol's early years times when we had trouble, big trouble, and when I felt that my main charge was to keep up the courage of our men," Rousseau later recalled. "I could not allow myself a moment's despair."[15]

Despite numerous setbacks, Sasol's chemists and engineers succeeded in getting Sasol I on line, producing gasoline, diesel, and synthetic feedstocks for fertilizers and secondary chemicals.

By 1973, as the first oil crisis threatened supplies from the Middle East, and South Africa's apartheid government was threatened with consumer boycotts and the possibility of government sanctions, Sasol supplemented its first eight-thousand-barrel-a-day plant with a second on a site located 130 kilometers northeast of Sasolburg, called Secunda, Latin for "second." As the downfall of the Shah of Iran precipitated yet another localized oil crisis for former ally South Africa, Sasol immediately embarked on Sasol III. At Sasol's Secunda plant, the firm is producing 160,000 barrels of gasoline, diesel fuel, and jet fuel a day—just enough, according to *BusinessWeek,* "to cover 28 percent of South Africa's needs, without using a single drop of crude oil, imported or otherwise."[16]

Billions were spent in the United States on large synfuels projects during the late 1970s but most of these plants were mothballed when the price of oil declined because technology at that time was still unable to produce synthetic oil on a cost-efficient basis.

PUTTING THEORY IN PRACTICE
AND MAKING IT COMMERCIALLY VIABLE

Although anyone can use the eighty-year-old German invention, Sasol is the world's largest producer of synthetic fuels, and the only company that has real-life experience operating and optimizing large plants using coal-to-liquid (CTL) and gas-to-liquid (GTL) technology on a commercial basis. Royal Dutch/Shell is the only other company that operates a small GTL plant in the deep sea port of Bintulu, Malaysia. Other global oil and gas players, such as Exxon Mobil, Conoco Phillips, and Marathon maintain pilot plants.

Only Rentech in Alaska and Texas-based Synfuels (which uniquely uses a process not based on Fischer-Tropsch) claim to have developed new GTL processes but have no more than experimental facilities. Chris Motterhead, a technology vice president at BP, calls GTL "an important contingent technology for BP. . . . We do believe that there are places around the world where the technology becomes economic to apply. . . . Our strategy is to drive down the cost of GTL."[17] His endorsement, while far from enthusiastic, appears to reflect the fact that most oil companies—even if BP (British Petroleum) proclaims that its initials now stand for "Beyond

Petroleum"—still stand to lose from alternative sources of energy. Cavan Hill, Sasol's investor relations manager, points out that there is a major difference between a small pilot plant and a large commercial facility that has been honed to highest efficiency for half a century. "Try to prepare a dish you had in a great restaurant from the chef's recipe book. You quickly realize that you have to practice a lot of times and, even then, it is still not as good." With the pride of an engineering-oriented company, he added: "We have become more efficient because we know the process so well and have brought down costs by building larger facilities with better economies of scale. We now also know how to use different catalysts (cobalt instead of iron) and we learned over the years how we can make money from by-products while minimizing pollution from the dirty coal."

DIVERSIFICATION INTO CHEMICALS

In 2001 Sasol took over Condea, a large, Europe-based chemicals company with operations in the United States and a subsidiary in Nanjing, China, in an effort to become less dependent on its coal-to-liquid coal, mining, and oil refining businesses. Although Sasol found it hard to make money in chemicals that are just commodities, it became the largest producer of olefins (used in detergents) in Europe and the #2 player in the United States. Sasol also makes 30 percent of the world's hexene from coal for use in new materials that gives them stretch and tear resistance (used, for example, in Saran wrap). With over $11 billion in sales and $1.5 billion in net earnings in 2005, Sasol remains small in comparison with the oil majors but large in its own special niche that has been studiously avoided by these same majors until very recently.

THE GAS-TO-LIQUID PROCESS—MORE THAN A PIPE DREAM

Gas is either used locally, flared, transported by pipeline (as Gazprom does to Europe), or liquefied into LNG and shipped by LNG carriers to a small number of expensive LNG terminals. That leaves plenty of gas without a home and many smaller gas fields without a market. The GTL process has opened up many new opportunities. Hill claimed that: "When it comes to gas, we don't even need the current high oil prices to liquefy it on a profitable basis as long as we can get the gas at a reasonable price. That is not a

problem in countries like Nigeria where they would flare the gas otherwise. We are a great and safe alternative to liquefied natural gas (LNG)
because oil is so much cheaper and easier to ship and, unlike LNG, does
not need specialized terminals." When I asked him why others had not
become involved earlier in what seemed to be a no-brainer, he joked:
"Anyone who can spell GTL is now trying to build a plant in Qatar. The
time of GTL has come. And I am sure this will become a big area if oil
prices stay so high and even if they don't. Fortunately, we have the benefit
of a good head start."

Not so long ago, John Ford, the former communications director of
Syntroleum in Tulsa, Oklahoma, put it differently in a candid moment:
"Everybody wants to be second, nobody wants to be first."[18] Sasol has
clearly decided to be the first and, now that a new CEO is selling most of
the former Condea business, its poorly performing chemicals acquisition it
has thrown in its lot with the global future of the gas-to-liquid and coal-to-
liquid processes. The immediate promise is greatest in gas-to-liquid (GTL)
but the longer term potential for coal-to-liquid (CTL) in China and other
countries is even more enormous.

For many years, people snickered at the idea of building GTL plants.
Existing pilot plants were small and the cost of capital seemed high as long
as oil prices remained below $25. Sasol has started to export its GTL tech-
nology aggressively, with several "majors" following its lead. Qatar holds
10 percent of the world's gas reserves with enough gas for over 100 years,
and plans six new GTL plants. Sasol's first plant there opened in June
2006 as a 49–51 percent joint venture with Qatar Petroleum. While a GTL
refinery may cost more than twice as much as a traditional refinery to
build, its feedstock tends to cost less because the gas is otherwise flared or
unused. Synthetic fuel is also virtually pollution-free with no sulfur, few
other emissions, and a low aromatic content. As part of its fifty/fifty joint
venture with Chevron, Sasol has begun construction of two other GTL
projects in Qatar for completion after 2010, which will bring the total
capacity of the Sasol-Chevron plants to over 200,000 barrels/day.

Another plant is under construction in Nigeria, a country that flares vast
volumes of natural gas. Owned 75–25 percent by ChevronTexaco and the
Nigerian National Petroleum Corporation, Sasol-Chevron will be the
licensor and provide the technical support.[18] The project is located 60 miles
southeast of Lagos and will produce 34,000 barrels per day. Now that the
GTL process is being taken seriously, there are plans afoot for some ten
plants with 1–1.5 million barrels/day capacity.[19] Sasol's Hill told me that

"Sasol plans to be the leader with 450,000 barrels/day of new capacity by 2014 in three or four locations such as Qatar, Nigeria, Australia, Algeria, and possibly even Iran."

CHINA BECOMES A PROMISING CANDIDATE FOR COAL-TO-LIQUID CONVERSION

More than just about any other country, China is eager to use its huge coal reserves (the largest in the world) to diminish its dependence on the 100 million barrels of oil it imports, largely from the volatile Middle East. It plans to invest some $15 billion in coal-to-liquid projects[20] over the coming decade of which projects worth $6 billion with Sasol have been announced. Acording to Sasol's new CEO Pat Davies, "the Chinese had been inviting us for years and we have had a few small operations that have at last led to a consortium between the National Reform Commission, two provincial governments and their two local coal companies, Chinese oil company Sinopec, the UK engineering firm Foster Wheeler, and a Chinese engineering company. We have contracts to build two plants in China that will together be as large as Sasol's entire South African production." Sasol will have a major equity stake in both projects and will "need to have our hands in there to make it work" with the hope of producing oil from coal at well under $20 per barrel, giving the project a good return on invested capital as long as oil prices stay above about $45 per barrel. He added that "we have our hands full now but India is equally interesting and next on the list."

The two Chinese plants would provide coal-rich China not only with greater energy security but at a price that is well below current import prices. Of course, synthetic oil cannot compete with the less than $5 it costs to produce oil onshore in the Middle East but a growing share of new oil reserves are found deep under water, in poorly accessible, cold regions or politically unstable countries where the cost is much higher. The future of a technology that was once out of the mainstream now looks very promising. Higher oil prices and tighter emission standards should focus the world's attention on an area where Sasol is well ahead of the crowd.

An Investor's view
The Bull Case
- *After years of promise but no action, large plants using the GTL process are being built and more are planned.*

- *There is significant interest in China in coal-to-liquid.*
- *Sasol has unique operating experience in a promising field.*
- Sasol's *new CEO took the hard decision to re-focus on GTL and CTL.*
- *The demand for virtually pollution-free fuel will rise.*

Bear Case
- *A sharp drop in oil prices would diminish current interest.*
- *Chinese projects are only at the design stage.*
- *GTL technology is not proprietary and is still unproven on much larger scale*
- *More focused Sasol is less global.*
- *The process to convert coal is expensive, requires enormous energy input, and needs to go further in reducing carbon-dioxide emissions.*

Lessons

- *Just as necessity was the mother of invention for oil-poor but coal-rich Germany and South Africa, a globalized world with plenty of well-distributed coal but scarce oil that is often found in politically sensitive spots may again turn attention to an old process to turn coal into oil.*
- *The rise of oil prices, China's need for dependable energy, and global tightening of emission standards give rise to new niche industries that have stayed outside the field of vision of major industry players.*
- *Overcoming difficult technical problems may be costly for a while but may lead to solutions that can be used for many years.*
- *If industry leaders do not have a vested interest in promoting a new technology, smaller outsiders have a chance to innovate and get a significant head start.*
- *One technology (coal-to-oil) may lead to another technology (gas-to-oil) with unexpected new applications.*

TENARIS
Seamless Pipe Maker and Logistics Provider

As oil becomes scarcer and harder to find, many of the sizable deposits of petroleum that remain still untapped are located in inaccessible environments: farther offshore, in deeper water, farther beneath the ground, close to the Arctic Circle, or in other remote and costly locations. The deeper an oil well needs to be dug into the earth or under the ocean, the more critical it becomes that a drilling rig be equipped with seamless steel pipe that keeps the oil flowing without leakage from the drilling hole deep below the surface, which may require as many as 25,000 linear feet of steel pipe of various shapes and sizes.

The highly specialized seamless steel pipes used in oil rigs—or "tubular technologies" as Tenaris prefers to refer to them—share little in common with the pipes running through houses or beneath roads. These are precision products, subject to exhaustive testing before qualification for use by oil and gas companies in their drilling operations. As Carlos San Martin, director of technology at Argentinean seamless pipe maker Tenaris, proudly showed me around the Siderca plant in Campana, outside Buenos Aires, he insisted that "Our production process is as fast, hi-tech, and efficient as anyone's anywhere." With the boyish enthusiasm of a born engineer, he demonstrated the speed with which his red-hot pipes completed the production cycle.

It had not always been like that. San Martin painfully recalled a Chinese petroleum engineer at an oil field pointing at a pile of Japanese oil and gas pipes and witheringly announcing to his Latin American visitor, "those are *real* tubes!" San Martin and his team were repeatedly forced to suffer the humiliation of haughty oilfield managers "literally throwing our catalogues at us," as they ceaselessly traveled the globe calling on major companies to promote their seamless steel pipes from Argentina. Prospective customers candidly advised the Latin Americans not to return until they could offer internationally certified products that could compete with the best in the business: premium seamless steel pipes from top-tier firms like Sumitomo and Kawasaki Steel of Japan, or the equally formidable offerings from German Mannesmann and French Vallourec.

In a process akin to Hyundai's rapid recovery from being the butt of Jay Leno jokes, Siderca ultimately prospered from being forced to endure innumerable pitiful and painful slights at the hands of skeptical clients. San Martin recalled with a visible wince a 1988 meeting with a procurement manager at Royal Dutch Shell. "I suggest that you and your colleagues," he gruffly advised, "only return to this office when you can do better than copying your competitors. . . . Too much is at stake for us to buy these pipes from you just to get a price discount!" Today—San Martin observed with a sly smile—Siderca's parent company Tenaris has become the top supplier to Shell in ten countries. "He steered us in just the right direction," San Martin noted of his old pal from Shell. "Wounded pride sometimes can be the best push." This, I silently reflected, could well be the mantra of countless managers of emerging markets multinationals. The harsh message from prospective customers was painfully clear: Either Siderca had to improve its quality to a level capable of competing with the big boys, or confine its ambitions to Argentina.

ACQUIRING A GLOBAL MIND-SET

Siderca's origins dated back to prewar Italy, when an engineer by the name of Agostino Rocca joined the Dalmine seamless steel pipe plant in the industrial city of Milan. Several years after becoming managing director of Dalmine in 1935, Rocca left to establish his own engineering firm in Milan, called Techint.

In 1948, seeking to escape the limitations of badly battered postwar Italy, Agostino's son Roberto Rocca relocated to Argentina, where the family established the Siderca seamless steel pipe manufacturer after constructing a plant that was a virtual copy of the Dalmine facility in Milan. Arch-protectionist Argentinean strongman Juan Peron was pursuing a policy of industrial independence that demanded domestically manufactured steel pipes to supply Argentina's burgeoning energy industry.

For the following three decades, the new company became a classic example of the then-popular practice of import substitution. Local companies, effectively obliged to buy from Siderca, were in no position to pressure the firm into improving its products or maintaining any sort of technological edge. Not surprisingly, its proprietary technology became outdated, and its products ultimately suffered by adverse comparison with foreign rivals. In the early 1980s, Siderca's problems worsened as the local economic environment deteriorated. After suffering through months of runaway 20–30 percent inflation, the Argentinean market became too volatile for local producers to survive by relying solely on domestic consumption. To qualify as a serious exporter, Siderca required a larger plant. Even more critically, it needed to learn more about how to produce seamless pipes that matched the quality of its Japanese and German competitors.

> "We want to create an island of technological excellence in Argentina by hiring a new generation of the brightest engineering graduates in the country."
> —Roberto Rocca

In 1986, Techint, now led by Roberto Rocca, Agostino's son, made a substantial investment in the expansion of the Siderca mill, tripling its size and production capacity. Siderca had in the meantime gained a controlling share of Argentinean welded pipe maker Siat.

CREATING AN ISLAND OF TECHNOLOGICAL EXCELLENCE

With an eye toward ramping up production to enter major export markets in the United States and Latin America, Roberto Rocca vowed to create an island of technological excellence in Argentina by hiring the brightest engineering graduates in the country. "He didn't want old people here but a new generation," San Martin explained. "That's how I got here." That first wave of graduates was destined to form the backbone of Tenaris's future management team.

Not only would the firm's seamless steel pipes undergo rigorous testing; the company itself would face a series of painful tests before it was prepared to take its own giant steps onto the world stage. Over the succeeding decade, Techint acquired a cluster of foreign manufacturers in a bid to become a global producer and consolidate the industry. Techint had been close to Tamsa, Mexico's sole producer of seamless steel pipes ever since it had been involved in building its plant. In 1993, when Techint acquired control, Tamsa was suffering the severe stress of a slowdown from Pemex, Mexico's national oil producer and its major customer, due to Pemex's buildup of surplus inventory of seamless steel pipe. After Dalmine was privatized by the Italian government in 1996, Techint acquired control of the firm with which it had old family ties. In 1998, Tamsa secured a presence in Venezuela by taking over its only seamless pipe producer Tavsa. Virtually locked out of the Brazilian oil and gas market by a local subsidiary of Mannesmann, Siderca gained entry to Brazil by taking a controlling stake in welded pipe maker Confab in 1999. NKK in Japan made extremely high-quality pipes (including drilling pipes) but found it difficult to survive, let alone thrive, against stiff competition from Japanese rivals like Sumitomo and Kawasaki. Sensing its rival's weakness, Siderca/Techint gained effective control of NKK by forming a joint venture with it in 2000, thereby gaining access to its state-of-the-art technology. Further timely acquisitions soon followed in Romania and Canada.

In the wake of its 1990s acquisition spree, Techint's local production units operated largely on a stand-alone basis. But after a period of half-hearted integration, the company's fragmented state created confusion with the firm's increasingly global clients. In December 2002, aware that a loose alliance was not enough to maintain a cohesive global presence, Paolo Rocca, grandson of the firm's founder, pulled off his most audacious gamble to date. With the help of consulting firm McKinsey, he thoroughly reorganized the company from top to bottom, by cobbling together three separately listed firms (Agentinean Siderca, Mexican Tamsa, and Italian Dalmine) under its new brand name: Tenaris. The reconstituted firm was listed on the New York Stock Exchange. Today Rocca claims that "we are managing Tenaris as one company. I call it 'The Tenaris Way.' We are not managing different profit centers. I have to admit that for a while it was like changing engines in a flying Boeing. Our managers needed to adjust to no longer being kings in their own plant."

After just a few years operating under its new name, Tenaris is now the world's leading producer of seamless steel pipe for the oil and gas industry, boasting a 20 percent global market share of the seamless oil country tubular goods (OCTG) category. By 2005, Tenaris was selling over 3 million metric tons of steel pipe with sales of US $6.7 billion and net profits of US $1.4 billion. As we spoke, Rocca's business was occupying a red-hot niche in the market, caused by a tectonic shift in the world energy supplies. In a world of $60-plus spot oil prices, with more and more drilling taking place in remote and inaccessible locations, the sophisticated steel pipes Tenaris was forging in its plants around the world were in remarkably high demand.

> *Tenaris has become the world's leading producer of seamless steel pipe for the oil and gas industry, boasting a 20 percent global market share.*

MERGING CULTURES AS WELL AS
STEEL PIPES: TENARIS BLUE

With the creation of Tenaris, Paolo Rocca began to think long and hard about how to differentiate the new firm from its competitors while repositioning itself as a unified, single, global brand. As described in a Stanford Business School case study, "the [Tenaris] brand would convey the concept of a global company with strong local roots and a proud tradition of multiculturalism, signified graphically by the multi-colored bars to the left of the Tenaris brand logo."

As Carlos San Martin put it to me, "We come from multicultural stock, we have executives located on four continents, and we have all learned to work well together." Early on, he and his colleagues grasped that his firm's emphatically multicultural character could be a key to their strategic competitive advantage. San Martin had spent some time living in Japan, and had thoroughly enjoyed assimilating various aspects of Japanese corporate culture, in particular its legendary obsession with precision, quality, and discipline.

San Martin firmly believes that the *key to success in the future of a modern, global company will be its ability to create a corporate culture where people feel comfortable sharing experiences*. A prime example of this philosophy, he contends, is the multicultural, cross-functional team he and his colleagues assembled to create a critical new breakthrough product, designed not only to gain market share, but to define Tenaris and put it on the map as a *technological* company, rather than just a commodity producer.

The challenge was clear, if not necessarily easy to execute: to develop and bring to market a breakthrough new product that would serve to integrate the firm's far-flung business units into an organization as seamless and precise as its products.

San Martin recalled how an energy industry analysis revealed the changing nature and location of oil and gas reserves around the world. With oil reserves located further out in the field, in deeper water and colder climates, requirements for the seamless steel pipes needed to service these wells were becoming even more precise and exacting than before. One area in which the industry competition has heated up dramatically was in the production of "premium connections," the connections between pipes that are virtually guaranteed to be flawless, leak-free, and tight. As San Martin explained, the American Petroleum Institute has standardized different kinds of threads forged into the male and female ends of pipe. Different manufacturers of stainless steel seamless pipes, from Germany's Mannesmann to Japan's Sumitomo, have developed their own proprietary premium connections, with threading displaying unique attributes that can be certified as maintaining a tight seal under extremely high pressures and at extremely high temperatures. These are typically marketed as "families" of connections.

Prior to the formation of Tenaris, Siderca contented itself with reverse engineering, copying an existing premium connection that lacked patent protection. It then moved to licensing rights to a family of premium connections from an American manufacturer. Following the acquisition of Dalmine, it marketed the Antares family of connections. Finally, it established a joint venture with the Japanese NKK company to license technology for premium connections developed by NKK. But to position Tenaris as the leading premium company, it needed to develop its *own* advanced and proprietary premium connection.

Rocca established a research team consisting of the two Japanese engineers who had designed the NKK premium connections, two Italian engineers who had designed the Antares family of connections, and a group of Argentinean computer engineers. Moving from concept to prototype to stress testing according to a rigorous ISO-sponsored regime of thermal cycling, high pressure stress testing, metallurgical tensing, compression, and testing the mechanical resistance of the connection, the resulting design was eventually marketed under the brand "Tenaris Blue."

Besides passing the most exacting tests with flying colors, the Tenaris Blue team came up with a breakthrough new "dopeless" technology, a seamless joint that permits oil service companies to dispense with the often costly and toxic lubricants typically required to make a seal tight and seamless at high pressures and temperatures. In the North Sea, the presence of toxic lubricant is contaminating and messy, while in Saudi Arabia, a desire to avoid having to clean grease off the pipes using large quantities of scarce pressurized water has prompted a keen interest in dopeless technology.

The motto of the Tenaris Blue research team was: "It's not hopeless, it's dopeless." San Martin proudly recounted how the team members worked in different locations but remained in constant email contact and met regularly in different countries. Melding all these different nationalities and cultures together allowed the team to build on each other's strengths. "The Italians are great designers, the Mexicans expert at welding technology, but nobody surpasses the Japanese in product testing, and one of the Argentineans, with a PhD from MIT, invented some of the complex models that are part of the Finite Element Analysis computer modeling we used."

SUPPLY CHAIN MANAGEMENT
AS TENARIS'S COMPETITIVE EDGE

Apart from high technology, Tenaris began to differentiate itself on a service as well as a product basis. This new approach dated from a former setback. The acquisition of Tamsa in Mexico prior to the 1994 Tequila Crisis occurred just as the Mexican oil giant Pemex was forced to stop most drilling and cancel multiple orders for Tamsa's seamless steel pipes. The situation deteriorated further after the devaluation of the peso gave rise to an anti-dumping suit in the United States designed to keep low-priced Mexican steel pipes out of price-sensitive U.S. markets. Yet in a result no doubt unanticipated by the proponents of anti-dumping legislation, Tamsa's rapid reaction to the dramatic change in circumstances set the company on a fresh course that ultimately transformed it into the global producer it is today.

As a means of remaining competitive, Tamsa offered Pemex "just-in-time" service to all its wells, an unheard-of innovation at that time. The priceless experience gained with Pemex would be later applied to customers elsewhere in the world and made Tenaris into something more than a sophisticated steel pipe producer: it was now a globally nimble logistics company. "We felt proud that Sumitomo started to imitate us," Rocca told me, "but, until recently, they worked through a trading company and, for example, could only ship their pipes to a Nigerian port while we brought them to the well head. We provide 'just in time' supply chain management and have begun to operate more like an oil service company."

An Investor's View
The Bull Case
- *Tenaris's success is based on state-of the-art technology, a global organization model, low-cost production, and innovative logistics solutions.*
- *Demand in the seamless pipe industry depends on oil prices, drilling activity, and how deep and far away reserves are.*
- *During the Emerging Markets Century, drilling in emerging markets will increasingly be done by companies from emerging markets.*

The Bear Case
- *A downturn in oil prices would quickly affect this notoriously cyclical industry.*
- *Tenaris competitors have quickly copied its "logistics" model and know they have to do everything to remain at the forefront technologically.*

Lessons
- *Wounded pride can be the best push.*
- *Emerging multinationals can succeed in technologically demanding businesses but only if they are willing to invest heavily in product testing and development.*

- *Companies can leapfrog competitors in businesses with global clients operating in many countries by moving to an equally global organization structure and using information technology to deliver products from wherever it is quickest and most cost-competitive.*
- *Making top-notch products is not enough any more to be competitive; companies of the future must also provide logistics solutions, including just-in-time service.*

CHAPTER 11

The Revolution in Cheap Brainpower

India's Infosys and Ranbaxy transform
the worlds of software design and generics

Strategy
- *Use cheap brainpower as a competitive edge*

For twenty-five years, nations aspiring to status in high-technology industries have sought with varying degrees of success to cultivate the cultural miracle of Northern California's Silicon Valley on their own soil. Particularly in Asia, national leaders, industrialists, and policy makers spent decades standing by as the best and the brightest of their technological graduates flocked to Silicon Valley and other high-tech brain-magnets in the West, drawn to high-paying jobs in the fast-growing computer and software industries. This dispiriting social phenomenon became so widespread in the reeling economies of the former Third World that it acquired a sad name: "The Brain Drain."

One of the most successful attempts to reverse the Brain Drain was mounted by K. T. Li, Taiwan's visionary minister of technology in the 1980s, who single-handedly strong-armed his government into supporting the development of the Hsinchu Science Industrial Park on the outskirts of Taipei and invited TSMC's Morris Chang to return "home" to Taiwan to jump-start Taiwan's semiconductor industry.

By the late 1990s, such silicon-seed-planting efforts verged on commonplace, especially in Asia. In Malaysia, controversial Prime Minister Mahathir Mohamad proudly inaugurated Cyberjaya, a 15-by 50-kilometer high-technology zone and multimedia super corridor constructed from scratch on a former oil palm estate south of Kuala Lumpur. In China, the government aimed to duplicate not just the success of Silicon Valley but also Taiwan's Hsinchu Science Park in a dusty northwest corner of Beijing. Not far from the Chinese emperors' Summer Palace, the central government designated Beijing's Zhongguancun District to become "The Silicon Valley of China." Today, with sleek modern buildings rapidly rising around prestigious Tsinghua University, the neighborhood is home to high-tech firms Microsoft, Sun, Siemens, and NEC. In Dubai, whole new medical, science, and media "cities" have arisen in an effort to create a similar critical mass of "brainpower" for the post-oil period.

The recipe for high-tech incubation strikes policy makers as deceptively simple:

1. Construct a cluster of clean, lean, low-slung university-style buildings surrounding lush lawns and courtyards in campus-like surroundings, preferably within a stone's throw of as many universities and technical institutes as can be planted on the periphery.
2. Attempt to emulate Stanford University's storied role as the incubator of Hewlett-Packard and other spin-offs like Intel and Apple by constructing technical institutes from scratch, focusing on such promising high-growth disciplines as software, hardware, aerospace, and biotech.
3. Toss in as many basketball courts, gymnasiums, cafeterias, and free soda dispensers as practicable to make the recent graduates feel right at home, as if they have only just transferred to another university, as opposed to a private firm in the free-market economy.

Stand inside the well-tended grassy courtyards of many of these postindustrial "new towns," whether they be in Brazil's Sao Jose dos Campos or the Ang Mo Kio neighborhood of Singapore (which—surprise, surprise!—styles itself "The Silicon Valley of Singapore"), and imagine yourself anywhere in the postindustrial world. Here's Apple's description of its Singapore campus in Ang Mo Kio: "The campus features a cozy and spacious work environment, a health club with up-to-date gym facilities, and a cafeteria that offers balanced meals for breakfast and lunch. The neighborhood is so attractive that many of the top technology companies also built office space nearby."

Sounds familiar? Looks familiar? That's precisely the point.

In India, the city currently vying for the title of local "Silicon Valley" (although sticklers for geography more accurately term it a "Silicon Plateau") is Bangalore. The capital of the state of Karnataka is the fifth

largest city in the country and by repute the fastest-growing urban agglom-
eration in Asia. Legend has it that Veera Ballala II, a prosperous king of the
eleventh century, was hunting in the thick forest of his peaceable kingdom
when he lost his way and took refuge in an isolated hut, the home of a
lonely poor woman who had nothing to offer her lord save a dish of fragrant boiled beans. The king was so grateful at being served this humble
meal that he named the town he founded on the site "Benda Kalooru,"
which means "town of boiled beans" in the local dialect. An Anglicized
corruption of the original name morphed into "Bangalore."[1]

By the late seventeenth century, the town had blossomed into a graceful
city with fragrant gardens famed throughout Southern India, and four
sturdy stone watchtowers guarding its bastions are still visible in the congested city center. The city's mild climate, strategic location, and lush vegetation lured the Colonial British to move in, under whose administration
the city acquired a reputation as a "pensioner's paradise," with its wide
tree-lined streets, ornate buildings and palaces, ceremonial gardens and
lakes. Today, by far the greatest and richest resource in this bustling and
overcrowded megalopolis of six million plus is a seemingly infinite, reliable, renewable crop of freshly baked university graduates.

Knowledgeable citizens of Bangalore date their city's love affair with
technology back to 1909, when pioneering industrialist J. N. Tata, founder
of the respected Tata industrial and services conglomerate, was persuaded
by the region's well-developed hydroelectric capacity to establish a science and technology university on a 372-acre site in northwestern Bangalore known today as the Indian Institute of Science. The IIS is one of the
nation's leading technical institutions and its graduates are said to be the
cream of the crop of India's significant technical talent base.[2] Bangalore
boasts an unusually diverse menu of educational institutions, including
BIT (Bangalore Institute of Technology) and dozens of other, lesser-
known schools that produce their fair share of young, educated, ambitious,
and aspiring "information workers" eager to land jobs at the 1,500-odd
technological firms[3] that have put down roots on native soil. More often
than not these firms were established by local entrepreneurs who, after
earning experience overseas, came home to lead a revolution in the construction of indigenous Brain Hubs. This has been the most effective antidote to date to the drag of the Brain Drain.

Ironically, Bangalore's headlong development into a magnet for the IT
services industry and a bustling center of India's "new economy" was
based on an old socialist government planning initiative. Jealous of Singa-

pore, Taiwan, and Korea, the Indian government chose Bangalore for the development of its electronics industry in part because it was sufficiently far south to be out of range of Pakistani or Chinese bombers. A further inducement, as the British discovered a century before them, was that Bangalore boasts one of the mildest climates on the subcontinent.

Only a decade ago, few could have anticipated that some of the largest companies in the world would one day rely on programmers thousands of miles away to develop their software solutions. By 2001, the same prediction could have made you a millionaire. Today, India churns out over 100,000 highly qualified and eager engineers[4] every year, many of them with outstanding software skills. A substantial number of these end up in Bangalore, even if at some point they accept the lure of often unscrupulous "body shoppers" who prowl the back alleys and pubs of India's Silicon City, dangling offers of lucrative coding work in the United States and Europe.

A closed Indian economy, closed minds, closed borders, and a lack of telecommunications made it impossible for ideas to move freely until the early 1990s. Plagued with poor roads, red tape, congested ports, inflexible labor laws, petty corruption, and power outages, India was the opposite of a draw for both foreign and domestic investment. That Indian computer scientists made a major contribution to the buildup of Silicon Valley was well known, but in the great scheme of things it hardly counted that brainpower was cheap and highly qualified in India.

In the early 1990s, prompted in part by free-market reforms instituted under the leadership of Finance Minister Manmohan Singh (India's prime minister in 2006), India's economy opened dramatically. Globalization, the Internet, and overinvestment in fiberglass telecommunications wires allowed people not sitting next to each other to communicate easily and cheaply through email while digitization rendered the paper files in the office obsolete and electronic information ubiquitously available. Add to these advances the fact that superior search engines made it possible to find the proverbial needle in the haystack of data and that growing standardization of systems facilitated the easy real-time connection of not just people but networks. Before long, the time-honored concept of the "work week" had edged toward a 24/7 world. Companies that for other reasons had elected to outsource some of their back office work to India found, to their delight, that it was not only cheaper but more expedient to have work sent out in the evening and be returned in the morning, an otherwise unheard-of luxury. The rules of the game in our new global world had permanently changed—for some for the better, for others for the worse.

India's economic reforms unshackled many eager young professionals who not only spoke excellent English but had received a good, sometimes even superb education at a fraction of the cost of that in Europe or the United States. Education became India's new competitive edge and made its inadequate infrastructure of roads and ports less of a logistical bottleneck. Research and IT services require neither highways nor machinery but computers and Internet lines. Initially, trained programmers were available in India at less than one-tenth of the cost in the United States or Europe. Even today, it may cost around $50,000 to $80,000 to hire an American IT specialist, while it costs $7,000 to $10,000 to hire a similarly if not better qualified Indian developer to perform the same task.

The indisputable foundation of today's tidal wave of IT outsourcing is the fact that American firms spend $2.20 on software and IT services for each $1 they spend on hardware.[5] With Indian salaries about one-sixth the price of similarly qualified U.S. or European engineers, Western firms can no longer ignore the siren song of this huge pool of brainpower available at substantial cost savings. The United States currently provides the largest market for offshoring and outsourcing of services (especially for English-speaking India) with a 70 percent share, followed by Great Britain. But demand in the rest of Europe is catching up quickly. Morgan Stanley economist Stephen Roach has called this phenomenon "a new and powerful global labor arbitrage."[6] Suddenly the old brain drain went into reverse: brainpower is being put to work at home. A study by the Cambridge, Massachusetts-based Forrester Research warned in 2002 that as many as 500,000 IT American jobs might be "offshored" to places like India by 2015. But the Institute of International Economics (IIE) has pointed out that job "losses" are hard to quantify due to the fluctuations of economic cycles and high "job churn." It cites American losses of 500,000 to 1 million jobs from outsourcing since the peak of the technology boom in 2000. In an economy where 130 million are employed, a comparable number of 7–8 percent of all private jobs are created and destructed each *quarter.* While the U.S. economy lost 545,000 jobs in call center and low-wage technology between 1999 and 2003 with average salaries of $25,000, it *gained* 402,000 jobs for computer software engineers and network administrators with average earnings of about $70,000 during the same period, based on Bureau of Labor statistics.[7] IIE makes a compelling argument that while many such white-collar and other jobs are moving abroad, many are also being *created* as a result of the growth in emerging markets.[8]

The unexpected success of the software industry provided a model for other brainpower industries in India to spread their wings globally. Not just manufacturing but services have become mobile and global. Numerous companies like Ranbaxy are involved in drug research. Investment banks are outsourcing some of their stock research and data maintenance. News agencies like Reuters have Indian researchers update information. Highly trained radiologists read and interpret medical scans. Accountants prepare tax statements for smaller auditing firms. Many thousands of young college graduates work nightly in call centers, answering questions on computers or dealing with credit card problems. When I visited one of these many call centers, Mphasis in Bangalore, I found floor upon floor of young college graduates in neat rows of cubicles whose activities were monitored in a room that reminded me of a NASA space center—quite different from the widespread perception of sweatshops.

Indian firms like Infosys have captured only a portion of the work. Companies like General Electric, Intel, Motorola, American Express, Accenture, IBM, EDS, and British Airways all set up their own operations in India in the 1990s and compete for bright graduates. Bangalore, as a sign of the times, now has direct international flights to a growing number of cities around the world. Driving through the city, you wonder whether you are in India or the United States as the signs on brand-new buildings display many familiar brand names. There is little question that the list of services that is now part of the global marketplace is growing every day. Just as China is dubbed the world's manufacturing hub, some are calling India the back office of the world. "Brainpower hub" might be a better name.

The key competitive edge that India continues to maintain over China is the English language, combined with decades of experience with democracy and a stream of graduates from elite universities. However, this edge has been dramatically blunted by China's awesome drive to improve its infrastructure, at just about any cost. Anyone who visits both countries knows that India faces a serious competitive threat from China just as the United States and Europe do, because just about everywhere in China the phone lines work, the roads are new, the trains run on time, and the general impression is one of order and security. In equally ancient India, infrastructure is still woefully behind. Roads and ports are congested, there is a lack of mass transportation, and a sense of urban decay—a contrast literally sensed by the nostrils—frequently overpowers the flashy go-go high-tech veneer of its teeming cities. Although China remains well ahead, in the past few years, India has begun an ambitious effort to deal with this infrastructure gap. Major new highways are under construction, new mass transit systems are planned for five cities, and mobile phone towers are sprouting in many areas.

China is ahead of India on most parameters*

	China	India
Population (Billion)	1.3	1.0
Urban population (% to total)	32	28
Net birth rate (per 1000)	8	16
Population below poverty line (%)	10	25
GDP per capita-PPP(US$/ person)	4,324	2,420
Household savings rate (% of GDP)	12	24
Electricity production (Bn kWH)	1,347	527
Port handling capacity (Mn Tons)	1,426	287
Expressways (1000 Km)	>16	<1
Exports (US $ Bn)	266	61
FDI inflow (US $ Bn)**	46.8	3.4
Adult literacy (%)	84	57
Education expenditure (% of GNP)	2	3

Source: World Development Indicators, The World Bank; CIA Factbook
*Data as of 2001; ** Data as of 2002

The New York Times reports that forward looking Indian companies like software powerhouse Infosys keep a close eye on China. Salkumar Shamanna, head of human resources for Infosys in China, explained his firm's recent decision to invest $65 million to expand its facilities in China, construct a new corporate campus in Pudong (a part of Shanghai), and hire thousands of new low-cost Chinese software engineers according to the same harsh calculus that caused Infosys to flourish in its home country: "Today, options for people are increasing in India so rapidly that hiring has become a matter of who's willing to overpay the most." At one Infosys corporate campus in the Indian city of Mysore, as well as the firm's sprawling headquarters in Bangalore, a *Times* reporter observed hundreds of the new Chinese hires "most of them recruited from its best universities . . . taking training classes in English."[9]

INFOSYS TECHNOLOGIES
Programmers to the World

No experience in bustling Bangalore so vividly illustrates the surreal contrasts on view in India today as the agonizingly slow rush-hour car trip through the city's congested, noisy, and polluted streets to the calm, squeaky-clean corporate campus of software outsourcing pioneer Infosys. When it first opened in 1995, the firm's new headquarters lay some fifteen miles outside the city center. Today urban sprawl has extended out to reach it.

The suburban landscape surrounding the provincial government-sponsored, 330-acre Electronics City industrial park to which Infosys relocated is now filled with American-style subdivisions that would not look out of place in Palo Alto. Today, Electronics City is also the Bangalore address of Hewlett-Packard, Motorola, Siemens, Wipro, and Satyam. The development of a suburban commercial zone to rival the city center's centuries-old core, combined with the return of thousands of Indian software engineers from overseas, has created a new Americanized India that epitomizes its startling leap from bureaucratic past to a possible future as a full-fledged member of the post-industrialized world.

A CAPITALIST IN MIND AND A SOCIALIST AT HEART

Infosys's lush and well-watered corporate campus (in a region habitually roasted by droughts) boasts all the predictable amenities, including cafeterias and restaurants, a gymnasium, pool hall, basketball and volleyball courts, a mini golf course, a sauna, a library, a videoconferencing center, and classrooms named after Nobel laureates. The overwhelming presence is of bright college students continuing their top-notch educations in "the real world," not unlike the young people one might meet at Microsoft. Narayana Murthy is the principal founder of the firm, one of India's largest outsourcers with the title of chairman[10] and "chief mentor" now that he (not unlike Bill Gates of Microsoft) has passed the operational reins and CEO title to his younger co-founder Nandan Nilekani. "I am a capitalist in mind and a socialist at heart," Murthy brightly announced at the outset of one of our conversations—an unusual statement for the head of a major corporation who happens to be one of India's richest men, but also a sincere one.

The first time Murthi and I met, at an India Growth Fund board meeting we attended together in the early 1990s, I was immediately impressed by the polite but pointed questions he asked on a wide range of subjects, from benchmarking to transparency and corporate governance. Today, Murthy is the role model for every bright Indian student, voted several times as India's best CEO and named by Time/CNN as one of the twenty-five most influential global executives. Even if he is genuinely humble, that doesn't mean he fails to grasp the fact that humility—particularly in spiritually inclined India—can be a useful approach to quietly wielding enormous power and influence behind the scenes.

The simple secret of Infosys's success is that Narayana Murthy and his co-founders not only spotted the opportunity in "cheap brainpower" as early as the 1980s, but that their collective "skill sets" left them in a position to do something about it.

Murthy was a bright student who studied electrical engineering and received a degree in computer science from the Indian Institute of Technology in Kanpur, one of seven IITs founded by Prime Minster Pandit Nehru, another socialist of high ambition. But after working as a programmer in Paris on the Sophia software project for handling air cargo at the newly opened Charles de Gaulle Airport in 1976, Murthy returned to India deeply disillusioned with socialism. The international bid had been awarded to an American firm but the French government had insisted on the participation of a French IT design firm that was supposed to gain experience. Curiously, Murthy was part of the "French" team. As he told me: "I met many French Communists during my days in Paris but came to the conclusion that the only way to fight poverty was by creating good jobs. I wanted to conduct an experiment."

What little dwindling enthusiasm he retained for his socialist past promptly evaporated after he was arrested and jailed overnight in Bulgaria on the train back to India, when its secret service overheard some innocuous statements that were considered controversial by the local Communist authorities.

Neither he nor the other six founders of Infosys had the money to start Infosys in 1981, but Murthy's wife Sudha, a bright computer engineer at the Tata Group, came to the rescue with her secret nest egg of Rs 10,000 ($500). Today, she is the driving force behind the Infosys Foundation, a charitable organization focused on improving life for India's rural poor, to which Infosys donates 1.5 percent of its net profits.

A TOUGH START BEFORE THE ECONOMIC REFORMS

Having an idea is different from making it work in a difficult environment. Infosys was anything but an instant success. The Indian business environment was far from favorable in Murthy's youth to the growth of a small software company from obscurity to world-class status. Competitive edge, global orientation, quality control, and client orientation were not the watchwords of the day. The Indian economy was shut tight as a drum; the notoriously sluggish bureaucracy often succeeded in stifling, if not strangling, business initiative through a dizzying welter of licenses and regulation. Murthy recounted to me how "it would take two to three years to even get a phone line, and international telecommunications were prohibitively expensive and difficult. Importing a computer required a license that took forty visits all the way to Delhi and more than three years. There was no venture capital. Banks wanted collateral against which to lend that we, as a software firm, did not have. Because the currency was not yet convertible, even an application to travel abroad took more than a week. When I tell this to my children now, they can't believe it."

> *Infosys went from $2 million in sales in 1991 and $100 million in 1999 to $2 billion in 2005.*

The fact that India was virtually strangling its productive sector in red tape actually provided an opportunity for the little-noted software sector to flourish. "While it is not a zero-sum game, the fact that manufacturing in India suffered from lack of infrastructure, a long supply line, and red tape made our factories less efficient. This led to a migration of the best brains in the country to the IT services sector."

Lacking available funds, the infant Infosys joined forces with a small American software company, Databasics Corporation, which provided support for Murthy in India while six of his co-founders labored on software projects in New York. After ten years, the firm had slowly built up to $2 million in annual revenues and employed one hundred people. In the closed Indian economy, corruption flourished, while private conglomerates and state enterprises formed an impenetrable network that was inefficient and heavily protected. Then even more than now, roads, power, and telecommunications were all woefully inadequate to commercial development.

In another perverse way, the existence of government restrictions and the reaction of multinationals against them provided young software companies in India with an unanticipated edge. IBM pulled out of the country in 1977 after being faced with a demand by the socialist government of then-Prime Minister Morarj Desai to renounce its majority ownership or be sent packing. IBM chose to leave. "Is IBM smarter or is India smarter?" the prime minister is said to have asked a senior IBM executive, whose no doubt sputtering response "has been lost to history," according to *Wired* magazine.[11]

The resulting vacuum left by IBM gave smaller Unix machines and other minicomputers a chance to fill in the gap. Indian companies were quick to spot the opportunities these cheaper, more accessible computers afforded, while Indian software code-writers acquired a well-deserved reputation for improvising simple, streamlined, highly sturdy and practical code. IBM's departure created an opportunity for an entire generation of young, highly trained computer engineers from the Institutes of Technology (IITs) and numerous local engineering colleges to flourish without competition from prestigious foreign firms.

Although Tata Consulting Services, from the venerable Tata Group, took an early lead, it would take practical visionaries from outside the inbred "club" of Indian business to spot the new opportunities emerging in the IT sector subsequent to IBM's and other foreign firms' abrupt departure. These visionaries had to ignore conventional wisdom, demonstrate confidence in their ability to do things cheaper and better, gain experience working with an international clientele, and have the stamina to resist the demands of petty corruption. Offshore software development did not take off quickly or immediately. It took Infosys nearly two decades of persistence to win the confidence of initially skeptical clients.

A POSTER CHILD
IN THE INDIAN ECONOMIC REFORM STORY

By 1991, the Indian economy was finally liberalized and opened up in a desperate response to a serious foreign exchange crisis that brought India to the verge of bankruptcy. Licenses were no longer required. Companies were allowed to do new share issues at market prices rather than at par. Trips to Delhi were no longer needed as local government authorities could give most needed approvals. A convertible currency made business dealings, finance, and travel less onerous. Murthy calls it "the finest thing that ever happened to business in India. There was much less friction and bureaucracy, the market became the leveler, and quality and competence came into play.

Infosys is the best example of all that came from the 1991 reforms." True
enough, after a decade of frustration and slow growth, revenues soared to
$100 million in 1999 (before Y2K put India on the map). As Murthy put it:
"It took us ten years before the reforms to grow fifteen times from $130,000
to $2 million in revenues, but in the past fourteen years since the opening up
of the economy we have grown a thousand times. That is a good indicator of
how free markets give you the opportunity to grow."

It was not that Murthy's beliefs and faith in the future were never tested.
"In 1990, we received an offer from a major company to buy us out for $1
million. Some of my colleagues felt we should accept what looked like a
huge amount of money at that time. There was a heated discussion and I
finally told everyone I would buy them out if they wanted. That did it. We
never sold. Imagine that we would have!" Infosys had a market value of
$18 billion as of December 2005. As Murthy put it, "For me it came down
to what my father had always told me: if you look for respect, everthing
else will become easy. More than anything, the respect from Indian society
was important to me. I believe that we are the most respected company in
India now—and respected around the world."

From a work force of less than 4,000 in 1999, Infosys has grown to over
49,000 employees today, and is India's leading software exporter. The first
Indian firm to be listed on NASDAQ, Infosys has enjoyed an amazing 71
percent annualized growth of net income over the past five years. The
company realized early on that the country's rapidly growing pool of
bright graduates could prosper in a virtual world. Although it was neither
the first nor, for a long time, the largest source of offshore talent to the
developed world, Infosys is today the country's most impressive IT services firm, leveraging India's massive pool of talent to achieve 2005 sales of
$2.1 billion with net profits of $551 million. Infosys is also remarkable for
gradually moving up the value chain, and expanding into more complex
and lucrative businesses such as IT consulting. Despite the political rhetoric against outsourcing in the West, business is booming.

While the shift of *manufacturing* to low-cost locations abroad has obviously been going on for decades, a similar shift in *services* was regarded as
unlikely, because conventional wisdom long held that they were too
closely integrated with other business functions to be as easily outsourced
as the production of sneakers or notebook computers. Once again, conventional wisdom proved wrong.

Infosys continues to lead its competitors in India and elsewhere. After
the urgency of Y2K activities dissipated, the company nimbly changed

gears, survived a tightening of IT budgets in the global economic down-turn in 2001, and continued to function when visas in the United States became harder to get post-9/11. Clearly, the company's success has not been an accidental by-product of the global IT outsourcing trend but is based on hiring and nurturing top-notch staff, being obsessed with process discipline, benchmarking against the most demanding standards in the world, and ensuring that everyone in the organization believes in a corporate culture of transparency and meritocracy.

Infosys believes that a company cannot be world-class without excellent financial transparency and has become well recognized for the quality of its financial statements, guidance to investors, and even its user friendly and informative website: www.infosys.com.

Success Factors

- *Management with unusual vision and commitment to meritocracy*
- *Hiring and nurturing the "best and the brightest" for a world-class work force*
- *A corporate culture stressing integrity, imagination, and speedy adaptation*
- *An uncompromising focus on process discipline*
- *Solid, well-diversified client relationships with high retention*
- *Unusually good corporate governance and transparency*

HIRING AND NURTURING THE BEST AND THE BRIGHTEST

Ever since his early socialist days, Murthy understood that imaginative thinkers required freedom to flourish, and that wealth could not be distributed without first being *created*. Back in India, Murthy had an unpleasant interaction with his boss at an Indian IT firm, who made it clear to him that he was being paid not so much to make a meaningful contribution as simply to "do as he was told." These experiences stayed with Murthy, and helped shape his attitude toward running Infosys. He was determined to create a company that valued people purely on merit rather than background and that would not only turn in strong profits but would do so in an ethical way. This philosophy (not unlike Hewlett-Packard's storied HP Way) persists within the company today.

> *Murthy did not fear people who were smarter than he was—rather, he embraced them.*

Hiring at Infosys is highly selective: less than 1 percent of the more than one million people who apply each year for jobs receive offers. Management and clients alike look on this extremely talented pool of employees as the company's greatest asset. From the beginning, Murthy hired engineers from the preeminent IITs, convinced that the most important element of a successful company was the quality of its people. Unlike many other managers in India at the time, Murthy did not fear people who were smarter than he was, but rather embraced them and gave them the room and the freedom to thrive. In 1985, he was instrumental in creating the "learnability test," a series of IQ puzzles used to test a job candidate's ability to extract information from one situation and apply it to another. This test is still in use today as an integral piece of the recruitment process.

> *Infosys received 1 million job applications in 2003. Fewer than 1 percent were accepted.*

Right from the start, Murthy realized that a strong, effective work force meant not just *hiring* the best and the brightest—an even bigger challenge was *retaining* them. Murthy was deeply concerned with keeping his staff happy and motivated. Anyone arriving through the congested streets of Bangalore on the main campus of Infosys suddenly feels in a different world and there is no question that this must be a big draw for India's bright, young "Infoscions." The huge main campus at global headquarters in Bangalore wants to rival Microsoft's in Seattle. Infosys has many such campuses throughout India that have helped create a collegial and friendly environment, a place where performance, continuous learning, and the free flow of ideas are valued. Another key benefit offered by Infosys is its employee stock option plan, common in the software industry but still a novelty in India when Infosys launched it in 1993. In addition, awards to top performers at Infosys are handed out by every business unit each quarter. Annual awards of excellence are presented by the chairman to the highest performers and awardees are recognized in the company annual report. All of this makes Infosys one of the most sought-after companies by India's smartest graduates, and the company has consistently been rated the #1 Indian employer across various sur-

> *"When IBM and Digital came to Bangalore, I decided that we should not try to keep them out but play by their rules and learn lessons from them. If you can't compete with [multinationals] in India, you can't compete with them anywhere."*
>
> —*Narayana Murthy*

veys. In an industry where staff turnover is usually 15–20 percent, Infosys has managed to keep its attrition rate to 10 percent.

Murthy told me proudly how everyone warned him that "your staff will leave in droves as soon as multinationals discover India's brainpower assets," but that has not happened. "It was a question of mind-set. When IBM, Digital, etc., came to Bangalore, I was the chair of our industry association. We could have pleaded with the government to keep them out or we could have thrown in the towel. I decided that we should not be afraid but play by their rules and learn their lessons. After all, if you can't compete with them even in India, you can't compete with them anywhere. From day one I believed in benchmarking on a global scale. The result was that we became much more open-minded, discussion-oriented, and 'walked the talk' of our convictions on meritocracy, speed, and imagination. Only when the leaders do so will everyone on your staff believe in your dream. But you can never stop."[11]

NEAR-OBSESSION WITH PROCESS DISCIPLINE.

Both Nandan Nilekani, a founder and now CEO of Infosys, and Satyendra Kumar, head of quality, have expressed their belief that "each of the founding members is close to being obsessed with process discipline."[12] The management goes to great lengths to ensure that this focus on process discipline is a mind-set that permeates the entire company. As a result, process has become a way of life at Infosys. Management spends as much as one quarter of its time dealing with issues such as setting quality and process goals, monitoring quality performance, guiding various improvement initiatives, and attending management reviews. The founders conduct regular "values" workshops and participate in monthly Management Council meetings chaired by Nilekani. The programs for these meetings are planned as far as eighteen months in advance and participation is mandatory.

> *"Each of the founding members is close to being obsessed with process discipline."*
> —*Nandan Nilekani, CEO, Infosys*

CUSTOMER RETENTION

Infosys has long understood that it must constantly move up the value chain beyond the rapidly commoditizing body-shop applications of design and maintenance in order to retain its competitive advantage. Few other Indian software companies can match its broad range of IT business solutions, including software package implementation, engineering and testing services, the more lucrative consulting and engineering services, and a recent move toward helping companies develop a vertical market strategy.

The trust clients have in Infosys shows in its impressive client retention rate of over 90 percent and the fact that it has billed more hours than its Indian competitors for work done in India (which is generally more profitable) vs. in clients' offices. Among its clients are companies such as AT&T, Reebok, J.P. Morgan, Goldman Sachs, and Verizon. This client base has been rapidly growing, from 145 in 1999 to over 350. On top of its strong growth, Infosys has been careful to keep its client portfolio broadly diversified. In 1997 Infosys refused to take more business from GE, one of its key clients, and held firm when GE balked. Infosys now has thirty sales offices in seventeen countries and twenty-six global software development centers.

Infosys has grown into a major player in the global IT software and services industry. The firm is a shining example of how the willpower, dedication, and vision of a few can infect an entire company, and how strong business principles help rather than hurt business success. As Murthy puts it: "We always ask ourselves the question: are we doing things faster today than yesterday? Are we bringing better ideas? Are we executing better? In the end, the success of a business should be judged by its longevity."

An Investor's View

The Bull Case	The Bear Case
• A *long record of growth and profitability*	• *No bargain, a well recognized success story*
• *Successful at scaling up the business*	• *Many new players are now crowding the field*
• *Able to select and nurture the brightest graduates*	• *Compensation pressures are rising*

- *Clients are loyal and pay a premium*
- *Significant growth potential remains*
- *Margins are always under pressure*
- *Industry is maturing*

Lessons

- *Value systems can make or break a business.*
- *Creating a mind-set that seeks global benchmarking builds confidence.*
- *Good corporate governance is a sign of integrity and often helps the stock price.*
- *There's no need to wait for others in an industry or home market to become transparent—it is a goal worth pursuing by itself.*
- *Scalability is key to the success of a growing business.*
- *The key question is: are we doing things better today than yesterday, bringing better ideas, executing better?*
- *The ultimate test of a business is its longevity.*

RANBAXY LABORATORIES, LTD
From Bulk and Generics to Full-Scale Drug Inventions

"We can't be satisfied with just reengineering drugs whose patents will soon expire nor with being the ninth largest generics company in the American market," insists Brian Tempest, an Englishman who, during my early 2005 visit, was the CEO[13] of Ranbaxy Laboratories. Within a remarkably short period of time, this firm has pole-vaulted from a small, basic pharmaceutical company producing largely for the local market into a global generics company. Tempest, a thirty-three-year veteran of the drug industry with a PhD in chemistry from Lancaster University, held major positions with industry giants Beacham, GD Searle (where he presented his budgets to then-CEO Donald Rumsfeld) and Glaxo Holdings before joining Ranbaxy in 1995.

"We certainly have the research talent and, with $1 billion in sales, we are now big enough to take chances on developing our own drugs," Tempest told me. Earlier, he had announced a hike of the firm's R&D spending to 10 percent of sales (from 7 percent now) so that 40 percent of revenues will come from its own drug inventions.

Tempest firmly intends to grow Ranbaxy into a $5 billion company within the next seven years. "Otherwise," he noted grimly, "we will never be a big enough player to be taken fully seriously." As a sign of his seriousness about playing with the big boys, he would be flying to the United States the week after our meeting to attend the annual get-together in San Diego "of the five or so largest buyers from the major drug store chains, who together purchase 80 percent of all drugs in the United States." Because the industry he plays in is consolidating so rapidly, Tempest is convinced that Ranbaxy must grow rapidly or risk being swallowed up or sidelined and marginalized as an almost-contender.

Copying or reverse engineering patented drugs and selling them in their home market (in blatant violation of intellectual property rights) used to be the main activity of nearly all small Indian pharmaceutical companies. This was the default position of the drug industry in emerging markets generally. The appeal of the generics market, growing R&D efforts and manufacturing expertise, and a tightening of intellectual property protection laws in India in 2005 have all challenged the Indian drug industry to move beyond the manufacturing of generics into the costlier and trickier business of proprietary drug research, testing, distribution, and production.

Making bulk raw materials for drugs is one thing. Becoming a major presence in the generics market is another. Inventing proprietary new drugs is an even more difficult process, which is why it remains dominated worldwide by a comparative handful of huge multinational pharmaceutical firms. Ranbaxy does all three quite capably, but Dr. Tempest makes it clear that his firm is putting a lot of effort into making this last great leap forward in a big way. To put such matters in a global perspective, and to see where Dr. Tempest is coming from and where he hopes to be heading, Ranbaxy's R&D budget will, in seven years, still be less than 10 percent of Pfizer's $5 billion budget today. G.V. Prasad, CEO of Dr. Reddy's Laboratories (one of India's other leading drug companies), has told pretty much the same story to investors and the press: "If you want to be a serious pharmaceutical company, you have to play in drug discovery."[14]

Ranbaxy Laboratories was established in 1961 and went public in 1973. The singular event that catapulted Ranbaxy from small local generics manufacturer to big global generics manufacturer with ambition to do greater things occurred in 1984, when the U.S. Congress passed the Hatch-Waxman Act. Although heavy lobbying by the pharmaceutical industry added provisions to protect innovation in the brand name industry, the main aim of the act was to promote the entry of cheaper generic drugs into the market. Key measures in the landmark legislation to make it more attractive for generics producers to enter the lucrative U.S. market were (1) the right to develop generics prior to patent expiration without having to undergo large and prohibitively costly clinical trials and (2) the right to six months of competition-free marketing for the first generic producer who filed and successfully challenged the validity of a brand drug patent.

In 1987 Ranbaxy became the largest manufacturer of antibiotics in India when it set up a modern plant in the Punjab to make bulk raw materials for drugs (called active pharmaceuticals ingredients or APIs) that received approval from the Food and Drug Administration (FDA) for the American market the next year. In 1990 it received its first U.S. patent for Doxycycline.

In 1994, Ranbaxy entered the U.S. generics market with the filing of five abbreviated new drug applications (ANDAs). Today, it files over twenty-eight applications each year that typically take seventeen months to receive approval. In comparison, Israel's Teva, the largest generics company in the world, files thirty to thirty-five American applications each year. Ranbaxy's specialty is antiinfectives such as Amoxicillin and Cipro but it also makes central nervous system drugs, gastrointestinal products, cardiovasculars, and antiinflammatories, prepared in bulk or in all the ready-made forms of capsules, tablets, bottles, and injectables. Its pipeline of first-to-file applications includes blockbuster anticholesterol drugs like Lipitor with its $8 billion market. It tries to specialize in generics that are difficult to develop (like isotretinoin, sold under the brand name Accutane). Ranbaxy has developed enough of a reputation that it now even cooperates with major pharmaceutical companies like Tempest's former employer Glaxo, whose blockbuster patents Ceftin and Augmentin Ranbaxy has challenged.

Even the threat of frequent patent-infringement litigation can no longer stop the momentum of generics, because the skyrocketing cost of pharmaceuticals has led to mounting pressures on governments worldwide to capture the cost savings offered by generic drug producers through legislative reform and deregulation. As a result, since 1996 sales from the once fledgling generics market have grown at a rate of 16 percent, much faster than the 6 percent growth for the brand name market. The share of generic drugs in the U.S. market, the largest market for generic drugs, climbed from 19 percent in 1984 to 51 percent in 2003. The share of generics is set to grow: between 1995 and 1999 only $10 billion in drug patents expired, but this number will swell to $82 billion between 2002 and 2007.

"Backward integration is the key to streamlining the process," Dr. Tempest tells me. By performing every step from producing the active ingredient to processing, manufacturing, and delivering the finished dosage form, Ranbaxy has total and unusual control of all the steps its products go through. Not surprising for an emerging market company, it has a special interest in malaria for which it has developed a synthetic form of artemisinin, a Chinese drug used in areas that have become resistant to older generations of malaria drugs. The new medicine is not only cheaper but needs to be taken for fewer days. In brand name products, the company's most promising drug is RBx 14255 for infectious diseases.

As India's largest pharmaceutical company with nationwide drug distribution in a crowded field, the firm now has plants in seven countries and exports to over seventy. Overseas markets account for 78 percent of sales, led by the United States with 36 percent. Interestingly, it was the first company I ever visited that had a "formal strategy" to become a major presence in the BRICS countries (Brazil, Russia, India, China, and South Africa) which are already their second largest combined market with 26 percent of total sales, including 20 percent in its home country. For example, Ranbaxy is the largest foreign supplier of generics in Brazil. It is strengthening its position in Europe where it took over RPG Aventis SA to become a leader in the French generics market. Europe is a large potential market for the company, as European governments are growing increasingly interested in generic drugs to save on huge and rising public health costs. In fact, the European generics market is slated to grow by 10 percent annually to a size of $5 billion in 2006.

As more and more consumers and countries turn to cheaper generic pharmaceuticals in an effort to avoid increasingly expensive brand name drugs, Ranbaxy is following close on the heels of Teva in Israel in submitting new generic drugs for approval to the FDA and to European and BRICS authorities well before patents expire on brand-name drugs. It produces them in India (in FDA approved plants) at a fraction of the price.

An Investor's View

The Bull Case	The Bear Case
• *A growing company*	• *Like many drug companies, Ranbaxy is highly valued*
• *A strong product portfolio*	• *Outcome of new approvals is always uncertain*

- *Strong commitment to new drug inventions*

- *Ranbaxy is a major generics company*

- *Drug research is prohibitively expensive if not resulting in blockbusters*

- *But not the largest in a consolidating industry*

Lessons

- *A legislative change halfway across the globe may open up huge new opportunities to alert emerging market companies.*
- *Only a strong commitment to R&D allows a company in the drug industry to compete globally.*
- *Just focusing on developed markets (or the home market) is not enough. Companies must develop strategies to conquer the new markets of rising economic powers.*
- *Having experienced international managers within the leadership team is key to becoming a globally successful company.*

CHAPTER 12

New Global Media Stars

Mexico's Televisa, India's Bollywood, and Korea's game makers appeal to worldwide audiences

Strategy

- *Being in touch with local culture and language increasingly matters while going global in the Emerging Markets Century*

Not long ago, I found myself seated at a dinner party in Washington beside a silver-haired congressman obviously intrigued by the rapid rise to power of emerging Asia. Yet when I told him about my recent visits to Asian companies, which were showing signs of becoming leaders in technology, design, and even fashion, he sighed skeptically. "I'll believe it when I see people watching Chinese and Indian movies."

By "people" the congressman obviously meant American citizens. From his inside-the-beltway perspective, the rising strength in the global media universe of India's burgeoning "Bollywood," the exploding world-wide popularity of Hong Kong–produced cinema, combined with a comparable stream of new international hits from Shanghai, could somehow still be pigeonholed into a narrow slot labeled "marginal, off the radar screen, of no real importance in the greater scheme of things."

Talk about conventional wisdom getting it wrong.

The congressman had moved on to the next subject before I had a chance to tell him that today more people watch Bollywood movies than Hollywood movies, that Mexican TV shows are wildly popular beyond the Spanish-speaking world, and that Chinese movies have huge audiences both at home and abroad. Demographics matter in media. I could have also reminded him that Hollywood only gained its dominance in Europe after

248

the recipients of Marshall Plan aid were forced to import only Hollywood movies. That recollection might not have played well in the nation's capital, where much is made of the French being culturally protective, despite the fact that foreign films encounter such major distribution roadblocks in the United States that their audience share has plummeted from 10 percent to 1 percent over the past decade.[1] This was not the first time that I had run into an otherwise broad-minded citizen of the world who was oblivious to the fact that the dominance of American companies was slipping in ways hitherto unimagined.

As Joseph Nye of the Kennedy School of Government at Harvard has pointed out, "soft power" matters as much as economic and military power in the dominance of nations. The culture business produces and reproduces the images, symbols, and ideas of just about everyone on the planet, and frequently sends those images and beliefs around the world for other cultures to consume at their leisure. And in perhaps no other industry on earth are the current tensions between globalization and local affinity more profoundly pronounced than in the mass media. While major media players all aspire to be global producers, most must still tailor their products to appeal to local tastes. Striking the right balance between the two poles typically spells the difference between success and failure in the culture industry.

Just as the worldwide electronics and high-tech industries have long emulated Silicon Valley, so the global media conglomerates have created Hollywood knock-offs around the world to produce their own versions and visions of the myths and symbols that audiences will line up for (and pay handsomely) to listen to and see. But even as they admire Hollywood's commercial clout, many more tradition-bound cultures are horrified by what they see reflected in its offerings. While the accoutrements of the digital age—television sets, DVD players, mobile phones, movie screens, even Internet cafes, Blackberries and satellite dishes—have all advanced into the remotest corners of the globe, the pull of local language and culture has not retreated in the face of encroaching modern technology. In some cultures, in fact, nostalgia for the glories of past history has actually grown in the face of the relentless onslaught of Western media images. Such cultural defensiveness frequently goes hand in hand with traditional concerns about the seductive impact of consumerism, violence, and sex in cinema and TV, and the impact of mind-numbing video games. Among the other pertinent facts I would like to have shared with my skeptical dinner partner that night were the following:

- Latin American *telenovelas* currently attract an audience estimated by *Foreign Policy* magazine at 2 billion and climbing.
- Playing Internet games in huge distributed groups is a fashion raging in Korea and China that is likely to spread east to west, as opposed to west to east.
- News in the Middle East is now more likely to come from Al Jazeera than either local government-controlled stations or CNN.
- Local business news in various Asia capitals is often far more extensive than in Europe or the United States.
- Venezuela is trying to capture the Latin American market with a new 24/7 news channel.

BOLLYWOOD

Monsoon Wedding (a low-cost Bollywood production) and *Bend It Like Beckham* (produced by an Indian-born director) gave Western viewers a chutney-flavored taste of what Asian audiences numbering in the millions have long recognized: the distinctive charm and flair of Indian cinema. Yet another Bollywood movie, *Lagaan,* was nominated as best foreign film at the 2002 Academy Awards. Indian director Deepa Mehta's film trilogy, *Earth, Fire,* and *Water,* has recently attracted attention in the West.

Movies were long thought (by Westerners) to be the exclusive preserve of Hollywood. But "Bollywood," named after the center of the Indian film industry Bombay (now Mumbai), currently produces more movies (nearly a thousand per year) and sells more tickets than Hollywood. In 2001, as many as 3.6 billion tickets were sold for Bollywood movies compared with 2.6 billion to Hollywood moviegoers.[2] Viewers are clearly massing in vast numbers, not just in urban centers but in rural communities where Bollywood melodramas have been popular for decades.

Nearly as old as Hollywood, Bollywood produced twenty-five or more movies by the 1920s and put out about two hundred annually by the 1930s. In recent years, the Indian film industry has been growing at a healthy annualized clip of 15 percent. Its stars are revered as much by poor, uneducated farmers as they are by well-off, young, urban call center attendants and software professionals. Some of the increasing sums of disposable income not spent on cell phones, motorcycles, cars, and homes are now available for entertainment, allowing room for ticket prices to begin to catch up with richer countries. As a result, populations in India and China have begun to consume media products in significant quantities, tilting the balance of economic power toward Mumbai and Shanghai, and away from New York, London, and Los Angeles.

Bollywood's global revenues of under $1.5 billion may still seem small in comparison to the $50 billion-plus earned in Hollywood,[3] but as audience numbers and ticket prices (now Rs 30–120 or $0.70–2.80) inevitably rise, these modest box office revenues will expand exponentially in the coming decades. Like their Hollywood equivalents, Bollywood movies are beginning to earn increasing amounts (now well over $100 million) from DVD and TV sales. Yet Bollywood still has a long way to go before it threatens Hollywood's dominance: its top-grossing 2004 movie, the love story *Veer Zaara* (named after the two lead characters) earned a mere $15 million at the box office. Of this, about half came from the domestic Indian market, which remains a drop in the bucket compared to the nearly $400 million hauled in by *Shrek 2,* Hollywood's highest-grossing film of that year.

Most Indian movies are tailor-made for mass appeal and stick to tried-and-true formulas of love triangles and family dramas interspersed with occasional outbreaks into dance and singing. Well-known stars are referred to as *"paisa vasool"* ("money's worth"), a home-grown version of the Hollywood epithet "bankable," out of respect for their multiple talents and broad appeal. The new urban dwellers seem to want mostly more of the same familiar work, but there is a rising interest among the more sophisticated set for artier films, a refined form of Bollywood output for which veteran filmmakers like Satyajit Ray have long been lionized.

Bollywood is not an exact replica of Hollywood, but rather resembles the Hollywood of years past, before the advent of the "majors." There are no major studios in Mumbai, the industry remains poorly organized, and much of the production and distribution capacity has been quasi-controlled by organized crime. Despite the difficulties, banks and venture capital firms have finally begun to provide financing. Few movies ever become profitable, in part because the public demands marquee-name stars, who typically command as much as 40 percent of the movie budget, earning more than twice the Hollywood average.

Bollywood films are mainly produced in Hindi, interspersed with Urdu poetic passages as a nostalgic reminder of former glories. Occasional scenes shot in English rudely yank escapist subcontinental audiences back to modern life. Due to widespread nostalgia for off-limits Kashmir, some key exterior scenes of Bollywood epics are shot in the Swiss Alps.

THE CHINESE MOVIE INDUSTRY

In 2000, *Crouching Tiger, Hidden Dragon* was the best-selling foreign language film in the United States. Although about half of its modest $15 million budget came from Hollywood,[4] it was widely perceived as a Hong Kong production. Its Taiwanese director, Ang Lee, went on to produce *Brokeback Mountain* in the United States for which he won an Oscar as best director. Much as *Monsoon Wedding* did for the Indian film industry, the surprising success of *Crouching Tiger* in Western markets trained a fresh spotlight on the Chinese-language film industry, despite the fact that Hong Kong–produced Kung Fu movies have been popular beyond the Asian hemisphere for years. *Crouching Tiger, Hidden Dragon* not only displayed higher aspirations, creative and commercial, but it fulfilled them magnificently. Just as modern Mumbai built on the traditions of the Bollywood movie boom of the 1930s, modern Shanghai became the center of the Chinese movie industry based on the success of its Depression-era predecessor that flourished on the same site. Over the past few years, Chinese-made movies have made more money at the domestic box office than European or Indian movies, leveraging their vast home market to cover their basic budget, and earning windfall profits overseas.

GROUP INTERNET GAMES

Anyone who drops by an Internet cafe in China will see dozens if not hundreds of young Chinese not only sending email or surfing the Web, but deeply engaged in playing computer games. They aren't playing alone or even in small groups against a handful of competitors but are connected to as many as *several hundred thousand concurrent users*. Get ready for a new techno-term: 3D MMORPG, which stands for "three-dimensional massive multiplayer online role playing games." Even though broadband is not quite as widespread and fast enough for these games to be popular in the United States or Europe, they have become all the rage in Korea, China, and Taiwan.

Video games first gained popularity in Japan and the United States but were exclusively based on individual consoles such as Sony's PlayStation and Microsoft's Xbox. Korea has taken the lead in producing this new type of online game, in which numerous players are simultaneously playing the same game, trying to outsmart or outplay each other.

The popularity of Internet games in Korea should not be surprising, as Korea rolled out broadband faster than the United States and now has a far higher household penetration. Korean game makers like NCsoft and Webzen quickly jumped into this popular area because young Koreans, followed by the Chinese, are among the most active group Internet game players in the world. NCsoft launched its first big hit Lineage as early as 1998, following up with a livelier and more sophisticated version called Lineage II. Both Lineages are medieval fantasies of dungeons and dragons. These remain the most popular group game genre in Korea, but also enjoy numerous followers in China and Taiwan, where a single game may attract as many as 300,000 concurrent users. Lineage's lead designer Hyung Jin Kim and producer James Bae explain that "both Lineages center on castles and the political and economic systems they support. The new edition of Lineage shares the same world view but takes place 150 years earlier."[5]

On the back of the lavish proceeds derived from these two successful games, NCsoft has grown into the world's leading independent online gaming company. According to its founder and CEO Tack Jin Kim, the company is now aggressively targeting the global market, seeking to expand its players in the United States and Europe. Kim had grown bored after creating a successful Korean word processor and developing an Internet portal site at Hyundai Electronics. He kept dreaming of his university days when he played some of the early, primitive games, and yearned to recapture that spirit in a new, more sophisticated offering.

Like many other creative Koreans, it was the Asian financial crisis that gave him the push to set up a new company when his employer abandoned projects he was working on. NCsoft's founder finds it only logical that his games should appeal not just in Asia and the United States but also in Europe because they are so rooted in European medieval history. Redbus Interhouse in Germany, Europe's biggest name in co-location and managed services, provides the backbone of high capacity servers to its audience of online gamers throughout Europe. This is yet another example of a European company supporting the creative inventions of emerging market producers.[6]

The Korean electronic game market is rapidly morphing into one of the largest and most dynamic in the world, closely followed by China where this "addiction" has spread so widely that the authorities regularly speak out about and against it.

GRUPO TELEVISA
Selling Soaps to the World

When Veronica Castro's plane touched down at Moscow's Sheremetyevo Airport in late 1992, she was shocked to see the size of the crowd that had gathered at the gate to watch her disembark. She was even more surprised to be escorted by a large security contingent through the cheering throng and whisked away, to be received like royalty by Russia's top political and economic leaders. For fifteen extra bonus points (and a chance to win a major cash prize in the Emerging Markets Century Sweepstakes), *who* is Veronica Castro?

Before the buzzer rings—and you lose—it may be worth pointing out that this fifty-something Mexico City native may be the most famous Latino actress in the world today. Yet she is that rare anomaly in the global media universe, a brand name and major box-office draw few non-Hispanics (in the United States at least) have ever heard of. Born in 1952, this buxom brunette first gained fame at the age of sixteen by posing nude for the men's magazine *Caballero*. Although she played minor parts in Mexican films from the age of four on, her big break was being cast as the poor orphan maid in *Los Ricos Tambien Lloran* ("The Rich Also Cry"), a 1979 Mexican *telenovela* that became the first true international hit of this uniquely Latin American genre: a big moneymaker not just in Latin America, Spain, and other Hispanic markets, but also a "crossover" hit in dubbed translations in France, Russia, China, Bosnia, Croatia, and the Philippines.

Originally scheduled for once-a-week Saturday showings, its runaway ratings quickly led to it being broadcast five days out of seven, as Russians at every level of society fell madly in love with Veronica Castro's spunky, upwardly mobile, socially challenged lead character, a Cinderella-like maid. On that same whirlwind tour of Russia when she was swamped by legions of fans at the Moscow airport, Castro told a Russian fanzine that she ascribed the universal appeal of her scrappy heroine to the fact that she "knows how to fight for her happiness . . . [she] is both a woman and a winner."[7]

The overwhelming success of Veronica Castro and *The Rich Also Cry* prompted *the Moscow Times* to report: "When the film started, streets became desolate, crowds gathered in stores selling TVs, tractors stopped in the fields and guns fell silent along the Azerbaijani-Armenian front." *Los*

Ricos, as it became known even in overseas markets, decisively swept the U.S.-produced soap *Santa Barbara* off the Russian charts, permanently altering the media landscape by shattering the fiction that the entire world was hankering for American media products, and only had to be shown them to be wowed and won over. Once maybe true, but no longer.

Produced in just about every major Spanish-speaking country as well as Brazil (where they are filmed in Portuguese before being dubbed into Spanish for the Latin American market), *telenovelas* have recently enjoyed stunning popularity in Russia, China, India, Eastern Europe, and in just about every corner of the world, including Africa. Manifestations of the immensity of their cross-over appeal are legendary. After the Chinese police arrested one of our company's Mexican brokers for trying to change money on the black market, his sole punishment (once they discovered that he was Mexican) was being forced to spend a few hours of "prison time" watching the latest episode of a popular Mexican *telenovela* in the company of his enchanted captors.

While Veronica Castro's 1979 *The Rich Also Cry* was wildly popular in such disparate environments as South Africa, Senegal, Bosnia, and China (and quickly became post-Communist Russia's top-rated show), Mexico's 1994 *Miramar* blossomed into an even greater global phenomenon, prompting millions of ardent fans around the world to hit the pause button on their lives during the airing of 148 heart-wrenching episodes. Not only did *Miramar* make a major star out of Mexican pop artist Thalia Sodi, but in the Ivory Coast its episodes were reportedly fortuitously timed away from the Muslim call to prayer so that no one missed out on a single scene.[8]

So how could serialized, stylized, melodramatic *telenovelas* produced in Mexico, but based on a Cuban model, find fans by the millions in Russia, Eastern Europe, India, and China? As a recent article in *Foreign Policy* described it,[9] "When Communism fell, television executives in Eastern Europe and the former Soviet Union faced a crisis. For decades, turning the television dial brought viewers nothing but state-sponsored programming." When those states and the sponsorships that went with them imploded, Latin American producers were quick to fill the gap at bargain-basement prices their United States–based competition proved hard-pressed to meet.

The fact that Mexican, Brazilian, and Venezuelan producers of media were able to deliver high quality at budget prices provided them with a critical edge at a critical time over comparable products made in the

United States and Western Europe. Yet there were even more powerful cultural forces and influences at work in this equation, not the least being that the products emerging from emerging markets producers were culturally more reflective of popular concerns in developing economies than American and Western European TV serials and films, which aim squarely at those nations' vast middle classes.

The Cinderella stories that provide the theme and inspiration of many a Latin American TV serial feature strong, spunky young women from working-class backgrounds whose deepening romantic attachment to a handsome young man of a higher class is thwarted by the machinations of the young man's family (typically his diabolical mother or sisters). Inevitably, the heroine's female rivals use all the sexual wiles at their disposal to thwart true love and make class differences triumph over the heart. Over numerous episodes, the lovers are kept apart by a combination of class and circumstance until in the end true love prevails over prejudice. These dramatic narratives vividly reflect and portray the deep social divisions and wide gaps between rich and poor that characterize developing economies.

The term *telenovela* (derived from the Spanish and Portuguese terms for "novel" and "television") is the Hispanic equivalent of an American soap opera. The origins of this popular genre date back to Colonial Cuba, when the island's patriarchal cigar factory owners realized that an effective way to boost productivity was to hire a story reader *(lector de tobacco)* to help the bored cigar workers wile away the hours as they rolled and shaped tobacco leaves into meticulously hand-crafted cigars. In the 1920s, '30s, and '40s, radio serials produced in Havana supplanted these on-site story readers, giving rise to *"culebrones"* (serpents), radio narratives known for their tendency to tenuously wind like a snake through multiple episodes and plot lines.

In the 1950s, culturally sophisticated Havana became the epicenter of the radio *culebrone,* but the Cuban revolution of 1959 caused a number of well-known women writers of radio soaps such as *Caridad Bravo* and *Delia Fiallo* to migrate to Mexico. As was the case with American soap operas, they found sponsors among American consumer companies. Indeed, the first Mexican *telenovela, Gutierritos,* sponsored by Procter & Gamble, aired in 1960, while the next major Mexican *telenovela, Senda Prohibida* ("Forbidden Path"), was endowed with the enticing slogan, "Your *Colgate* novela."

Today, the indigenous *telenovela* departs from its American soap-opera cousins in a number of critical respects. The most notable differences are that *telenovelas* air during prime time as opposed to daytime, and are designed to appeal equally to men and women. In contrast to the U.S.'s famously open-ended daytime dramas, they always have a distinct beginning, middle, and end.

Despite the intimate involvement of U.S.-based sponsors and their Latin American affiliates, *telenovelas* developed their own thematic integrity. Here is a summary (drawn straight from the Televisa website) of a current *novela* called *Rubi:*

> In Rubi's heart lays a constant fight between every woman's desire to find true love and a desperate obsession for fortune and extravagance. Destiny has blessed Rubi with an extraordinary physical beauty instead of money. She is determined to use her beauty in order to marry a wealthy man who can offer her the life of luxury she so much desires.[10]

Although I've never laid eyes on Rubi I would be willing to bet a hatful of pesos that she ends up getting her handsome, swarthy guy in the end. Unlike the more sexually explicit Brazilian soap operas, the *telenovelas* produced by the Mexican media giant Televisa tend to be romances often laden with social justice overtones, inherently popular—even populist—in their appeal. Emilio Azcarraga Jean, Televisa's young CEO, has observed that "television must show nice stories and give people something to dream of because in everyday life there is already too much suffering."[10] Rich-versus-poor is another resonant theme, in accordance with which Televisa owns two soccer teams. One sports the best players from around the world; another can only afford local players. "There is great rivalry and it works," a Televisa official confided to me. "Everyone [presumably both rich and poor] can identify with their favorite team."

Watched by an eager global audience, the success of this popular genre astonishes left-leaning media commentators who for years have reflexively rued the dominance of Western media in general and American media in particular as a prime example of "cultural imperialism." Indeed, *telenovelas'* triumph has often been cited as a form of "reverse cultural imperialism," in which a mass-appeal product from the developing world trumps its upper-and-middle-class "first world" rival in a real-world imitation of the populist plots of these narratives.

AT THE HEART OF GLOBAL ROMANCE

The sprawling corporate headquarters of Televisa, set high on a rugged hill in Mexico City's chic Santa Fe neighborhood, is a symphony of saturated color. Its pristine plazas, executed with customary finesse by Mexico's leading architect, Ricardo Legoretta, reflect all the cultural influences of modern Mexico, from Mayan to Moorish to Spanish Colonial to the stark Cubistic lines of Pablo Picasso. The outlying Santa Fe neighborhood provides an airy escape from the smoky congestion of the world's megalopolis, with the Mexican headquarters of GE, EDS, IBM, and Daimler-Chrysler all crowded around the palm-tree-studded estate owned by Televisa. The nearby Universidad Iberoamericana, a Jesuit university, is popular with the sort of upper-class Mexicans who fill the ranks of the country's leading media firm, which—not so ironically—derives the lion's share of its revenues by artfully devising media products of intense appeal to the impoverished masses of Latin America.

The rich tangled roots of Mexico's #1 TV broadcaster, the largest media company in the Spanish-speaking world, date back to 1954, when Emilio Azcarraga Vidaurreta, a Mexican radio and movie pioneer, who got his start as the Mexican representative of RCA Victor Records, formed the Telesistema Mexicano network with two associates. After parlaying a lucrative stake in a string of live vaudeville theaters into a controlling interest in a fast-growing cinema chain, Mexico's first media tycoon used his theater chain as a platform to branch out into record and music production, cleverly leveraging his ownership of artists' management firms and artistic rights to promote his talent on his own network of radio stations.

By the advent of World War II, Emilio Azcarraga Vidaurretta controlled, through alliances with CBS and NBC, Mexico's two leading radio networks. Within a decade of the end of World War II he and his family firm owned more than 50 percent of the nation's radio stations along with an estimated 70 percent of national radio revenues.[11] As the nation's leading private broadcaster, Azcarragas enjoyed a cozy relationship with Mexico's ruling PRI party, which dominated Mexican politics virtually unchallenged from the early 1930s to the watershed year of 2000, when the National Action Party (PAN) took over under former Coca-Cola executive Vicente Fox. Few in positions of power down the PRI decades ever thought to challenge the validity of the Azcarraga family's possession of monopolistic media power, which over time swelled into a south-of-the-border empire mirroring the monolithic nature of the one-party state.

After expanding into TV in the mid-1950s with the tacit support of the Mexican government, Azcarraga took strong steps to ensure that Latin American broadcasting entrepreneurs adapted the U.S. commercial broadcasting model as opposed to the noncommercial, government supported, public service model pioneered by the British and other European countries. In 1972, Azcarraga's Telesistema Mexicano took over one of its only real rivals, Television Independiente Mexicano, launched four years earlier by a coalition of Monterrey-based business interests. The new combination was renamed Grupo Televisa. After Emilio Sr. died the following year, control of the family media empire passed into the hands of his oldest male heir, Emilio Azcarraga Milmo, then forty-three, a 1948 graduate of Culver Military Academy in Culver, Indiana.

Nicknamed El Tigre ("The Tiger") for the white streak in his hair as well as for his ferocious manner and reputation for romantic conquests, Emilio Azcarraga Milmo was a family patriarch worthy of his own *tele-novela*—or, for that matter, *Dallas* or *Dynasty*. He was widely held to be the spitting image of his father, not just in looks but in his monarchical, dictatorial managerial style. He married four times; his fourth and final wife, Adriana Abascal, was a former Mexican entrant in the Miss Universe pageant. After serving loyally as his longtime mistress, Adriana finally won the ultimate prize, marrying El Tigre and, in the wake of his death in 1999, becoming one of his numerous heirs.

During his expansive and expensive career as a media tycoon, "El Tigre" spent quite a bit of time across the border tending to his budding U.S.-based Spanish-language TV empire. Branded the Spanish International Network, in 1976 SIN became the first U.S. network to be connected by satellite—long before the Big Three had taken full advantage of this latest advance in broadcast technology. Back at home, El Tigre amused himself by snapping up the sports daily newspaper *El Nacional* along with the largest stadium in the Southern hemisphere, a gaggle of sports teams, publishing and recording companies, a cable television venture, a cellular telephone company, and acre upon acre of premium downtown Mexico City real estate, including the immense HQ in Santa Fe and an equally capacious Hollywood-style studio in the District's equally upscale (yet older) San Angel neighborhood.

When El Tigre died in 1999, he left his twenty-nine-year-old son,

Emilio Azcarraga Jean, a tangled web of conflicting interests that amounted to not much more than a major migraine headache. According to a piece in *The New York Times*, "What he did bequeath to his only son was the presidency of a bloated and stumbling enterprise saddled with debts estimated at $1.3 billion [along with] a tangled estate that quickly generated a struggle among the heirs."[12] El Tigre's embattled heir spent years wrangling with his father's former wives and myriad mistresses (who were as numerous as his entertainment ventures) before finding himself seated—initially rather tenuously—in the saddle.

Success Factors of Televisa

* *The success of telenovelas in the Spanish-speaking world*
* *Dominance in the Mexican media market*
* *An old-style studio system with its own school for future stars*
* *Early recognition of the importance of the U.S. market*
* *Imposition of business discipline on a company with a studio mentality*
* *Active distribution abroad*

At the time, media analysts and observers speculated that the third-generation heir to the family fortune was little more than a spoiled playboy and a lightweight. But shortly after his tumultuous arrival on the scene, he displayed his own patriarchal mettle by issuing two statements, each of which deftly put a strong personal stamp on Televisa's unfolding future:

1. "If someone wants to drink water, they should bring it from their own house."
2. "Our real competitors are Disney and CNN."

In both instances, Emilio Azcarraga Jean was only stating a new if harsh reality: Televisa was no longer a monopoly, and no longer (following the stunning upset of the PRI party in 2000) the pampered pet of the party in power. As we have seen with other emerging markets monopolies, Televisa was obliged to confront the need to refashion itself to adapt to a tougher, more competitive, more unrestrained market. Televisa under Emilio Azcarraga Jean not only flourished in the new atmosphere, but actually emerged as a stronger, leaner, more integrated operation.

From the outset, the brash young Azcarraga intuitively grasped that in a world where Televisa no longer enjoyed an effective monopoly, discipline and performance would have to become not the exception but the rule. "I didn't have a strategy for gaining control," Mr. Azcarraga told *The New York Times,* explaining that upon his succession to the presidency, he owned a mere 10 percent of Televicentro, the holding company that his father had controlled and that, in turn, controlled 26 percent of Televisa. "But I had a strategy for restoring the company."

While his father and grandfather, both archetypal men of their times, had ruled Televisa as lone and distant dictators, the young Azcarraga Jean adopted a more collegial if not exactly easygoing management style. Instead of a one-man dictatorship, he instituted a three-man triumvirate composed of old school buddies and close friends, team-players whom he could implicitly trust as a result of relationships dating back decades.

To all willing to listen, the young CEO made it clear that the sloppy habits of the past would no longer be tolerated. The days of prima donnas, coddled producers, and feudal, baronial studio bosses able to simply shrug off corporate financial controls were over. He laid down a pattern early on by jettisoning battalions of managers chosen by his father, pink-slipping forty-six vice presidents, and revolutionizing the operating culture by imposing strict cost controls and laying off 6,000 of the company's 20,000 employees.[13] Under the new regime, business units were to be held accountable for sales, market share, profit margins, collections, and above all, customer satisfaction. Displaying a wry sense of humor he even joked about dying his hair gray so that investors would take him seriously, but Emilio Azcarraga Jean ultimately proved to be as effective a manager as his formidable father.

Early on, the young Azcarraga was forced to face down members of the powerful Aleman family, longtime major Televisa shareholders and scions of Miguel Aleman Valdes, a former president of Mexico. In a cunning deal that startled observers and dramatically reshaped his public perception, Emilio Azcarraga Jean won the backing of Mexico's most successful business tycoon, Carlos Slim Helu, who had built a vast empire through a series of shrewd investment moves that resembled the style of Warren Buffett, with the telecommunications giants Telefonos de Mexico and America Moviles at its core. Slim not only bought out the Aleman family holdings but guaranteed that he would reliably vote his 23.9 percent block of shares with management. He thus ensured that Azcarraga's hold on Televisa would remain secure as long as he was there to prevent any further instability.

HOLLYWOOD ACROSS THE RUBICON

Televisa has continued to operate like an old-style Hollywood studio long after the decline of the studio system in its own country. Just as Louis B. Mayer's stars were chattels of management, Televisa's stars are made—and if they get ornery, unmade—at the iron will not of talent agents but rather of executive management. Stars and starlets with the temerity to get too big for their britches—in the case of Televisa's wildly popular period pieces, many do wear britches, at least on camera—are known to be dealt with by a strict form of discipline that demands that their characters get into "accidents" and vanish abruptly from the airwaves, perhaps to miraculously return from the dead if they cave to the terms set by their masters.

In keeping with this old-style studio system, Televisa's great trump card is its school for aspiring actresses and actors, the only one of its kind in the Hispanic world. With admission more competitive than Harvard or Yale, each year over 20,000 young would-be stars and starlets apply to "Centro de Estudios Artisticos" (CEA), but only fifty to sixty are accepted for a two-year program that teaches them acting, dancing, makeup and other necessary skills for *telenovela* stardom. For writers, Televisa has regular contests to spot the most promising talent.

TELEVISA'S INFLUENCE IN MEXICO AND ABROAD

When I recently visited Vice President Alfonso de Angoitia, the architect of Televisa's financial restructuring in the spacious boardroom of Televisa, my colleagues and I joked that, with his swarthy good looks and the liquid charm of a matinee idol, he could easily take the place of one of the stars of his own soap operas. "What makes Televisa such an interesting company," de Angoitia observed, "is not only its profound impact on the political and social life of Mexico, but also that we export Mexican culture to virtually every corner of the world. We sell our products to more than one hundred countries, not just our famous soap operas but also Spanish-language children's shows, game shows, reality shows, news, the World Cup, and other soccer matches—all beamed into living rooms around the world. As a result, the way people in other countries now view Mexico has been heavily influenced by Televisa productions."

With its extensive interests in television, radio, and publishing, Grupo Televisa—already the largest media company in the Spanish-speaking world—owns four TV networks with nearly 260 affiliated stations in Mexico. It reaches the Hispanic population in the United States through its partly owned affiliate Univision—for greater control of which it made an unsuccessful tender offer in the spring of 2006. Univision receives over 70 percent of the advertising dollars spent on Hispanic media in the United States.[14] Its original content, including *telenovelas,* comedies, game shows, movies, documentaries, concerts, and sporting events, is sold not just in the Hispanic world but is dubbed into twenty-seven languages. Editorial Televisa, the world's largest Spanish-language magazine producer and distributor, boasts sixty titles in eighteen countries, commanding an approximate annual circulation of 127 million. The company also operates eighty-one radio stations serving thirty-seven Mexican cities. Televisa also owns a 51 percent stake in Mexico's Cablevision, a cable joint venture, a 60 percent stake in Innova, and maintains operational control of the direct-to-home satellite system SKY. Apart from its core operations, Televisa owns an Internet portal, three professional soccer teams, and a feature film production and distribution company.

With its stable dominance of the Mexican TV market—in 2004, Televisa aired 91 out of the top 100 television programs in Mexico—its 70 percent audience share compares to 30 percent commanded by Televisa's only viable rival on the domestic scene, TV Azteca. Owned and operated by the aggressive but unscrupulous entrepreneur Ricardo Salinas Pliego—yet another typical *telenovela* character—TV Azteca once aimed to steal market share from Televisa by inaugurating a new type of edgier, sexier, more violent *novela.* During years of bitter struggle, Azteca aggressively poached Televisa's stars and producers in a blatantly no-holds-barred attempt to conquer a greater chunk of the domestic TV market but Azteca and Televisa some time ago declared an informal truce. "We have both agreed not to fight using prices," notes de Angoitia, "because it won't change our market shares in the long run anyway. Sometimes we even cooperate. For example, we buy the World Cup together and air it at the same time. We both show the national soccer team and we each show half of the local football games. We don't steal talent from each other any more. And as for movies, they have a deal with Disney and we have a deal with Warner."

STRUGGLE FOR CONTROL
OF THE U.S. HISPANIC MARKET

During my visits, Televisa's leaders made no bones about their long-term goal of acquiring a controlling share in one of the richest prizes of the media universe: the leading U.S. Spanish-language TV network Univision. The fast-growing forty-million-plus Hispanic audience in the United States represents aggregate annual spending power of something on the order of $650 billion. Televisa has owned 11 percent of Univision with Venezuela's media firm Venevision owning a similar share. The controlling stake of the voting shares is held by the 75-year-old entrepreneur A. Jerrold Perenchio, a Texas-based promoter of boxing matches and other sporting events who became known as a shrewd dealmaker and protégé of Hollywood legend Lew Wasserman. Univision regularly beats other major channels in the Nielsen ratings, largely due to the popularity of Televisa's soap operas.

Televisa has been engaged in its own soap opera-like duel for control of the U.S. based network. One of the few setbacks suffered by the ferocious El Tigre occurred in 1986, when the U.S. Federal Communications Commission ruled that his effective 75 percent control of the Spanish-language TV network SIN in Texas contravened the 25 percent restriction on foreign ownership of radio and television stations. Heartbroken at being forced to sell SIN to the greeting card company Hallmark, which renamed it Univision. El Tigre could at least console himself that, despite the change of ownership, most of the programming on Univision continued to be provided by Televisa, the most popular content being its trademark *telenovelas.*

"The original sixteen SIN stations became popular because Mexicans on this side of the border have the same likes and dislikes as Mexicans do on the other side," de Angoitia told me. "Even though it is two countries, in reality it is more like two states. Mexicans who come to the U.S. want to see what they were watching in Mexico." In contrast, the new American management installed by Hallmark believed that Hispanic Americans had developed more Anglicized tastes and preferences than their cousins south of the border and made an effort to save money for their financially strapped operations financed with junk debt. Despite the high ratings enjoyed by the Televisa-produced programs, they committed the cardinal commercial sin of shifting a good portion of the programming to shows produced in the United States like *Starsky and Hutch* that were clumsily dubbed into Spanish. According to de Angoitia, they were clueless about what Hispanic viewers really wanted. Mexican Americans had next to no interest in watching shows that were not produced in Latin America and tailored to their specific tastes. The new programming proved commercially disastrous and, four years after they bought it, Hallmark was forced to sell Univision for $550 million[15] to a group that included its original owner Televisa together with the American entrepreneur Jerrold Perenchio and Venezuela's Venevision.

The participation of Jerry Perenchio (as he prefers to be called) was a necessary prerequisite to maintaining a facade of U.S. ownership of the network. In 1996, Televisa merged its ownership in a Spanish-language cable channel called Galavision with Univision, and the combined entity floated an IPO. Perenchio was awarded a sizable block of "super-voting" shares, whose special powers would be destined to dissipate upon either his decision to sell them or his death.

Despite the fact that Televisa provided the overwhelming majority of the successful network's prime-time content, the fifty/fifty royalty arrangement with Televisa and Venevision remained unchanged for a decade in an exclusive programming deal that ran to 2017. In 2003 Emilio Azcarraga Jean decided to play hardball with his American partner and demand higher royalties. Ultimately, the royalty arrangement was renegotiated 60–40 percent in Televisa's favor. In another demonstration of the growing bargaining power of emerging market companies, Televisa yanked NFL football games, including the Super Bowl, off the air in Mexico for an entire season after a thirty-five-year run, until the NFL renegotiated the royalty arrangement.

After its competitor Telemundo came close to bankruptcy in 1992 under the assault of Univision's more successful programs, NBC attempted to gain entry into the hard-fought territory of Spanish-language programming in the United States by acquiring control of Telemundo, backed by the virtually infinite resources of industrial giant GE. Yet according to de Angoitia, who has publicly proclaimed that Telemundo remains a serious threat, "We killed Telemundo with our novelas. Our programming is a tested product. Whatever works in Mexico works in the U.S. As long as Mexicans continue to be the dominant population within the Hispanic community in the U.S., our programming works. In Latin America, Mexican Spanish has become the neutral accent. Mexican programs can be used in any place in Latin America. Even though they can tell it is Mexican, it's the most neutral one."

In February 2004, Emilio Azcarraga Jean earned extra space in gossip and business columns worldwide when he married his blushing bride who was rumored to be American, but is actually Mexican, before an audience of 1,500 guests at his palatial Mexico City residence. This led to speculation in the business press that he would strategically pull a "Rupert Murdoch" to quickly gain U.S. citizenship in a bid to wrest control of Univision from Jerry Perenchio. In an interview with *Business Week,* Azcarraga dispelled the rumor that his new wife was not Mexican and dampened speculation that they might shortly take up extended residence in their South Beach Miami condominium to hasten the day that he could enjoy U.S. citizenship, and thus privileged access to U.S.-based broadcasting properties. "Right now, it's not feasible, although I am spending more time [in the United States]. It would completely change my life—it's not that easy to move myself and my wife and stop seeing her family." [16] Moreover, Mexican law has similar restrictions on foreign ownership of media.

After months of rumors, Univision was finally put on the auction block in June 2006 but the growing competition from modern media like the Internet for advertising revenues made its force felt even in the growing Hispanic media market. Perenchio was reportedly disappointed by the lukewarm interest shown by media giants for his sixty-two TV stations, sixty-nine radio stations, and a music unit. Even though the sale was timed to take place during the popular World Cup soccer period, private equity firms and bankers proved more cautious than expected. Televisa had put together a financially and politically well connected group consisting of Bill Gates's Cascade Management, Bain Capital, Blackstone, Kohlberg, Kravis Roberts (KKR), and the Washington-based Carlyle Group, as well as its original partner Venevision. However, its offer was submitted, late in the game, half of its group dropped out before the final bid was submitted, and Televisa's bid was finally trumped by media mogul Haim Saban's $13.7 billion offer made together with the Texas Pacific Group and other private equity firms. Despite the objections from the board members representing Televisa and Venevision, the Univision board, in a surprising move, quickly accepted the Saban-led bid that was only $0.50 per share higher, leaving Televisa stunned that it would not be given an opportunity to improve its offer and hinting that it would sell its shares in Univision. Unlike *telenovelas*, with their clear beginning, middle and end, this story may have an unknown sequel as Univision remains heavily dependent on Televisa for its programming.

A FORMULA WITH GLOBAL APPEAL

Non-Spanish-speaking fans of *telenovelas* in the United States were thrilled to hear that the Fox network intended to broadcast two *telenovelas*—"Americanized without destroying the integrity of the story," according to a New Corporation spokesman—in the United States. One, entitled *Table for Three,* which originated in Colombia, "tells of the of the tragic destruction of a family when two brothers compete for the same woman." The second "Americanized" product, originally from Cuba, *Fashion House,* "focuses on glamour and unscrupulousness in the fashion industry." Apparently, fashionistas in Fidel Castro's Havana possess striking cultural and behavioral similarities to their finicky counterparts in New York, London, Berlin, and Paris.[17]

Sony Entertainment Television is broadcasting an Indian-language adaptation of the Mexican *telenovela My Sweet Fat Valentina* (the narrative theme of which—surprise, surprise—was "an ugly duckling turning into a beautiful swan") adapted for Indian audiences. "Hispanic audiences like the same high-voltage family drama that Indians do," The Telegraph of Calcutta, India quoted an unnamed participant in the production that "most of these serials are high on drama and surcharged with emotion. Audiences here identify much more easily with such tele-dramas than with American or British soaps, which appeal to just some of the viewers."[18]

"Culturally, Latin Americans are close to Indians. The characters and the story line match our sensibilities," added Tarun Katyal, the executive vice-president of programming for Sony Entertainment Television in India. "The key word here is adaptation . . . a successful adaptation that has been sufficiently spruced up to suit Indian sensibilities."

An Investor's View
The Bull Case
- *Dominance of the Mexican and U.S. Hispanic television markets*
- *Growing purchasing power of the U.S. Hispanic market in which Univision is well-positioned.*
- *Success of* telenovelas *in international markets, even outside the Spanish speaking world.*

The Bear Case
- *Already dominant in Mexico, political changes always represent risks to Televisa.*

- *Future control of Univision in the United States remains a question mark.*
- *Growing competition in non-Hispanic international markets.*

Lessons

- *Shows produced for the Spanish-speaking world have found ready audiences in non-Hispanic countries.*
- *The success of* telenovelas *shows that emerging market media have an opportunity to tap into growing new markets thanks to being on the same "wavelength" as their audience.*
- *The onetime dominance of Hollywood and Disney in entertainment and Western news media like CNN and BBC is giving way to home-grown or regional sources of entertainment and news*

PART III

TURNING THREATS INTO OPPORTUNITIES

CHAPTER 13

A Creative Response

Don't be defensive or stick your head in the sand— develop new policies and strategies

"The only thing we have to fear is fear itself."
—Franklin D. Roosevelt, First Inaugural Address, March 4, 1933

"It is not the strongest of the species that survive, nor the most intelligent, but the ones most responsive to change."
—Charles Darwin

All over the world, government officials and business executives are beginning to seek new solutions to the competitive challenge posed by rapidly emerging markets. In a single week in late March 2006, *The New York Times* reported on a number of American efforts to turn the one-way flood of products coming from Asia into a two-way street, by capturing a larger share of the Chinese and Indian consumer dollar.

- In a clear demonstration of the strength of its distribution formula, WalMart—which purchased about $14 billion in goods from China in 2004—now plans to hire 150,000 employees in China over the next five years. This is five times the number of workers currently employed at its fifty-six Chinese stores.[1]
- Dell, the world's largest marketer of personal computers, already maintains four call centers employing roughly 10,000 in India. It recently announced its intention to double the size of its work force in this rapidly growing computer market to 20,000. But this time around, the focus will be on locally manufacturing and selling its brand in India. "There is a fantastic opportunity to attract talent, and

271

we will insure a major recruitment push in engineering talent,"
explained Michael Dell, the firm's founder and chairman, at a news
conference in Bangalore.[2]

Both announcements demonstrated the degree to which American firms
are beginning to respond nimbly to Darwinian change by selling (and in
Dell's case, manufacturing) more products that would appeal to the growing middle classes of India and China. Since a fair portion of that profit
would likely accrue to U.S.-based entities, wasn't that good news for the
American economy, even if American jobs were created only indirectly?

During that same week India's finance minister confidently announced
his plan to expand the convertibility of the rupee against global currencies
"as its economy surges." He not only signaled that rising foreign reserves
give India room for new policies but also implicitly recognized the new
reality that outsourcing would inevitably lead Indian corporations to invest
(and create jobs) in the United States and other First World countries. Not
just trade but also capital is starting to flow in both directions. Chinese officials displayed a similar kind of confidence. While Chinese officials
bluntly reminded the United States not to hold China responsible for
American economic policy failures in resolving its budget and current
account deficits, they also subtly wined and dined key U.S. senators in
Beijing who had earlier proposed legislation to more forcefully deal with
the widening bilateral trade deficit. Several days later, the news that
Lenovo—still majority-owned by the Chinese government's Academy of
Sciences—had been granted a $13 million contract to provide 15,000
ThinkPad computers to the U.S. State Department prompted a rumble of
criticism from "a diverse group of liberal and conservative critics who
have been warning about China's growing power for several years,"
according to *The New York Times*.[3] Larry Wortzel, chairman of the little-
known United States–China Economic and Security Review Commission,
created by Congress to monitor the unfolding U.S.-China relationship,
bluntly observed that "while he would not be concerned if Airbus moved
an aircraft production line to China, he would be worried if Lenovo ever
started to sell computers to American government agencies involved in
foreign affairs." The notion of State Department officials somehow threatening U.S. national security by typing out memos and cables on Lenovo
computers defied rational analysis, especially when most other computers
are also made in China.

Earlier news reports of threatened Congressional action on everything from trade deficits with China to foreigners running U.S. ports seemed to confirm that, in the post-9/11 world, both protectionist sentiment and political posturing were alive and well. Upon closer inspection, however, a more realistic attitude is beginning to take hold of governments and companies. When the French president visited India shortly after the popular outcry raised by Mittal Steel's plans to acquire European steel maker Arcelor, he was diplomatically reminded of India's large Airbus orders, and therefore of his own government's interest in quieting primordial and chauvinistic fears. American corporations that rely on China's manufacturing prowess lobbied just as quietly against import tariffs and the push for a sharp revaluation of the yuan. After Hurricane Katrina, decades-old anti-dumping charges against CEMEX (already the largest cement distributor in the United States) abruptly dropped tenfold when cement supplies in southern states tightened, while the authorities in Alabama welcomed Hyundai's large new car plant (along with several other plants being planned by Asian manufacturers nearby) with open arms.

A TWO-WAY STREET
OF OUTSOURCING AND INSOURCING

A harsh reality faces just about every working person on the planet today. The reality is that since the Internet has reduced data transmission costs to nearly nothing, many jobs can be done at any time, in any place, if not by anyone, threatening the jobs of assembly line and white collar workers alike. In the future, there may be a good deal of truth to Daniel Pink's contention in *Revenge of the Right Brain* that in the future anything routine will be automated or outsourced. Even some nonroutine activities like design and tech innovation can now be outsourced, if not yet fully automated.

But outsourcing and offshoring are just one side of the story. The Institute for International Economics (IIE) has made a persuasive case that not just China and India but the entire First World has reaped huge gains from globalization. The IIE cites net economic gains of $1 trillion dollars (or 10 percent of GDP) for the United States alone, a percentage only likely to increase for European economies commanding a stronger global orientation.[4] The management consulting firm A.T. Kearney has estimated that by 2015, there will be 900 million more middle-class consumers in emerging markets with incomes over $10,000, a level approaching close to half of the two billion global consumers expected to enjoy such income levels at that time.[5] Each of these new customers will be capable, even eager, to pay for products and services originating in the former First World. Yet the question hanging over these rosy predictions of a rising tide lifting all boats is whether those nearly one billion new customers will continue to prefer products and services with First World imprimaturs and brands, or choose more locally tailored homegrown varieties. In the end this will depend on the adaptability of First World economies and firms.

Besides low-cost imports, job losses from outsourcing are the most visible component of globalization, at least when examined from a First World perspective. But as we have seen, they constitute an incomplete part of a more complex global dynamic. Just as H. Ross Perot's "giant sucking sound" after NAFTA became more of a two-way street than some feared, outsourcing is creating thousands of new jobs in the United States and Europe. An article in *Foreign Affairs* by George J. Gilboy cites an independent study by the Information Technology Association of America, to the effect that "outsourcing to countries such as China and India created a net 90,000 new U.S. jobs in information technology in 2003." The same report estimated that "outsourcing will create a net 317,000 new U.S. jobs by 2008."[6]

The fact is that not just *imports from* but also *exports to* emerging markets have risen so fast that they have become the most dynamic parts of the global economy. This other side of the two-way street all too often gets overlooked in the frenzy of policy debates.

Exports to Emerging Markets (in $ billions)

Exports from	1984	1994	2004	20-year growth (1984–2004)
United States	86	218	377	338%
Developed countries	336	809	1,598	376%

Source: International Monetary Fund, Direction of Trade Statistics

Many of these economic gains and jobs created in mature economies are the direct or indirect result of growing exports to emerging markets, which provide a stimulus to new jobs in exporting countries. But these newly created jobs lack a political constituency and press coverage because they are so much harder to measure than the more obvious job losses. More visible are the still small but growing number of jobs created by emerging multinationals investing directly in the mature economies, as evidenced by the dramatic expansion of companies such as Hyundai, Samsung, CEMEX, and Tenaris into global players. Of the twenty-five emerging multinationals profiled in this book, Hyundai, CEMEX, TSMC, Sasol, and Samsung are the largest employers in the United States. Together with Haier and others, they account for more than 30,000 jobs in the United States and more than 70,000 in the First World. These numbers have been growing fast and are, at best, an incomplete count because they ignore the numerous part suppliers, car dealers, handset marketers, advertising creators, designers, lawyers, and others employed by these emerging multinationals indirectly. A number of other emerging multinationals employ significant numbers of workers in the United States, including Mexico's Gruma, which has 5,000 American employees to serve—even dominate—the U.S. packaged-tortilla market. Grupo Bimbo, another Mexican company, maintains 8,000 American employees in its U.S. Bakeries division. Already in 2003, a total of 160,000 worked for emerging multinationals in the United States. This number has grown rapidly in recent years and is likely to grow further in the future.[7] That is the good news: a classic win-win for all sides.

Although the data for emerging multinationals are not broken out, 5.3 million Americans who work for foreign companies in the United States have a total payroll of $318 billion and an average compensation per employee of over $60,000. Not at all incidentally, these foreign companies contribute a whopping 21 percent to total U.S. exports.[8]

Even if this reverse wave of jobs remains—at least for now—a drop in the bucket compared to the north-south shift of manufacturing work to low-wage economies, it is easy to underestimate the impact of the more diffuse wave of exports stemming from the higher income levels that these outsourced jobs generate in emerging markets. For example, every "outsourced" job created in India generates a reputed eight more for night watchmen, household servants, and other more menial laborers, contributing to an expansion of those economies that ultimately benefits everyone.

Simple demographics (in the form of graying populations in the First World) combined with a lack of willingness of First World citizens to perform many menial or low-paid tasks would in any event *necessitate* exports of jobs to countries with lower wages and faster growing populations, a problem made all the more acute by increasingly commonplace political constraints on immigration.

THE FEAR FACTOR

When President Franklin D. Roosevelt announced in 1933 to an anxious United States citizenry that the only thing they had to fear was fear itself, he spoke not long after the Crash of 1929 and in the midst of a major banking crisis and global recession. Due to a combination of the president's own optimism, charisma, and unorthodox industrial-policy initiatives, the U.S. economy eventually revived from that psychological and economic low point.

While neither the United States nor Western Europe today faces a comparable crisis, the former First World is with good reason suffering from occasional bouts of self-doubt, at times descending into outright xenophobia masquerading as somewhat dubious national security concerns (such as China's CNOOC, Dubai Ports World, and Lenovo–U.S. State Department). These fears are prompted by the combined competitive challenges of outsourcing, offshoring, and the growing prowess of a new breed of world-class corporations threatening to "eat their lunch."

Yet even the recent history of the United States presents not just grounds for optimism but models for a "creative response," which can provide all of us with the proverbial "win-win" for both sides. During the 1950s, the nuclear threat from the Soviet Union followed by the launch of Sputnik frightened people into believing that the Russians were "winning" not just the Cold War but the Space Race. When Sputnik provided its shocking demonstration that the Soviet Union possessed the aerospace technology to pose a serious threat in space in October 1957, a perfectly predictable period of saber rattling was followed by a far more inherently creative and productive response. Following President Kennedy's call to put a man on the moon, the United States created a civilian space program, which over the next decade put the bellicose rhetoric of Nikita Khruschev and his successors to shame. Not only did NASA's great adventure enhance U.S. prestige at the time, it produced incalculable long-term value for U.S. society in the form of space spin-offs: a dazzling array of new technologies from the high-speed computer to new synthetic materials to the emergence of new industrial hubs in the South.

While the underground home shelters built in response to the Soviet nuclear threat are long gone or under water, the massive government research and development programs and promotion of the sciences stimulated by the Soviet space threat provided the United States with a powerful technological edge for decades to come. To cite just one example, Pentagon efforts to ensure continuous communications during a nuclear first strike ultimately led to the creation of the Internet.

During the 1970s, the success of Toyota, Sony, and other Japanese corporations capped by the Japanese acquisitions of trophy properties Rockefeller Center and the Pebble Beach golf course frightened Americans into the seemingly inexorable belief that "the Japanese were winning." Yet the politically popular protectionist response that ensued—slapping tariffs on imports of steel, cars, and consumer electronics—scarcely aided those industries most threatened, and in fact aided those doing the threatening. The more nuanced and creative adaptive response was the widespread adoption of quality circles, just-in-time manufacturing, total quality management (TQM), and Six Sigma. By emulating Japanese companies—while simultaneously avoiding some of the worst traps that Japanese and other Asian firms had fallen into, namely trying to be all things to all people—U.S. corporations themselves learned to become leaner and more productive, setting the stage for the rapid increases in productivity in the 1990s.

So what's the lesson? In essence, it's simple: when faced with a competitive challenge, we can ignore it, respond defensively with subtle or overt protective measures, or react creatively by matching innovation with innovation. Past experience suggests that we are better off rejecting the temptation to lower the protectionist boom even if it may seem like the easier course in the short term.

THE PROTECTIONIST'S DILEMMA

The examples of Samsung, CEMEX, Tenaris, and Embraer cited in this book provide ample evidence of how easily anti-dumping measures can backfire. Samsung benefited from an American anti-dumping suit against the competitive threat of growing Japanese semiconductor sales. Locking out the Japanese allowed Samsung to become the world's leading producer of memory chips. When a coalition of Southern cement companies instigated a suit against Mexican cement maker CEMEX, triggering punitive anti-dumping charges over 50 percent, it was forced to diversify into Spain and buy up Central American cement producers. The immediate result was higher cement prices in the United States at a high cost to consumers and taxpayers, as half of U.S. cement is purchased by the government. But anti-dumping also taught CEMEX the art of acquisition and ultimately transformed it into the largest cement maker in the United States. When Tamsa's seamless pipes for the oil industry threatened U.S. producers, a 21.7 percent anti-dumping charge was levied on their imports. This punitive policy forced the merged group Tenaris to seek innovative solutions that ultimately made it into a global producer with an edge in logistics. Small plane makers in the United States tried to keep Embraer from selling its planes, but ultimately Embraer succeeded. While some of these plane makers went bankrupt, many other companies—including American ones—now supply Embraer.

Looking for protection is a sign of weakness, not confidence. Protection may temporarily save jobs but it often defers much-needed efforts to shake up companies and force them to reinvent themselves. Adjustment to new competition is as old as economic history rather than something that is special about today's world. Cries for protectionism are equally old. The challenge of cheap labor is not anything new either. As late as 1959, Japan's skilled and disciplined workers were paid 10 percent of American wages,[9] about the same gap that currently exists between Indian and American software engineers. The only constant in life is the continual pressure to change. Less than a century ago, agriculture dominated employment in most countries. Now many of the agricultural workers in the United States are legal or illegal immigrants. Agricultural production has not fallen but its share in the economy has plummeted because other sectors have grown much faster. Fifty years ago, the United States, Japan, and Europe were the industrialized countries. Now, manufacturing as a percentage of GNP is higher in many emerging markets than in the former First World.

Protectionism not only stifles innovation but ignores the strengths of developed economies, institutional weaknesses of emerging nations, and the usual rapidity with which wages and currencies in competing nations adjust. Shouldn't strengths such as the well developed rule of law, mature political institutions, superb universities, the freedom to try out new ideas and build new businesses, and a flexible labor market (more in the United States than Europe and Japan) inspire some confidence?

And of course, it pays to recall that no matter how impressive many emerging multinationals may seem, they are hardly invincible giants. Emerging multinationals still have to contend with political restrictions, stubborn and recalcitrant bureaucrats, piracy by competitors, dysfunctional court systems, inflexible labor rules, and an uncertain regulatory environment. The ongoing progress of the emerging economies has not been—and still is not—entirely based on tailwind. Wages, for example, have a tendency to rise fastest in the fastest growing economies. When discussing the establishment of an office in Mumbai recently, I was struck by the fact that experienced Indian analysts (at least in the recent bubble) are already being paid compensation comparable to First World packages, a phenomenon that would have been unthinkable just a few years ago. Nevertheless, the flow not just of funds but also of ideas (and idea generators) coming increasingly from the East to the West is inescapable.

The answer is not to seek to stem that inexorable flow by stamping it out, but rather to stimulate a counterflow through reinvention and innovation. At the same time, those most affected by the flow should not be consigned to the dustheap, but rather provided with the benefits of retraining and a safety net for those unable to adjust to the Darwinian pressure to change.

LESSONS TO BE LEARNED FROM EMERGING MARKETS

1. Public-private partnerships have value.

The first lesson to be learned from emerging markets and the successful firms that are creating those markets is to set aside our chronic skepticism about permitting local, state, regional, and national governments to become partners in launching and sustaining private enterprises. While far from advocating a return to state enterprises or industrial policy, we have documented that there is often a high payoff from *enabling* new industries through a combination of support for entrepreneurial clusters and attractive environments for the best, most innovative minds. Underwriting basic research, support of high-quality education, special industrial zones, a push toward the early use of technology in schools, and small-scale, targeted interventions to help new industries get off the ground have also paid dividends.

The outstanding success of the Taiwanese and Korean governments in jump-starting key and strategic industries and firms, from TSMC in Taiwan to Posco, Hyundai, and Samsung in Korea, has not gone unnoticed by U.S. and European policy makers and economists. The fact that Bangalore's preeminence in India's software explosion was helped along by the early establishment of elite schools and Bangalore's designation as a new high-tech cluster—in productive partnership with private enterprises—has raised the profile of government guidance and forced a reexamination of a prevalent bias against government intervention in all forms. Without government guidance and support, Brazil's Embraer or ethanol industry would never have gotten off the ground and South Africa's Sasol would never have gained its present preeminence in the alternative energy arena.

Education policies in China and India and Korea's first nationwide network of wireless Internet access provide other examples of productive government support for entrepreneurial activity. Many Korean schools even mandate that students submit their homework over the Internet. Taiwan's Hsinchu Science Park, China's Shenzhen industrial zone, and the endeavor of the Estonian government to make its bureaucracy paperless are also examples of successful departures from hard-core market economics.

2. Protectionism stands in the way of excellence.

Lest the policy pendulum swing too far the other way, the second lesson to be gleaned from this book is that, while many companies *initially* benefited from local protection, those who continued to rely on its cozy comforts inevitably drifted toward mediocrity and obscurity. Only those firms that no longer could or wanted to rely on the protectionist "moat" progressed on the hardier route to world-class status. Thorough analyses of the temptation to protect a variety of American industries such as cars and steel have drawn the same conclusion.[10]

3. Learn from the first adopter—in an emerging market.

The First World routinely used to be the first in adopting new technologies or introducing new designs and fashions. Yet as the anchor economies of the future shift, this learning process will increasingly become a two-way street. Telecom operators in the United States are learning from first movers Korea and Japan how consumers play games, watch TV, pay bills, and get traffic information on the small screens of their smart phones. Banks need to learn from their experiences in emerging markets how they adjust to unexpected competitors. For example, phone companies in Asia were among the first to let their customers not just talk and search the Internet but also pay parking meters, vending machines, and groceries with their handsets. In Brazil and Mexico, retail chains with more credit information about low-income consumers than banks are setting up banks or becoming de-facto banks themselves.[11] The "prepaid" phenomenon has swept emerging markets but was only later followed by "smart" prepaid debit cards issued to Hispanic immigrants in the United States who do not always find it easy to get a bank account. Yet another financial novelty finding its way from poor communities in Bangladesh and Africa to the United States are microfinance institutions that have broadened the concept of retail lending to a whole new level of clients whose credit is not based on their assets or personal history but the collective strength of a peer group.

4. Figure out what clients need all over the world.

The fourth, perhaps most obvious but also most often ignored lesson is that countries that want to avoid current account deficits and companies that want to grow must remain in tune with the ever changing demands of their clients wherever they are. Gas guzzlers do not sell in countries with high gasoline prices. Big stoves and refrigerators do not fit in small kitchens. Besides planes and semiconductors (in part for re-export), it is striking how many American exports to China are agricultural commodities, waste paper, and scrap metal rather than innovative, high-technology items.

Success in today's global environment requires smart firms to act like chameleons and constantly move up the value ladder. From Samsung and Hon Hai to Embraer and Ranbaxy, companies that are successful in regularly reinventing themselves sustain success.[12]

C. K. Prahalad, author of *The Fortune at the Bottom of the Pyramid*, believes that companies that try to sell their products in the same old way to the same customers won't succeed any longer but that new products and new ways of selling and packaging are required to succeed in the new global environment. Ilkone Mobile in Dubai sells phones that alert Muslim users to the daily prayer times and help to point them toward Mecca.[13] Modern Islamic banking principles will soon crowd out western-style banking in the Middle East and Pakistan and have made their entry even in London. Nike, once one of the most insular firms in the world, recently entered into a creative partnership with the United Nations Refugee Agency to design an athletic uniform—a streamlined *hijab*—that permits young female Islamic athletes to play competitive sports without compromising their religious modesty.[14] With citizens from Gulf countries unable to obtain visas to the United States, Bumrungrad hospital has stepped into the void by attracting patients from the Middle East. Located in Buddhist Bangkok, its hospital staff has been trained in how to deal with Islamic customs and dietary practices.

TURNING A THREAT INTO AN OPPORTUNITY

Endless complaining and hand wringing about outsourcing to India, towering trade deficits with China, government debt held in Taiwan and China, shoes made with cheap labor, dependence on oil from Venezuela, Nigeria, and the Middle East or gas from Russia, and unmatchable high math and science scores in Singapore and Korea will not make any of these challenges and threats vanish into thin air. Like all successful people, firms, countries, and civilizations, we should actively seek to turn these threats into opportunities. As discussed in previous chapters, grabbing such opportunities involves developing a new set of attitudes:

- Emerging multinationals will become important clients for all kinds of high-value products and services, including—to name just a few— machinery, mining equipment, investment banking services, advertising, design, and political forecasting.
- College and MBA students will seek out emerging multinationals to do summer internships in interesting new environments and for globe-trotting careers.
- Just as Belgian beer brewer Interbrew did with Brazilian Ambev or Miller Beer with South African Breweries, companies will join to revitalize their marketing strategy and even learn about efficiency from their peers in emerging markets.
- Complex new research projects will increasingly be undertaken jointly by North-South (or East-West) groups of companies following the example of Sony and Samsung.
- As emerging multinationals become more global and First World corporations seek a foothold in new markets, they will not only build their own distribution networks but will rely on each other to provide them with local knowledge.
- Rapidly growing investment funds in emerging markets will seek to diversify their holdings in the First World while institutional and retail investors from the United States, Europe, and Japan will increasingly find investment opportunities in emerging markets.

Although recognizing opportunities is an important part of any truly creative response, dealing with the new competitive challenges will involve not only corporations adapting nimbly but also governments rallying the deep reservoirs of national enthusiasm and universities becoming more global.

A NATIONAL COMPETITIVENESS CAMPAIGN: THE NEED FOR BIG, INSPIRATIONAL GOALS

It does not matter whether you want to become a National Merit scholar, a world-class corporation, or a competitive nation: you need big ambitions and inspirational goals. I believe that the United States as a nation must formulate a concise and clear set of such national goals akin to the earlier effort of putting a man on the moon and perhaps less visible but similar campaigns in Japan, Korea, and China. One example of a major national goal would be the invention of a new, alternative car engine not dependent on fossil fuel. Neither energy independence nor any progress toward a cleaner environment is possible without a radical redesign of the car engine (or possibly the whole car concept). Other countries are already in this race.

Six elements are crucial in a National Competitiveness Campaign.

* *Tackling legacy issues:* Health care and pension costs have spiraled out of control for many older corporations, as a result of inflated and unrealistic past promises. This is a crisis waiting to happen—in fact, already in full swing in some sectors—and the ultimate cost to resolve it will simply climb higher the longer we wait to address it. In the meantime, these legacy costs of an aging work force are placing a crushing burden on too many major corporations, have lowered their credit rating to "junk bond" status, and made it difficult for them to invest in innovation. The beginnings of a solution would be to separate the "operating" and "insurance" functions of companies so that companies can focus on what they do best (or disappear if they cannot succeed) without this constant burden on their shoulders. During "good times" many companies agreed with unions on future benefits for health and pensions that have proven to be, in retrospect, unrealistic.[15] I would propose research into converting pension liabilities of so-called defined benefit plans through the use of newly designed financial instruments similar to zero coupon bonds. These could be pooled, customized, and then traded in ways similar to the secondary market for home mortgages. Instead of waiting for companies that are

burdened with legacy costs to go bankrupt, employees should be given the choice to exchange their health care package for enrollment in some form of "basic" national plan that allows them to contribute more for additional services.

- *Supporting basic research in a new type of "Bell Lab" for the twenty-first century:* Basic research has yeilded huge, unanticipated dividends in the United States and many other countries. A broad consensus is already developing that it needs to receive more government support[16] and cannot rely largely on business funding. Close cooperation betwen state/local authorities and universities has also demonstrated its effectiveness. Surprisingly, a major potential source of funding for creative thinking and new inventions has gone untapped. Corporations once supported more of the freewheeling inventiveness that led to a host of new inventions at research labs like that of Bell Laboratories. For the twenty-first century, there is roon for a prestigious new type of Bell Lab where the best minds would interact. This time, it should be funded by or in alliance with private foundations of entrepreneurs who have accumulated fortunes and have a natural interest in innovative thinking. Encouraging this type of giving would help national competitiveness more than abolishing the estate tax.

- *Eliminating the current account deficit:* A self-respecting global power cannot afford to be dependent on foreign finance and foreign energy simultaneously, especially if its technological edge is steadily eroding. Large current account and budget deficits have forced the United States to be dependent on China to, in fact, fund its debt by buying treasury bills and bonds, thereby keeping interest rates low and, in turn, funding the housing boom and consumer economy in a manner that is nonsustainable in the long run. Only a major currency devaluation, energy independence, or greater competitiveness of exports can make a country like the United States less dependent, unless it would resort to the less desirable alternative of hiding behind protective walls.

- *Emphasizing creativity in education and fusion of design and technology:* The United States will no longer be able to compete with leading emerging markets in the *numbers* of college graduates, engineers, and scientists but it can ensure that it remains ahead in *quality* of education. Its "human capital" will maintain a competitive edge by continuing and even broadening the American educational focus on creative, "fuzzy" areas that require the integration of many skills. This left-brain/right-brain interaction is equally important in the fusion of design and technology that helps companies to achieve a competitive edge.[17]

- *Creating special "ideas" zones:* Local and state governments should create new twenty-first century economic hubs by smoothing the two-way street in job migration. As Alabama has done in the case of Hyundai Motor, state and local governments should welcome emerging multinationals in their efforts to create new industrial hubs or high technology zones. Just as Taiwan and China learned from Silicon Valley, state and local officials could form close partnerships with emerging multinationals, local businesses, universities, real estate developers, and innovative architects to facilitate clusters of twenty-first century industries and living environments that would attract the best and the brightest from all over the world.
- *Reinvesting in infrastructure to give it a much-needed face lift:* Infrastructure is an area in which a number of emerging markets like China and Korea are beginning to leapfrog, from airports, wireless broadband, and mass transit to efficient modern power plants which are beginning to use alternative energies. Innovative new architecture for public buildings (like the libraries of a past age) should rekindle pride, perhaps built in partnership between local governments and the many private foundations established by wealthy individuals.

NORTH-SOUTH ORIENTED CORPORATIONS

Some (yet still just a few) corporations have developed an explicit North-South, or "BRICs" strategy in a world dominated by global competition, and in which much of the future demand growth lies in the emerging markets. If most of the first one billion computers were sold in developed markets, most of the next billion will be sold in emerging markets, where sales of technology products are growing at 11 percent, or nearly twice the rate of the First World.[18] Emerging markets are already way ahead in the sales of mobile phone handsets (outstripping the sales of computers by nearly ten to one) where developed markets are playing a catch-up game. Even though local brands and products will become increasingly competitive, there is plenty of room for companies from everywhere to compete.

- *Embedding:* Like journalists and photographers embedding with the military in Iraq, young corporate executives are now asked to do the same, but elsewhere in high-growth locales. John Pepper, the former CEO of Procter & Gamble, cited the example of young marketing specialists in the company spending months in the households of Chinese consumers to observe everything they do, from how they brush their teeth to their eating habits.

- *International focus groups:* Focus groups are widely used to test the appeal of new products but, despite being the fastest growing group, emerging market consumers are still often ignored in these tests. Companies will increasingly need to hire a new breed of young executives who either come from new markets or speak local languages and are not just superficially but thoroughly familiar with different environments. For example, *Business Week* recounts how HP learned that Indian photographers needed portable solar battery chargers for their cameras and printers to take wedding pictures in villages. Strong brands need to be constantly refreshed. In the future, the taste and design preferences of emerging market consumers will become not just more important but even dominant in many cases.

- *Forging alliances:* Lenin once said that a capitalist is someone who will sell the rope to hang himself. He underestimated the capitalist as much as he did the ability of market economics to adapt and thrive. First World corporations are becoming well aware of the opportunities in new, growing markets that can offset the threats from emerging multinationals in those often stagnant markets they have traditionally called their own. We may expect First World corporations to enter into many different forms of alliances, ranging from equal partnerships like joint design (favored by Hon Hai) to playing the lucrative but noncontrolling part of outsourcee instead of outsourcer (as in the case of Embraer). In the process, some American companies may lose their reluctance to form the types of partnerships already existing between European and Japanese companies and their counterparts in Asia, Latin America, and Eastern Europe. Just as the earlier experience of overseas plants (and especially outsourcing) familiarized traditional multinationals with their counterparts in emerging markets, the future will bring not just more competition but also new forms of closer cooperation in which the classic need to ensure best practices will continue but the outdated "we know best" attitude will erode.

Taking the opportunity-knocks approach, the Silicon Valley–based venture capital firm Norwest Venture Partners has developed a "hybrid" investment strategy in Bangalore, by which it "marries" entrepreneurs of Indian origin with Western executives. The firm estimates that 40 percent of its portfolio companies have set up software development operations in India. Many of these new firms have been launched by former Indian denizens of Silicon Valley. Still others are run by entrepreneurs of all ethnic backgrounds and stripes looking for the next big thing. One example of this trend is a start-up called Read-Ink Technologies, a producer of sophisticated handwriting-recognition programs that is the brainchild of Thomas O. Binford, a retired computer science professor from Stanford, and his wife Ione, a former manager for Hewlett-Packard, who four years ago decided to migrate from Silicon Valley to Bangalore to put down roots in India's fast-sprouting Silicon City.[18]

What are the offshoots of these new approaches? These are neither "Indian" companies nor "American" companies but exciting hybrids of both. Is this a net loss for the developed world or a welcome sign that globalization is producing a cosmopolitan entrepreneurial culture that is no longer bound by national boundaries? Many more American college graduates may find attractive jobs in such unabashedly global companies than they can imagine today.

GLOBAL UNIVERSITIES

The relatively small populations of the developed world (which are, in fact, a small and declining minority of only 15 percent of global population today) will be unable to turn out anywhere near the numbers of university graduates, engineers, scientists, and computer specialists emerging nations will produce. The curriculum, student body, and faculty of many American universities have become increasingly international, with Asian students and professors leading the charge.[19] It would be an exaggeration to say that these institutions already reflect the global environment that the next generation of students and scientists is likely to face in their careers. Yet if the key skills of the future are to be less routine and mechanical, university graduates of the future must be endowed with a different competitive edge than before. Creativity and advanced problem-solving skills—already strengths of American education—must be honed further. At an early stage, scientists, generalists, and artists should be brought together in workshops to learn from each other's approaches to a problem, thereby learning early on to fuse technology and design. Fluency in at least one other language and first-hand experience of living in very different cultures and countries should become an integrated part of the curriculum of top universities. Instead of the low-key, vacation-type "junior year abroad" experience, students should immerse themselves in an intense learning-work experience that is lengthy enough to leave them with a solid understanding and a high level of comfort with operating in a different environment.

A REVERSAL OF CAPITAL FLOWS
AND TALENT POOL MIGRATION

A few decades ago, the great concerns of policy makers in developed and emerging nations alike were emerging market debt, currency crises, high interest rates, dependence on foreign aid and bank credit, capital flight, the threat of multinationals, and the brain drain. But today, those concerns have shifted. The questions preying on the minds of interested observers worldwide are now dramatically different:

- How will central bankers in emerging markets invest their huge and constantly rising reserves; and how will it affect the dollar and other major currencies?
- How will the abundance of foreign investment and easy money in China affect the "hurdle rate" of corporate investment decisions and perhaps lead to overinvestment and low profitability of many companies?
- What are the risks in having so many U.S. treasury bills and bonds in the hands of a few governments of emerging markets in Asia?
- How will the huge flow of workers' remittances to emerging markets effect the balance of payments of developed markets? (which now outstrip capital flight many times over)
- What will happen to innovation in Silicon Valley if more and more software engineers return to India to start their own firms?

In this changed world, there is less room for effective protectionism and a greater need to remember that—to paraphrase Darwin—creative adaptation is the key to successful survival.

Harvard professor Samuel P. Huntington's insightful *Clash of Civilizations*[20] struck a chord in the post-9/11 world with his controversial theory that "the fundamental source of conflict in this new world will not be primarily ideological or primarily economic. . . . The fault lines between civilizations will be the battle lines of the future." But battle lines—while sometimes unavoidable—leave no middle ground. We forget that Europeans who had lost track of the classical lessons absorbed by the Greeks and the Romans underwent their Renaissance after contact with the Islamic civilizations of the Middle East, which had done a better job of preserving the cultural literacy of Europe during the Dark Ages than the Europeans had themselves. A more optimistic view of the positive benefits of cultural clash and collision was set forth by the Budapest-born British immigrant author and philosopher Arthur Koestler in his 1964 book *The Act of Creation*. In contrast to Huntington's battle lines, clashes, conflict, and war, Koestler celebrates the fact that many truly creative acts are grounded in clashes of individual, group, and cultural viewpoints, as "creative collisions," when as Koestler puts it, "two reference frames collide." Previously advanced China fell behind when its inward orientation (despite the Silk Road trade) made it ignore the lessons of the Industrial Revolution. New contacts may result in bloody as well as creative collisions in our present globally interconnected world.

From the different, less political perspective of the world of business and economics, this book—I hope—underscores some fundamental points: (1) When faced with a competitive challenge, viewing the world as a zero-sum game of conflict is usually a recipe for failure; instead, adaptation and a creative, proactive response are key to successful survival. (2) There is much that people, companies, and countries can learn from each other if they adopt a truly open and global mind-set. (3) Partnerships and joint ventures between parties in the developed world and emerging markets often serve both parties well. As we have seen in this book, unconventional thinking, a proactive response to globalization, and the evolution of a truly global mind-set and corporate culture have produced success after success in navigating the dynamic landscape of our current era. Time and again, the visionary founders and ambitious executives I interviewed stressed that thinking and acting in a global context is no longer some exotic abstraction, but a living and breathing requirement for survival. Their success demonstrates that the ultimate edge—in not merely surviving but thriving—goes to those who summon the will to seek a creative response rather than digging in their heels, and who act nimbly and confidently as opposed to rigidly and fearfully.

PART IV

AN INVESTOR'S RESOURCE

CHAPTER 14

Investing in the Emerging
Markets Century: Ten Rules

A long-time investor looks at pride and
prejudice in emerging market investing

In an interview with *Forbes* magazine,[1] Fred Smith, the founder and CEO of Federal Express, recounted the story of Nobel laureate Dr. Hans Selye, who as a young medical student became frustrated when one of his cultures in an experiment was consumed by ugly green mold. This eminent researcher—author of the modern theory of stress and trauma and its relationship to disease—felt that a year of his life had gone down the drain. In 1928, the young Scottish bacteriologist Alexander Fleming observed precisely the same phenomenon, saw the lifesaving properties of an ugly mold that consumed bacteria, and went on to invent . . . penicillin. Fred Smith recounted this tale as a way of describing the value of seeing gold where others see dirt. He did so himself when conceiving of Federal Express.

A story like this also illustrates a basic lesson in investing. *Just looking at things a bit differently* can make all the difference because even—and sometimes especially—experts don't always know best. I believe that this is true as much in creating successful new companies as it is in investing. For example, the Asian crisis of the late 1990s was, in some ways, like this mold. Too easily dismissed at the time by many as a destructive force that would end the Asian Miracle, it instead proceeded to weed out the strong from the weak, transforming the survivors into stronger and more globally competitive companies.

Another lesson was illustrated by a preview I watched years ago for an Italian movie. Its name has long since escaped me but its message has stuck with me because it so neatly sums up where many investors go wrong. As a red-hot Maserati speeds away, the driver insouciantly pulls off the rearview mirror and tosses it into the road. "The first rule of Italian driving," he advises his blond companion, "is never to look backward."

Yet following conventional wisdom and looking backward at past stock performance or proven success are precisely what too many investors spend too much time doing. They follow broker opinions slavishly or use their Bloomberg monitors like a rearview mirror, obsessed with following markets and impatiently tracking stock prices by the hour, instead of using them as valuable analytical tools to shed light on areas others ignore. Because we believe that analyzing companies is more important than following markets, the portfolio managers in our office must walk to a central area for access to a terminal rather than having one on their desktops.

If obliged to sum up a simple tripod of emerging markets investing, I would hazard the following: (1) seeing things a little differently, (2) recognizing that *proven* success is typically already reflected in stock prices, and (3) focusing intensely on company fundamentals instead of wasting too much time on stock market developments.

I am often asked for the "secret" to investing in emerging markets as if it were possible to bottle such a formula. But just as shortcuts inhibit the quest for excellence in companies so does the illusion that there is a universal, simple recipe to investing. Not long ago, I was reminded of this same, very human urge to find such formulas for success when I attended a class on leadership taught by John Thornton, the former co-CEO of Goldman Sachs, at the prestigious Tsinghua University in Beijing. The class was composed of some of the most promising future leaders of China. Thornton often invites CEOs and top managers from around the world to share their experiences and the guest lecturer that afternoon was Yale University president Richard C. Levin. After his presentation on the raft of challenges he faces daily while managing a world-class university and an intellectually stimulating give-and-take with these very bright students, one final hand shyly shot up.

"What" the questioner wanted to know, "is Yale's special secret for producing so many American presidents?" Following the inevitable round of laughter, Levin offered a few plausible ideas on why the Yale experience encouraged public service but he admitted that there was no single secret.

What, then, is the secret to investing in emerging markets?

The only truly accurate response would be that the real secret is that the secret is always changing. One early secret to investing in the markets of the future was simply: *Don't be afraid of investing in them.* As emerging nations and companies have gained increasing prominence, that is no longer a secret and the question today is no longer *whether* or *where* but rather *how much* to invest. In the emerging markets context, two conventional approaches have shown their limitations:

Conventional Wisdom Rule #1

Picking the right countries is key to successful emerging market investing. During the early "discovery" phase of emerging markets investing in the 1980s as well as during the crisis years of the 1990s, zip code was often the main reason why a company performed well or poorly. All along, it has remained crucial to tread carefully and diversify your bets, but during these early days it was often essential to use a "top down" approach to investing which holds that investors should focus first on selecting countries before they pick stocks. Avoiding huge devaluations, real estate bubbles, or market runs while moving early into undiscovered or out-of-favor countries usually made all the difference.

Conventional Wisdom Rule #2

The second conventional wisdom in emerging market investing has been to focus on *finding companies with a proven, successful record of growth*. If one invests in them early enough before they become household words, and if they maintain their excellence, one will do very well over the long haul, thank you.

Both rules are valid only up to a point. Certainly, investors in search of corporations with a sustainable competitive edge are following the right path. And certainly, it makes sense over a ten to twenty year period to invest in healthy, growing countries while constantly watching out for overvalued currencies, high inflation, bubbles, budget deficits, and current account problems. But the best market performance is instead often found in countries recovering from crises. The Chinese example of recent years has taught us that strong economic growth is no guarantee for high market returns. Sometimes the opposite is even true for several years. Competition is often so fierce in countries with rapid growth that it is tough for many companies to achieve profitability. In a contrasting example, on my last visit to Nigeria, we were taken from the airport to the center of the capital in a convoy with armed guards. Yet the highest profit margins are often found in countries like Nigeria that have economic or political problems. Based on our experience and that of other investors, investments in Africa have performed better over the past decade with lower volatility than our investments in supposedly "safer" markets.

In the end, proven success is less important than the fact it is not yet fully recognized by other investors. Thus, I like to identify and invest in companies with a *sustainable competitive edge* that are *not (yet) widely perceived to be world-class*. In investing, it does not pay to get "married" to stocks but it is better to move on when they become too popular.

I would be the first to point out that this is hardly an original recipe, but that doesn't make it any less true or any easier to follow. In fact, to do so consistently over time takes a loner instinct, insatiable curiosity, and a healthy appetite for risk. If there *is* a secret to investing, it lies in achieving the right mixture of discipline and determination, in judiciously ignoring rather than following the fashions of the market, in pursuing the pure pleasure of discovering a company before others do, and in a stubbornness to hang on when others lose heart while possessing the ruthlessness to sell without remorse whenever serious problems arise or others begin to over-rate the company.

The real problem with following this time-honored approach to invest-ing—a problem not unlike following the rules of dieting—is that so few people find it possible to execute on the rules without falling victim to fashion, consensus conceptions, and powerfully distorting emotions such as greed and fear.

When I started out as a professional investor years ago, I was either arrogant or inexperienced enough to believe that it might be possible to consistently pick companies that would be winners as companies as well as stocks. Today, I continue to believe that lesser known markets and stocks offer unusual opportunities but, like most investors, I have also learned that *consistent* results are tough to achieve: an impressive technol-ogy may disappoint, demand for a product may dry up, a sudden devalua-tion may trigger a default, a formidable competitor may show up out of nowhere, or a serious-looking manager may in fact be betting on horses or may abandon his core business to get into real estate. It is easy to be fooled by companies that grow fast but find it a fundamental challenge to keep doing so. Others may be cheap but for the good reason that they have something to hide. And successful company executives easily fall victim to the hubris that if they are successful in one business they should also do well in others. Fortunately, investing is not brain surgery where a single mistake can spoil a promising career. The best investors are those who consistently learn from their mistakes, and who don't spend too much time being impressed by their occasional successes.

Any reader will immediately understand that I am skeptical of any rules or the thought that any formula can be bottled. Instead I believe that investors—like any world-class company—must constantly reinvent their approach. The ten rules presented here have, at least for me, stood the test of time as they helped me run and grow a portfolio now worth billions of dollars without losing too many nights' sleep or too many clients. In fact, these rules have helped us add value for clients over the long haul during periods of both growth and crisis. My rules are simply commonsense reminders and may, more than anything, point the reader to *what to avoid.*

A NOTE FOR INDIVIDUAL INVESTORS

Individual investors should definitely include emerging markets in their portfolios but should recognize that they are at a disadvantage in picking stocks. Several of the world-class companies discussed in this book are not available for investment through American depository receipts (ADRs). It is even more difficult to buy lesser known stocks. A large number of mutual funds investing in emerging markets are offered to individual investors, from low-cost index funds like Vanguard's to actively managed funds. There are broadly diversified funds, regional funds, and individual country funds. I personally avoid buying funds that have recently performed well, have a high turnover, or are saddled with high fees. Investors in closed-end funds should avoid buying those that do not trade at discounts to their net asset value. Exchange traded funds (ETFs) are another cost-efficient way of gaining exposure to individual stock markets. My practical advice would be:

- *For those who have never invested in emerging markets, "average in" rather than buying all at once, putting in money each month or quarter until you reach your target level (more about this later in this chapter).*
- *Avoid emerging markets when everyone talks about them and invest twice as much as usual when nobody likes them.*
- *Over the next twenty-five years, gradually add 1 percent of your total stockholdings to emerging markets each year, until it reaches the share of emerging markets in the global economy (now 21 percent)*
- *Invest no more than 10 percent of your emerging markets exposure through individual stocks and invest the remainder through funds or ETFs.*

MY TEN INVESTMENT RULES

1. Buy only stocks that are underrated

The key to successful investing in any market, emerging or mature, is not finding cheap, high-growth, or even world-class companies but finding and investing in those that are *underrated by the market.* Investors who simply avoid overpriced and uncompetitive companies are already way ahead of the game. But the true art of investing is to zoom in on whether a company is underrated for the *right* or the *wrong* reason. Is there a valid reason for "cheapness" like lack of competitiveness, lousy corporate governance, a fragmented industry, or poor management? Or is it an invalid reason, such as simple obscurity, the fact that investors had a bad experience with the country or industry, or that few brokers follow it or because it is still undiscovered, too small, or out of favor? The distorting power of conventional thinking and the resultant irrational prejudice are among the major reasons why some stocks are underrated. A variant on the same theme is that if anything seems too obvious or easy, others have probably discovered it.

2. Do your own homework and dig deep

Good investors learn the hard way that true insight only comes after one conducts a great deal of painstaking research. Edison's rule concerning "99 percent perspiration and 1 percent inspiration" is as true in investing as in inventing. I have yet to find a supposed "no brainer" that turned out to be a good investment. Any serious investor must know all the basic information about a company and its industry but will use this only as the starting point. While most investors and brokers love income statements, I have learned to prefer the information I can glean from balance sheets. The notes in the back of financial statements often reveal more than the management reports in the front.

To decipher these often cryptic statements takes time and effort. As a professional investor, I enjoy the luxury of making frequent plant visits, meeting with managements and talking to competitors. In all my years of investing, I have yet to meet any successful investor who does not love constantly researching companies, industries, and countries, frankly to the point that others call obsession. But you do not need to be a full-time investor to read industry reports or to surf the Internet for unusual tidbits of information that have not yet become part of the consensus view.

3. Distrust the wisdom of the markets

Just because most market participants believe something does not make it true. Market prices reflect imperfect information and manias more than they do perfect data. Evolution has hardwired us to feel better when we follow the herd but if it feels good to run with the bulls or the bears, it is often the wrong choice or moment. If you feel lonely in your choices and a bit scared, you probably have a better chance of success than those who perceive their choices to be safe and risk-free. Investing flies not only in the face of just about every other lesson we learn in life, it runs counter to much of our evolutionary history and makeup.

4. Use crises to get in and investment fashions to get out

Here again we directly address the often yawning gap between perception and reality. Periods of crisis frequently create the richest investment opportunities. Conversely, risks run highest when things seem to be at their best. As fallible human beings, we tend to know (and then just as quickly forget) how wildly popular stocks always seem to make money for our neighbors but never for us. Yet stocks that plummet precipitously in the wake of a crisis tend to bounce back after a while.

5. Be skeptical of proven success

The fact that other investors as well as competitors rapidly recognize proven success is a major reason why stocks become overrated and companies lose market share or profitability. Although world-class companies are typically good at keeping competitors at bay, even the best companies are not immune to competition. Once again, the notion that proven success predicts future success is simply off the mark.

6. The next generation of world-class companies offers the greatest potential and their competitiveness really matters

Picking companies *on their way to becoming* world-class offers the highest returns over the long term. Once fully recognized (and not all the companies in this book are yet fully recognized), great companies are no longer cheap. The point is not to simply identify great companies, but to understand what makes a company world-class before everyone else recognizes it as such. And the great definer of world-class companies is that they do not just survive but thrive in the cauldron of global competition. Companies and countries that prefer to hide from global competition are bound to self-destruct.

Only companies that are serious about being competitive and becoming world-class have a chance to earn sustainable profits and high rates of return for investors. Conversely, companies that rely on government hand-outs and protection for survival, or that don't constantly work on improving their costs and competitive edge, will rapidly disappear from the map.

7. The best insights come from unusual sources

Occasionally, I've found that listening to badmouthing is the most efficient road to the truth. I tend to take the word of competitors and customers over company managements when it comes to assessing their future prospects. It pays to listen to interesting tidbits heard on a ski lift or picked up at an industry conference or while surfing the Internet. Much as broker's reports are full of useful information, I prefer to tear off the first page with the "Recommendation" and put it on the bottom of the pile. Company websites are useful for updates and background but beware of the spin zone. Newspapers tend to be overly event-oriented while news magazines frequently hype industry trends. I find it safe to assume that when more than one newspaper reports a development, it is already discounted in the price of a stock. In fact, too much sudden attention is often a sure sign of investor overreaction. Of greatest value to investors are facts or trends that most sources ignore or carefully avoid. When interviewing executives, I always try to answer the question: "What did he or she *not* say?"

8. Assume that events—good or bad—are always overblown

Like most investors, I never give up trying to figure out major economic and industry trends and have found that the effort alone is worth it. But I have learned that it is impossible to forecast when and where the next crisis will hit and that, by the time a crisis hits, one is rarely able to do much but roll with the punches. Fortunately, it is easier to spot investment fashions—and to avoid them—even if it takes effort (and a strange kind of loner mentality) to avoid the infectious enthusiasm of others and to deliberately sell a stock, industry, or market that everyone else likes. Iron discipline is needed. One way to distance oneself from the market obsession of the week is to employ not just one valuation indicator (like a price/earnings multiple), a single year of growth, or unique measure of economic health (like GDP growth) but a very broad, standardized list of fifteen or more "ratios" for companies, industries, and countries.

Some of My Favorite Ratios

Companies	*Countries*
• *Price/cash earnings*	• *Foreign reserves/debt trend*
• *Price/net asset value*	• *Budget + current account*
• *Net debt/equity*	*balance as % of GNP*
• *Growth in free cash flow*	• *Momentum of economic growth*
• *Return on equity trend*	• *Inflation trend*
• *Operating margin trend*	• *Export growth trend*

9. Write down why you make investment decisions

Not surprisingly, we all remember our "winners" much more clearly than our "dogs." Over the years, I have found it particularly useful to look up old investment reports and analyze whether the reasons to invest actually turned out to be correct or, even more importantly, why they were mistaken. We have a natural tendency not to do that—a psychological phenomenon referred to as "hindsight bias"—but it is the only way to learn from mistakes. It also helps to come to terms with the fact that every investor makes mistakes. Only investors who constantly monitor, discuss, and learn from their own mistakes have a chance to get better at investing and survive in the profession. It would be even better if we could learn from the mistakes of others but very few people are capable of this, certainly not independently minded investors.

10. Look for unusual or unexpected South-South connections

Things are rarely what they seem and it pays to spot unusual connections, particularly often overlooked links between companies in emerging markets. For example:

- China's economic boom affected its own stock market less than commodity driven markets like Brazil, Chile, and the Middle East, which produce the iron ore, copper, gold, and oil that a growing China is consuming in vast gulps.
- Peru has become one of the top ten exporters of vegetables to China.
- Most Taiwanese technology firms have the bulk of their operations in China even if the continuing political rhetoric between the two might make that seem impossible.
- Just as aircraft maker Embraer sources and sells in the United States

and elsewhere in the world, a European oil company like Shell has most of its resources in emerging markets while the American oil-service giant Schlumberger derives much of its revenues from Russia and other emerging markets.

- Kazakhstan is building roads and railways from East to West (to supplement the North-South roads that lead to Moscow) in order to cut transportation time for goods from China to Europe, creating new opportunities for its mining and cement companies.
- The Asian market is overtaking the United States as the main export market for countries like South Korea.

The rise of new markets creates a host of new connections. Among them are the increasingly important but often overlooked South-South connections that are creating investment opportunities for those who can identify and act on them.

THE NOT-SO-SECRET RECIPE

During the early days of emerging market investing, searching for stocks that others had never heard of or investing in countries others disdained was enormous fun. Apart from being intellectually and emotionally stimulating, it gave me the feeling that this was more than a job but something that made a difference in the world. Suffering through crises years when we lost nearly half of our clients' money was anything but an amusing experience, even if we more than earned it back again in the recovery that followed. Yet even the most intense perturbations in markets never once shook my core conviction that if we stuck to competitive companies and took advantage of crisis opportunities, we would come out all right, as indeed we, and most importantly, emerging markets investors, have done.

These crises taught me my three most important investment lessons:

1. The past is often a poor predictor of the future.
2. Good times create bad habits[2] but crises and bad times create great companies (and many losers).
3. Only competitive companies survive crises, while companies that can't compete die out. This process of culling and selecting for the most adaptive among the species is simply the essence of natural as well as corporate evolution.

FLAWS, MYTHS,
AND OUT-OF-DATE BENCHMARKS

While commonsense investment rules may be of special interest to individual investors, there are some investment theories used by investment managers and institutional investors that may need a fresh look even if they are held as nearly sacred investment dogmas:

- The efficient markets hypothesis[3] (dear to financial theoreticians) holds that market prices reflect all available information, but in my experience, this runs counter to the actual behavior of markets, which are—fortunately for some investors and active investment managers—anything but efficient.
- Modern portfolio theory's[4] "efficient portfolio" aims at achieving maximum return with minimum portfolio risk but is based on some questionable premises about the relevance of short-term correlations between assets and past volatility for the future.
- Frequently used benchmarks focus backward rather than forward.

MARKETS ARE MORE EMOTIONAL
AND EVEN OBSESSIVE THAN "EFFICIENT"

While it is true that information travels fast, especially with trading desks operating at all hours around the world, I have learned from experience that markets react less to the information itself than to the instantaneous reaction of those who hear or see it. In an instant, facts are turned into opinions and interpretations. The herd instinct takes over. Perception colors reality. With most people reacting the same way, the pull of this herd instinct is so strong that it typically drives markets in new directions, trumping cool analysis and rational calculations. Often for no good reason, the newest fact quickly crowds out other, older information that just as quickly is forgotten but may be much more relevant.

A seasoned analyst quickly learns to use models or explicit rules that enforce a disciplined approach. A standardized data format forces you to pay attention to a *whole range* of data rather than just the newest fact and provides an automatic context. While traders and hedge funds may benefit from instantaneous reactions, investors are usually better off taking some distance. In order to accomplish that, articulating and writing down reasoning is so important. The effect could be compared with taking Prozac. The highs may be lower but the lows will be higher. In any case, the end result will likely be better. Instead of monitoring whether a *stock* has done well or agonizing about whether it will go up, an investor is better off focusing on whether a *company* (1) has the right stuff or, if not, is turning around and (2) is underrated by others.

MODERN PORTFOLIO-BASED MODELS ARE BUILT ON SOME DUBIOUS PREMISES

Modern portfolio theory postulates that the best way to diversify risk is to combine several types of assets that move in different directions over a market cycle. By focusing on the risk and return of entire *portfolios* of assets, portfolio theory marked an enormous advance over the traditional theory that investors should examine the risk of each individual investment separately. Its greatest achievement is that it has allowed investors to move beyond investments that were deemed safe only because they were familiar.

Emerging markets have provided a classic test of this theory, as they have undergone four distinct phases during which they moved faster, slower, or even in a different direction from the American or other developed markets. During the early "discovery" phase (1988–1994), emerging markets equities as an asset class outperformed both the American and other more developed markets. Then they dramatically underperformed during the "crisis" phase of the mid–1990s. They fluctuated in tandem with the American market during the years of the Internet boom (1998–2001). During the "renaissance" phase of the early years of the twenty-first century they uncoupled again. Over the past five years, emerging markets equities have demonstrated robust returns while the American and many other developed markets have by comparison languished. During the next decade we should expect "tailwind" from the growing importance of emerging markets and their middle-class consumers in the global economy, but there will continue to be occasional periods during which emerging markets will underperform the more established markets.

Emerging Markets Go Their Own Way

MSCI and S&P 500 (Total Return) since April 1988

Source: Emerging Markets: Morgan Stanley Capital International Total Return (including gross dividends) through May 31, 2006
US Market: Standard & Poor's 500 Total Return through May 31, 2006
(The MSCI Emerging Markets (EM) IndexSM is a trademark of Morgan Stanley Capital International.
The S&P 500 (500 leading U.S. stocks) is a trademark of Standard and Poor's)

The approach most frequently adopted by modern portfolio theorists is to measure the extent to which assets move up and down together through monthly correlations. It would *seem* to be common sense that diversification should increase when correlations are low. That was more true for emerging markets and the American market well over a decade ago than it is today. Monthly correlations have increased from 0.18 to 0.82 which looks like a dangerous rise. Yet, when I analyzed the data more extensively, I found that monthly correlations were virtually the same during one market cycle (September 1994 to August 1998) when emerging markets declined 55 percent while the American market had a remarkable total return of 125 percent as they were during the years of the Internet boom when both went up and down together but ended up virtually the same with returns of 12 percent and 13 percent respectively. The monthly correlations during these two periods were .51 and .52 respectively. This similarity demonstrates that using monthly correlations (which simply measure whether markets move together during short periods) as a tool to measure risk diversification is of little use. Why should a long-term investor care about short-term correlations? What matters more is the way markets behave over a full market cycle.

> *Correlations were practically the same during one market cycle (September 1994 to August 1998) when emerging markets declined steeply while the American market was up sharply, as they were during the Internet boom (1998–2001) when both went up and down together and had virtually the same returns.*

Returns were hugely different from period to period
Emerging Markets vs. US Market (MSCIF vs. S&P 500)

	Relative Performance	Correlations
Dec. 1987–Sept. 1994	390%	.18
Sept. 1994–Aug. 1998	-165%	.51
Aug. 1998–Sept. 2001	-4%	.52
Sept. 2001–Dec. 2005	127%	.82

Monthly correlations reveal little about longer-term returns or diversification potential

Source: Bloomberg monthly correlations

The other basic premise of modern portfolio theory is to require higher returns for assets that are more *volatile*. Because data series on emerging markets are relatively short, some measure this by looking at the experience of the past three to five years. When I looked into this, I found to my surprise that the much dreaded "volatility" of emerging markets in the years before the crises of the mid-1990s was *the same* as the 19 percent volatility for the American market just five years earlier. Based purely on this measure and without looking more deeply into the fundamental market characteristics, an investor might have been tempted to underestimate the true volatility of emerging markets, which increased sharply to 26 percent during the crisis years. As the Italian driver already knew, the back mirror may be a poor guide for the future.[5] Just when past years show a historic peak, volatility often drops dramatically. Crises do not persist but neither do good times.

Volatility

	S&P	EAFE	MSCI Emerging Markets
1986–1990	19%	23%	25%
1991–1995	10%	15%	19%
1996–2000	16%	14%	26%
2001–2005	15%	15%	21%

Source: EMM Research using index data, average monthly volatility for 5-year periods (The MSCI EAFE [Europe, Australia and Far East] Index TM is a trademark of Morgan Stanley Capital International.)

The concept of not putting all of our eggs in one basket makes eminent sense but the tools we are using are clumsy. Worse, they may even point us in the wrong direction.

HOW DIFFERENT ARE EMERGING MARKETS?

When making the original case for emerging markets twenty-five years ago at the International Finance Corporation,[6] I focused on the following arguments:

- *Diversification* should lower portfolio risk even if individual invest-ments are more risky because emerging markets had traditionally moved in different directions from developed markets (correlations were extremely low then and I had not yet discovered the difference between monthly correlations and longer term market moves).
- Developing countries were *growing* faster. Local consumers would have more money to spend and local companies would be well-positioned to serve this demand while exporters would gain market share.
- *Valuations* were much lower than in the major markets.
- Companies were still *undiscovered and underresearched* but had the potential to become future blue chips.
- Global investors had few investments and were likely to invest more, leading to additional demand from those new investment plans.

Of course, I also highlighted many risks of investing in emerging mar-kets. Local markets were more protected, political regimes were less sta-ble, economic policies were often undisciplined, companies were generally much smaller and less well-managed, while investors were less well protected.

"OLD" AND "NEW" RISKS ARE NOT THE SAME

As we enter the Emerging Markets Century, the time has come to rethink what we mean by "risk." Gazing back in the rearview mirror, we once regarded emerging markets as crisis-prone, volatile, desperately poor, small in the global economy to the point of irrelevancy, dependent on

Western consumer markets, and heavily protected. Stock markets were poorly regulated and prone to manipulation; a lack of participation by institutional investors and pension funds left much room for speculation and insider trading; corporate disclosure was notoriously poor.

More developed markets, in contrast, led in economic stability, technology, market size, and transparency. A better legal framework and corporate governance protected investors while domestic pension funds and a large mutual funds industry were ready buyers of stocks and bonds. And, of course, a huge gap remained in the size, sophistication, and quality of companies between the West and "the Rest."

During the past few decades, much has happened to change this situation, even if our perceptions have not truly caught up with this new reality and thus with the "risk" of investing in emerging markets. In 1991, I emphasized in a *Wall Street Journal* interview that "the key to investing in emerging markets is to pre-position yourself in stocks and markets that are not yet popular and to look for companies nobody is interested in."[7]

Today, the case for emerging market investing is different precisely because (1) these markets themselves are *less* different and more global than before and (2) a growing number of companies are becoming world-class. While emerging markets were until fairly recently regarded as a small yet risky niche, the increasing importance of these countries and the quality of these companies has propelled emerging markets from being the spice of an investment portfolio to a more central role that is more mainstream and less of a gamble. The practical implications of this broad-based shift both in real and perceived risk are that emerging markets should be a core component of investors' portfolios rather than an afterthought but that they will also be less exciting going forward.

> *Improved macroeconomic policies, vastly increased foreign exchange reserves, and healthier corporate balance sheets have made emerging markets less crisis-prone while the United States, much of Europe, and Japan all run large budget deficits and current account deficits in the United States keep increasing. Instead of being debtors, leading emerging markets now are large creditors to the United States. Macroeconomic risks have shifted.*

- *Risk* has decreased: market volatility is lower, economic policies are sounder, and companies are not only more competitive and better managed but in much better financial shape.

- *Valuations* are still better but the gap has decreased and will continue to decrease.

Emerging market valuations in a global context

| | Relative valuations (historic 2005) | | | |
	P/E	P/BV	P/CE	Yield
North America	17.3	2.8	11.6	1.9
Europe	14.0	2.3	8.7	3.0
Japan	18.2	2.0	9.3	1.2
Emerging Markets	13.7	2.3	8.3	2.5

As of June 16, 2006
Source: Morgan Stanley and EMM calculations
P/E - price/earnings multiple
P/BV - price/book value
P/CE - price/cash earnings
Yield - dividend yield

- *Companies* are no longer second rate but are becoming more world-class. The leading emerging market companies are often as global and as competitive as their developed country counterparts and many have returns on equity, operating margins, and debt to equity ratios that are in line with or even better than their counterparts.
- *From debtors to creditors:* Developing countries *repaid* more loans to "official" lenders like the World Bank and IMF than global portfolio investors put into emerging markets in 2005.[8] Their central banks are now major official creditors to the United States and other deficit spenders rather than the other way around. Workers' remittances back to emerging markets are now higher than the capital flight from these markets in the past. Acquisitions of companies in both directions keep growing while emerging market investors are active investors in their own markets and are slowly beginning to diversify their portfolios into developed markets.
- *A reversal in macroeconomic discipline:* Improved macroeconomic policies, vastly increased foreign exchange reserves, and healthier corporate balance sheets have made emerging markets less crisis-prone (but of course, not crisis-proof). Many emerging markets, having undergone privatization, now have smaller state sectors than developed markets. In contrast, the United States, Europe, and Japan all run large budget deficits while current account deficits in the

United States keep increasing. Large debts of the United States and other developed countries are increasingly held by emerging markets. When will investors begin to worry about this *shift* in macroeconomic and corporate risks?

- *Corporate governance:* Scandals in the United States from Enron to WorldCom have not only undermined the trust in accounting and investment data but also demonstrated that losses can be hidden or earnings sometimes overblown. Curiously, better disclosure and corporate governance have had the opposite effect in emerging markets (even if they still have a long way to go) with investors waking up to the fact that it provides emerging multinationals with fewer opportunities to hide earnings. As a result, earnings have risen rather than been downgraded. The Internet boom and bust also taught many investors that it is just as easy to lose a lot of money on well-known stocks in major markets as on unknown companies in emerging markets. Disclosure of information by individual companies in emerging markets, while still inferior to that in Anglo-Saxon countries, is rapidly improving. Many more companies follow international accounting standards like GAAP. Even the notoriously poor disclosure of Russian companies has improved while the Chinese Securities and Exchange Commission (under the leadership of the now-governor of the Central Bank) has made major efforts to improve the quality and flow of information. Most of the world-class companies cited in this book boast world-class corporate governance. The greatest problem for active investors in emerging markets today is no longer a lack of quality information but the difficulty of finding information that is not yet well known or widely publicized in research.
- Emerging markets are *no longer undiscovered.* My old friend and colleague George Hoguet of State Street Global Advisors has conducted some interesting research showing that there are more broker estimates now for the average emerging market company than for Japanese companies or for the two thousand companies included in the Russell-2000 universe.[9] Fortunately for active investors, only a tiny portion of the 15,000 emerging market listings are included on the radar screens of brokers and investors. This dynamic segment (that could be called the "new emerging markets") is constantly expanding with a growing stream of new issues.

NO MORE CRISES?

While it would be a stretch to describe emerging markets today as crisis-immune, they are certainly less prone to crisis than before. There is an amazing difference in the financial health of the four major emerging economies (China, India, Brazil, and Russia) in 1990 and 2005, as illustrated in the table with Key Data below. The same progress on all vital indicators, from inflation, foreign debt, reserves, and exports to current accounts and budget deficits, is visible for emerging markets included in the MSCI indexes as a group.

Key Data

$ billion	BRICS		Emerging Markets (including BRIC's)	
	1990	2005	1990	2005
GDP	2,255	4,577	4,092	9,292
Inflation	594%	4.9%	468%	4.7%
Foreign Reserves	45	1,201	213	2,205
Foreign Debt	359	760	1,016	2,236
Exports	182	1,220	694	3,392
As % of world	6%	12%	21%	34%
Current Account	-2	206	-14	+217
Budget surplus (deficit)	-221	+19	-249	-29
MSCI Market Cap - float	183**	482	98	1,650
MSCI Full Market cap	222**	1,489	1,072	3,882
# of stocks included	159**	195	1,031	828

Source: IMF Direction of Trade Statistics, J.P. Morgan data, MSCI data
*1994 MSCI market capitalization is adjusted for "float," i.e., only counts investable shares.
**1996

Emerging nations now own over 75 percent of all foreign exchange reserves (led by China, Taiwan, and Korea) while the reserves of the BRICs are now nearly double their foreign debt, which is practically the reverse of the situation in 1990. With few exceptions (Venezuela and, until recently, Turkey), emerging markets no longer suffer from high inflation as many did before the crises of the 1990s. Their exports have skyrocketed and their current account deficits have often turned into surpluses. With greater budgetary discipline they are no longer mired in budget deficits, even as *new* debtors like the United States rack up massive current account and budget deficits, which are effectively financed by the newly wealthy and more frugal nations of the developing world.

For better or worse, emerging markets are becoming less and less different from the mature markets as they themselves mature, which is not to say that economic crises cannot be triggered unexpectedly. An energy crisis could disrupt economies. A pandemic like the avian flu could lay waste to not just an entire agricultural sector in several countries but lead to a reversal of trade relations, as SARS did in a less destructive way. A nuclear conflict or even nuclear stalemate could create huge geopolitical tensions. A massive terrorist attack could lead to severe disruptions. If the world suddenly woke up to the fact that nuclear nonproliferation might well be dead as a doornail, scientific and high-technology exchanges between members and nonmembers of the nuclear club could be dramatically reduced. Any sudden slowdown in China or, worse, a financial or real estate crisis, major political unrest, or a military conflict over Taiwan would undermine the dynamism of the Asian region and could lead to a sharp reversal in the strong uptrend in many commodity prices.

ARE WORLD-CLASS COMPANIES
GREAT INVESTMENTS? IT DEPENDS. . . .

The companies discussed in this book are all success stories, the proud survivors of first local then increasingly global competition. Achieving a competitive edge has been an obsession for all of them. Their most common trait is that they *sought out* competition before their own borders opened up by exporting. They knew that competitors would find them anyhow and that the global marketplace is a great testing ground of the brave. They adapted, experimented, and became bigger and better. Each in their own way became world-class but not without missteps and crises.

Are the world class companies in this book likely to be *the* best investments in the future? Probably not. Even if most of the companies discussed in prior pages *have been* excellent investments in the past. But if we know anything about investing, it is that past performance is no predictor of future performance. The more relevant questions today are (1) how sustainable is their competitive edge, whether it is a market niche, design, technology, cost advantage, efficiency, brand, or natural resource, and (2) are they *still* underrated?

The twenty-five world-class companies discussed in this book have a good chance to grow and do well in the future. Many of them belong in a well-diversified global stock portfolio.

Even today, many of these companies still have a "zip code" problem. If their headquarters were in New York, London, or Tokyo, investors would look at them differently. Compared to their industry peers in developed countries their valuations often remain lower. In other words, many still suffer from an *excessive emerging markets discount* even if the gap has understandably shrunk over the past years. Many are still underrated. This lingering prejudice helps investors even now. But they are no longer the bargains they were a decade or so ago because they have been *discovered* by emerging market specialists and even global investors.

Moreover, just as they once challenged major traditional multinationals in the West and Japan, they in turn are now being challenged by newcomers in places like China and India. Those that continue to be industry leaders, keep costs competitive, and innovate should not only be admired and feared by others in their industry but remain good investments. Those that falter in the global market will be punished with lower stock prices.

What is more interesting is that I am convinced that an understanding of how these companies became successful provides a series of clues to investors to (1) avoid companies that do not have "the right stuff" and (2) identify the *next generation* of world-class companies, as yet underrated, which will make for successful investments in the future.

I believe that the *real* questions investors should ask themselves today are:

- In building an investment portfolio, how does it matter that we are entering the Emerging Markets Century?
- Why is it helpful to understand what has made these companies successful?
- What should we look for in the next generation of world-class companies?

Stock Market Returns (December 1995–December 2005) of World-Class Companies

Company	Country	Founded	2005 Sales ($mn)	2005 Earnings ($mn)	Company Total $ return (Incl. Gross Dividends)	Local Market Total $ return (Incl. Gross Dividends)	Difference (Total Return)	Company 10-year Annualized $ return (Incl. Gross Dividends)	Local Market 10-year Annualized return in $ (Incl. Gross Dividends)	Difference (Anualized)	Companies that have overseas listings	Note
Samsung Electronics	Korea	1969	56,700	7,413	514%	105%	408%	20%	8%	12%	GDR	
Petrobras	Brazil	1953	56,324	9,753	894%	331%	563%	26%	16%	10%	ADR	
Hon Hai	Taiwan	1974	28,300	1,268	2523%	23%	2500%	39%	2%	36%	GDR	
Hyundai Motor	Korea	1967	26,743	2,262	312%	105%	207%	15%	8%	8%	GDR	
POSCO	Korea	1968	25,680	3,922	311%	105%	205%	15%	8%	8%	ADR	
Reliance	India	1958	17,673	1,903	689%	221%	468%	23%	10%	13%		
America Movil	Mexico	***	16,753	2,969	374%	155%	219%	48%	26%	21%	ADR	(5 years)
Telmex	Mexico	**	14,986	2,592	540%	425%	115%	20%	18%	2%	ADR	
CEMEX	Mexico	1906	14,964	2,062	406%	425%	-19%	18%	18%	0%	ADR	
CVRD	Brazil	1942	13,958	4,841	786%	331%	456%	24%	16%	9%	ADR	
Sasol	South Africa	1950	11,150	1,541	533%	104%	429%	20%	7%	13%	ADR	
Hyundai Heavy	Korea	1972	13,577	171	660%	232%	428%	29%	14%	15%		(9 years)
TSMC	Taiwan	1987	8,239	2,900	682%	23%	659%	23%	2%	21%	ADR	
Tenaris	Argentina	2003	6,736	1,278	541%	106%	435%	86%	61%	25	ADR	(3 years)
Modelo	Mexico	1922	4,549	669	249%	425%	-176%	13%	18%	-5%	ADR	
Embraer	Brazil	1960	3,758	292	3293%	331%	2962%	42%	16%	26%	ADR	
Yue Yuen	Taiwan	1988	3,155	310	539%	23%	516%	20%	2%	18%	ADR	
Televisa	Mexico	1954	2,987	563	267%	425%	-158%	14%	18%	-4%	ADR	
MISC	Malaysia	1968	2,995	801	186%	-20%	206%	11%	-2%	13%		
Lenovo	China	1984	2,892	144	2209%	-31%	2240%	37%	-4%	40%	ADR	
High Tech	Taiwan	1997	2,266	366	686%	18%	668%	99%	19%	80%	GDR	(3 years)
Haier****	China	1984	635	56 (E)	368%	-31%	399%	17%	-4%	20%		
Infosys	India	1981	2,020	551	18942%	221%	18721%	69%	12%	57%	ADR	
Aracruz	Brazil	1972	1,345	340	255%	331%	-75%	14%	16%	-2%	ADR	
Ranbaxy	India	1961	1,315	143	220%	221%	-1%	12%	12%	0%	GDR	
Concha y Toro	Chile	1883	360	34	405%	74%	331%	18%	6%	12%	ADR	

	Companies	MSCI EM Free	MSCI World
10-year Annualized Return	19.9%	7.9%	6.7%
Total Return	512.4%	113.6%	90.4%

*For America Movil, Tenaris, Hyundai Heavy and HTC data is less than 10 years and Benchmark data has been shortened to match the time period since listing

**Privatized 1990

***Spun off from Telmex in 2000

****Full information on Haier group not available; information on Hong Kong listed company only, which is incomplete.

Sources: MSCI, Bloomberg, Company Annual Reports, EMM Analysts.

GDR: Global Depository Receipt

ARDR: American Depository Receipt

INVESTING WILL BE DIFFERENT
IN THE EMERGING MARKETS CENTURY

Most institutional investors now have a portion of their portfolio in emerging markets, although some feel they are being daring when in fact they are still timid. Investors vividly remember past crises, volatility, lack of liquidity, and the peripheral place of emerging markets among the world's assets, but they should also look forward and focus on a long-term, secular trend: the improved quality, economic importance, and growth of this asset class.

When deciding where to put their money, a typical starting point for investors is to ask how much emerging market stocks are worth as a share of all global stocks ("market capitalization"). Yet in attempting to determine this "neutral benchmark," the MSCI (Morgan Stanley Capital International) Emerging Markets Index immediately sows confusion. According to MSCI, which is widely used by the institutional investors, the share of emerging markets stocks of all global market capitalization is 6.5 percent,[10] but this only includes just over 800 of the larger listed stocks. In a major adjustment announced in 2000 and implemented in 2001 when trading activity in emerging markets was low following a major correction, MSCI curtailed the number of stocks included in the Emerging Markets Index in a realistic effort to count only the "float" (shares not owned by founding families and, in the case of state enterprises, major government ownership). In another major index, originally compiled by IFC and now called the S&P Emerging Markets Index, the share of emerging markets is a more realistic 12 percent.[11]

> *Investors who do not have a reasonable chunk of their portfolio in emerging markets simply do not see where the world is going, while those who feel valuations of world-class companies require a huge "risk premium" have an outdated perception of risk*

I believe that MSCI seriously understates the share of emerging markets among global stocks for several reasons.

First, there have been few major additions to the MSCI index despite many new share issues and even though liquidity, market capitalization, and trading of once-smaller stocks have increased fairly dramatically since 2000.

Second, we overlook that institutional investors in developed markets in practice "lock up" many shares so that they can only nominally be counted as "float" while there are many fewer institutional investors (and more international investors) in most emerging markets.

Third, the earnings of emerging market companies make up well over 12 percent of the world's total earnings.

And finally, the MSCI benchmark includes only about 830 or just over 5 percent of the more than 15,000 stocks actually listed on the emerging stock exchanges.[12] *More than one out of every three stocks listed in the world is now from emerging markets.* Some would say that many of the stocks not included in the major indices used by investors are small, illiquid, and hard to buy. On the other hand, this is precisely the segment of the market bound to become the most dynamic in the future. If we use a broader list of markets and the more comprehensive listings of the International Federation of Stock Exchanges, around 19 percent of the value of all stocks is in emerging markets and this share has been growing steadily.[13] Even so, this is still below the 21 percent emerging markets contribute to the global economy. As emerging economies continue to outgrow the

> *If large and small stocks are counted, around 18–19% of the world's market capitalization is in emerging markets—and that share is likely to keep growing over the next few decades.*

developed countries, their share of the world economy will overtake the industrialized countries over the next twenty-five to thirty years. The same will happen with stock markets—possibly even faster—as emerging multinationals begin to benefit from "tailwind" and emerging market investors have more money to invest in their own markets through pension funds and mutual funds.

Over the next years, I expect that many investors will gradually adjust their "neutral" benchmarks from below 5 percent today to around 20 percent. Over the next decade, this benchmark will probably approach 50 percent of all global stocks. For most investors, I believe that it would make sense to "average in" and add about 1 percent year-in year-out for the next few decades to keep up with the growing share of emerging economies in the world economy. A variant on this approach would be to add 2 to 3 percent following a year of negative performance of emerging markets and not add at all the year following three years of outperformance of developed markets. Investors are always tempted to invest after several years of good performance of an asset class while they should do just the opposite. Unfortunately, risks are always highest when things look best and there is a danger of some investors going overboard again in their enthusiasm. Investors who were early believers and already allocated more than 15–20 percent of their equity portfolio to emerging markets should give thought to technically "underweighting" their neutral benchmark after a series of years (such as 2002–2005) in which emerging markets outperformed the developed markets until a major correction occurs.

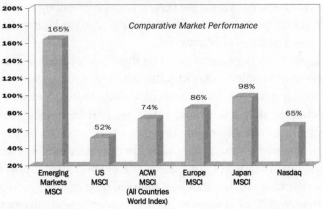

Strong Emerging Markets Performance During December 2002–2005 Period

Comparative Market Performance

Source: MSCI (Total Return)

WHY COMPETITIVENESS MATTERS, AND IS USUALLY "MAN-MADE"

Does it make a difference to know whether a company is second-rate or world-class? Absolutely. Is grasping the difference sufficient to ensure that investors will make money investing in these companies? Surely not. It is worth repeating the essential investment message of this book: *The ideal investment is a company that not only has "the right stuff" but is still underrated, turning around, or undiscovered.* If everyone else (this consensus thinking is often called "the market") feels the same as you, there is little chance you have picked a true winner. In contrast, if no one else likes the stock, there is no guarantee that the stock is not an abysmal pick.

> *Often the best investment is a company that not only has "the right stuff" but is underrated, turning around, or still undiscovered.*

WHAT TO LOOK FOR IN THE NEXT GENERATION
OF WORLD-CLASS COMPANIES

The world-class companies profiled in this book did *not* become leaders in their industries just because they relied on cheap labor, natural resources, or protection. "Man-made factors" were always crucial to differentiate them from their competitors. Ambitious goals, savvy management, a global mind-set, a willingness to ignore conventional wisdom, an eagerness to test themselves against the best, a "can-do" mentality, and constant adaptation (in retrospect often called "strategy") are the hallmarks of virtually all of these successful companies.

The lessons from the examples set by these companies should not only be an inspiration to other companies that aspire to become world-class but should also help investors pick companies likely to be the *next generation* of world-class companies, which, I believe, will be among the greatest investment winners of the coming decade.

A disciplined investment approach always examines key valuation, growth, and quality ratios of companies. But beyond these ratios, there are always "soft" factors that cannot be expressed quantitatively in addition to industry trends, and, of course, political, economic, and currency risks. I have found that some of the key soft factors to watch are:

- A corporate culture that rewards unconventional thinking, pride in work, and speed in getting products to market
- An obsession with quality
- Bold but disciplined ambition, including hiring the best and the brightest and a willingness to invest large amounts in R&D for the future
- A strong desire to test themselves in global markets with the most demanding customers and outflank competitors through novel rather than textbook solutions
- An unwillingness to cut corners with tax authorities, shareholders, and clients
- A high speed of adaptation to crises, new industry trends, and customer demands
- A constant search for products and market niches that others overlook
- The ability to translate strategy to others—clients and staff
- Benchmarking against the best in the world

To sum up: Those who do their homework, dig deep, don't jump to conclusions, are not easily scared or overenthusiastic but keep a cool head, read everything from newspaper articles to broker reports with interest but healthy skepticism, diversify their choices, have patience, and learn from their mistakes can't go far wrong and have a chance to do better than the "market" or the average investor.

Sound easy? Perhaps. Yet it is a surprisingly tall order and harder to follow than one might expect. Successful investing requires three intangible attributes that are not in abundant supply: the discipline to dig deeper, never-ending curiosity, and a "cool" mind-set. Keeping your cool in the Buddhist as opposed to the fashionable sense, of course.

INVESTMENT LESSONS

1. *Buy only stocks that are **underrated** rather than "hot," cheap, fast-growing, safe, or even world-class. Prejudice is an investor's best friend. Conventional wisdom often reflects lazy thinking.*
2. *Always do your own research and dig deep.*
3. *Distrust the "wisdom" of the markets.*
4. *Use crises to get "in" and investment fashions to get "out."*
5. *Be skeptical of proven success because it is quickly recognized by other investors and competitors.*
6. *The greatest potential is in the **next** generation of world-class companies and their competitiveness really matters.*
7. *The best insights come from unusual sources. What you hear from companies, read in newspapers, or are told by brokers is often already reflected in market prices.*
8. *Spend more time studying economic and industry trends than reacting to events that—good or bad—are always overblown.*
9. *Always write down **why** you made a decision to invest or sell. Later, take the time to look back at your notes and analyze why an investment **really** worked or didn't work.*
10. *Look for unusual and unexpected South-South connections.*

FINANCIAL PROFILES OF 25 WORLD-CLASS EMERGING MULTINATIONALS

America Movil
Wireless communications leader in Latin America

BACKGROUND
America Movil is Latin America's #1 mobile telecommunications provider (and #4 globally) with over 100 million subscribers as of March 2006. It plans to add another 50 million by 2008 (or half of all new subscribers in the region). America Movil dominates the Mexican market with a 70% share but is also active in Brazil (#3, 23%), Argentina, Colombia, Peru, Uruquay, Paraguay, Venezuela,* Puerto Rico,* Dominican Republic,* and Central America.
*upon completion of its acquisition of Verizon's regional holdings

HISTORY
Carlos Slim, the world's third richest man, owns a controlling interest in America Movil along with minority partner Southwest Bell Communications (now ATT). After acquiring Telmex, a fixed-line monopoly in one of Mexico's earliest privatizations in 1990, Slim expanded its network and quickly recognized the potential of mobile. America Movil was spun off in 2000 to focus exclusively on the mobile business in Latin America. After watching American and European operators overpay for telecom assets and then fight the early battles, Slim has acquired $10 billion worth of mobile assets from ATT, Bell South, Verizon, Hutchison, and others.

INDUSTRY
Wireless telecommunications have taken emerging markets by storm because of poor fixed-line infrastructure and the flexibility of pre-paid plans. Penetration rates are catching up with developed markets. Mobile users now often exceed fixed-line subscribers and global handset sales growth is led by emerging markets. Voice communications still dominate revenues but 3G broadband access with "smart" phones will spread rapidly. The top five wireless providers include Vodafone, China Mobile, China Unicom, America Movil, and Telefonica Moviles.

COMPETITION

2005 Data	Market Cap ($bn)	Revenues ($bn)	Net Earnings ($bn)	ROE	P/E	Net Debt/Equity
America Movil	53.1	16.7	2.9	38%	17.7	0.6
China Mobile	93.9	29.7	6.5	21%	14.1	(0.3)
Telefonica Moviles	45.5	20.5	2.4	41%	20.0	1.7
China Unicom	10.2	10.6	0.6	7%	16.7	0.4
Vodafone Group	181.4	62.9	(13.9)	(7%)	NA	0.1

SUCCESS FACTORS
- Dominant position in Mexico
- Many low-cost acquisitions
- Increasingly regional footprint
- Huge cash flow to finance acquisitions

CHALLENGES
- Keeping dominant position in Mexico
- Intense competition in Brazil
- Competing with Telefonica in major markets like Argentina and Chile

Aracruz Celulose
All pulp, no paper

BACKGROUND

Aracruz pioneered the idea of "stand-alone" pulpwood produced for the global market rather than for an integrated in-house paper mill. Previously, most pulpwood came from pines in colder climates and integrated mills in Scandinavia, the United States, and Canada. The pulp industry has moved South—mostly to Brazil, Chile, and Indonesia—because eucalyptus trees, which are prevalent in tropical climates, grow much faster and their pulp is more suitable for tissue and other paper. Aracruz owes its success to low wood costs, a focus on improving yield through sophisticated forest management and genetic engineering, large scale self sufficiency in energy, integrated logistics, and long-term contracts with customers, with products tailored to their needs.

HISTORY

Aracruz was born in 1967, when it planted its first eucalyptus trees in Brazil. The company's first mill opened in 1978 and two more mills had been added by 2001. In 2005, another mill owned jointly with Finland's Stora began operations in Brazil. Today, Aracruz is the world's largest and lowest cost market pulp maker for tissue, printing, and photographic paper, with 30% of the global supply of market pulp. With 98% of its production directed towards exports, Aracruz has customers on five continents and is one of Brazil's large exporters. In 2006, the company became one of only a few Brazilian companies considered "investment grade" by the rating agencies of Moody's and Standard & Poor's.

INDUSTRY

The integrated paper and pulp industry is centuries old but didn't become international until after World War II. As the demand for tissue and toilet paper expanded around the globe and paper mills increased in size while easily accessible forests disappeared, new suppliers for pulp in bulk form were able to establish a rapidly growing market niche. In recent years, demand from China and the Asian Tigers has grown in addition to growth from Europe and Japan.

COMPETITION

2005 Data	Market Cap ($bn)	Revenues ($bn)	Net Earnings ($mn)	ROE	P/E	Net Debt/Equity
Aracruz	5.1	1.4	340	31%	16.6	0.4
Votorantim	2.4	1.1	264	14%	10.1	0.6
Stora Enso	11.0	16.4	(162)	(2%)	NA	0.7
Weyerhaeuser	16.3	22.6	733	8%	18.6	0.8

SUCCESS FACTORS

- Use of fast growing eucalyptus
- Superior forest management
- Tight operating management focused on efficiency, technology, and IT
- Close, long-term customer relations

CHALLENGES

- Pulp's highly cyclical nature
- Risk of Chinese slowdown impacting pulp market
- Unstable shareholder structure with competitor VCP vying for control

CEMEX, S.A. de C.V.
Mexico's global cement champion

BACKGROUND
CEMEX's rise to global status began with the acquisition of two Spanish cement companies in 1992. An anti-dumping suit that imposed a 58% tariff on U.S. imports had forced the company into a more global focus. CEMEX has continued its acquisitions in Latin America, Asia, the United States, and Europe with the backing of strong free cash flow from its existing operations and continued dominance of the Mexican cement market. Its latest acquisition of RMC has doubled its revenues, broadened its product line, and made CEMEX the #1 cement producer in the United States and #2 in the United Kingdom. CEMEX is well known for highly centralized management, strong IT, and effective post-merger integration teams. CEMEX's aim is to transform cement from a commodity into a branded product.

HISTORY
CEMEX was founded in Mexico in 1906 under the name Cementos Hidalgo. The company grew rapidly in the 1960s, building its own plants and making acquisitions throughout the country. In 1976 CEMEX went public and acquired its main competitor Cementos Guadalajara, making it Mexico's top cement producer. In 1989 it consolidated its dominance of the Mexican market by acquiring Mexico's #2 cement producer, Cementos Tolteca, and in the 1990s, it began a global acquisition spree. By 2004 the company was operating in over fifty countries and today CEMEX is the third largest cement producer worldwide.

INDUSTRY
Prior to CEMEX's Spanish acquisition in 1992, the cement industry was dominated by a select group of European companies. In the United States, cement imports now account for 25% of the market, compared with a mere 10% twenty years ago. Global cement production is rising but the industry is rapidly consolidating, with CEMEX among its leaders.

COMPETITION

2005 Data	Market Cap ($bn)	Revenues ($bn)	Net Earnings ($bn)	ROE	P/E	Net Debt/Equity
CEMEX	21.0	14.9	2.1	23%	9.9	1.3
Lafarge	15.7	19.8	1.4	12%	11.9	0.6
Holcim	15.6	14.8	1.2	15%	13.3	0.9
Siam Cement	7.1	5.4	0.8	53%	9.1	1.4

SUCCESS FACTORS
- Dominance of Mexican market
- Emphasis on global competitiveness
- Systematic acquisition strategy
- Effective post-merger integration
- Industry leader in the use of IT

CHALLENGES
- Highly centralized management of increasingly sprawling operations
- Managing huge cash flow profitably
- Expanding into Asia
- Turning a commodity into a brand

Concha y Toro
A global wine brand from the South

BACKGROUND
Concha y Toro has built a successful export business based on modernization of its wine-making process, aggressive distribution, and global brand recognition. The company seeks a balance between producing affordable wines in competition with other global wine brands and catering its high-end brands (such as Don Melchor) to the preferences of fine wine connoisseurs. In the 1980's, Concha y Toro doubled the size of its vineyards while hiring a separate renowned wine expert for each one to maintain quality control. During the 1990's, Concha y Toro gained control of major vineyards in Argentina and became a major exporter there. It also created a trendy boutique vineyard in Chile, catering to the British market. In cooperation with Bordeaux's Philippe de Rothschild vineyard, it is focused on creating Latin America's first Grand Cru.

HISTORY
Concha y Toro has been making wine since 1875 but it did not become an active player in the global wine market until new Chilean economic policies in the 1980s forced the company to compete internationally under new ownership. By 2004 the company was selling its wine in 110 countries. In 1994 Concha y Toro became the first vineyard to be listed on the New York Stock Exchange. The company has been named "the most important vineyard in Chile and Argentina" *(Wine Spectator)* and rated the best-selling Chilean wine in leading American restaurants (*Wine and Spirits* survey). With revenues of over $300 million, Concha y Toro ranks among the twenty largest winemakers in the world, is South America's leading wine brand, and the #2 import in the United States.

INDUSTRY
After traditional wine producers like France, Italy, and Spain first lost ground against new winemaking methods in the United States, the global wine industry moved from North to South, with Australia, Chile, and South Africa becoming major players. The exports of Chilean wineries grew from a mere $10 million in 1985 to $835 million, 60% of their production, in 2004, making Chile the #5 wine exporter worldwide.

COMPETITION

2005 Data	Market Cap ($bn)	Revenues ($bn)	Net Earnings ($mn)	ROE	P/E	Net Debt/Equity
Concha y Toro	1.1	0.4	34	12%	28.5	0.5
Constellation*	0.5	0.5	33	11%	16.1	0.8
Robert Mondavi*	0.6	0.5	26	5%	20.1	0.7

SUCCESS FACTORS
- Understanding need to export its wines
- Focus on improving quality
- Strong marketing and distribution of its brand
- Focus on favorable ratings in prestigious wine publications

CHALLENGES
- Battling prejudices against New World quality
- Raising prices
- Growing competition from Australian ("Yellowtail") and South African wine brands

*Data as of February 2006 (February year-end)   **Data as of June 2005 (June year-end)

CVRD
Feeding the furnace

BACKGROUND

CVRD currently harbors the world's largest and richest supply of iron, the Carajas mine, making it by far the largest and lowest-cost producer of iron worldwide with 30% of global exports. CVRD is also the world's #2 manganese producer, #5 in copper, and has ambitious plans in bauxite and nickel. Its 5,600 miles of rail and eight marine terminals transport two thirds of Brazil's freight. The company has sales offices in all major markets and mining operations in fourteen countries in the Americas, Africa, and Europe but 90% of its mining still takes place in Brazil. CEO Agnelli's goal is to make that 30% within the next ten years.

HISTORY

CVRD began in 1942 as a publicly-run company with the hope that Brazil would become a major steel producer. After a contentious privatization in 1997, new management sold off unrelated businesses and turned the huge mining and logistics operations into a world-class company. Chinese ambitions to establish the world's largest steel industry have driven up the demand for iron ore in recent years. The resulting huge cash flow allows CVRD to diversify and modernize its mining operations.

INDUSTRY

The economics of mining have changed fundamentally. Traditional mining reserves are being exhausted while new reserves are discovered, strip mining in more densely populated areas has become unpopular, the center of global manufacturing has moved South, and huge vessels make transportation of commodities over sea feasible. After decades of small, monotone price increases, rapidly increasing Chinese demand has suddenly made the iron ore market and other commodities red hot. CVRD still remains behind other giants such as Anglo-American, BHP-Billiton, and Rio Tinto as a diversified global producer but a takeover bid of Inco in Canada, the worlds #2 nickel producer in August 2006 may soon change this.

COMPETITION

2005 Data	Market Cap ($bn)	Revenues ($bn)	Net Earnings ($bn)	ROE	P/E	Net Debt/Equity
CVRD	45.6	14.0	4.3	12%	28.5	0.5
Anglo-American	50.3	29.4	3.5	15%	13.8	0.2
BHP Billiton*	31.5	29.6	6.4	41%	12.2	0.5
Rio Tinto	23.1	19.0	5.2	39%	13.2	0.1
Alcoa	25.7	26.2	1.2	9%	17.4	0.4

SUCCESS FACTORS
- Unmatched natural assets at low costs
- Focus on mining and efficient production

CHALLENGES
- Risk of hard landing for China
- Loss of focus with diversification
- Becoming a global mining operation

*Data as at June 2005 (June year-end)

Embraer
Flying high after a tough ride, it is helping airlines to "right size"

BACKGROUND
Embraer is not yet a household name like Boeing or Airbus, but it already dominates the regional jet market—competing with Canadian Bombardier, and its former competitors Fairchild-Dornier and Fokker bankrupt. Embraer has grown into the world's fourth largest airplane producer, building over 5,400 planes since 1969 at a current rate of over 140 per year. Its most popular models are regional jets that seat 50–110 made for clients such as US Air, JetBlue, Cross Air, and Chinese Southern Airlines. Its niche is expanding fast and it is beginning to manufacture in China as well.

HISTORY
Embraer was founded by the Brazilian government in 1969 to produce military and commercial aircrafts. After initial export success in its state-sponsored years with its Bandit turboprop, the company saw its sales plunge from $700 million to $177 million between 1989 and 1994, and was forced to privatize. Embraer then focused on the development of its new fifty-seat twin-engine jet, the ERJ 145, whose success prompted further focus on small regional jets. After eleven years in the red, Embraer returned to profitability in 1998 and now has a $10 billion order book, including nearly 900 orders for the new E170–190 series.

INDUSTRY
The major players in the airplane industry are Boeing and Airbus. However, they have had little interest in aircrafts suited for short regional flights. Their focus has been mostly on large planes best suited for flying longer distances. The entire industry has struggled since the terrorist attacks in late 2001.

COMPETITION

2005 Data	Market Cap ($bn)	Revenues ($bn)	Net Earnings ($mn)	ROE	P/E	Net Debt/Equity
Embraer	6.6	3.8	291	15%	23.3	(0.2)
Boeing	53.4	54.8	2,572	23%	29.4	0.4
EADS (Airbus)	30.1	42.5	2,083	11%	15.1	(0.3)
Bombardier*	4.6	14.7	249	11%	23.7	0.8

SUCCESS FACTORS
- Finding a market niche ignored by big plane makers
- Taking advantage of greater competition and regulatory changes
- Strong, low-cost engineering
- High quality planes which are cheaper to buy and more cost-efficient to run

CHALLENGES
- Vulnerable to cyclical setbacks
- New shareholder structure
- Competition with Boeing and Airbus in 100+ seater arena

*Data as of January 06 (January year-end)

Grupo Modelo
Taking Corona Beer global

BACKGROUND

Corona took the American market by storm in the 1980s, becoming the leader among imported beer brands (with over 30% of this market) thanks to its distinctive bottle, slice of lime, and beach beer image. In the process, it beat Heineken and numerous other brands and formed the basis for building a global brand. Corona is the leading beer brand in Mexico, the world's seventh largest beer market. It ranks fourth among all beer brands worldwide (after Bud Light, Bud, and Inbev's Skol), with leading positions among imports in countries such as Canada and Australia.

HISTORY

Pablo Diez Fernandez founded Modelo in 1925, although the beer market in Mexico did not really take off until after World War II, when Modelo began to broaden its network of domestic distributors and, through a series of acquisitions, expanded from its stronghold in the Southern part of Mexico to the North, just as the Pan American Highway began to allow national distribution. Over time, Modelo became Mexico's largest beer company with 56% of the domestic market today.

INDUSTRY

Even if beer taste is often local, the global beer industry has been rapidly consolidating with all the leading companies now seeking a global presence. Modelo has tied up with the world's largest brewer, Anheuser Busch, which has a 35% stake. Its larger and more efficient competitor, Ambev in Brazil, has a 50–50 tie-up with Belgium's Interbrew (of Stella Artois, Becks fame) and South African Breweries bought Miller Beer. Corona and other Modelo brands are now sold in 150 countries.

COMPETITION

2005 Data	Market Cap ($bn)	Revenues ($bn)	Net Earnings ($mn)	ROE	P/E	Net Debt/Equity
Grupo Modelo	12	4.5	669	14%	17.2	(0.3)
Anheuser Busch	33	15.0	1,839	61%	17.7	2.3
Inbev	27	14.5	1,123	9%	24.4	0.4
Ambev	23	6.6	635	8%	31.8	0.3
Sab-Miller*	30	15.3	1,440	14%	18.8	0.5
Heineken	16	13.4	946	21%	17.2	0.6

SUCCESS FACTORS
- Initial focus on local market
- Building a global brand with a distinct, non-Mexican image
- Active marketing in export markets

CHALLENGES
- Keeping control of its home market
- Maintaining its iconic brand image
- Merger of Ambev with Interbrew and other global brewer consolidations

*Data as at March 2006 (March year-end)

Haier

A rising Chinese brand in household appliances

BACKGROUND

Haier is the undisputed market leader in China, the world's biggest appliance market, with a 34% market share. Haier's rising global brand can be found not only in Wal-Mart but in stores in many countries. By 2004, Haier was one of only a handful of emerging market brands to make the World Brand Laboratory top-100 brands list. Haier has made a big export push with factories in twenty-two countries from Italy and the United States to the Philippines and Iran, eighteen international design institutes, and 30,000 employees worldwide. It now produces over 6 million refrigerators a year, as well as air conditioners, TVs, washing machines, handsets, and other home electronics.

HISTORY

In 1984, Zhang Ruimin, a senior manager at a refrigerator plant owned by the munici-pal government in Qingdao, China, took over Haier and quickly set about reforming the struggling operation. Within a year, Haier almost broke even, turned a profit by the next, began to export in 1991, became listed in Shanghai in 1993, and had nearly $2 billion in sales by 2004. It caught global attention by an ambitious, albeit unsuccessful, bid to take over Maytag in 2005.

INDUSTRY

Whirlpool, Electrolux, and Bosch-Siemens are the top three producers of household appliances worldwide. Haier comes in fourth (third in refrigerators). More household appliances are now sold in China than in the United States.

COMPETITION

2005 Data	Market Cap ($bn)	Revenues ($bn)	Net Earnings ($mn)	ROE	P/E	Net Debt/Equity
Haier	0.5	0.6	(56)	(76%)	NA	(0.2)
Whirlpool	5.7	14.3	422	25%	12.4	0.4
Electrolux	11.0	16.4	(162)	(2%)	NA	0.7

SUCCESS FACTORS

- Dedication to quality and reliability
- Global branding
- Alliances for best global technology
- Dynamic and ambitious management
- Active global distribution
- Innovative design of niche products

CHALLENGES

- Risk of over-diversification
- Lack of top brand perception
- Poor transparency of financial infor-mation and complicated corporate structure

High Tech Computer Corp. (HTC)
On the cutting edge of wireless communications

BACKGROUND

As smart phones are beginning to take the world by storm with the roll-out of third-generation telecommunications networks, designers of sophisticated, converged hand-held devices are becoming more important. HTC has an early lead in this field with its 1,100 research engineers strong focus on R&D, history of designing and producing winning products like the iPaq, TREO, and Pocket PC, close relationship with Microsoft, and established presence with leading telecoms in the United States and Europe. HTC is now one of the leading firms in this industry niche and recently launched its own HTC brand in Europe.

HISTORY

Unlike many Taiwanese companies, HTC has focused on design and R&D from the start. In 1997, a team of engineers originally with DEC Taiwan designed the bestselling iPAQ, one of the early successful personal digital assistants (PDA), and sold its idea to Compaq. By 2001, the company was shipping nearly 1.5 million iPAQs, with sales of over $450 million. In 2002 HTC designed and manufactured its first wireless PDA, went public, and shipped its 2 millionth iPAQ. By 2003, HTC had a global market share of more than 50% for Windows CE-based PDAs. It has continued to design a new series of smart phones for the third generation of wireless communications, making its stock a strong performer in recent years.

INDUSTRY

Early in the PC age, Taiwanese companies took the lead in notebooks and many types of PC accessories by developing a reputation for being cost-efficient producers. Currently, an edge in design and R&D are equally important. As wireless communications continue to grow in popularity, smart phones will increasingly take center stage with sales of over 200 million forecast by the end of the decade, as multi-function handheld devices are becoming the wave of the future.

COMPETITION

2005 Data	Market Cap ($bn)	Revenues ($bn)	Net Earnings ($mn)	ROE	P/E	Net Debt/Equity
HTC	6.7	2.3	366	69%	19	(0.7)
Palm	1.4	1.3	66	12%	18	(0.6)

SUCCESS FACTORS

- Production of a broad line of products
- Speed in marketing with new technologies
- Active R&D and extensive testing
- Expertise with Windows based OS
- Close relations with telecom carriers

CHALLENGES

- Pricing pressures from the increasing popularity of smart phones and wireless PDAs
- Product coomoditization
- Fending off mass producers
- Successfully introducing its brand name

Hon Hai Precision Industry Co., Ltd.
The factory behind the brand

BACKGROUND

Hon Hai produces many of the everyday electronics that Western consumers buy from big brand names. Dell computers, Nokia phones, Sony PlayStations—Hon Hai silently makes parts or all of these products in its factories in China and ships then to its clients. Hon Hai has experienced remarkable growth over the last twenty years and today is the world's largest electronics contract manufacturer, after passing previous leader Flextronics in sales in 2004. Having developed solid relationships with its customers through low prices with rapid and high-quality execution, Hon Hai continues to grow at a high rate today, as more and more products—and clients—are added to its portfolio.

HISTORY

Known as Foxconn in the United States, Hon Hai was founded in Taiwan in 1974. Producing plastic parts for TVs, it operated out of a garage. The company developed its first connector product in 1981. With the PC boom, the company soon moved up the food chain and began manufacturing modules and circuit boards, opening a plant near Taipei. By 1991 the company was listed on the Taiwan Stock Exchange and, a year later, it established R&D centers in the United States and Japan. In 1996 Hon Hai began producing PC enclosures, and by 1999 it had established production facilities in Scotland, the United Kingdom, Ireland, and the United States. In 2003 the company went on an acquisition spree that has positioned it to make mobile phones, servers, and networking gear and today it is the #1 electronics producer in Taiwan.

INDUSTRY

Most of Hon Hai's global peers have focused more on margins than top-line growth. Since 2000, Hon Hai's revenues have grown many times faster than those of Intel, Microsoft, and Dell. The industry's current consolidation benefits the big players.

COMPETITION

2005 Data	Market Cap ($bn)	Revenues ($bn)	Net Earnings ($mn)	ROE	P/E	Net Debt/Equity
Hon Hai	22.1	28.3	1,268	27%	18	(0.1)
Solectron*	3.9	10.4	3	0%	24	(0.4)
Flextronics**	5.9	15.3	141	3%	15	0.1

SUCCESS FACTORS

- Early move into China
- Seeking demanding customers
- Huge plants with modern machinery
- Special molds, which allow for flexibility and speed in producing new models

CHALLENGES

- Lack of transparency
- Maintaining growth without constant acquisitions
- Competition from China

*Data as of August 2005 (August year-end)
**Data as of March 2006 (March year-end)

Hyundai Heavy Industries (HHI)
Korea's heavyweight shipbuilding champion

BACKGROUND

Korea's HHI is the world's largest shipbuilder, building LNG tankers, oil supertankers, bulk carriers, containerships, and high-tech chemical carriers in its sprawling 1,000 acres of facilities, which include the world's largest shipyard. The company also produces maritime diesel engines, electrical products such as circuit breakers, switchgears, and transformers, and construction equipment including excavators, forklifts, and loaders. HHI continues to dominate the shipbuilding market, with 236 orders for new ships in 2005 alone, totaling $18 billion, through a strong focus on product quality.

HISTORY

Hyundai Heavy began in 1972 as part of the Hyundai group. In the early 1980s the company enhanced its R&D abilities and by 1989 HHI was delivering the world's biggest jacket (the base of an oil platform) to Exxon. That same year, the company merged with Hyundai Engines and in 1991 started building Korea's first LNG carrier. In 1999 the company built the world's largest 200 MW diesel power plant in India, and got listed on the Korean Stock Exchange. By 2000 their orders had reached $7.7 billion, an all-time record. In 2001 the company began breaking its ties to the Hyundai group. HHI reached a major milestone in 2002, completing its 1000th ship in its thirtieth year of existence.

INDUSTRY

Hyundai Heavy is the industry leader in shipbuilding, Samsung Heavy comes in the #2 spot but #3 Daewoo Shipbuilding is more profitable. Mitsubishi Heavy is the leader in Japan, although at lower profitability. While Japanese yards have superior labor productivity, the disparity in wages more than makes up the difference. Japanese companies also face higher steel costs. In 2000 Korean shipyards received 50% of the industry's orders, as compared with 27% in Japan and just 11% in the European Union.

COMPETITION

2005 Data	Market Cap ($bn)	Revenues ($bn)	Net Earnings ($mn)	ROE	P/E	Net Debt/Equity
Hyundai Heavy	4.9	13.6	171	5%	25	(0.4)
Samsung Heavy	4.0	5.4	71	3%	55	(0.3)
Daewoo Shipbuilding	4.5	5.0	398	18%	11	0.0
Mitsubishi Heavy	16.0	24.7	263	2%	63	0.7
Mitsui Eng & Ship.	2.7	5.0	50	5%	56	1.0
Sumimoto Heavy	5.8	4.9	262	20%	23	0.7

SUCCESS FACTORS

- Engineering culture
- Discounts for large steel orders
- World's most efficient steel producer as main supplier

CHALLENGES

- Disconnection with Hyundai Group
- Cyclicality of industry
- Rising raw material prices; won strength

Hyundai Motor Company
Surging in quality and global manufacturing

BACKGROUND

In 2005, Hyundai Motor, together with its affiliate Kia Motors, sold over 3 million cars worldwide with large plants in the United States, China, and India, making it the seventh largest car manufacturer in the world. Following the example of Japanese car makers, Hyundai made an early splash in the United States with low-cost compact cars but consumers soon realized that they were not as reliable as their Japanese counterparts. Catching the entire industry by surprise, Hyundai recently surged up the J.D. Power quality survey, even overtaking Toyota in 2006. The indictment of HMC's charismatic chairman, the son of the Group's founder, has been a recent setback.

HISTORY

The Hyundai Group was formed in 1947 and Hyundai Motor Company (HMC) was established in 1967. In 1968, Hyundai, in conjunction with Ford Motor Company, introduced its first car, the Cortina. In 1974 Hyundai launched Korea's first independently designed and manufactured car, the subcompact Pony, which became an immediate success. The Asian financial crisis forced the Hyundai Group to split in 1999. As an independent company, joined with its Korean competitor Kia and benefiting from a devalued currency, Hyundai struggled back to sell 1.6 million vehicles in 2001.

INDUSTRY

The car market in the United States, Europe, and Japan has shrunk in recent years, with all new growth coming from emerging Asia. 20% of revenues are from emerging markets and that is expected to grow to 40% by 2015. China is expected to become a car exporter within a few years.

COMPETITION

2005 Data	Market Cap ($bn)	Revenues ($bn)	Net Earnings ($bn)	ROE	P/E	Net Debt/Equity
Hyundai	20	58	2.3	17%	9	0.8
Toyota	177	186	12.1	14%	15	0.1
Honda	57	88	5.3	16%	11	0.1
GM	11	192	(11.0)	(50%)	NA	1.5
Ford	14	177	2.0	15%	5	8.0
Volkswagen	21	118	1.0	5%	15	2.0

SUCCESS FACTORS

- Overhaul in automobile quality
- Focus on good design
- Global manufacturing
- Image makeover from notorious underperformer to top quality player

CHALLENGES

- Succeeding in being a global producer
- Keeping its competitive edge in China
- Overcoming the image problem of the indictment of its Chairman

Infosys Technologies
Programmers to the world

BACKGROUND
India is home to many well-qualified engineers and IT specialists who are willing to work at almost one sixth the price of their counterparties in the United States and Europe. Infosys was among the first to jump on the opportunities for outsourcing IT services in a world connected through the Internet. Today, India's software companies, led by Infosys, Tata Consulting Services, and Wipro, receive billions of dollars in business from the developed world. The Internet has provided a shortcut to the world in a country that lacks infrastructure but can leverage its massive pool of "cheap brain-power." Infosys has since moved up the value chain into more complex and lucrative businesses such as IT consulting.

HISTORY
It took nearly two decades for Infosys to become a major presence on the international scene but its workforce has grown tenfold since 1999 to over 49,000. Over the past five years, Infosys has become a leading player in the global IT outsourcing trend. It changed gears adroitly after the urgency of Y2K activities disappeared, overcame the malaise in the aftermath of the Internet boom, and survived the tightening of IT budgets in the global economic downturn. It has managed to beat its top line guidance figures for each of the last five years.

INDUSTRY
India is acquiring the reputation of becoming the "back office of the world," just as China has become the manufacturing hub. Despite the political rhetoric against out-sourcing, business is booming and the trend is likely to continue. The industry has experienced consistent growth over the past five years.

COMPETITION

2005 Data	Market Cap ($bn)	Revenues ($bn)	Net Earnings ($mn)	ROE	P/E	Net Debt/Equity
Infosys*	18.4	2.1	551	40%	33	(0.5)
Wipro*	17.8	2.4	455	30%	33	(0.5)
Tata Consulting*	21.0	3.0	649	62%	31	0.0
Accenture*	22.5	17.1	940	59%	17	(1.1)
Cognizant	7.0	0.9	166	28%	48	(0.6)

SUCCESS FACTORS
- Hiring the "best and the brightest"
- Stressing integrity, imagination, and speedy adaptation
- Strong focus on process discipline
- Nurturing of solid client relationships

CHALLENGES
- Moving up the value chain to such activities as consulting
- Dealing with the political backlash against outsourcing
- High staff turnover and rising wages

*Data is calendared

Lenovo
The Chinese company that swallowed IBM's ThinkPad

BACKGROUND
Lenovo has quickly gone from unknown upstart to the #1 computer brand in China with its home base located in the fastest growing computer market in the world. After the daring purchase of pioneer IBM's ThinkPad in 2004, Lenovo became the #3 PC producer in the world, after Dell and HP.

HISTORY
In 1984 Liu Chuanzhi of the Computing Institute of the Chinese Academy of Sciences, founded the New Technology Development Company. Its early success came from developing its own hardware-based Chinese-language software known as the "Legend Chinese Insertion Card," spotting a market void in desperate need of being filled. Within a year, the Legend Card became a huge success, and NTD changed its name to Legend in 1989. By 1992 Legend's aggressive distribution business had helped AST secure the #1 PC vendor position in China, overtaking HP, IBM, and other foreign brands. In 1993 the company began manufacturing its own PCs (the first Chinese company to do so). By 1995, Legend was the fifth largest manufacturer of PCs in the world. The company was renamed Lenovo in 2003 as part of its global push.

INDUSTRY
With sales already near the $3 billion mark, Lenovo's purchase of IBM's ThinkPad will increase total sales to $12 billion. With a 27% market share, Lenovo is also the second-best known electronics brand in China, after home appliance maker Haier.

COMPETITION

2005 Data	Market Cap ($bn)	Revenues ($bn)	Net Earnings ($mn)	ROE	P/E	Net Debt/Equity
Lenovo*	2.5	2.9	144	23%	17.7	(0.5)
Dell**	102.0	49.2	3,043	48%	31.8	(1.4)
HP***	79.5	86.7	2,398	6%	17.0	(0.2)
Toshiba****	18.7	56.0	683	9%	28.1	NA
Acer	5.3	9.9	264	13%	21.5	(0.5)

SUCCESS FACTORS
- Daring decision to make and sell its own brand in China
- Innovative products and thinking

CHALLENGES
- Integrating IBM's PC business
- Making Lenovo a global brand
- Introducing attractive new models
- Surviving new competition in China

*Data as at March 2005 (March year-end)
**Data as at January 2006 (January year-end)

***Data as at October 2005 (October year-end)
****Data as at March 2006 (March year-end)

Malaysia International Shipping Corporation (MISC)
Malaysia's leader in LNG shipping

BACKGROUND

Malaysia International Shipping Corporation is the global leader in shipping liquefied natural gas (LNG). It has nineteen LNG tankers, all of which operate under long-term contracts. In total, MISC owns 107 vessels, including fifty-two petroleum tankers, twenty container ships, thirteen chemical tankers, and two bulk carriers with a combined tonnage exceeding 7 million deadweight tons. Producers of a wide variety of goods rely on MISC to ship their products worldwide, from woodchips, fertilizer, and grain to crude oil, gasoline, and jet fuel. MISC's fleet operates in Japan and emerging Asia, Europe, the United States, the Middle East, South Africa, and Australia.

HISTORY

MISC was founded in 1968 and established its shipping agency in 1975. In 1991 the company entered the container trade. MISC Trucking and Warehousing subsidiary opened shop soon thereafter in 1992. After being purchased by Petronas, Malaysia's oil and gas company, in 1997, MISC expanded its global operations through a series of acquisitions and alliances and took over Petronas Tankers. In 2003 the company purchased American Eagle Tankers, a petroleum tanker company. In 2004 MISC purchased five new LNG carriers for $900 million.

INDUSTRY

MISC's biggest competitors are Shell and NOL. LNG production and shipping will grow substantially over the next decade with new supplies in Qatar, Iran, Russia, and elsewhere coming on-stream, as well as the need for a cleaner environment. With growing global trade and need for commodities, other shipping needs will also grow.

COMPETITION

2005 Data	Market Cap ($bn)	Revenues ($mn)	Net Earnings ($mn)	ROE	P/E	Net Debt/Equity
MISC*	9.6	2.9	801	18%	12.9	0.2
Evergreen Marine	4.9	13.6	717	5%	25.3	(0.4)
Teekay Shipping	3.0	1.5	571	24%	7.6	0.8
Mitsui OSK*	8.5	11.6	1,005	24%	8.4	1.0
Golar LNG	0.9	0.2	35	8%	32.5	1.9

SUCCESS FACTORS
- Relationship with Petronas
- Long term LNG contracts
- Focus on growing energy sector
- Dynamic and focused new management

CHALLENGES
- Increasing fuel costs
- Over reliance on Petronas (nearly 70% of profits)
- Environmental legislation

*Data as of March 2006 (March year-end)

Petrobras
Brazil's oil and gas champion

BACKGROUND
Petróleo Brasileiro (Petrobras), a partly state-owned company is the largest Latin American company and the world's fifteenth largest oil and gas company. Although the company lost its monopoly in Brazil in the mid 1990s, Petrobras is still the dominant player in its home market, controlling over 20% of Brazil's gas stations. While the majority of its sales are domestic, 89% of its reserves are offshore with operations in fifteen countries. Petrobras is now recognized as an industry leader in deep-water drilling.

HISTORY
In 1953 the Brazilian government founded Petrobras as a state-run oil and gas monopoly. By 1973 it was producing less than 10% of national needs. The company later shifted its priorities to overseas exploration, striking oil deals in Angola and the Gulf of Mexico.

INDUSTRY
While BP, Shell, and Exxon Mobil remain dominant players in the oil and gas industry, emerging multinationals like Petrobras, Gazprom, Lukoil, and Petrochina are now giving them a run for their money. The industry currently enjoys high oil and gas prices and growing demand from new markets, but also faces geopolitical risks. As Brazil imports 55% of its natural gas from Bolivia, a Bolivian government takeover could lead to soaring prices there.

COMPETITION

2005 Data	Market Cap ($bn)	Revenues ($bn)	Net Earnings ($bn)	ROE	P/E	Net Debt/Equity
Petrobras	70	56	9.8	34%	7.2	0.5
Shell	204	307	25.3	29%	7.9	0.0
Exxon Mobil	345	328	36.1	34%	10.5	(0.2)
BP	220	247	22.3	28%	10.0	0.2
Lukoil*	25	34	4.2	22%	5.8	0.1
Gazprom	155	48	10.8	13%	NA	0.3

SUCCESS FACTORS
- Expertise in deep water drilling
- Partnerships with industry leaders
- Increased financial transparency
- Dominance in Brazilian market
- Regional expansion of exploration

CHALLENGES
- Updating antiquated infrastructure
- Restrictive labor regulations
- Vulnerability to political cycles
- Bolivian state control of gas assets

*Data as of December 2004

POSCO
Korea's unlikely steel giant

BACKGROUND
South Korea was determined to achieve industrial development even without many natural resources. Today, POSCO is one of the largest, most efficient, and most profitable steelmakers in the world. Originally learning from the Japanese, POSCO is now the teacher, exporting its homegrown technologies to both developing and developed markets. POSCO is a remarkable example of the stunning growth seen in East Asia over the last half-century, and a true symbol of Korea's transformation into a modern industrialized nation.

HISTORY
Pohang Iron & Steel Co. (POSCO) was incorporated in 1968. With training, technology, and loans from the Japanese, a plant in Youngil Bay, far away from Seoul, was completed in 1981 with an annual capacity of 8.5 million tons. It was followed by a second plant in Kwangyung in 1986 with an 11.4 million ton capacity. By the mid 1990s, POSCO exported 6 million tons, 30% of its production. Today POSCO produces 30.5 million tons of steel and is expanding its production capacity into China and India. In addition to its integrated mills, POSCO has its Finex mini-mill technology.

INDUSTRY
While steel production in the United States, Europe, and Japan is languishing, it is growing rapidly in emerging nations led by China. POSCO was an early entrant and is now one of the largest steel companies in the world, second only to Arcelor in profits.

COMPETITION

2005 Data	Market Cap ($bn)	Revenues ($bn)	Net Earnings ($bn)	ROE	P/E	Net Debt/Equity
POSCO	16.0	25.7	3.9	23%	4.0	(0.1)
Mittal Steel	18.6	28.1	3.4	42%	6.0	0.5
Arcelor	15.4	38.6	4.6	30%	3.4	0.1
Nippon Steel*	25.8	34.5	3.0	24%	8.9	0.6
US Steel	5.2	14.0	0.9	26%	6.9	0.1

SUCCESS FACTORS
- Broad commitment to training
- Focus on technological innovation
- Early government subsidies
- Alliances with leading steelmakers, suppliers, and customers
- Relentless emphasis on productivity
- Low-cost production

CHALLENGES
- Bringing new FINEX technology online
- High raw materials prices
- Long term risks of "leapfrogging" posed by China's growing and sophisticated steel production
- Industry consolidation led by Mittal

*Data as of March 2006 (March year-end)

Ranbaxy
Global player in generic drugs

BACKGROUND
Ranbaxy is a pharmaceutical company based in India. The company has a strong global focus, manufacturing in seven countries around the world and selling its products in 100. Three quarters of its 2005 sales were international, with 36% in the United States and a growing presence in major emerging markets. Ranbaxy produces both prescription and over-the-counter drugs.

HISTORY
Ranbaxy was established in 1961 and went public in 1973. In 1984, the U.S. congress passed an act promoting the entry of (cheaper) generic drugs into the market. This act transformed Ranbaxy into the major player in the pharmaceutical industry it is today. Its modern plant in Punjab set up in 1987, made it the largest manufacturer of antibacterial drugs in India. Its products received U.S. FDA approval a year later and Ranbaxy got its first U.S. patent in 1990, for Doxicyclin. In 1994 the company entered the U.S. market with five ANDA's and today the company submits over twenty each year.

INDUSTRY
The generic drug industry has experienced consistent growth, in recent years, although brand names are fighting back with sharp price decreases once drugs go off-patent. New FDA policies making generic drug approval easier could lead to more investments in the industry, while the generics market in Europe is slowly opening up. Among the major players in generics are Teva, Amgen, Biogen Idec, and Chiron.

COMPETITION

2005 Data	Market Cap ($bn)	Revenues ($bn)	Net Earnings ($mn)	ROE	P/E	Net Debt/Equity
Ranbaxy	3.1	1.4	143	23%	28.0	0.3
Dr Reddy's*	2.4	0.5	33	7%	74.1	1.0
Teva	33.9	5.3	1,072	19%	25.3	0.3
Chiron	8.7	1.9	180	6%	33.9	0.1

SUCCESS FACTORS
- Focus on drugs that are difficult to develop
- Global focus
- Retention of the local market

CHALLENGES
- Competing with major players
- Competing with name brand drugs
- Consolidation in generics industry
- Approvals for new product pipeline

*Data as of March 2006 (March year-end)

Reliance Industries
A global leader in petrochemicals and a leading Indian business conglomerate

BACKGROUND
Reliance Industries is involved in exploration, refining, and marketing of oil, gas, and petrochemicals. It remains one of India's leading private sector business groups even though, after a family dispute, other businesses such as telecom and financial services were split off in 2005. It is the world's second largest polyester fiber and yarn producer, third largest in paraxylene, fifth in PTA, and seventh in polypropylene. Reliance is the market leader in each of its major businesses in India, one of the world's largest consumer markets.

HISTORY
Dhirubhai Ambani founded a commodity trading and export house in 1958, built his first textile mill in 1966, and soon after entered the polyester fiber business, establishing several filament yarn and staple fiber plants over the next decade. The company went public in 1968 and its shares became among the most widely held in India. In 1991, Reliance integrated backward by building a petrochemical complex. The company continued to grow, adding the world's largest multi-feed cracker, largest polypropylene plant, fifth largest refinery, and India's largest port. In 2002 Reliance bought control of India's second largest petrochemicals company, Indian Petrochemical Corporation Limited, and launched Reliance Infocomm, a leading telecom services provider. In 2004 the company moved into Europe by acquiring German specialty polyester manufacturer Trevira.

INDUSTRY
As consumption and production of textiles in emerging market grows, raw materials are increasingly sourced from large-scale, world-class, petrochemical facilities in the region. Energy needs are rising even faster with larger fleets of cars.

COMPETITION

2005 Data	Market Cap ($bn)	Revenues ($bn)	Net Earnings ($bn)	ROE	P/E	Net Debt/Equity
Reliance*	25	18	1.9	25%	13.9	0.4
India Oil	12	30	1.2	21%	9.4	0.7
Sinopec	43	99	5.1	20%	8.5	0.6
Dow Chemical	42	46	4.5	33%	10.0	0.4
Formosa Petrochemical	16	14	1.7	29%	9.1	0.6

SUCCESS FACTORS
- Low-cost, huge scale production
- Highly diversified product mix
- Vertical integration
- Financial muscle
- State-of-the-art facilities
- Vast undeveloped oil and gas blocks

CHALLENGES
- After the break-up, Reliance Industries is no longer the largest Indian group
- Decreasing tariff protection
- Competition in petrochemicals from the Middle East with lower energy and feedstock costs

*Data as of March 2006 (March year-end)

Samsung Electronics
The premier brand name in Emerging Markets

BACKGROUND

Samsung has painstakingly built its brand name over many years and is now better known than Sony or Philips. It made a name for itself in stylish-looking handsets (sales of over 100 million in 2005, #3 globally). It is also the undisputed global leader in memory chips (DRAM and flash) as well as flat screens, and hopes to become recognized as a global trendsetter in the new digital multimedia world. Samsung Electronics' R&D budget is larger than Intel's and the company ranks #5 globally in patent applications.

HISTORY

Samsung General Stores opened in 1938 and exported Korean fish, vegetables, and fruit to Manchuria and Beijing. By the 1990s, the Samsung Group had become Korea's most influential conglomerate *(chaebol)*, active in many industries, from consumer electronics and insurance to cars, shipbuilding, and petrochemicals. Founded in 1969, Samsung Electronics merged with Samsung Semiconductors in 1988. After the Asian Crisis of 1998, Samsung Electronics' aggressive deleveraging and determined shift from low-end electronics and commodity memory chips to specialized semiconductors, mobile handsets, TFT-LCD screens, and digital media led the company to world-class status.

INDUSTRY

Samsung has led Korea in wrestling away the dominant position in electronics from Japan. The company has overtaken Sony in Interbrand's brand value rankings as one of the fastest climbers on that list for several years.

COMPETITION

2005 Data	Market Cap ($bn)	Revenues ($bn)	Net Earnings ($bn)	ROE	P/E	Net Debt/Equity
Samsung*	107.0	56.7	7.6	20%	13.2	0.2
Intel	147.7	38.8	8.7	23%	17.6	(0.2)
Nokia	76.3	42.5	4.5	27%	18.7	(0.8)
Philips	15.2	9.8	0.5	8%	28.2	0.3
Sony	46.4	66.0	1.1	4%	44.4	0.3
Motorola	56.5	36.8	4.6	31%	19.0	(0.6)
Matsushita*	49.2	78.6	1.4	4%	37.6	(0.1)
LG Electronics	12.6	43.4	0.6	11%	23.5	0.9

SUCCESS FACTORS

- Corporate culture attracting the best and the brightest
- Early government support
- Relentless drive for excellence
- Early focus on exports, R&D, and the importance of a "brand"

CHALLENGES

- Competition from lower-cost China will force continued movement up the technology ladder
- LG is making inroads

*Consolidated revenues. Unconsolidated revenues are $56 bn.

Sasol
Turning cheap coal into global profits

BACKGROUND
In 1923 two German scientists discovered the process of converting coal into liquid (Fischer-Tropsch), a great breakthrough for oil-poor but coal-rich Germany. Soon after its discovery, the South African government established a company to take advantage of this technology. Today, Sasol produces 40% of South Africa's fuel needs and has become a diversified energy and chemical company with operations throughout the globe. The company remains the global leader in synfuels and now focuses on exporting its technology, for example, through joint ventures to convert gas into oil (GTL) in gas-rich Qatar and Nigeria and coal-to-liquid (CTL) plants in China.

HISTORY
As a result of White Paper, which dated back to 1927, in coal-rich but oil-poor South Africa, the South African Coal Oil and Gas Corporation was established in 1950. By 1955 the company produced its first car fuel. In 1967 construction began on the National Petroleum Refinery of South Africa and in 1979 the company was privatized. Starting in the 1973 oil crisis, Sasol built two large CTL plants in South Africa. After taking over European chemicals company Condea in the mid-1990s, Sasol now operates in over twenty countries, with exports to over 100.

INDUSTRY
Sasol is the world's largest producers of synthetic fuels, and the world's only company that uses coal-to-liquid technology on a commercial basis. Other global oil and gas players, such as Shell, Exxon Mobil, Conoco Phillips, and Marathon have had only small GTL plants in operation but GTL is becoming an increasingly popular technology.

COMPETITION

2005 Data	Market Cap ($bn)	Revenues ($bn)	Net Earnings ($bn)	ROE	P/E	Net Debt/Equity
Sasol*	18	11	1.5	24%	10.5	0.4
Exxon Mobil	345	328	36.1	34%	10.5	(0.2)
Royal Dutch/Shell	204	307	25.3	29%	7.9	0.0
Chevron	127	185	14.1	26%	8.7	0.0
Petrobras	70	56	9.8	34%	7.2	0.5

SUCCESS FACTORS
- Determination to make synfuels commercially viable
- Promising GTL technology
- Operation of coal mines
- Strong competitive edge in process technology of GTL and CTL

CHALLENGES
- Interest in capital-intensive GTL and CTL projects would wane with low oil prices
- Oversupply in chemicals industry
- Risk of imitation

*Data as of June 2005 (June year-end)

Grupo Televisa
Exporting Mexican soap operas to the world

BACKGROUND
Grupo Televisa is the largest media company in the Spanish-speaking world, with television, radio, and publishing companies. In Mexico, the company owns four TV networks and nearly 260 affiliated stations, airing over 90% of Mexico's top programs. It also provides most of the programming for Univision, the leading Hispanic network in the United States, and produces original content for over 100 countries. Televisa's historic success has been based on the popularity of its *telenovelas,* a Latin form of soap operas. Televisa's current industry domination is, in part, a result of its school for aspiring actors, which gives the company a first look at future *telenovela* stars.

HISTORY
Grupo Televisa began in 1954 as the Telesistema Mexicana network. After gaining strong control of radio and TV in Mexico, Televisa launched SIN, a Spanish-language station for U.S. broadcast, in 1976. Ten years later it was forced to sell the network due to U.S. foreign ownership regulation and SIN was renamed Univision. Televisa went public in 1991 and bought back into Univision in 1992. After struggling in the late 1990's, Televisa reclaimed its success through more focused management under the leadership of Emilio Azcarraga Jean, the son of "El Tigre" who had put Televisa on the map.

INDUSTRY
Televisa dominates Mexico's TV market with a 70% audience share. Its Latin-produced shows have been much more successful among the Hispanic population in the United States than American programs dubbed into Spanish. The Hispanic media industry in the United States has been growing steadily and Univision dominates the Spanish-speaking audience there.

COMPETITION

2005 Data	Market Cap ($bn)	Revenues ($bn)	Net Earnings ($mn)	ROE	P/E	Net Debt/Equity
Grupo Televisa	10.4	3.0	562	21%	17.9	0.1
Time Warner	79.4	43.7	3,364	(34%)	NA	3.2
Viacom	31.7	9.6	(17,462)	12%	24.5	0.7
News Corp*	53.6	23.9	2,128	8%	23.7	0.2
Univision	9.0	2.0	187	4%	35.0	0.3
TV Azteca	2.0	0.8	112	30%	17.0	1.1

SUCCESS FACTORS
- Global appeal of *telenovelas*
- Growing purchasing power of Hispanic population in the United States
- Old-style studio system with its own school to train future stars

CHALLENGES
- Maintaining dominance in Mexico in a politically pluralistic environment
- Relationship with Univision
- Ownership restrictions on non-U.S. citizens in the U.S. market

*Data as of June 2005 (June year-end)

Taiwan Semiconductor Manufacturing Company (TSMC)
Changing the way the world makes semiconductors

BACKGROUND

TSMC is an example of how determined and successful industrial policy can revolutionize an industry. Before TSMC, silicone wafers were made by giants such as IBM and Intel in expensive (then $1 billion) in-house "fabs." By introducing the dedicated chip foundry, TSMC allowed smaller, fabless design houses to flourish. Today, TSMC is the world's premier independent maker of semiconductors in a highly cyclical industry with a reputation for innovation and superior quality and reliability.

HISTORY

The Taiwanese government lured away former Texas Instrument executive Morris Chang from Silicon Valley to move the island up and away from low-end electronics. TSMC was formed in 1987 as a joint investment with Dutch electronics giant Philips and the Taiwanese government in a spin-off from Taiwan's Industrial Research Technology Institute (ITRI) to become the island's first six-inch wafer fabrication facility (or "fab"), and the world's first independent "pure play" chip foundry. While "in-house" fabs depend on the success of the products of a single parent, the independent fab can constantly shift its output to newly developing sectors. In this way, TSMC was able to partner with rather than compete against such IC giants as Intel, NEC, and Siemens.

INDUSTRY

Manufacturing of consumer electronics has shifted largely to Asia, first to Japan, then to Korea and Taiwan, and increasingly to China. Korea now dominates the "memory" semiconductor ("chip") industry and Taiwan the independently produced "logic" semiconductors used in everything from graphic boards to handsets. The first out of the gates, TSMC, has managed to maintain its market dominance, remaining one of the most successful and profitable semiconductor companies in the world.

COMPETITION

2005 Data	Market Cap ($bn)	Revenues ($bn)	Net Earnings ($bn)	ROE	P/E	Net Debt/Equity
TSMC	47.0	8.3	2.9	22%	16.5	(0.3)
UMC	10.7	3.1	0.2	3%	48.0	(0.2)
Chartered	2.0	1.0	(0.2)	(11%)	NA	0.4
Intel	147.7	38.8	8.7	23%	17.6	(0.2)
Texas Instruments	51.2	13.4	2.3	19%	22.5	(0.4)

SUCCESS FACTORS

- Visionary management
- Economies of scale and technology
- Clear focus on efficiency and success rates
- Full service offerings

CHALLENGES

- Interpreting and timing industry cycles
- Growing competition from China

Tenaris
Introducing advanced logistics to the world of oil pipes

BACKGROUND
Tenaris focuses on seamless steel pipes for oil-related industries. The global nature of the oil industry has made Tenaris a worldwide operation, with plants in four continents, distribution networks in over twenty countries, and proven high-quality products combined with sophisticated logistics including on-time delivery. Tenaris also targets consumers in other industries such as generating plants and car manufacturers.

HISTORY
In 1935 Agostino Rocca started Techint, an engineering firm, in Milan. His son, Roberto, moved to Argentina to establish a stainless steel pipe manufacturing company, Siderca, in 1948. Heavily protected and tied to the local oil and gas industry, Siderca began to lose its technological edge and suffered from Argentina's bouts with bad economic conditions and high inflation. It tripled in size with a 1986 expansion and was then forced to compete globally. Siderca gradually merged with other Techint ventures in Mexico (Tamsa), Brazil, Europe, and Japan under the new name Tenaris in 2002.

INDUSTRY
The oil pipe industry is heavily dependent on oil and gas exploration and the depth at which it takes place. Less accessible oil and sharply rising oil prices have favored the industry of late. Tenaris's main competitors are Sumitomo Metal, Mannesmann, and JFE.

COMPETITION

2005 Data	Market Cap ($bn)	Revenues ($bn)	Net Earnings ($bn)	ROE	P/E	Net Debt/Equity
Tenaris	13.9	6.7	1.3	43%	11	0.0
Sumitomo Metal*	20.6	13.7	2.0	37%	11	0.8
JFE*	23.7	27.4	2.9	30%	9	0.9
US Steel	5.2	14.0	0.9	26%	7	0.1

SUCCESS FACTORS
- Dedication to quality and reliability
- Global focus
- Edge in logistics and on-time delivery
- Tenaris Blue's "dopeless" connections to deepwater and arctic regions

CHALLENGES
- Cyclicality of oil drilling
- Raw material prices
- Maintaining a competitive edge in logistics
- Gaining a foothold in China and Russia

*Data as of May 2006 (May year-end)

Yue Yuen
The unseen face of global athletics

BACKGROUND

Yue Yuen has been the world's leading producer of athletic and casual footwear for every major brand for over ten years, making over 186 million or one out of six pairs of athletic shoes globally, far more than any competitor. Yue Yuen accounts for 30% of Nike's orders, over 25% of Adidas's, and over 20% of Reebok's. Growing at twice the industry rate, it has benefitted from a consolidation of suppliers as requirements by its brand-name clients for environmental and labor conditions have become more stringent. Yue Yuen's early move into China, huge factories, a management team of seasoned footwear executives, design capabilities, efficient production, and quick reaction to the image requirements of the brands for which it produces propelled it to the top of the competition.

HISTORY

While most shoemakers and their customers were still focusing on Taiwan, Yue Yuen was the first to realize that China was the way of the future and set up a plant in Zhuhai. It was a gamble that paid off. By the early 1990s, when the major brands realized the potential benefits of doing business in China, Yue Yuen, a subsidiary of the well-established shoemaker Pou Chen in Taiwan, was among the few companies that were able to meet their needs. Besides its first mover status, Yue Yuen was also able to produce large quantities at low costs without sacrificing quality.

INDUSTRY

Throughout the 1970s and 1980s, Taiwan took pride in being the world's low-cost shoe manufacturer, but later the industry sought lower cost labor in China, Vietnam, and Indonesia. With its huge labor pool, improving infrastructure, and potential market, China now dominates the competition. All major brands of athletic and boat shoes now outsource their production

COMPETITION

2005 Data	Market Cap ($bn)	Revenues ($bn)	Net Earnings ($mn)	ROE	P/E	Net Debt/Equity
Yue Yuen	4.4	3.2	310	17%	14.4	0.2
Nike*	20.6	15.0	1,392	23%	14.9	(0.3)
Reebok	9.6	7.9	454	18%	17.5	(0.2)

SUCCESS FACTORS	CHALLENGES
• Experienced, first mover into China • Economies of scale in huge plants • Integrated but diversified production • Superior design capability • Speed-to-market	• Reliance on large athletic brands. • Limitations on China's low cost labor pool • Selling China under own brand name • Diversifying into sportswear

*Data as of May 2006 (May year-end)

Notes

PART I

1. Cited in Jeffrey E. Garten, *The Big Ten* (Basic Books, HarperCollins Publishers, New York, 1997) from William Safire, *Lend Me Your Ears: Great Speeches in History* (W.W.Norton, New York, 1992), p. 888

CHAPTER 1

1. Before the Industrial Revolution, China was the world's largest economy and India ranked among the major ones.
2. Goldman Sachs, *Global Economics Paper #134,* December 2005, an update of an earlier published paper
3. Ranked by current size; among the emerging markets, the GNP of China stands out with nearly three times the size of its next competitors; the four BRICs do not even include Korea, Mexico, and Taiwan which have relatively smaller populations and less potential to be ranked among the largest economies well into the twenty-first century.
4. Korea, Mexico, Turkey, Indonesia, Iran, Pakistan, the Philippines, Nigeria, Egypt, Bangladesh, and Vietnam, ranked by current size of their economies. This does not yet include major economies such as Argentina and Taiwan.
5. *International Herald Tribune,* July 18, 2005, Claudia H. Deutsch "GE: A General Store for Developing World."
6. *New York Times,* July 23, 2005.
7. *Wall Street Journal,* February 13, 2006.
8. "Name Goods in China But Brand X Elsewhere," David Barboza, *New York Times* June 29, 2005.

CHAPTER 2

1. "Unabashed Romp," Greg Sandow, www.meetthemusic.org, cited in Robert Greenberg, *Great Masters, Tchaikovsky—His life and Music*, The Teaching Company.
2. "Nowhere is this bias—the gap between participants' views and the actual state of affairs—more noticeable than in economic theory . . . I have [therefore] focused on the gap between perception and reality." George Soros, "A Failed Philosopher Tries Again," *The Critical Rationalist,* Vol. 1, No. 1, 1996.
3. Amsden, Alice H., *Asia's Next Giant: South Korea and the Late Industrialization* (Oxford University Press, London, 1988), p. 29.
4. An update of the original list which compared 1988 and 2003, using full market capitalization of the top 100 companies of the MSCI Emerging Markets Index for 2005.

Because the MSCI Index for 1990 excludes many countries and companies as noninvestable, I used the IFC Global Emerging Markets Index, which has a much broader representation to make sure I did not understate the overlap.

5. Based on year-end 2004 data.
6. Out of a total of thirty-eight in emerging markets in 2005.
7. Out of a total of fifty-nine in 2005.
8. Gazprom is larger but most of its shares were not accessible to international investors until late 2005.
9. S&P–IFC Emerging Markets Index.
10. Institute for International Finance.
11. National Public Radio, January 23, 2006.

CHAPTER 3

1. With its sleek design, Motorola's new Razr cell phone is a classic example of a creative competitive response to Samsung.
2. Including $102 billion by U.S. corporations, $56 billion by Japanese, and $31 billion by German corporations. The top spenders in the UK spent 10.7 percent of revenues, in the Netherlands 8.2 percent, in Switzerland 7.9 percent, and in the United States just over 6 percent.
3. Cientifica Survey, October 2005: *Global R&D Spend 2002–2004.*
4. "Top ten organizations receiving most U.S. Patents," U.S. Patent and Trademark Office, press release, January 10, 2006.

CHAPTER 4

1. "A Technology Legend in China," *Harvard Business School,* April 5, 2004.
2. Ibid.
3. "Dell Finds Success in China's Maturing Market," *Wall Street Journal,* July 5, 2005.
4. I was unsuccessful in arranging a visit to the Haier plan in Qingdao or interviewing its CEO Zhang Ruimin, so I had to rely more than usual on various outside sources including case studies of the Harvard Business School and the ICFAI Center for Management Research, and articles in *McKinsey Quarterly, Forbes, The Economist* and *Business Week.* Direct quotations came from such outside sources. Financial information of the Hong Kong-listed affiliate of Haier does not reflect the whole group, on which information is much less transparent.
5. "The Haier Group," *Harvard Business School,* July 27, 2001.
6. *BusinessWeek* online, June 14, 1999.
7. David Barboza, "Name Goods In China But Brand X Elsewhere," *New York Times,* June 29, 2005.
8. Cited in Ang Li, The Internationalization of Chinese Enterprises Compared with Japanese Enterprises (Fall, 2005)
9. "The Haier Group," *Harvard Business School,* July 27, 2001.
10. "China's Refrigerator Magnate," *The McKinsey Quarterly,* 2003, No. 3.

CHAPTER 5

1. Jane Skanderup, "Taiwan's Cross-Strait Economic Strategy and the WTO," Center for Strategic and International Studies (CSIS), January 2004.
2. While the Koreans and Japanese invest more (although not exclusively) to gain access to the large Chinese market, the Taiwanese focus mostly on industries that export globally rather than the domestic Chinese market.
3. "Why Taiwan Matters," May 16, 2005 (International edition cover story).
4. *Asia Times,* February 15, 2005.
5. Chinese Academy of Foreign Trade and Cooperation, Ministry of Commerce: 2005 Report of Transnational Corporations in China.
6. Ibid.
7. According to *Forbes* magazine's list of the "World's Richest People" in 2004, March 2005.
8. Since my last visit, Hon Hai has constructed a brand-new building next door.
9. *Economics Daily,* July 11, 2001.
10. Based on data from key industry source International Data Corporation (IDC); this includes its Hong Kong affiliate Foxconn.
11. Based on data from China's Ministry of Commerce.
12. Jessie Shen, "Foxconn to lay off Finnish force while Investing in India" DigiTimes.com, March 9, 2006.
13. Cited by Ken Fleck, Fleck Research Associates.
14. At 2004 annual meeting.
15. Three years later, Hon Hai closed down many of its production units in Finland and moved production to Chennai in India after failing in its original plan to use Finland as a base for high-end, smart phone components or achieving the closeness to Nokia it aimed for.
16. Robert Collier, "Labor Rights and Wrongs: Some U.S. Firms Work to Cut Abuses in Chinese Factories," *San Francisco Chronicle,* May 17, 2000.
17. Stephan Schmidheiny, Charles Holliday, and Philip Watts, *Walking the Talk—The Business Case for Sustainable Development.*
18. April 22, 2005.
19. David Hall, "Yue Yuen Industial Plans Entry into Sportswear," *Footwear News*, March 2003

CHAPTER 6

1. The value of U.S. IP—including copyrights, patents, brands, trademarks and other protected forms of innovation was recently valued by economists Robert Shapiro and Kevin Hassett at a whopping $5 trillion.
2. U.S. Department of Commerce, United States Patent and Trademark Office (USPTO), May 1, 2006. IpIQ, cited by *International Herald Tribune,* November 19, 2005; based on extrapolation from first three quarters of 2005.
3. Emerging Markets Management LLC research.
4. Singapore, Taiwan, Korea, and Hong Kong (as well as japan) in Asia and Hungary among European emerging markets scored consistently ahead of the United States, while Malasya, Indonesia, and the Philippines, among the countries included, scored

lower, according to studies for 1993, 1999, and 2003, according to the Institute of Education Sciences, U.S. Department of Education, "Trends in International Math and Science Study."

5. World Economic Forum (2005). The United States "maintains global leadership in the business readiness component of the rankings as well as in variables such as the quality of its scientific research institutions and business schools—which have no peer in the world—and the availability of training opportunities for the labour force as well as the existence of a well-developed venture capital market, which has spurred innovation."

6. "Outsourcing Innovation," *Business Week*, March 21, 2005

7. Peter Clarke, "ATI produces first x architecture chip, says Cadence," EETimes, June 13, 2005

8. Nikkei article

9. A bottleneck that companies often face when launching new products is a delay in the new product certification process. If a product does not meet certification requirements, it may often be returned to the drawing board for a period of up to six months, a near fatal delay in a fast-moving industry of converged data devices. Due to the prohibitive cost of much of the testing equipment (often $1–2 million or more), not many small companies are willing or can even afford to invest in such testing capabilities.

10. Including the CeBIT, Comdex, Spring, and PC Expo shows.

CHAPTER 7

1. In 1993, H. Ross Perot cited a study by Pat Choate, "U.S. Jobs at Risk: Vulnerable Industries and Jobs Under NAFTA," in claiming that six million American workers would lose their jobs if NAFTA was implemented.

2. "NAFTA: Setting the Record Straight," The Brookings Institution, Policy Brief # 20—1997, by Nora Claudia Lustig.

3. J.D. Power & Associates, Annual Survey, June 8, 2006.

4. "Hyundai gets Hot," *Business Week International,* December 17, 2001.

5. Moon Ihlwan, "Hyundai's Hurdles," *Business Week,* July 21, 2003.

6. Ibid.

7. USNews.com, June 10, 2005. GM Vice Chairman Bob Lutz: "What we are re-learning as a company is that we are not simply in the transportation business; we're in the art and entertainment business. So, what we've got at GM now, is a general comprehension that you can't run this business by the left intellectual, analytical side of your brain alone, you have to have a lot of right side creative input."

8. "Building a Camry Fighter," *Business Week,* September 6, 2004.

9. "For Hyundai, China is the Highway," *Business Week,* March 29, 2004.

10. "Hyundai Arrest Shakes Foundation of South Korean Industry," *New York Times,* May 20, 2006.

11. "Hyundai Hits A Speed Bump" *New York Times,* June 11, 2006

12. Daniel Dombey, "Well-built Success," *Industry Week,* May 5, 1997.

13. *Financial Times,* November 7, 1997.

14. Kevin Kelleher, "The Wired 40," *Wired,* July 2003.

15. National Public Radio.

16. This percentage is adjusted on an annual basis. After nearly two decades of huge anti-

dumping charges (and after Hurricane Katrina tightened already tight cement supplies in Southern states), the charges were lowered in early 2006 and are expected to be phased out over the coming three years.

17. Pankaj Ghemawat and Jamie L. Matthews, "The Globalization of CEMEX," Harvard Business School, November 29, 2004.
18. Daniel Dombey, "Well-built Success," *Industry Week,* May 5, 1997.

CHAPTER 8

1. Kirby J. Harrison, "JetBlue's new EMB 190 fills blue-yonder niche," *Aviation International,* October 2005.
2. Jeremy W. Peters, "JetBlue Sets a Shuttle to Boston," *New York Times,* October 12, 2005.
3. "Brazil's Embraer Hits the Stratosphere," *Business Week,* April 19, 2004.
4. Ibid.
5. "Plantations and Planes," *New Internationalist,* February 1990.
6. "The Realities of Modern Hyper Inflation," *Finance and Development,* June 2003
7. Andrea Goldstein, "From National Champion to Global Player: Explaining the Success of Embraer," University of Oxford, 2001.
8. "On the Record with Mauricio Botelho," *The Chief Executive,* January–February 2003.
9. Harvard Business School, Case study October 20, 2000, *Embraer, the Global Leader in Regional Jets.*
10. Juarez Wanderley, former president of Embraer, quoted in *Financial Times,* June 6, 1995.
11. Embraer, Market Survey, Spring 2006.

CHAPTER 9

1. Tracey Ober, "CVRD sees Amazon-friendly mining as industry trend," Reuters News Service, September 13, 1999.
2. Ibid.
3. Alice Amsden, *Asia's Next Giant,* p. 297.

CHAPTER 10

1. Cited by CLSA report on The Global Outlook for biofuels, source EIA.
2. David Luhnow and Geraldo Samor, "As Brazil Fills Up on Ethanol, It Weans Off Energy Imports," *Wall Street Journal,* January 16, 2006.
3. Ibid.
4. According to Citigroup energy analyst David Raso, the top five ethanol producers in 2006 are by volume order, Brazil, United States, China, EU, and India. Brazil is the lowest-cost ethanol producer at about 25–30 cents per gallon cheaper than the United States and over $1.00 cheaper than the EU. Current estimates are that the United States will supplant Brazil as the top ethanol producer in 2006, but U.S. production is based on costly corn, while Brazil's is all based on sugar.
5. *Wall Street Journal,* January 16, 2006.

6. Consulting firm Datagro, which counts Brazil's biggest sugar companies as its clients, estimates that Brazil spent at least $16 billion in 2005 dollars from 1979 to the mid-1990s on loans to sugar companies and price support. Cited in *The Wall Street Journal,* January 16, 2006.

7. "Industry Note," Citigroup Analyst Report by David Raso, February 22, 2006.

8. "How Brazil Broke Its Oil Habit," *The Wall Street Journal,* February 6, 2006.

9. Holman W. Jenkins, "What's Wrong with Free Trade in Biofuels?" *The Wall Street Journal,* February 22, 2006.

10. Rocky Mountain Institute: Setting the Record Straight on Ethanol, Newsletter, 2005 Fall-Winter 2005.

11. CLSA, ibid.

12. Contrary to detractors' claims that ethanol made from cellulose uses a lot of energy in its production by counting (free) solar energy, the U.S. Department of Energy estimates that it only uses 0.2 units of fossil energy rather than 1.23 units in gasoline. Source: DEA, *Ethanol: The Complete Energy Life Cycle*

13. Perry A. Fischer, Natural Gas: Monetizing Stranded Gas, November 2001. Over 450 Tcfg of stranded gas is found in fields greater than 50 Bcf (often considered the economic minimum) and can be produced for under $0.50/MMBtu.

14. Even earlier, in 1902, Paul Sabatier and Jean Senderens in Switzerland had first made liquid out of gas

15. "Historical Overview of the South African Chemical Industry: 1896—2002," *The Chemical and Allied Industries Association,* February 20, 2003.

16. "What The U.S. Can Learn From Sasol," *Business Week,* February 27, 2006.

17. "Alchemy in Alaska," *Frontiers Magazine,* December 2002.

18. Chevron Press Release, April 8, 2005.

19. David Brown, *Explorer* magazine.

20. *Fuels* magazine, November 16, 2004.

CHAPTER 11

1. Bangalore, Historical Notes, State of Karnataktaka.

2. Richard Rapaport, Bangalore: "The Silicon Valley of India," *Wired,* February 1996.

3. "Indian Challengers Sneak Up on Bangalore," Reuters, November 7, 2005.

4. *The New York Times* reported that China graduated 600,000 engineers, India 350,000 and the United States only 71,000 but, according to National Public Radio (Steven Inskeep, *Morning Edition,* June 12, 2006), a study at Duke University has shown that the numbers are closer to 137,000 for the United States, 100,000 for India, and 351,000 for China.

5. Catherine L. Mann, "Offshore Outsourcing and the Globalization of U.S. Services: Why Now, How Important and What Policy Implications." In C. Fred Bergsten and the Institute for International Economics: *The United States and the World Economy,* 2005, p. 301.

6. *Economist,* December 11, 2003.

7. Catherine L. Mann, ibidem.

8. See Fred Bergsten, ibidem.

9. Howard French, "India and China Take on the World and Each Other," *The New York Times,* November 8, 2005.

10. Bangalore," *Wired* magazine, February 1996
11. Murthy relinquished the "chairman" title in August 2006 but remains chief mentor and is actively involved. "
12. Satyendra Kumar, "Managing Excellence the Infosys Way." Available at www.seana tional.com.au
13. On January 18, 2006 he became chief mentor and executive vice chairman, making way for a Malvindev Mohan Singh, a descendant of the original founder.
14. "India's little Drug Makers that Could," *Business Week,* March 3, 2003.

CHAPTER 12

1. National Public Radio, December 2005.
2. "Bollywood," *Business Week,* December 2, 2002.
3. Ibid.
4. *The Wall Street Journal,* September 14, 2005.
5. www.uopowergamers.com, May 2002
6. Redbus Interhouse, January 2005.
7. David MacFadyen, "Literature Has Left the Building: Russian Romance and Today's TV Drama" (University of California, Los Angeles), *Kinokultura # 8,* April 2005.
8. Ibsen Martinez, "Romancing the Globe," *Foreign Policy,* November/December 2005.
9. Ibid.
10. *Televisa* website
11. KetUPA.com Media Profiles.
12. Julia Preston, "Executive Has Firm Grip on Mexico's Top Broadcaster," *New York Times,* April 25, 2000.
13. Ibid.
14. Kristin C. Moran, "The Development of Spanish-Language TV in San Diego," *The Journal of San Diego History*
15. "Univision Peers into Cyberspace," *Business Week,* January 17, 2000.
16. "Here Come the Telenovelas," *New York Times,* December 15, 2005.
17. "Indian Television Is Stretching Across Continents to Latin-American Production Houses for Scripts to Suit the Tube," *The Telegraph* (Calcutta, India), New Delhi, November 14, 2005.
18. Emilio Azcárraga on "Televisa's Advantage," BusinessWeek.com, October 4, 2004.

CHAPTER 13

1. "Wal-Mart to Ratchet Up Hiring in China," *New York Times,* March 20, 2006.
2. "Dell to Double India Work Force," *The New York Times,* March 21, 2006.
3. "State Department Is Criticized For Purchasing Chinese PCs" *The New York Times,* March 24, 2006.
4. Institute for International Economics, *A New Economic Policy for the United States,* February 2005.
5. Cited in *"Tech's Future,"* *Business Week,* September 27, 2004.
6. George J. Gilboy "The Myth Behind China's Miracle," *Foreign Affairs,* July 2004.
7. Bureau of Economic Analysis, U.S. Department of Commerce, *Survey of Annual Business,* August 2005.

8. Data for the year 2003 from the website of the Organization for International Investment, Washington DC. Source: Bureau of Economic Analysis, U.S. Department of Commerce.

9. Daniel Trefler, *Offshoring: Threats and Opportunities,* Brookings Trade Forum 2005.

10. Paul London, *The Competition Solution: The Bipartisan Secret behind American Prosperity,* AEI Press, 2005, and Nathan Nunn and Daniel Trefler, *The Political Economy of Tariffs and Growth,* 2005

11. For example, Grupo Elektra in Mexico sells appliances and electronic goods to low-income consumers on credit and has used its vast database and efficient collection to set up a bank oriented toward low-income consumers.

12. Although reinvention is often considered a special American strength, there are, despite the frequently cited Euro-sclerosis, many examples of European firms reinventing themselves. Under the slogan "The shoes in Spain are anything but plain," eco-friendly Camper shoes from Spain turned around a sleepy footwear company, and are now sold in fashionable stores in New York, Boston, Paris, and Milan. The oldest Dutch ceramic manufacturer, Koninklijke Tichelaar Makkum (established in 1594) saw its business decline rapidly until it commissioned fresh new designs by young artists like Hella Jongerius, which now sell in the prestigious Moss Gallery in New York.

13. "Tech's Future," *Business Week,* September 27, 2004.

14. "Where Showing Skin Doesn't Sell, a New Style Is a Hit," *The New York Times,* March 20, 2006.

15. During the early 1980s, accounting rules were changed by the Financial Accounting Standards Board allowing companies to delay the funding of their liabilities until their work force grew older. In the meantime, Congress (unwilling to take away popular tax deductions but facing large, growing deficits) adopted the *Tax Equity and Fiscal Responsibility Act* in 1982 that, among other provisions, froze or reduced contributions (and their deficit-burdening tax-deduction impact) until the future. During the 1990s, good stock market returns led many companies to, in effect, raid their pension funds. Defined contribution plans such as 401K plans have grown rapidly and constituted about half of all pension fund assets and over 90 percent of the number of pension funds by 1997. As of 1997, about 23 million or one-third of all pension fund participants were enrolled in defined benefit plans, down from nearly two-thirds in 1980. Only 16 percent of these were underfunded but the actual or feared bankruptcy of several major steel, airline, and car companies has created concerns that the Pension Benefit Guaranty Corporation may not have adequate funds to deal with future potential losses. See Sylvester J. Schieber, "The Evolution and Implications of Federal Pension Reguation," in *The Evolving Pension System,* The Brookings Institution, 2005.

16. In reaction to the success of India in general and Bangalore in particular in attracting top-drawer technology talent, California Congressman Jerry Lewis, who also happens to be chairman of the House Appropriations Committee, announced that he is seeking a government agency "to sponsor projects in areas like nanotechnology, semiconductors, energy and pharmaceuticals and possibly to collaborate with agencies in India." See: "Is The Next Silicon Valley Taking Root in Bangalore?" *The New York Times,* March 20, 2006.

17. "Tech's Future," *Business Week,* September 27, 2004, cites data compiled by IDC, a global market intelligence firm specialized in information technology.

18. Saritha Ray, "Is the Next Silicon Valley Taking Root in Bangalore?" *New York Times,* March 21, 2006.
19. Richard C. Levin, the president of Yale University, in an article in *Newsweek* ("Universities Branch out," August 21, 2006) cites that "the number of students leaving home each year to study abroad has grown from 800,000 in 1975 to 2.5 million in 2004. Most travel from one developed nation to another, but the flow from developing to developed is on the rise, too. Today foreign students earn 30 percent of the doctoral degrees awarded in the United States and 38 percent of those in the United Kingdom. In the United States, 20 percent of newly hired professors in science and engineering are foreign-born, and in China the vast majority of newly hired faculty received their graduate education abroad. Since Deng Xiaoping first permitted Chinese students to seek education in the West in 1978, no country has made a more deliberate effort to send its most talented students abroad for a top education—especially at the graduate level . . . (and) . . .most Chinese students return after graduation."
20. Samuel P. Huntington, *The Clash of Civilizations and the Remaking of World Order* (Touchstone, 1996), first published as a seminal essay in *Foreign Affairs* in 1993.

CHAPTER 14

1. *Forbes*, with Gretchen Morgenstorn, *Great Minds of Business,* John Wiley, 1997.
2. I am indebted to Robert Ford of Merrill Lynch for pointing this out to me.
3. The efficient market hypothesis (EMH) evolved in the 1960s from the PhD dissertation of University of Chicago business school professor Eugene Fama, who argued that in an efficient market, no information or analysis can be expected to result in outperformance of an appropriate benchmark because securities will be priced to reflect all available information.
4. Originated by Nobel prizewinner Harry Markowitz in the early 1950s, modern portfolio theory defines an "efficient portfolio" as one that achieves a maximum rate of return with minimum risk by allocating assets according to varying levels of risk and return. All assets—stocks or asset classes—behave differently; the measure used to quantify this variation is called a "correlation coefficient."
5. EMM Research on the volatility of emerging markets (MSCI) in comparison with other developed markets (EAFE) and the American market (S&P 500).
6. See, for example Antoine W. van Agtmael and Vihang Errunza, "Foreign Portfolio Investment in Emerging Markets," *Columbia Journal of Business,* 1982.
7. *Wall Street Journal,* June 19, 1991. I cited two examples of companies: CVRD which indeed became a highly successful, world-class iron ore producer, and C.P. Pokphand, a Thai-Chinese company that dominated agribusiness (from feedstock to chicken and shrimp exports) in Thailand and thought it could do the same in the much larger Chinese market. It never lived up to expectations because of its overly ambitious strategy in China, diversification into many noncore activities (from retail to motorcycle manufacturing), and poor corporate governance.
8. Institute for International Finance, Private Capital Flows to Emerging Markets, January 2006.
9. George Hoguet, *Availability of Earnings Estimates in Emerging Markets,* State Street Global Advisers, January 22, 2006, shows that 3,100 analysts made 17,000 estimates on the 824 emerging markets stocks included in the September 2005 MSCI Emerging

Markets Index. After excluding companies under $100 million, there were nine estimates for the companies in the MSCI Emerging Markets universe (even more, ten, for the top 300 companies which make up 85 percent of the MSCI market cap), compared with eight for the companies in the MSCI Japan and 5.2 for the 2,000 companies in the Russell 2000 universe of American companies. An earlier study by J. Chang, T. Khanna, and K. Palepu, *Analyst Activity Around the World,* SSRN, January 2000, showed that estimates before 2000 were often less accurate. The Russell 2000 Index is a trademark of the Frank Russell Company.

10. At year-end 2005, adjusted for "float."
11. *S&P Emerging Markets Fact Book,* 2005.
12. FIBV, Federation of International Stock Exchanges; data exclude markets such as Russia, Czech Republic, most Middle Eastern markets (even though Iran is included), Pakistan, and various others that I have added.
13. FIBV data are still available only for 2004 but I have adjusted them for the increases in markets during 2005.

Bibliography

Amsden, Alice, *Asia's Next Giant: South Korea and the Late Industrialization* (Oxford University Press, London, 1988).

Amsden, Alice, *The Rest* (Oxford University Press, London, 2001). *Challenges to the West from late-industrializing economies.*

Boston Consulting Group, The, "The New Global Challanges: How 100 Top Companies from Rapidly Developing Economies Are Changing The World," March 2006. *Implications for both challengers and incumbents.*

Das, Gurcharan, *India Unbound* (Alfred A. Knopf, New York, 2001). *An account of the dramatic change in India's economic life and corporate world from the "Licensing Raj" to today by a former Procter & Gamble executive.*

Friedman, Thomas L., *The World is Flat: A Brief History of the Twenty-First Century* (Farrar, Straus and Giroux, New York, 2005). *An introduction to globalization, the impact of new technologies, offshoring, and outsourcing.*

Garten, Jeffrey E., *The Big Ten: The Big Emerging Markets and How They Will Change Our Lives* (Basic Books, HarperCollins Publishers, New York, 1997). *An investment banker and policy maker describes how the big emerging markets will reshape the world.*

Hiscock, Geoff, *Asia's Wealth Club: Who Is Really Who in Business, The Top 100 Billionaires in Asia* (Nicholas Brealey Publishing Ltd., Hong Kong, 1997). *Written before the 1998 Asian crisis, it provides an overview of the founding families of many Asian corporations.*

Hufbauer, Gary C., and Jeffrey J. Schott, *NAFTA Revisited, Achievements and Challenges* (Institute for International Economics, Washington D.C., October 200). *An analysis of the real impact of the North American Free Trade Agreement between the United States, Mexico, and Canada.*

Khanna, Tarun, and Krishna Palepu, *Emerging Giants: Building World Class Companies From Emerging Markets* (Harvard Business School paper, October 2004). *Case studies on how several emerging multinationals have succeeded.*

Mobius, Mark (with Stephen Fenichell), *Passport to Profits* (Warner Books, New York, 1999). *Visits on the ground to companies from Russia to Brazil with rules from an experienced emerging markets investor on how to invest in them.*

Sina, J., *Emerging Champions,* McKinsey Quarterly, March 2005. *Using Samsung, HSBC and Ranbaxy as examples, the article explores how emerging multinationals can use their countries of origin as a springboard to global success by learning how to transfer hard-to-imitate capabilities to new countries.*

Sulls, Donald N., *Made in China: What Western Managers Can Learn From Trail-blazing Chinese entrepreneurs* (Harvard Business School Press, Cambridge, 2005). *How eight Chinese companies made it to the top, ranging from Legend in computers and Haier in home appliances to Wahaha in beverages and Ting Hsin in noodles.*

Sull, Donald N., and Martin Escobari, *Success against the Odds: What Brazilian Champions Teach us about Thriving in Unpredictable Markets* (Elsevier/Editora Campus, 2005). *An exploration of what it takes to survive and prosper in a highly volatile economic environment by examining how Brazilian corporations like Embraer, Ambev, and VCP succeeded.*

Wells, Louis T., Jr., *Third World Multinationals: The Rise of Foreign Investment from Developing Countries* (MIT Press, Cambridge, 1983). *An early analysis of foreign investments by emerging multinationals from Hong Kong, Singapore, the Philippines, India, Korea, Brazil, Venezuela, and other countries.*

Acknowledgments

Entrepreneurs tend to be overly optimistic when they embark on a new venture, restless to get it done but then relying heavily on those around them. I am no exception. I could have never written this book while simultaneously running an investment management firm that went through an unexpected growth spurt without a colossal amount of help in both endeavors. At Emerging Markets Management, L.L.C., Felicia Morrow made sure that everything ran smoothly even when I was away writing, researching, interviewing, or simply preoccupied. When the book itself was only at the concept stage, I had the good fortune to hire Nowshad Rizwanullah, a bright young Yale graduate from Bangladesh as researcher and special assistant. For the next two years he was intimately involved with the book, from researching numerous ideas and helping me write the individual analyses of emerging multinationals to transcribing the interviews and checking facts. Later on, my agent, David Kuhn, had the great idea to get me in touch with Stephen Fenichell, who is, unlike me a professional writer whose help in recalling events and, most important, giving color to my blander, less anecdotal style of writing was absolutely indispensable. I owe him a huge debt. At later stages, virtually all of the portfolio managers and analysts at our firm organized meetings, shared their detailed knowledge, and commented on drafts while others, in particular Danielle Menichella, Marios Athanasiadis, and Justin Machata helped out with researching data and preparing charts. In the final stages, my summer research assistant Ben Morgenroth helped me with proofreading and fact checking as well as revisions to the financial profiles. And throughout the process, my trusted executive assistant, Sue Ellen Wells, patiently made corrections to draft after draft while keeping my life organized.

This book is largely based on my experience at Emerging Markets Management LLC (EMM) these past 19 years. Ever since we began to discuss the idea of establishing an investment firm in 1987, at the initiative of Hilda Ochoa-Brillembourg, I have had the great fortune to work closely with her and my other founding partners Michael Duffy, Mary Choksi,

Carol Grefenstette, and George Alvarez Correa and also with K. Georg Gabriel, as we ultimately started two firms, Strategic Investment Management (a global investment firm led by Hilda) and Emerging Markets Management LLC (of which I became the CIO). Each firm—with its own staff and clients—grew to a size way beyond our wildest imagination.

I am also immensely grateful to numerous friends and several family members who encouraged me and commented on drafts. Strobe Talbott was among the first to review chapters and provide extensive guidance, Donald Sull (who has himself written insightfully on some of the companies in this book) generously shared his advice, while Jeff Garten, David Swensen, Eugene Rotberg, Bob Pastor, and Moises Naim also helped me with their comments. During two summer vacations, which served as writing stints in Lenox, Massachusetts, my whole family read drafts and provided useful comments including my niece Alanna Kaufman, herself a budding editor, who helped edit several chapters, and spelling champion Elinor Baker, whose sharp eye caught a number of typos.

And, of course, many CEOs and other key executives of the companies profiled in this book candidly shared their thoughts with me in interviews that often went way beyond their allotted time. Their investor relations staffs were helpful in chasing down answers to specific questions and details as well as reviewing drafts for inaccuracies.

My superb agent, David Kuhn, patiently sent me back to the drawing boards until he felt the manuscript was ready to be shown to publishers and guided me throughout the process. At Simon & Schuster, I was lucky enough to have Fred Hills as my editor just before he retired. I quickly understood why he is legendary as he was as insightful as he was rapid in his edits. I was grateful to have Emily Loose and Carol de Onís help me at the later publishing stages.

Finally, writing a book eats time and absorbs full attention. My wife, Emily, not only suffered through my mental absences that were even worse than usual but, recalling her own editing days, helped me clarify my thoughts. There is no way I can adequately express my admiration, love and gratitude for how she always stands by me and did so again during this busy period.

Despite the help of so many and my own arduous attempts to be accurate, errors will be inevitable for which no other than me bears the responsibility.

Index

A.T. Kearney, 273
Abascal, Adriana, 259
Accenture, 36, 232
Acer, 86, 102, 110
Act of Creation, The (Koestler), 289
Adidas, 54, 111–113, 115, 116
Aeronautical Training Centre (CTA), 172,
    174
Agnelli, Roger, 53, 194–197
Aguiar, Carlos, 187, 189
Airbus, 54, 163, 165, 166, 180, 182, 273
Airlines industry, 13, 16, 43, 52, 53, 55,
    61, 163–182, 278
Akbank, 32
Al-Attiyah, Abdullah Bin Hamas, 210
Alckmin, Geraldo, 166
Alcoa, 36, 192, 196
Aleman Valdes, Miguel, 261
Alfa, 41
Algeria, 211, 217
Allende, Salvador, 77
Almaviva Winery, Chile, 79
Alternative energy producers, 205–226
Amazon.com, 155
Ambev, 13, 36, 96–98, 282
Ambit, 109
Amelio, William, 86
America Movil, 36, 44, 261, 323
American Airlines, 178
American depository receipts (ADRs), 297
American Express, 232
American Petroleum Institute, 223
Anglo American, 36, 193
Anglovaal, 213
Angola, 211
Anheuser Busch, 36
Antares, 223, 224
Anti-dumping issue, 156–158, 174, 273,
    277–278
Apple Computer, 60, 63, 84, 102, 104, 108,
    109, 228
Aracruz, 37, 43, 50–51, 184–190, 324

Arcelor, 12, 36, 273
Argentina, 19, 24, 29–34, 37, 41, 43, 44,
    49
    Tenaris, 19, 24, 29, 30, 37, 41, 43,
    47, 49, 54, 218–226, 277, 278,
    346
Art of War, The (Sun Tzu), 135
Asian financial crisis of 1997–1998, 6, 27,
    33, 34, 41, 42, 51, 64, 65, 67, 71, 91,
    141, 144, 148, 253, 293
ASICs (application specific ICs), 126
AST, 85
Asustek Computer, 37, 102, 138
ATI Technologies, 129
AT&T Company, 36, 242
Audi A6, 149
Audiovox, 132
Australia, 77, 78, 80, 97, 188, 192, 217
Automobile industry, 22, 32, 36, 42, 47,
    53, 72, 120, 140–153, 173, 208–209
Azcarraga Jean, Emilio, 257, 260–261,
    265–266
Azcarraga Milmo, Emilio, 259–261, 264
Azcarraga Vidaurreta, Emilio, 258–259,
    261

Bacardi, 63
Bae, James, 253
BAE Systems, 180
Bain Capital, 23, 83, 88, 266
Banco Itau, 45
Bandeirante, 174
Banfi Vintners, 75
Bangalore, 20, 228–230, 232, 234, 240,
    241, 279, 287
Bangladesh, 2, 281
Bankers Trust Company, 1–3
Banking industry, 1–5, 32, 34, 44–45, 195,
    280–281
Barger, Dave, 164
Baron Philippe de Rothschild Winery, 79
Barton & Guestier wine, 79

Batista, Eliezer, 193
Bauxite, 196, 198
Beacham, 243
Beechcraft, 173
Beer industry, 13, 36, 43, 54, 61, 83, 93–98
Beko, 25
Belgium, 97, 122, 181
Bell Laboratories, 123, 124, 284
BenQ, 24, 102, 138
Berkshire-Hathaway, 61
BHP Billiton, 36, 192
Binford, Ione, 27
Binford, Thomas O., 27
Biofuels, 208–210
Bismarck, Otto von, 7
Blackberry, 134, 137, 139
Blackstone Group, 23, 83, 88, 266
Blu-Ray technology, 73
BMW, 69
BNDES, 196
Boeing, 54, 163, 166, 167, 180, 182
Bolivia, 207
Bollywood, 248, 250–251
Bombardier, 52, 166, 178–179, 181
Botelho, Mauricio, 165, 167, 176–182
Bowerman, Bill, 113
Bozano Simonsen, 176
BP (British Petroleum), 36, 214
Bradesco, 194, 195, 197
Brands, 59–98
    Concha y Toro example, 75–81
    Grupo Modelo example, 93–98
    Lenovo example, 83–86
    Qingdao Haier example, 86–92
    Samsung example, 64–74
Bratt, Nick, 6
Brazil, 19, 25, 34, 38, 44, 55, 96–98, 108,
    208–210
    Aracruz, 37, 43, 50–51, 184–190, 324
    Companhia Vale do Rio Doce (CVRD),
        19, 32, 36, 37, 43, 53, 184, 327
    Embraer (Empresa Brasileira de Aero-
        nautica S.A.), 13, 16, 27, 37, 39, 43,
        49, 52, 53, 55, 61, 163–182,
        277–280, 286, 328
    Petrobras, 32, 36, 38, 43, 46, 173, 175,
        176, 209, 338
Brazilian National Institute for Space
    Research (INPE), 170
BRICs (Brazil, Russia, India, and China),
    11, 13, 33, 53, 207, 246, 285, 311
British Airways, 232

British Burmah Company, 213
Büchi, Hernan, 77
Budweiser beer, 60
Buffett, Warren, 61, 261
Burr, Donald, 165
Bush, George H.W., 142, 156, 206
Bush, George W., 206–208
BusinessWeek, 59, 60, 63, 69, 100, 105,
    146, 165, 200, 214, 266, 286
Butterfield, Peter, 149

C.P. Pokhpand, 63
Cadence Design Systems, 129
Canada, 25, 96, 98, 193, 221
    Bombardier, 52, 166, 178–179, 181
Canadair, 179
Canon, 71
Capital Investment, Inc., 5, 6
Cardoso, President of Brazil, 194
Carlsberg, 96
Carlyle Group, 266
Carrefour, 44
Cascade Management, 266
Case, Steve, 21
Casillero del Diablo wine, 76, 79, 80
Castro, Veronica, 254, 255
Cathay Financial, 32
CBA-123, 175, 176, 178
Cement industry, 13, 19, 29, 32, 36, 54, 63,
    154–162, 273, 277–278
CEMEX, 13, 19, 26, 27, 29, 36, 43, 47, 49,
    54, 63, 154–162, 273, 275,
    277–278, 325
CEMEXNet, 160
Cessna, 173
Chaebols, 33, 152, 201
Chameleon strategy, 52
Chang, Morris, 29, 40, 122–131, 227
Changh Hwa Bank, 32
Chartered, 129
Chen Shui-bian, 99
Chevrolet, 147
Chevron, 23, 210, 216
ChevronTexaco, 216
Chiang Kai-shek, 99, 119, 123
Chile, 34
    Concha y Toro, 38, 44, 61, 63, 64,
        75–81, 326
China, 2, 9, 10, 13, 20–26, 34, 43–45, 48,
    51–53, 55, 64, 73, 81, 83–92,
    99–106, 109–115, 118, 120, 121,
    129–131, 151, 152, 184, 189, 197,

204, 208, 217, 227–228, 232–233, 271–274
film industry, 252
Harbin Embraer Aircraft Industry Company, 167
Lenovo, 22, 43, 54, 83–86, 92, 272, 276, 336
Petrochina, 25, 36
Qingdao Haier Ltd., 16, 23, 25, 27, 43, 54, 55, 61, 63, 83, 86–92, 330
Yue Yuen, 16, 37, 43, 54, 111–118, 347
China Construction Bank, 32
China Entrepreneur magazine, 89
China Mobile, 32, 36
China Southern Airlines, 167
China Steel, 32
Choi, Changsoo, 68
Choi, Harry, 151
Chou, Peter, 133–137
Chu, Woo-Sik, 73
Chung, Eui Son, 152
Chung, Ju-Yung, 145
Chung, Mong Koo, 42, 144, 147, 149, 152
Cingular, 136
Cisco, 109, 155
Citibank, 155
Clash of Civilizations (Huntington), 288–289
Club de Marques, 79
CNOOC, 23–24
Coal, 196, 198, 212
Coal-to-gas (CTG) process, 212
Coal-to-liquid (CTL) process, 214, 216–218
Coca-Cola, 61, 93
Cold War, 26, 175, 178, 276
Comer, Clarence, 156
Commerce, U.S. Department of, 156
Commodity producers, 183–204
Communist economies, 33
Compal, 138
Companhia Vale do Rio Doce (CVRD), 19, 25, 32, 36, 37, 43, 53, 184, 327
Compaq Computer, 85, 126, 135
Computer Science, 36
Concha y Toro, 38, 44, 61, 63, 64, 75–81, 326
Concha y Toro, Don Melchor, 76
Condea, 215, 216
Confab, 221
Confucius, 90
Cono Sur winery, Chile, 79

Conoco Phillips, 214
Consumer electronics industry, 14, 16, 24–25, 42, 51–53, 59–61, 63–74, 82–83, 100, 103–111, 119–122
Continental Airlines, 179
Copa Airlines, 167
Copper, 195–196, 198
Corona beer, 13, 43, 54, 61, 63, 83, 93–98, 329
Cortina, 145
Craig, Russell, 100
Crandall, Robert, 178
CSN, 194
Cuba, 196, 256, 267
Cultural Revolution, 86
CVRD. *See* Companhia Vale do Rio Doce (CVRD)
Cyberjaya, 227
Cydsa, 41
Czech Republic, 108

Daewoo, 41
Daimler-Chrysler, 143, 258
Dalmine, 220–223
Damasceno, Fernando, 209
Darwin, Charles, 271, 288
Dassault, 182
Databasics Corporation, 236
Davies, Pat, 217
de Angoitia, Alfonso, 262–265
Dell, Michael, 272
Dell Computer, 13, 16, 36, 49, 51, 54, 83, 86, 102, 104, 107, 108, 136, 271–272
Delta Airlines, 61
Deng Xiaoping, 86, 101
Derobert, Eric, 192
Desai, Morarj, 237
Deutsche Bank, 1
Digital Equipment Corporation (DEC), 126, 134, 240, 241
Domino's Pizza, 49, 160
Don Melchor wine, 79, 80
Dreamworks, 72
Dubai Ports World, 24, 276
DuPont, 20

EADS, 182
Earth Summit (1992), 191
eBay, 155
Economist, The, 113, 161
Edison, Thomas, 120, 298

EDS, 232, 258
Efficient markets hypothesis, 303–304
Eimo, 109
Elantra, 151
Embraer (Empresa Brasileira de Aeronau-
    tica S.A.), 13, 16, 27, 37, 39, 43, 49,
    52, 53, 55, 61, 163–182, 277–280,
    286, 328
Emerging Markets Data Base, 5
Emerging Markets Growth Fund, 5
Emerging Markets Management, 6, 33
Empresa Brasileira de Engenharia, 177
Enron Corporation, 310
Ericsson, 73
Errunza, Vihang, 4
Estonia, 122, 280
Ethanol, 206–210, 280
Ethiopia, 2
Eucalyptus trees, 40, 43, 186–190
Excel, 146
Exchange traded funds (ETFs), 297
Execution and quality, obsession with, 46,
    47–48
Export orientation, 46–47
Exxon Mobil, 185, 214

Fairchild-Dornier, 52, 174, 180
Federal Express, 293
Fernandez, Carlos, 93–96
Fernandez, Pablo Diez, 95
Ficke-Wulf Aircraft, 172
Film industry, 248–251
Financial Times, The, 115
Finex, 203, 204
Finland, 109, 187, 190
Finlay, Francis, 5
First Financial Hld, 32
Fischer, Franz, 212–213
Fischer-Tropsch (FT) process, 211–212,
    214
Fisher, David, 6
Fleming, Alexander, 293
Flextronics, 103, 104, 106, 107
FNM, 173
Focke, Heinrich, 172
Fokker, 52, 180
Forbes magazine, 41
Ford, Henry, 180
Ford, John, 216
Ford Motor Company, 14, 143, 145
Foreign direct investment (FDI), 18–19,
    101

Formosa Plastics Group, 135
Forrester Research, 231
Fortune magazine, 15, 29, 38, 200
Fortune at the Bottom of the Pyramid, The
    (Prahalad), 281
Foster Wheeler, 217
Fox, Vicente, 258
Foxconn, 102, 332
France, 24, 76, 79, 80, 122, 160–161, 181,
    182, 219, 273
Friedman, Milton, 77
Friedman, Tom, 17
FSA, 29

G7 (United States, Japan, Germany,
    France, United Kingdom, Italy, and
    Canada), 11
Galavision, 265
Gap, 60
Gas-to-liquid (GTL) process, 211,
    214–218
Gates, Bill, 120, 132, 234
GATT (General Agreement of Tariffs and
    Trade), 157
Gazprom, 13, 31, 32, 36, 37, 205–206,
    211, 215
GD Searle, 243
GE Capital, 91
Geisel, Ernesto, 209
General Electric, 16, 20, 61, 89, 181, 232,
    258, 265
General Instruments, 122
General Motors, 20, 36, 143, 146, 149, 150
Geophysical Service Incorporated (GSI),
    124
Gerdau, 36
Germany, 77, 78, 88, 122, 211–213, 218,
    219, 223, 253
Getty Oil, 13
Ghana, 2
Gilboy, George J., 274
Gill, David, 3–4
Glaxo Holdings, 243, 245
Global Information Technology Report
    (World Economic Forum), 122
Global market share, 37
Global warming, 207
Goldman Sachs, 11, 242
Google, 63, 155
Gou, Terry, 49, 104–110
Goya, 97
Great Britain, 24, 122, 161, 180

Great Depression, 62
Great Leap Forward, 86
Gros, Francisco, 193
Gross national product (GNP), 10–11, 20
Grundig, 25
Grupo Bimbo, 63, 275
Grupo Modelo, 13, 36, 43, 54, 61, 83, 93–98, 329
Grupo Televisa, 44, 53, 257–268, 344
Guilisasti, Eduardo, 80
Guilisasti, Rafael, 75, 78–80
Gurgel, 208

Hafei Aviation Industry, 167
Haier. *See* Qingdao Haier Ltd.
Hallmark, 264, 265
Harbin Aviation Industry Group, Ltd., 167
Harbin Embraer Aircraft Industry Company, 167
Harley-Davidson, 60
Hatch-Waxman Act of 1984, 244
HDTV (high definition television), 73
Health care industry, 12
Heineken beer, 13, 36, 61, 95, 97, 98
Hewlett-Packard, 9, 51, 71, 83, 102, 108, 109, 121, 132, 135, 136, 228, 234, 239, 286
Hexene, 215
High Tech Computer Corporation (HTC), 9, 10, 30, 39, 43, 73, 102, 132–139, 331
Hill, Cavan, 215–217
Hitachi, 71
Hoguet, George, 310
Holcim, 161
Hollywood movies, 248–249
Holste, Max, 173
Home market advantage, 20
Hon Hai Precision Industry Company Ltd., 16, 26, 30, 36–38, 43, 49, 54, 99, 100, 102–111, 286, 332
Honda, 14, 141, 146, 149, 150
Honeywell, 181
Hong Kong, 2, 122, 248
Hong Kong and Shanghai Bank (HSBC), 44, 63
Hoogovens, 203
Housing Development Finance Corporation (HDFC), 44
Hsinchu Science Park, Taipei, 123, 227, 228, 280
Hua Nan Bank, 31, 32

Huang, Jack J.T., 25
Hungary, 108
Huntington, Samuel P., 288–289
Hwan, Oh Sung, 150
Hydrogen fuel cells, 207
Hyundai Construction, 145
Hyundai Heavy Industries (HHI), 37, 42, 145, 211, 333
Hyundai Motor Company, 16, 22, 27, 30, 36–39, 41, 42, 47, 53, 54, 63, 67, 140–153, 273, 275, 279, 285, 334

IBM Corporation, 14, 22–23, 50, 54, 71, 83–86, 102, 104, 121, 124, 126, 128, 155, 232, 236–237, 240, 241, 258
Ibuka, Masaru, 83
IC (integrated circuit), first, 124
ICBC, 32
ICICI Bank, 44
IDC, 85
Ikea, 60, 63
Ilkone Mobile, 281
iMate, 132
Immelt, Jeff, 20
Inbev, 13, 36, 98
Inco Ltd., 25, 193, 196, 197
India, 2, 10, 13–16, 21–22, 25, 26, 34, 43–45, 48, 52, 53, 55, 92, 108, 151, 167, 189, 203, 208, 217, 228–233, 271–274
    Bangalore, 20, 228–230, 232, 234, 240, 241, 279, 287
    Bollywood, 248, 250–251
    Infosys Technologies, 15, 19, 26, 30, 36, 39, 43, 47, 55, 232–243, 335
    Ranbaxy Laboratories, Ltd., 27, 38, 43, 53, 55, 232, 243–247, 340
    Reliance Industries, 38, 46, 341
    Tata Motors, 36, 120, 151, 153
Indica, 120
Indonesia, 34, 111, 113, 114, 116, 188
Industrial espionage, 116–117
Industrial Revolution, 10, 16, 17, 21, 289
Industrial Technology Research Institute (ITRI), 123–125
Infant-industry protection, 46, 120, 173, 200–201
Inflation, 33, 34
Information Technology Association of America, 274
Infosys Foundation, 235

Infosys Technologies, 15, 19, 26, 30, 36, 39, 43, 47, 55, 232–243, 335
Iniguez, Gelacio, 160
Institute of International Economics (IIE), 231, 273
Instituto Technologico de Aeronautica (ITA), 170, 172
Integrated device manufacturers (IDMs), 125–126
Intel, 13, 29, 36, 50, 70, 71, 108, 109, 121, 124, 126–128, 135–137, 228, 232
Intellectual property rights, 120, 121
Interbrand, 60, 62, 63, 80, 146
Interbrew, 97, 98, 282
Interest rates, 33, 34
International Federation of Stock Exchanges, 316
International Finance Corporation (IFC), 3–5, 40, 186, 196, 307, 315
International Trade Commission (ITC), 156, 174
Internet, 19, 55, 133, 137, 277, 280, 304, 305, 310
Investing, in emerging markets, 293–319
Ipanema, 173
iPAQ, 9, 135–136
Iran, 207, 217
Iran Air, 2
Iraq, 207
Iron ore, 19, 25, 32, 36, 37, 43, 53, 184, 191–198
Israel, 122, 245, 246
Italy, 76, 211, 220, 221

J.D Power & Associates, 146, 153
J.P. Morgan, 5, 11, 242
Jaguar, 146
Japan, 2, 48, 100, 111, 113, 120, 181
    Honda, 14, 141, 146, 149, 150
    Kawasaki, 181, 219, 221
    Matsushita, 13, 71, 73
    Mitsubishi, 91, 145, 180
    Nippon Steel, 36, 199
    Sony, 13, 14, 16, 26, 36, 51, 54, 60, 61, 63, 68, 71–73, 82–83, 88, 102, 104, 109, 135, 252, 277
    Sumitomo, 219, 221, 223, 225
    Suzuki, 147, 151
    Toshiba, 71, 72, 121, 136
    Toyota, 16, 26, 36, 42, 63, 141, 146, 147, 150, 151, 153, 277

Jet airplanes, 13, 16, 43, 52, 53, 55, 61, 163–182, 278
JetBlue, 163–166
Jobs, Steve, 120
Jones Day Company, 25
Jordan, Michael, 94
Just-in-time inventory management, 26, 49, 277

Kalam, A.P.J. Abdul, 22
Kalson, John, 143
Katyal, Tarun, 267
Kawasaki, 181, 219, 221
Kelleher, Herb, 165
Kennedy, John F., 276
Kepco, 32
Khrushchev, Nikita, 276
Kia Motors, 148, 150–152
Kia Motors America, 149
Kilby, Jack, 124
Kim, Eric, 69–70
Kim, Hyung Jin, 253
Kim, Tack Jin, 253
Kimberly Clark, 186
Kitchen appliance industry, 16, 23, 25, 27, 43, 54, 55, 61, 63, 83, 86–92, 330
Knight, Phil, 65, 111, 113, 114
Koestler, Arthur, 289
Kohlberg Kravis Roberts (KKR), 266
Korea. See South Korea
Korean War, 145, 199
Kraft, 97
Ku, Edward, 114
Kubler Ross, Elisabeth, 25
Kumar, Satyendra, 241
Kutaragi, Ken, 73

Labatte Blue beer, 96
Lafarge, 36, 161
Laozi, 90
Laurent Perrier wine, 79
Lee, Ang, 252
Lee, Byung-Chul, 65
Lee, Gregory, 66, 69
Lee, Jackson, 116
Lee, Kun Hee, 47–48, 66, 67, 71, 72
Lee family, 83
Legend, 84, 85
Legoretta, Ricardo, 258
Leno, Jay, 146
Lenovo, 22, 43, 54, 83–86, 92, 272, 276, 336

Levin, Richard C., 294, 357 [19]
Lexus, 146
LG, 15, 16, 22, 63, 70, 73, 74
Li, K.T., 40, 119, 120, 122, 123, 125, 227
Li, Steve, 115
Li Qin, 85
Liebherr-Haushaltsgerate, 91
Lindbergh, Charles, 171
Liu Chuanzhi, 84
Logistics, 48–49
Lorentzen, Erling, 40, 185–186, 188, 190
LOT Airlines, 167
Luft, Gal, 210
Lukoil, 13, 32, 36
Lula da Silva, Luiz Inacio, 208
Lun, Rita, 107
Lutz, Bob, 149

Magneti Marelli, 209
Malaysia, 32, 33, 37, 43, 44, 227
Malaysian International Shipping
    Corporation (MISC), 37, 43, 211,
    337
Manganese, 195
Mannesmann, 219, 221, 223
Mao Zedong, 86, 87, 91, 99, 119, 123
Marathon, 214
Marine Midland Bank, 44
Maruti, 151
Matsu, 99
Matsushita, 13, 71, 73
Maytag Corporation, 23, 54, 63, 83, 88–89,
    92
McElroy, Neil, 62
Mead, Carver, 126
Media, 248–270
Medina, Hector, 157
Mehta, Deepa, 250
Mercedes, 146
Messier, Jean-Claude, 21
Mexico, 6, 32, 93–98, 108, 142, 254–256
    CEMEX, 13, 19, 26, 27, 29, 36, 43, 47,
        49, 54, 63, 154–162, 273, 275,
        277–278, 325
    crisis of 1994, 27, 33, 34, 41, 95, 224
    Grupo Televisa, 44, 53, 257–268, 344
    Pemex, 41, 221, 224, 225
    Tamsa, 41, 221–222, 224–225, 278
Micron, 36, 71, 121
Microsoft, 13, 36, 132–133, 135, 136, 155,
    228, 234, 240, 252
Middle-class consumers, 20–21

Miele, 89
Miller, Alexei, 206
Miller Beer, 97, 98, 282
Mining industry, 19, 25, 32, 36, 37, 43, 53,
    184, 191–198
MISC. See Malaysian International Ship-
    ping Company (MISC)
Mitac, 138
Mitsubishi, 91, 145, 180
Mittal Steel, 12, 204, 273
Mobile phone industry, 9, 42, 43, 59, 60,
    68–70, 72–74, 82–83, 100, 102,
    121, 132, 133, 135–139
Mobius, Mark, 6
Modelo. See Grupo Modelo
Modern portfolio theory, 303, 304–307
Mohamad, Mahathir, 227
Montenegro, Casimiro, 171–172
Moore, Gordon, 29, 127
Moore's law, 29, 127
Morita, Akio, 83, 124
Motorola, 13, 61, 68, 73, 102, 109, 123,
    124, 126, 128, 136, 232, 234
Motterhead, Chris, 214
Mozambique, 196
MSCI (Morgan Stanley Capital Interna-
    tional) Emerging Markets Index,
    315–316
Mulvenon, James C., 130
Murphy, John, 62
Murthy, Narayana, 234–242
Murthy, Sudha, 235

Naim, Moises, 12
NAND flash memory business, 72
National Aeronautics and Space Adminis-
    tration (NASA), 276
NCsoft, 253
NEC, 228
Neeleman, David, 164, 165
Nehru, Pandit, 235
Nescafe, 61
Nestle, 14, 44
Netherlands, 122, 203
New Balance shoes, 112, 115
New Technology Development Company
    (NTD), 84
New York Times, The, 23, 73, 88, 152, 164,
    233, 260, 261, 271, 272
Newmont, 192
Niche strategy, 92
Nickel, 196, 198

Nigeria, 207, 211, 216, 217, 295
Nigerian National Petroleum Corporation,
    216
Nike, 16, 54, 60, 65, 94, 111–114, 116,
    117, 281
Nilekani, Nandan, 234, 241
Nintendo, 109
Nippon Steel, 36, 199
Nippon Tel, 36
NKK, 221, 224
Nokia, 13, 16, 36, 49, 51, 54, 60, 61, 63,
    68, 102, 104, 108, 109, 136, 139,
    155
North American Fair Trade Agreement
    (NAFTA), 142, 274
Norwest Venture Partners, 286–287
Nucor, 36
Nye, Joseph, 249

Odebrecht Automacao e Telecomunicacoes
    Ltda., 177
Oil and gas companies, 19, 23–25, 29, 31,
    32, 36, 43, 47, 49, 205–226
Oil and Natural Gas Corporation (ONGC),
    25, 32
Olefins, 215
Oliveira, José Auto Lancaster, 196
Olympic Games (2008), 117
One-stop shopping concept, 107
O'Neill, Finbarr, 148
OPEC oil shocks of 1973, 208, 214
Operation Paperclip, 213
Orange, 136
Oregon Weekly, The, 113
Original design manufacturers (ODMs),
    121, 132
Original equipment manufacturers
    (OEMs), 121
Outsourcing and offshoring, 13, 15, 19,
    34, 47, 52, 106–107, 109, 112–114,
    230, 231, 273–275, 282

P & O, 24
Pakistan, 2
Palm, 9, 132, 134–136
Panama, 167
Panasonic, 14, 60, 73
Paraguay, 196
Park, Chung-hee, 199–201
Park, Tae-joon, 200
PDAs (personal digital assistants), 132,
    135–139

Peixoto, Clecius, 172
Pemex, 41, 221, 224, 225
Pepper, John, 286
Pepsi, 60, 61
Perenchio, A. Jerrold, 264–266
Perez, Gilberto, 157
Peron, Juan, 220
Perot, H. Ross, 142, 143, 274
Petrobras, 32, 36, 38, 43, 46, 173, 175,
    176, 209, 338
Petrochina, 25, 36
Pfizer, 244
Pharmaceutical industry, 14, 22, 43, 53, 55,
    243–247
Phelps Dodge, 192, 193, 196
Philip Morris, 97
Philips, 13, 14, 60, 73, 128
Piaskowski, Joel, 150
Pink, Daniel, 273
Pinochet, Augusto, 77
Piper, 173
PlayStation, 135, 252
Pohang Iron and Steel Company (POSCO),
    29, 32, 36, 42, 50, 184, 198–204,
    279, 339
Poland, 167
Pony, 146
Population, global, 20
Porsche, 146
Porter, Michael, 90, 170
POSCO. See Pohang Iron and Steel Com-
    pany (POSCO)
Pou Chen, 115, 117
Prahalad, C.K., 281
Praj, 208
Prasad, G.V., 244
Press, James E., 147
Privatization, 33, 34
Procter & Gamble, 20, 62, 67, 256
Protectionism, 277–280
Pulp, 40, 50–51, 184–190
Putin, Vladimir, 205

Qatar, 210, 211, 216, 217
Qatar Petroleum, 216
Qingdao Haier Ltd., 16, 23, 25, 27, 43, 54,
    55, 61, 63, 83, 86–92, 330
Qualcomm, 134, 136, 138
Quality control circles, 145, 277
Quanta Computer, 37, 102
Quemoy, 99
Quotas, 34

Ranbaxy Laboratories, Ltd., 27, 38, 43, 53,
    55, 232, 243–247, 340
Rand Corporation, 130
Ray, Satyajit, 251
Read-Ink Technologies, 287
Redbus Interhouse, 253
Reebok, 54, 112, 114–116, 242
Reed, John, 154
Reis, Mauricio, 191
Reliance Industries, 38, 46, 341
Rendell, Edward, 212
Rentech, 214
Retail industry, 44, 280
Revenge of the Right Brain (Pink), 273
Reverse engineering, 48
Ricardo, David, 183
Rio Tinto, 192
Rizwanullah, Nowshad, 30
RMC, 161
Roach, Stephen, 231
Robert Mondavi wine, 78, 79
Rocca, Agostino, 220
Rocca, Paolo, 41, 49, 222, 224, 225
Rocca, Roberto, 220, 221
Role reversal, 19–20
Romania, 221
Roosevelt, Franklin D., 271, 276
Rousseau, Etienne, 213
Royal Dutch/Shell, 29, 214, 219
Rumsfeld, Donald, 243
Russia, 24, 26, 31, 37, 45, 197
    bond market collapse of 1998, 33, 34
    Gazprom, 13, 31, 32, 36, 37, 205–206,
        211, 215

SAB Miller, 36, 98
Saban, Haim, 266
Sadia, 44
Saldanha, 203
Salinas Pliego, Ricardo, 263
Salomon Brothers, 4, 5
Samsung Electronics, 13, 15, 16, 22,
        25–27, 30, 32, 36–39, 41, 42, 47,
        51–54, 59–61, 63–74, 82–83,
        87–89, 121, 136, 139, 275, 277,
        279, 342
Samsung Group, 6, 148
Samsung Semiconductors, 65, 67
San Francisco Chronicle, 114
San Martin, Carlos, 219–221, 223, 224
San Miguel beer, 63
Santa Fe SUV, 150

Santos-Dumont, Alberto, 171
Sarney, Jose, 175
SARS epidemic, 105, 106, 312
SASOL. *See* South African Coal, Oil and
        Gas Corporation Ltd. (Sasol)
Satyam, 234
Saudi Arabian Airlines, 167
Schumpeter, Joseph, 121
Schweitzer, Brian, 212
Scotland, 108
Scudder, 6
Seamless steel pipe, 19, 24, 29, 30, 37, 41,
        43, 47, 49, 54, 218–226, 278
Selye, Hans, 293
Semiconductor industry, 29, 30, 32, 36, 37,
        40, 43, 50, 66, 71, 74, 100, 104,
        122–132, 227, 277
Senge, Peter, 90
Shammanna, Salkumar, 233
Shanghai Bao Steel, 36
Sharp, 136
Shell Oil, 14, 36
Shinsegae, 44
Shipbuilding industry, 37, 42, 145
Shockley, William, 123
Shoe industry, 43, 54, 94, 100, 111–118
Siat, 221
Sichuan Airlines, 167
Siderca, 219–223
Siemens, 60, 126, 128, 228, 234
Siemens Mobile, 24, 102, 138
Silva, Ozires, 173–177
Silver bullet brand strategy, 78, 81
Singapore, 2, 104, 106, 122, 129, 228,
        229–230
Singh, Manmohan, 230
Singha beer, 97
Sinopec, 217
Six Sigma, 26, 90, 277
SK Telecom, 36
Slim Helu, Carlos, 41, 261, 323
Slovakia, 143, 151
Slovenia, 14
SMIC, 129
Smith, Fred, 293
Smith, Richard, 172
Snyder, Betsy, 164
Sodi, Thalia, 255
Software industry, 22, 36, 231–243, 279
Solar energy, 207
Solectron, 104, 106, 107
Sonata, 149, 150

Sony Corporation, 13, 14, 16, 26, 36, 51, 54, 60, 61, 63, 68, 71–73, 82–83, 88, 102, 104, 109, 135, 252, 277
Sony Entertainment Television, 267
Sorkin, Andrew Ross, 23
Soros, George, 28
Sossego Copper Mine, 195–196
South Africa, 77, 78, 80, 203
  South African Breweries (SAB), 97, 98, 282
  South African Coal, Oil and Gas Corporation Ltd. (Sasol), 37, 43, 46, 210–218, 275, 280, 343
South Korea, 2, 21, 30, 32–34, 37, 38, 41, 44, 48, 51, 59–61, 63–74, 89, 100, 102, 111, 122, 252–253
  Hyundai Heavy Industries (HHI), 37, 42, 145, 211, 333
  Hyundai Motor Company, 16, 22, 27, 30, 36–39, 41, 42, 47, 53, 54, 63, 67, 140–153, 273, 275, 279, 285, 334
  Pohang Iron and Steel Company (POSCO), 29, 32, 36, 42, 50, 184, 198–204, 279, 339
  Samsung Electronics, 13, 15, 16, 22, 25–27, 30, 32, 36–39, 41, 42, 47, 51–54, 59–61, 63–74, 82–83, 87–89, 121, 136, 139, 275, 277, 279, 342
Southdown, 156–158
Southwest Airlines, 165
S&P Emerging Markets Index, 315
Spain, 80, 122, 154, 155, 158–159, 181, 277
Spanish International Network (SIN), 259, 264
Spielberg, Steven, 72
Sprint, 136
Sputnik, 26, 276
Starbucks, 60, 61, 63
State, U.S. Department of, 272, 276
Steel industry, 14, 29, 32, 36, 40, 42, 50, 184, 193, 198–204
Stern, Walter, 6
Stora Enso, 190
String theory, 22
Stumpf, Urbano Ernesto, 208
Sudan, 25
Sumitomo, 219, 221, 223, 225
Sun Microsystems, 109, 228
Sun Tzu, 90, 135, 163, 168
Suntech, 208

Suzlon, 208
Suzuki, 147, 151
Swatch watch, 94
Switzerland, 161
Sylvania Electronics, 123
Synfuels, 214

T-Mobile, 136
Taco Bell, 97
Taiwan, 13, 21, 29–34, 38, 44, 49–51, 99, 100, 103, 119–120, 189, 227
  Asustek Computer, 37, 102, 138
  BenQ, 24, 102, 138
  High Tech Computer Corporation (HTC), 9, 10, 30, 39, 43, 73, 102, 132–139, 331
  Hon Hai Precision Industry Company Ltd., 16, 26, 30, 36–38, 43, 49, 54, 99, 100, 102–111, 286, 332
  Taiwan Semiconductor Manufacturing Company (TSMC), 29, 30, 32, 36, 37, 40, 43, 50, 100, 104, 122–132, 275, 279, 345
  Yue Yuen, 16, 37, 43, 54, 111–118, 347
Taiwan Semiconductor Manufacturing Company (TSMC), 29, 30, 32, 36, 37, 40, 43, 50, 100, 104, 122–132, 275, 279, 345
Tamsa, 41, 221–222, 224–225, 278
Tariffs, 34, 62, 277
Tata, J.N., 229
Tata, Ratan, 120
Tata Consulting Services, 15, 36, 55, 237
Tata Group, 120, 237
Tata Institute of Fundamental Research, Mumbai, India, 22
Tata Motors, 36, 120, 151, 153
Tchaikovsky, Piotr Ilyich, 28
TCL, 24
Tech Cominco Inc., 193
Techint, 220, 221
Telecommunications, 21, 33, 36, 44, 280
Telefonica, 136
Telefonos de Mexico, 261
Telemundo, 265
Telenovelas, 44, 53, 254–257, 260, 262–268
Telesistema Mexicano, 258, 259
Televicentro, 261
Televisa. See Grupo Televisa
Television Independiente Mexicano, 259

Televisions, 69, 70, 73
Telmex, 32, 41, 44, 46
Tempest, Brian, 27, 243–246
Templeton, 5, 6
Tenaris, 19, 24, 29, 30, 37, 41, 43, 47, 49, 54, 218–226, 277, 278, 346
Tequila Crisis of 1994, 34, 41, 95, 224
Teva, 245, 246
Texas Instruments, 36, 122, 124, 126–128, 133
Texas Pacific group, 266
Textile industry, 44
Thailand, 3, 12, 34, 63, 102, 111, 114, 281
ThinkPad brand, 22, 43, 54, 85, 86
Thomson, 24, 128
Thornton, John, 294
TIAA-CREF, 5
Tian Xi PC, 85
Timberland, 54, 112, 114
Time operation research, 90
Tinbergen, Jan, 1
Toshiba, 71, 72, 121, 136
Toy industry, 44
Toyota Motor Corporation, 16, 26, 36, 42, 63, 141, 146, 147, 150, 151, 153, 277
TQM (total quality management), 26, 90, 277
Transistor radios, 123–124
Trevino, Rodrigo, 161
Trinidad, 211
Tropsch, Hans, 212–213
Tsai, David, 118
Tsai Chi-jui, 114–115, 117
Tsai Chi-neng, 116, 117
Tsingtao beer, 97
Turkey, 25, 32, 311
TV Azteca, 263

Ukraine, 205–206, 211
UMC, 129
Unbundling, 50–51
Unconventional thinking, 40, 45
Unilever, 44
United States-China Economic and Security Review Commission, 272
Univision, 263–268
Unocal, 23–24
U.S. Army Corps of Engineers, 145
U.S. Steel, 36, 203
US Air, 61, 166

US Airways, 166
USS-POSCO Industries, 203
Uttam, 208

Vallourec, 219
Varig Airlines, 177
VCP, 190
Venevision, 264, 266
Venezuela, 157, 207, 211, 221, 250, 264, 311
Verizon, 9, 36, 136, 242
Vertical integration, 51, 107–108, 116
VIA Technologies, 135
Video games, 252–253
Vietnam, 111, 114, 116
Vitro, 41
Vodafone, 9, 136
Volkswagen, 36, 147, 173, 209
Volkswagen Beetle, 94
Volvo, 146, 147
VSL, 203
VSMPO, 181

Wal-Mart, 14, 44, 55, 68, 89, 92, 271
Walkman, 135
Wall Street Journal, The, 23, 86, 156, 208, 308
Wang, Cher, 135
Wasserman, Lew, 264
Wasserstein Perella, 176
Webzen, 253
Welch, Jack, 90
Whirlpool Corporation, 23, 83, 88
Winchester rifle, 51
Wind power, 207, 208
Windows, 132, 134–137
Wine industry, 38, 44, 61, 63, 64, 75–81, 326
Wipro, 36, 55, 234
World Bank, 3–5, 29, 40, 186, 198–199
World Brand Laboratory, 63
World Business Council for Sustainable Development, 191
World Economic Forum, 122
World Is Flat, The (Friedman), 17
World Semiconductor Trade Statistics, 37
World Trade Organization (WTO), 34, 101, 210
WorldCom Corporation, 310
Wortzel, Larry, 272
Wright Brothers, 171

Xavante, 173
Xbox, 252
Xiali, 151

Yahoo, 155
Yang, Ping, 129–130
Yang Yuanqing, 84, 85
Yellowtail wine, 80
Yokota, Satoshi, 172, 181
Young, Andrew, 113

Yue Yuen, 16, 37, 43, 54, 111–118,
    347
Yugo, 146
Yukos, 24
Yun, Jong Yong, 41, 64, 66
Yungching, Wang, 135
Yushchenko, Viktor, 205

Zambrano, Lorenzo, 29, 154–160
Zhang Ruimin, 86–92, 330